An Introductory History of British Broadcasting

'. . . a timely and provocative combination of historical narrative and social analysis. Crisell's book provides an important historical and analytical introduction to a subject which has long needed an overview of this kind.' *Sian Nicholas, Historical Journal of Film, Radio and Television*

'Absolutely excellent for an overview of British broadcasting history: detailed, systematic and written in an engaging style.' *Stephen Gordon, Sandwell College*

An Introductory History of British Broadcasting is a concise and accessible history of British radio and television. It begins with the birth of radio at the beginning of the twentieth century and discusses key moments in media history, from the first wireless broadcast in 1920 through to recent developments in digital broadcasting and the internet.

Distinguishing broadcasting from other kinds of mass media, and evaluating the way in which audiences have experienced the medium, Andrew Crisell considers the nature and evolution of broadcasting, the growth of broadcasting institutions and the relation of broadcasting to a wider political and social context. This fully updated and expanded second edition includes:

- The latest developments in digital broadcasting and the internet
- Broadcasting in a multimedia era and its prospects for the future
- The concept of public service broadcasting and its changing role in an era of interactivity, multiple channels and pay per view
- An evaluation of recent political pressures on the BBC and ITV duopoly
- A timeline of key broadcasting events and annotated advice on further reading

Andrew Crisell is Professor of Broadcasting Studies at the University of Sunderland. He is the author of *Understanding Radio*, also published by Routledge.

An Introductory History of

British Broadcasting

Second edition

Andrew Crisell

Routledge
Taylor & Francis Group

LONDON AND NEW YORK

First published 1997
by Routledge
2 Park Square, Milton Park, Abingdon,
Oxon, OX14 4RN

Simultaneously published in the USA
and Canada by Routledge
270 Madison Avenue, New York, NY
10016

Reprinted 2001
Second edition published 2002, 2005,
2006

*Routledge is an imprint of the Taylor &
Francis Group*

© 1997, 2002 Andrew Crisell

Typeset in Times by Keystroke,
Jacaranda Lodge, Wolverhampton
Printed and bound in Great Britain by
The Cromwell Press, Trowbridge,
Wiltshire

*British Library Cataloguing in
Publication Data*
A catalogue record for this book is
available from the British Library

*Library of Congress Cataloging in
Publication Data*
Crisell, Andrew
An introductory history of British
broadcasting / Andrew Crisell. –2nd ed.
   p. cm.
Includes bibliographical references and
index.
1. Broadcasting–Great Britain–History.
I. Title.
HE8689.9.G7 C75 2002
384.54'0941–dc21

ISBN 0–415–24791–8 (hbk)
ISBN 0–415–24792–6 (pbk)

To Brian Kennett

Contents

Contents

Contents

Acknowledgements to the first edition

I MUST FIRST DECLARE my warm gratitude to Rebecca Barden, my editor at Routledge, whose support for the idea of a single-volume yet fairly comprehensive history of British broadcasting has never wavered during the vicissitudes of its composition. For many years before I thought of this book, as well as while writing it, I benefited greatly from discussions with Ken Stephinson of Stephinson Television, who combines experience of virtually every aspect of television production and a long record of distinguished programmes for both the BBC and ITV with a larger, philosophical view of broadcasting. I owe a similar debt to Marjorie Lofthouse, also of Stephinson Television: as well as being an experienced radio and TV broadcaster in her own right, she directed me to certain sources of information about the BBC. Another who was able to tell me much about the corporation was Jane Bywaters, who has spent many fruitful years there as a researcher in the field of television arts programming.

For similar enlightenment about ITV I must express my warm thanks to David Thomasson of Yorkshire/Tyne Tees Television. A former student of mine, Anita Sharma, who is now a research assistant at the Open University, kindly briefed me about ITV's educational programming and aspects of the 1990 Broadcasting Act.

I am most grateful to two media consultants, Robert Palmer and Toby Syfret, who were generous with their time, first-hand knowledge and the printed materials at their disposal. Both directly and indirectly, they furnished me with much information about the recent history of independent, satellite and cable broadcasting and thus helped me to gain some perspective on the present state of the media.

I owe a double debt to my brother-in-law, Tony Humphreys. Through his work in information technology at the Post Office, he kept me as abreast of the latest developments in interactive television as my limited understanding would allow; and second, via telephone tutorials and with a patience verging on the saintly, he helped me to get to grips with a new computer and new software. Another redoubtable assistant was my daughter, Harriet, whose informatic skills are, thanks to the mystery of the genes, everything that her father's are not.

My employer, the University of Sunderland, readily granted me half a semester's leave during which I managed to write what was for me the hardest part of the book. My penultimate debt is to the students on the 'History of the Mass Media' syllabus – first, and quite simply, by making it clear to me that an introductory history of broadcasting needed to be written, and second by forcing me during our seminars to think long and hard about the main themes and issues that should shape it. Despite all these forms of assistance, I alone am responsible for any mistakes or omissions which the reader may detect.

My last and largest debt is to my wife and two daughters, whose stoicism in living with 'an author' was rewarded only by the fact that his abstracted silences during meals allowed them to talk animatedly to one another without risk of clumsy male interruptions.

Acknowledgements to the second edition

I AM ONCE AGAIN grateful to the University of Sunderland for granting me a semester's leave during which much of this book was written. And I must thank my daughter, Hattie, an avid but critical viewer, for sharing with me some of her extensive knowledge of modern television programmes. She was also able, in a matter of moments, to tease out the logic and coherence of a particular argument I had been struggling with for several hours – an instance of that easy filial superiority which fills so many parents with mingled pride and dismay. Again, I am indebted to my brother-in-law, Tony Humphreys. As well as a grasp of cable and digital technologies he showed that rarer gift, the ability to explain them patiently and lucidly to a none-too-clever pupil. I must further thank him for providing calm counter-measures when the threat of a computer virus to my almost-finished typescript had reduced me to a gelatinous wreck.

It is a pleasure to record my debt to Alex Thomas of Independent Television News, who supplied me with prompt and vital information on the TV coverage of sport, and to my friend and former colleague Gordon Robson for his energetic researches into the history of party political broadcasting. Among my colleagues at the University of Sunderland, Richard Berry and Victoria Ball made helpful observations on aspects of digitization, internet and cable technology. To another colleague, John Paul Green, who collated a mass of material about interactivity, cable, satellite and digital television, I owe special thanks. Without his cheerful and obliging researches the final part of this book would have been both harder to write and harder to read. However, none of my benefactors may be blamed for errors or omissions which the reader may encounter: the responsibility for these is entirely mine.

Acknowledgements to the second edition

As usual my greatest debt is to my long-suffering wife and daughters: Margaret, Ellen and Harriet. My preoccupation with this book was such that they were sometimes overlooked and unheard. But they were always my guiding light.

Preface to the second edition

THIS SECOND EDITION of *An Introductory History of British Broadcasting* was written with three main aims. The first was to try to bring it more or less up to date. I have added to the coverage of digital broadcasting and of that difficult, sprawling entity, the internet, suggesting some of the ways in which it might overlap with conventional forms of broadcasting. But updating is always more than a matter of simple chronological addition: new facts cast older ones in a different light, trends one confidently predicted a year or two ago fail to develop and are eclipsed by others which once seemed negligible. In broadcasting particularly, technological developments have come so thick and fast that the experts, let alone the laity, are hard put to make sense of them. Like most people's views about its future, my own change almost from moment to moment, for getting a clear view ahead is like trying to gain a foothold on shifting sand. In the last part of the book I suggest that the character of broadcasting is being so radically transformed that the word itself may soon cease to serve as an adequate description.

My other two aims were to remedy what I perceived to be the deficiencies of the first edition. One concerned that slippery term 'public service' – a phrase on every broadcaster's lips, from the Director General of the BBC to the captains of commercial radio. One might be forgiven for feeling that the less it is understood, the more it is talked about. Like a child's comfort blanket it is brought out and caressed on every occasion, a talisman against threats to cut the licence fee or complaints about pandering to the masses. My aim, then, was to trace the evolution of the concept more clearly, to note how it met changing conditions sometimes by shedding certain of its tenets, sometimes by acquiring new ones. I hoped not only to provide a clearer historical understanding of the concept but to determine what life may be left to it in an era of multi-channel 'narrowcasting', of interactivity and pay per view.

My other aim was to offer a fuller account of the political pressures on the BBC and ITV during the 1980s and 1990s. It could be argued that the broadcasting reforms envisaged by the government of that time turned out to be much less radical than was intended. But for their opponents at least, they threw the merits of the old duopoly into sharper focus, portending what would be lost as well as gained when it was breached by an inundation of cable, satellite and digital channels.

All of this means that the book has been extensively rewritten. Apart from the above changes, I have tried to clarify the overall historical narrative and sharpen some of my arguments about particular issues. I have also sought to improve the style in which the book was written. To make it both less bitty and more readable, I have written longer paragraphs but shorter sentences. And in the further interests of clarity I have added a timeline of key broadcasting events.

Introduction

THIS BOOK IS primarily intended for A level and undergraduate students of media studies but may also be of use and interest to students of social and cultural history. It may even appeal to those laypersons who have often wondered how broadcasting in Britain has come to be as it is: why, for instance, a licence-funded public corporation is its central feature when many other countries operate a full-bloodedly competitive, commercial system.

There are, of course, many perspectives from which a history of broadcasting may be written – the social, the political, the technological, the anecdotal – and from time to time I adopt one or other of them throughout this book. But what moved me to write it was a belief that there was a crucial element which other histories had insufficiently considered. They had offered searching analyses of media institutions, their cultural contexts, their ownership and social structure, their programming policies, and their relations with the state and with dominant ideologies; but what they had largely omitted, perhaps as being too elementary or self-evident, was an account of the broadcasting process itself and the way in which audiences experience it. This seems to be an important omission because whatever the political, cultural and institutional forces that shape broadcast content, the latter is in the first place constrained by the special characters of radio and television themselves. A TV news editor with the BBC may choose to cover a public sector strike in a way which favours either the state employers or the workforce, and her choice may in some measure be influenced by the fact that it is the state which determines not only the level but the very existence of the licence fee. But what she has no choice about is that the strike must be covered through a time-based medium using sounds and moving images, and for a large, remote and dispersed audience of varying abilities and attentiveness.

This history therefore takes the nature of broadcasting and the situation of the audience as its pivot, weaving a crowded chronology of events, facts, personalities and trends around a simple account of its technological evolution. Part I considers how broadcasting is distinguishable from the other modes of mass communication in being live and, for the most part, domestically or even individually received. Part II explores how in due course broadcasting began to be modified by a growth of audience *activity* (though I do not imply by this term that before the arrival of remote control and VCRs, the audience was inactive in the sense of being mentally inert). And Part III describes how broadcasting is now being confronted by a growth of audience *interactivity*. The audience will be able to use their radio and television sets to modify and respond to live broadcasting as well as for non-broadcast purposes such as internet access and home shopping. Moreover, they will, if they wish, be able to receive live broadcasts by computers and mobile phones – devices which boast interactivity as an inherent property. This growing media convergence means that the phenomenon of broadcasting is becoming rather harder to define: but it does, at least, mark a good point at which to bring our history to an end.

As part of my aim to illuminate the essential character of broadcasting, the reader will note the preoccupation with its various *genres*, both those which radio and television have borrowed or adapted from other media and those they seem to have originated. This has largely determined which programmes I have chosen to discuss, though choice is always an idiosyncratic matter. The reader will certainly question some I have included and others that I have omitted deliberately, accidentally or from sheer ignorance. I have also mentioned programmes and series which do not illuminate the medium particularly but which were extremely popular and successful in their time, reason enough for inclusion in a broadcasting history of any kind.

But, of course, a history of broadcasting cannot simply be a chronology of programmes. The paradox which seems to explain why so many studies of the media ultimately focus on media *contexts* rather than on the media themselves is that broadcasting is in itself a mere process, little more than an abstraction. Yet the conduct of it is so complex, costly and (in one way or another) so significant, that it is inevitably a highly social and political matter, too – and any history of broadcasting which did not reflect this could not even claim to be 'introductory'.

Great care has therefore been taken to set the process of broadcasting within its social and political contexts. Indeed, as the history approaches the present, an analysis of these almost entirely supersedes the discussion of individual programmes. This is partly because now that both radio and television are old media many of their original or distinctive programmes were made many years ago, and those that are more recent will in any case be known to the reader; but mainly because these broad contexts and their impact on media institutions seem to give a better perspective on broadcasting's growing convergence with other forms of communication.

My concern with development and perspective also implies, intentionally, that this history should not primarily be treated as a reference book to be dipped into in the way that its more scholarly sources can be. It is a continuous narrative, a matter of themes and of logical or causal connections rather than a mere chronological succession, and should be read as such. This is why, when it seemed appropriate to do so, I condensed certain aspects of broadcasting into one or two summary sections – often at their first or early occurrence in the history – rather than returned to them in a piecemeal way which would have denied the reader a coherent overview. This approach is particularly obvious in the case of the BBC's external services, which, since domestic broadcasting is the main subject of the book, are given only a single sketchy account in Chapter 2. One or two other subjects are similarly condensed: educational broadcasting, television advertising, the effects of TV on audiences, government policy on broadcasting. Television and politics also occupy separate if extended sections, but the reader will swiftly grasp that in one guise or another politics suffuse the entire history.

With the nature and experience of broadcasting firmly at the centre of our picture, certain other topics get little if any mention: labour relations within the broadcasting industry, programming budgets, media publications, the finer details of commercial media ownership. Though fascinating in themselves, it would be hard in a history as cursory as this to show what direct effects these have had on content or the audience. Yet, wherever possible, sources are provided for those who wish to pursue them.

In sum, this book aims to create in the reader a composite impression of British broadcasting as a single though luxuriant growth, ramifying and flourishing from relatively modest roots. Yet so inseparable is it from the society that it reflects, results from and partly shapes that (to change the metaphor) it often prompts us as we follow its route to peep into, and sometimes take a few steps down, side-alleys with tempting vistas – subjects whose relations with broadcasting would each make a book in themselves, and in most cases already have: advertising, rock and pop music, sport, debates about artistic value and its relation to highbrow and popular culture, media effects and influences, questions of authority, expertise and the public's 'right to know', patterns of leisure and employment.

Two points about style. I have been blithely inconsistent, though I hope not confusingly so, in my use of the word 'medium', sometimes applying it to radio and television individually but often, and less accurately, describing broadcasting in general as 'a medium' in order to stress what radio and TV have in common and how they differ from other media such as print, cinema or photography. I believe that the contexts make clear which meaning of the term is intended.

The second point relates to the vexed question of 'gendered language'. Since an important theme of this book is the frequent individuality of broadcasting consumption, it is not always helpful to refer collectively to 'the audience', 'the viewers', and so on. Since I do not wish to weary the reader with dualisms such as 'him/her' and 'he/she', and since there are as yet no singular epicene pronouns which will satisfy the gender politicians, I have quite arbitrarily referred to the viewer, listener, broadcaster, or whatever, as 'he' at some points and 'she' at others. I therefore assure the reader that when she/he encounters these feminine/masculine pronouns she/he may take it that where one gender is used the other is also implied.

Part I

The phenomenon
of broadcasting

It seems a good time to write a history of British radio and television because we can now see broadcasting as a distinct phase in the development of communications technology. Broadcasting followed upon print, the first automated mass medium, but is itself, after a relatively brief reign of some eighty years, being caught up in newer technologies that are bringing about a convergence, even a blurring, of mass and private media. Before offering an account of these eighty years we therefore need to isolate the distinctive characteristics and functions of broadcasting by locating it within the broader history of mass communication. Inevitably this historical sketch will be simple and crude, containing no room for specifics, subtleties and exceptions, but if it gives the reader a general and roughly accurate perspective it will have justified itself.

We might begin with a simple definition of mass communication: the sending of messages to a multitude of receivers. Its original mode was *live* in the sense that the receivers were in the presence of the sender – that is, within hearing and/or sight of him – and in a space which, in needing to be large enough to accommodate both parties, was most likely *public*. In these circumstances mass communication was inevitably a kind of *performance*, so we might term this public space a *theatre* even though it could accommodate almost any kind of message – political speeches, philosophical disquisitions, religious rituals, educational lectures, story-tellings or factual reports, spectator sports and circuses, as well as the more conventionally theatrical kinds of performance such as drama and light entertainment. Indeed it is probable that not only drama but poetry, that other great literary genre, was originally performed in this space. Before the advent of printing, literacy was very rare, and poetry's inherent acoustic features of rhythm and rhyme suggest that it was intended to be recited to numbers of listeners rather than silently read to oneself.

The first automated mode of mass communication was *print*, which was utilized in Britain from 1475. The cultural, intellectual and political consequences of printing were enormous – truly incalculable – but it was made possible only by a pre-existing and even more momentous technology: writing (Ong 1982: 81–2). For several thousand years writing had provided a way of fixing speech, of taking human utterance out of its natural, constantly dissolving element, *time*, and putting it into *space*, where it could remain permanently accessible. What print did was to turn writing into a mass medium by allowing an indefinite number of copies of an 'utterance' to be made. This was the first real instance of mass production, a process which is regarded as the distinguishing feature of industrialization but which in this case preceded the main 'Industrial Revolution' by several hundred years. Printing was none other than the mass production of writing or 'literature' in its broadest sense: the first stage in the industrialization of communication. Moreover, 'massification' entails the democratization of the product to which it is applied in

3

the sense of widening popular access to it. It is not just – perhaps not even primarily – the case that mass production meets a pre-existing mass demand; rather that in order to justify itself economically it must *increase* demand, and it was the arrival of print which was to prompt the growth of mass literacy.

But in creating numberless copies of its written messages print differed from the earlier mass medium of 'theatre' by introducing a gap in space and time between senders and receivers: a public, live medium was superseded by a private, 'lifeless' one whose receivers could withdraw into their own separate environments. A paradox thus arose which applied not only to print but to most subsequent modes of mass communication, and which terms like 'mass' and '*broad*casting' belie: for while these modes have enormously *increased* the size of the audience they have also 'atomized' it – reduced it to small groups or isolated individuals who read or listen or watch in their own private spaces.

From about 1839 print technology was complemented by *photography*, which could offer fixed images of reality; but what the next two mass media technologies did was to provide fixed messages or 'recordings' in which one or both of the two most important live or time-based elements of the communication act, sound and moving vision, would be re-created. We might usefully term the first of these *phonography*, which from the 1890s produced recordings of different kinds of sound, notably speech and music, and which over the years has variously taken the form of wax cylinders, graphite platters, vinyl records, several kinds of audio tape including cassettes, compact discs and minidiscs. Phonography was always a *private* mass medium in the sense that sound reproduction equipment and the recordings themselves were purchased and used by families, households or single individuals.

Cinematography, which developed from about 1895, was another quasi-live medium since, through its 'moving text' of pictures and (from 1927) sound, it could simulate the conditions of the earliest mode of mass communication. Not surprisingly, the kind of material that seemed most suited to it and likeliest to appeal to its audience was conventional drama, and in focusing upon drama 'film', as it came to be known, created a corpus of work – of definitive, 'best possible' performances which differed from those of the conventional theatre in being infinitely reproducible. However, like its predecessor, film was a *public* medium in the sense that its audiences gathered in theatres – 'cinemas', as they were called. Although individual cinema audiences were no larger than theatrical audiences, film was much more of a mass medium than theatre because the number of cinemas in which it was possible to show copies of a single film far exceeded the number of theatres to which it was possible to tour a single dramatic performance.

However, *broadcasting* was the first genuinely live mass medium since 'theatre' because it was instantaneous: its messages were received by its audience at the very moment they were sent; they were not fixed messages in the form of printed texts and photographs or recordings of sounds or moving images. From 1922 radio transmitted live sound to a private, domestic audience, and from 1936 television provided the same kind of audience with live sound and live moving pictures.

As in the case of print, the economic logic of all these communications technologies was to maximize their audiences, and to this end they resorted, wherever possible, to the modes of mass production. Since photography was a mass medium only as an adjunct to print – that is, when photographs appeared in books, newspapers and magazines rather than in family albums – its artefacts were mass produced in the same way as those of print. Phonographic artefacts, notably gramophone records, were also mass produced. The artefacts of cinema and broadcasting were not, of course, produced in quite the same way as those of print, photography and phonography, since they were not, at first, tangible objects which could be individually retained by their consumers. But in the sense that they were serially and multiply constructed, according to pre-set patterns or formulas and by teams whose workers each had a specialized role (scriptwriter, director, camera operator, performers, and so on), they too were mass produced.

And all these media had one important advantage over print. Quite apart from the high initial cost of books and pamphlets and the negative impact of certain social and political forces, a real barrier to the mass consumption or democratization of printed products was the fact that they required decoding skills: to enjoy or benefit from print consumers first had to learn how to read. Near-universal literacy was not finally achieved until the end of the nineteenth century (Cannon 1997: 582) and even now there are many who are either non-literate or do not find reading and writing easy or pleasurable activities. The media which have developed since printing, however, are all *iconic*: their products reproduce the sights and sounds of the world we experience directly and thus require from their consumers only the minimal decoding skills we need in our daily lives. They amply demonstrate the truth of the observation that many technologies are extensions of man's corporeal faculties (McLuhan 1962: 4), and leaving economic considerations aside it is hardly surprising that their democratic spread has been more rapid than print's. The Americans were the first to appreciate the democratizing tendencies of these iconic media and to use them to democratize culture, but as we shall see, this process was less straightforward – was, indeed, consciously resisted – in Britain.

The different characteristics of all these modes of mass communication, or 'mass media' as we have also termed them, can be summarized as in the table overleaf.

As we might expect, different media develop their own kinds of message – which we will term *genres* – but the relationships within and between media and genres are often complicated. One genre may be common to several media, and as well as operating separately different media may be contained one within another, like a nest of boxes. Print was the medium which fostered the third of our great literary genres, the novel, as well as news and current affairs. News is clearly not a genre

MEDIUM	LIVE	RECORDED		PUBLIC	PRIVATE
		Fixed text: (Writing; Pictures)	*Moving text: (Soundtrack; Film)*		*Domestic/ Individual*
'THEATRE'	*			*	
PRINT/ PHOTOGRAPHY		*			*
PHONOGRAPHY			*		*
CINEMATOGRAPHY			*	*	
BROADCASTING (RADIO/TV)	*				*

in the sense that the novel or poetry is, since these are *formal* categories whereas the term 'news' refers to *content*; but news has its own characteristic forms so we might for the sake of convenience refer to it, too, as a 'genre'.

To say that print fostered news and the novel is not of course to deny that they were very much the product of such contemporary social and cultural factors as the growth of capitalism, the political ascendancy of the middle class, the rise of literacy, and changes in the patterns of work and leisure. It is merely to say that print provided the technical preconditions for such factors to operate, as other media have in their turn. Since photographs in themselves are limited or ambiguous in meaning, photography became a mass medium as an ancillary to the print genres, enhancing the content of newspapers, books and magazines.

Though certain genres have remained peculiar to certain media, it is clear that many can be taken over by other media with varying amounts of adaptation and variable degrees of success. When records are broadcast on the radio it is reasonable to speak of one medium, phonography, being subsumed by another, sound broadcasting. Consequently the musical genres which make up the content of the former undergo no adaptation at all. On the other hand, the amount of adaptation may be so great that we might almost speak of a new genre being created. It is clear, for instance, that the cinema feature film has its origins in theatrical drama; but the difference which the physical flexibility, recording and editing techniques of the newer medium have made to acting methods and to the location and changes of scene is such that the two no longer seem closely related.

A genre may migrate to a new medium and become so at home there as to be no longer identified with the old one. Poetry moved from theatre to print, and though poetry readings are occasionally staged it is clear that the move has generally been for the better. Its acoustic elements of rhythm and rhyme can still be appreciated by the private reader even though she may internalize them, and its transformation into a fixed, visible text which she can mull over means that the genre is probably capable of a much greater sophistication of structure and meaning than it was in an oral medium.

For similar reasons, the novel remains largely confined to the print medium in which it was born. It is obvious that the medium of television can subsume that of print (as in the case of teletext): nevertheless, for the time-based characteristics of radio, cinema and television the novel is invariably turned into *drama* (though straight, abridged readings are sometimes heard on the radio). Only print is equal to the fact that the novel is quite as much concerned with the workings of the inner consciousness as with the sensory world of actions and events.

News has been a cosmopolitan genre. It has always flourished in its native medium, print, which affords the scope and depth that it needs. Photography added a useful visual dimension to the newspapers, but cinema brought the vivid illustration of sound and moving pictures. Later, television could match this illustrative power, and in addition offer the absolute up-to-dateness of a live medium, and cinema capitulated with the demise of Pathé News in 1969.

The rise and fall of cinema as a news medium is reflected in the fortunes of its word 'newsreel'. Though offering live sound, radio news, which evolved at much the same time, could not match cinema's visual power. The BBC therefore sought to borrow this power by titling one of its programmes *Radio Newsreel*, but once television news had established itself during the 1950s 'newsreel' implied something not up-to-date but merely recorded, and thus declined in status. We might also note in passing that because it can subsume the medium of print, television can borrow something of the stability and continuous accessibility of newspaper news as well as offering its own kind of news, for it gives us not only live bulletins but the fixed summaries of teletext.

Drama is another much-travelled genre. Although it has always remained in the theatre its dialogue and stage business were soon transposed to print, and several centuries later it was adapted for cinema, radio and television. Drama in the latter medium may take the form either of theatrical adaptation or feature film, and the genre is a good illustration of the fact that the historical development of the mass media has not been a simple matter of continuous improvement, but that what is in one respect an advantage is in another a limitation. Theatrical drama was hit by the cinema, cinema was hit by broadcasting, and for some time broadcasting has been feeling the effects of newer media; but because each of them has irreplaceable characteristics or functions the older media survive, albeit in reduced circumstances. Cinema and television incorporate the visual, auditory, temporal elements of theatrical drama in a way that a printed script cannot; but handy, portable print can 'stabilize' it and permit an overview of its structures and themes in a way that is beyond the other media. Thanks to this stability it is print, above all, which has facilitated the enormous expansion of scholarship and intellectual inquiry that has taken place over the last five centuries. The domesticity of radio and television is in general a great asset, but a visit to the cinema is a public, communal experience which can be much more pleasurable than an evening at home – and in addition to this pleasure, the theatre affords a genuinely live performance that the cinema cannot.

Even that most protean of the new media, the network of computers known as *the internet*, has its limitations. With varying degrees of effectiveness, the internet can subsume most older media – print, photography, phonography, film and broadcasting – and now offers many of their typical products: on-line newspapers and magazines, various literary texts, records, and both radio and TV transmissions. We shall have more to say about this hybrid and baffling medium later in the book, but for all its comprehensiveness and versatility the keyboard and screen through which it is accessed are – for the time being, at least – less wieldy and flexible than a book or newspaper, more physically and visually constricting than a radio set.

However contingent they might be, the advantages of broadcasting as it developed in the first half of the twentieth century were clearly considerable because they embraced so many of those of the earlier mass media. First, radio and then television domesticated various live or live-seeming genres which hitherto could be experienced only in public. Any kind of instantaneous performance that had been received in a collective, 'theatrical' space – talks, plays, narratives, debates, spectacles and light entertainment – could now be received at home. Likewise, television could domesticate the cinema film – an important achievement since film's earlier attempt to re-create the liveness of theatrical performance had resulted, almost incidentally, in a body of dramatic productions which were both optimal or definitive in themselves and capable of being shown many times over. Second, broadcasting was able to make live – to 'animate' – those genres that were already private because they were native to print, notably news. Radio and television conveyed the sound and sight of public events to audiences in an environment where they had previously been used only to written descriptions and fixed images of them. To spectator sport, which is both theatrical entertainment and 'news', broadcasting did a double favour, domesticating it as a spectacle and animating it as news.

As we would expect, it is older people who are more aware of the changes broadcasting has wrought, for they remember the original media from which its genres have been taken and still tend to conceive of them in those terms. For older people especially, radio and, above all, television have brought the cinema, theatre, sports stadium, or, in the case of news, the world itself into our living rooms – a perception which focuses upon the peculiarly invasive, irresistible quality of the medium and reminds us that the question of its effects and influences on the audience is not the less important for being complex and elusive.

Yet the perception also reminds us that the audience's experience of broadcasting is on one level ambiguous: it brings the outside world into our private space but there is also a sense in which it takes us out into the public sphere. This two-way process characterizes all acts of communication: when a sender seeks to impose her world on the receiver it is much the same as extracting the receiver from his own world and relocating him in hers. This latter effect may be less obvious if the receiver is face-to-face with the sender and/or her message refers to experiences they share. But it is more obvious if sender and receiver are physically separated. When reading a vivid news report, for instance, the receiver may well feel that he is being 'transported' into the sender's world. And it is very obvious when the medium of communication is iconic and the receiver can 'experience' the sender's world through his own faculties of sight and hearing. Even while we are sitting in our homes, radio and television make us present at other events – events which are inevitably 'public' because we are hearing or watching them as part of a mass audience.

But it is particularly when hearing or watching events which are literally 'in public', such as a major soccer match, state funeral or general election, that we gain a strong sense of participating in a collective, sometimes national experience (McQuail 2000: 395–6). In its early years broadcasting's coverage of public rituals and religious services could even cause behavioural dilemmas (Scannell 1996: 77–80, 91). Should domestic listeners stand during the national anthem? Did a conscientious Catholic fulfil her obligation to attend Sunday mass if she watched it on television? This is why scholars sometimes insist on speaking of radio and television as *public* rather than private media, arguing that the social experiences of many people are only partly first-hand: the remainder are derived through radio and television, allowing them to form an affinity with other people whom they are physically separate from and may never have met (Thompson 1995: 34–5). It has also been suggested that because broadcasting both domesticates the public sphere and socializes the private one it is neither a public nor a private medium in the traditional sense (Dahlgren 1995: 123).

Nevertheless, while its ambiguous effects should be kept firmly in mind, we may still reasonably describe broadcasting as in essence a *private* medium since its messages are received and understood in the listener's or viewer's home or personal space. In this respect it makes private experience out of what was formerly public or – as in the case of news, which was always private – richly enhances it; and we can see this achievement as part of a tendency towards that individualism of consumption or ownership which is one of the great themes of modern civilization. What broadcasting did for one kind of communication the motor car did for another, transforming travel from something public and collective into a private, atomistic activity; and the consequences of this general tendency have been so diverse and far-reaching as to be almost incalculable. The car has largely determined where and how people live, their modes of work and leisure; and the newer forms of electronic communication have had similar effects. Computers, the internet and now that great emblem of personal empowerment, the mobile phone, allow us to turn our personal space into an office and to access from it such traditionally public institutions as retail outlets, banks, travel agencies, libraries and educational establishments.

But our task in this book is to consider the particular historical impact of broadcasting. How were the genres and cultural forms which pre-dated it – news, information and various kinds of entertainment – adopted and modified by this new technology? Did it create genres of its own? In their private, separated spaces how did its millions of listeners and viewers respond to its content? And what were its influences and effects on them?

There can be no doubt that content is ultimately constrained by technology. In our discussion of media and genre we saw that new media could develop new genres and that while certain genres could migrate comfortably from an old to a newer medium, others needed varying degrees of adaptation, and yet others could not make the journey at all. But this is not the whole of the matter. If it is true that radio can take the traditional public lecture and successfully turn it into a talk, should that talk be on politics and unemployment or on how to bake a cake? If television can do drama should it be Shakespeare or soap opera? And if both radio and television are very effective news media what sort of news should they carry and how should they treat it? The answers to these questions depend on the nature of the broadcasting institution – and that, in turn, depends on yet larger questions. What is the relationship of the broadcasting institution to the state? What is the attitude of the government to broadcasting? And how is this unprecedented activity to be paid for, organized and regulated – by taxes and as a public utility, or by advertising and as a private enterprise?

All this means, then, that broadcasting is a matter of cultural values, politics and economics as well as of mere technology and that it can develop – and has developed – along different lines in different countries. As I hinted in my earlier remark about the democratization of culture, the history of broadcasting in Britain has been in marked contrast to that of the United States and, indeed, of most other parts of the world. It is this history which we must now begin.

Sources/further reading

Some of the vast intellectual and cultural consequences of the development of the technology of writing are succinctly indicated in Ong (1982), while the analogous consequences of the development of print technology are explored in McLuhan (1962) and Williams (1998). Briggs and Burke (2002) is a compendious and very readable social history of the media 'from Gutenberg to the Internet'.

For the genesis of media technologies and the tendency to domestic or private consumption which they created – also for the relationships between media and genre – see Armes (1988). The classic definition of literary genre based on the relationships between the communicator and the audience is in Frye (1971), and the relation between the development of print technology and the rise of the novel is explored in Watt (1963). Dahlgren (1995), Thompson (1995), Scannell (1996), McQuail (2000) and Moores (2000) all offer useful insights into the way in which radio and television are both public and private media. For essays which provide a composite view of media power in the twentieth century see Curran, Smith and Wingate (1987).

Finally, a history of broadcasting, like any other specialized history, needs to be set within its broader context. For a straight chronological account of the events of the twentieth century see Mercer (1988); for a magisterial overview of the movements which have shaped it, together with some percipient remarks on the role that broadcasting has played, see Hobsbawm (1994); and for individual topics such as 'literacy', 'radio' and 'television' refer to Cannon (1997).

The birth of radio

Chapter 1

The birth of radio

The development of radio technology

It was the great Australian operatic soprano Dame Nellie Melba who first demonstrated the power of radio broadcasting. On 15 June 1920, in the prosaic setting of the Marconi wireless works near Chelmsford and under the sponsorship of the *Daily Mail*, she gave a special concert in English, French and Italian. Her voice was heard throughout Europe and in parts of North America, and almost sixty years of trials and experiments were at an end.

In order to understand radio technology a little better we need to distinguish it from certain other technologies which were thrown up by the same long process of experiment and discovery. The first of these was *telegraphy*, the transmission of electronic impulses over distance. These impulses could be arranged into a code by the sender and then translated into words by the receiver. The most commonly used code was that which was named after its American inventor Samuel Morse. The transmission of sounds, particularly spoken words, over distance is known as *telephony*. *Wireless* telegraphy or telephony is transmission not by means of wire or cable but through the atmosphere. The final distinction we need to be aware of is between *point-to-point* transmissions, which take place between a sender and a single receiver, such as those which normally occur on the telephone, and *broadcast* transmissions, which take place between a sender and an indefinite number of receivers. Broadcast transmissions are usually offered to anyone who has the equipment to catch them.

Radio technology could thus be described as *broadcast wireless telephony*, and this helps to explain why despite being wreathed in wires the early radio receiver was known as a 'wireless', a paradox which was often celebrated by writers and cartoonists. One length connected the receiver to the aerial, another ran to the earth, and one or more went to the headphones; but *no* wire spanned the considerable distance between the station transmitter and the listener's aerial.

As we might expect, these communication technologies have a common ancestry but a number of progenitors, most of whom were at work in different parts of the world. In 1864 James Clerk Maxwell, a professor of experimental physics at Cambridge, expounded his theory of the existence of electromagnetic waves. During the 1880s the American Thomas Edison showed that an electric current could jump through space, and the German Heinrich Hertz that you could catch the waves with a receiver and reflect them with a metal sheet. In 1894 the Englishman Sir Oliver Lodge used wireless waves to send messages in Morse code, thus inventing wireless telegraphy, and three years later he showed how a receiver could 'tune' to a particular transmitting station.

However the Italian, Guglielmo Marconi, is justly regarded as 'the father of radio' because it was he who brought together so many of these discoveries and inventions. A man of endless energy, Marconi was adept not only at developing his own research and combining it with that of others but at exploiting the *business* potential of telecommunication. At the turn of the century he came to England and patented his own system of telegraphy; formed the first company for the manufacture of wireless apparatus (the Wireless Telegraph and Signal Company); saw his system adopted for ship-to-shore Morse communication; and in 1901 received a prearranged Morse code signal (the letter 'S') which was sent from the far side of the Atlantic. A year later the Canadian R. A. Fessenden used wireless waves to carry the human voice over the distance of a mile, thus inventing wireless telephony, and in the same decade work by J. A. Fleming in England and Lee de Forest in the United States led to better amplification and to wireless transmissions over greater distances. By 1910 ship-to-shore messages were common, and air-to-ground radio contact had also been achieved. Thanks largely to the experiments of Fessenden and de Forest the Americans began to take the lead in wireless telephony, and by 1915 the American Telephone and Telegraph Company was able to send speech signals 3,500 miles from Arlington, Virginia, to Paris, and later 5,000 miles to Honolulu.

At a political level point-to-point telegraphy and telephony were perceived to have enormous significance. They had strategic and military benefits which were only too obvious both in Britain and in the many other countries that were about to be engulfed in the Great War of 1914–18. Yet the secret communications they facilitated might also pose a threat to the security of the state and to public morality. For this reason private media have always been a source of anxiety to governments. National security was one of the reasons that the carriage of private mail was entrusted solely to the Post Office, which until 1970 was a government department whose head, the Postmaster General, was a government minister. To this day it remains a public corporation. More recently government fears about the seditious and immoral possibilities of the internet have resulted in the Regulation of Investigatory Powers Act (2000), which allows the police and security forces to monitor web-sites and intercept electronic mail.

When wired telegraphy and telephony developed in the nineteenth century they, too, were soon placed under the control of the Post Office. The Telegraphy Act of 1869 gave the Post Office the exclusive right to transmit telegrams within the United Kingdom, and in 1880 a court case established it as the universal licenser of wired telephone services. A further act of 1904 gave the Postmaster General control of point-to-point *wireless* telegraphy, and when wireless *telephony* developed he regarded that, too, as subject to his control (Briggs 1961: 95). This explains why the Post Office was later established as the licenser of *broadcast* wireless telephony – or 'broadcasting', as we simply term it.

But not only was the Post Office the licenser of wired telephone services: it used its position to become the sole operator of them. It decided to compete with the telephone companies it had licensed and established a near monopoly by taking over the trunk lines and refusing to extend the local licences of its rivals beyond the end of 1911. Only after the Great War was the Post Office able to develop a fully national service; the single system which managed to survive outside it was in Kingston-upon-Hull (Winston 1998: 254). Telephones were to remain a Post Office monopoly until 1984, when this area of its business was privatized as 'British Telecom' and subjected to competition from other operators.

The central role of the Post Office demonstrates that as *point-to-point* technologies telegraphy and telephony were closely regulated by the government from their very beginnings. However, their *broadcasting* potential was at first barely noticed and then as little more than a technical weakness, a negative side-effect which seemed to call for scientific remedy rather than government regulation. The problem with point-to-point (usually *wired*) communication was that it afforded privacy to those who were not entitled to it as well as those who were; the problem with broadcast (usually *wireless*) communication was that it afforded privacy to no one. Its messages could be picked up not just by designated individuals but by all and sundry, thus exposing the crudity of these technologies as well as their potential. And a tiresome consequence was that they were attracting a growing band of amateur enthusiasts, as new technologies often do, who were building their own receivers and were keen to listen to anything they could find on the airwaves.

Nevertheless, there were some radio pioneers, especially in America, who were able to see the broadcasting property of telephony, in particular, not as a weakness or liability but as the main justification for its existence: to re-cast the snoopers and busybodies who were the unintended recipients of its messages as a potentially valuable audience. David Sarnoff, a young employee of the American Marconi Company, was among them (even though Marconi himself was not), for in 1916 he pointed out that if telephony were used to broadcast regular entertainment and information this would act as a colossal stimulus to the sale of wireless receivers:

> I have in mind a plan of development which would make radio a 'household utility' in the same sense as the piano or phonograph . . .
>
> The receiver can be designed in the form of a simple 'Radio Music Box' and arranged for several different wavelengths, which would be changeable with the throwing of a single switch or pressing of a single button . . .
>
> The box can be placed in the parlor or living room, the switch set accordingly and the transmitted music received . . .
>
> This proposition would be especially interesting to farmers and others living in outlying districts removed from cities. By the purchase of a 'Radio Music Box' they could enjoy concerts, lectures, music, recitals etc., which may be going on in the nearest city within their radius.
>
> (quoted in Armes 1988: 107)

The seductiveness of this vision perhaps explains why sound broadcasting got off to a slightly earlier start in the United States than in Britain.

The establishment of a public broadcasting service

With the end of the Great War in 1918 it became harder for the British government to resist on military grounds the pressure from both wireless manufacturers and amateur enthusiasts to authorize some kind of regular broadcasting service. The enthusiasts, many of whom had already built their own receivers, were keen to have something informative or entertaining to listen to on a routine basis, rather than having to eavesdrop on messages intended for someone else. The manufacturers were keen to stimulate the sales of receiving equipment and were willing if need be to provide the service themselves. In its role of licenser the Post Office therefore gave the Marconi Company permission to make broadcasts from its transmitter at Writtle near Chelmsford, but instructed it to avoid encroaching on the point-to-point transmissions of the armed forces. As Raymond Williams points out, the situation was always

> complicated by the fact that the political authorities were thinking primarily of radio telephony while the manufacturers were looking forward to broadcasting . . . When the Marconi company began broadcasting in 1920, there were complaints that this use for entertainment of what was primarily a commercial and transport-control medium was frivolous and dangerous, and there was even a temporary ban, under pressure from radio-telephonic interests and the Armed Forces.
>
> (Williams 1974: 32)

In spite of the achievement of Dame Nellie Melba, it was not until 1922 that the Post Office accepted a distinction between wireless technology which addressed designated individuals ('point-to-point') and that which addressed all and sundry ('broadcast'). In the same year the Marconi Company began regular broadcasts from Writtle and opened a London station, known by its call-sign '2LO'. Another London station, 2WP, was opened by Western Electric, which also started 5IT in Birmingham, while Metropolitan Vickers began broadcasting from Manchester as 2ZY.

However, the Post Office refused to license any of these on a permanent basis. Why? Whatever the political case for its regulatory role, the technological case was even stronger: there was only a limited number of frequencies on which broadcasting could take place. In the United States, where regulation was weak, a kind of aerial anarchy developed during the early 1920s: too many stations crowded the waveband, some on pirated frequencies and some using stronger signals to drown out their rivals. But geography conspired with technology to make tight regulation even more necessary in Britain. Europe, scarcely as big as the United States, accommodated over a dozen different countries, each speaking its own language and wanting its own broadcasting frequencies. As the mere offshore island of this cacophonic subcontinent Britain would have to content itself with a very limited share of the waveband. The Post Office could not allow its few available frequencies to be permanently monopolized by a handful of the manufacturers, yet had to accept that there would never be enough frequencies to license every manufacturer who wished to broadcast.

Its solution was to invite the leading firms (six large companies and several small ones) to form a broadcasting consortium. The service they collectively provided would stimulate the sales of the receivers they made, which the government would protect from foreign competition. As a result of this scheme the manufacturers created the *British Broadcasting Company* to which the Post Office granted a *de facto* though never a *de jure* monopoly. The BBC began transmissions on 14 November 1922. The manufacturers guaranteed the company's solvency, and its funds came from three sources: the original stock, the royalties on the wireless sets which the manufacturers sold, and a share of the revenue from the broadcast receiving licences which the Post Office collected from the listening public on the company's behalf.

The person who was appointed general manager was an austere Scot of Calvinist upbringing, a thirty-four-year-old engineer named John Reith. When he applied for the post he scarcely knew what broadcasting was, yet through energy and force of personality he shaped it according to a moral vision whose traces are discernible even today. Reith soon formed the conclusion that broadcasting was a precious national resource – too precious to be used merely to deliver audiences to advertisers or even to wireless manufacturers. It should instead be developed into a comprehensive public service which was for him distinguished by five main characteristics:

1 It aimed to broadcast to *everyone* in the country who wished to listen.
2 It sought to maintain *high standards* – to provide the best of everything.

To achieve these two things the public service system needed to:

3 operate as a *monopoly* because competition would force it to abandon 'quality' programmes and programmes for minorities and simply seek to maximize its audience;
4 be funded by a *licence fee* to ensure that the costs of the programmes were not related to audience size – that if need be, expensive programmes could be made for minorities.

Both as an alternative to advertising revenue and as a hypothecated tax (that is, a tax raised for a specific purpose), the licence fee also allowed the system to achieve another aim alongside universality of provision and high standards of content:

5 to be institutionally and editorially *independent* – of commercial pressures on the one hand and, as far as possible, government influence on the other.

It is, however, important to understand that Reith did not conceive of these characteristics in a vacuum, that there were organizational precedents for the service he aimed to provide. During the first decades of the twentieth century the model of the public utility or public corporation was being developed as an alternative to both direct government control and private enterprise (Curran and Seaton 1997: 113–15). It was based on the view that if the former was over-bureaucratic and inefficient, the latter was materially wasteful, thanks to the duplications of competition, and socially painful in the insecurities that it bred in its workforce. The public corporation sought to combine the best of both civil and commercial values, rejecting political interference on one side and market forces on the other in favour of efficiency and planned growth. And events seemed to justify belief in it. The forestry, gas, water and electricity industries were all organized on this model, and during the Great War, with its urgent need for central planning and the conservation of resources instead of the rivalries of private enterprise, the model was applied to health, insurance, coal production and food rationing (Curran and Seaton 1997: 113–14). Moreover there was a growing political belief that a post-war economic depression, which could throw large numbers out of work, would also call for centralized and humane control.

The British Broadcasting Company already possessed some of the characteristics of the public corporation when Reith joined it in 1922, perhaps because the government sensed straightaway that broadcasting would be a cultural amenity like public libraries or adult education classes (Winston 1998: 83). Though set up to make money for its constituent manufacturers, the company offered a modest rate of return to its shareholders and was never driven primarily by the need to make a profit. Indeed the government had approved the licence system precisely in order to cushion it against this need.

The first programmes

Wireless enthusiasts and, it was hoped, the wider public wanted a regular broadcasting service. But what should it consist of? The broadcasters were confronted, so to speak, with a blank sheet of paper. This new medium transmitted live sound (but not vision) to multitudes of separate, mostly domesticated individuals. What could it do? And what should it avoid? In its attempts to do news, drama, light entertainment and talk, it instinctively fell back on traditional forms – the newspaper, the stage, the lecture theatre – yet not always appropriately because even content which seemed well suited to it would need adaptation. For certain other things it attempted, such as sporting commentary, there were no precedents. Broadcasting had to evolve its own conventions – and not all of these would be successful.

In the early years broadcasts were made for only a few hours each day. Typically, transmissions might not begin until the afternoon and would conclude well before midnight. But they were varied. Since it seemed ideal for radio there was music in abundance, much of it classical: but dance music, even though rather sedate by later standards, was often heard too. Yet even in music the medium would often modify what it borrowed. Singing, for instance, had traditionally been a sonorous and public activity for which 'sincerity' had not been a relevant criterion. But the microphone demanded a more intimate style of delivery which even acquired its own name – 'crooning'; and since the listeners were mostly alone, radio helped sincerity to acquire a new musical significance (Scannell 1996: 60–9).

Radio talks underwent a similar modification. 'The lecture, the sermon, the political speech, all had rhetorical styles that spoke to audiences constituted as a crowd, a mass. But radio must speak to each listener as someone in particular' (Scannell 1996: 24). Once this was understood, talks became frequent and covered a range of topics. While some were light and humorous, many were serious and instructive, embracing such subjects as literature, film and drama. In 1924 Reith affirmed his belief in broadcasting's potential to teach and train by approving the creation of a Central Education Advisory Committee to give guidance on schools programmes. These began in the same year, as did talks in the sphere of adult education. A year earlier he had approved an advisory committee to offer similar guidance on religious broadcasts.

Programmes for the young date from the very beginning of radio: *Children's Hour* originated in Birmingham in 1922. Entertainment for older listeners included live relays of song and comedy from the music halls, with a commentator on hand to describe inaudible acts such as jugglers and dancers. The first straight drama to be heard on radio was an adapted scene from Shakespeare's *Julius Caesar*, but the first to be written especially for the medium was *A Comedy of Danger* (1924) by the novelist Richard Hughes. In devising a play which could not be presented in a conventional theatre (it was set in a coal-mine where the lights have failed) Hughes perhaps showed an excessive concern for radio's limitation. On the other hand some drama producers ignored it to the extent of requiring their actors to broadcast in theatrical costume. This was presumably intended to help them enter into the spirit of the play despite the absence of spectators, but like the outside broadcasts from music halls it really shows that some years would pass before broadcasters could conceive of radio as a dramatic venue in itself rather than as the mere blind witness of events which were taking place on a stage. The company also covered sport, but its early relays of the major events in horse-racing, rugby, soccer and golf, among others, were not wholly successful: the commentators had trouble keeping pace with fast-moving events and had not yet learned what they needed to describe and what they could safely leave to the listeners to infer. Indeed its first attempt at an outside broadcast was not sporting at all but operatic – a 1923 performance of *The Magic Flute* from Covent Garden.

Though varied and popular, this programming diet suffered from one serious deficiency. All too aware that in its coverage of current affairs radio would prove itself much more fleet than Fleet Street, the Newspaper Proprietors' Association put pressure on the government to forbid any news broadcasts until 7 p.m. Even then, the company was obliged to take its news from the main agencies such as Reuters – and this was supplied in the form of bulletins which had evidently been drafted with newspaper readers rather than radio listeners in mind. The restriction on the supply of the news was not finally thrown off until 1938, and in the early years of broadcasting the Post Office also banned all political commentary and controversy and most political speeches.

The company's first programmes were transmitted not only from London (initially Magnet House and then Savoy Hill) but from such regional centres as Manchester, Birmingham, Newcastle and Glasgow, and from a number of smaller relay stations. Thanks to the relative compactness of Britain and the enormous popularity of the new medium, enough transmitters had been built by 1925 to reach about 80 per cent of the population. Reith exploited technology to create the unified image for the company that he desired, for a networking system was soon introduced which allowed any of the regional stations to supply all the others. Yet Reith's vision was not merely of a unified company, but one which was centred on London: the nation's broadcaster must emanate from the nation's capital. Hence the primary purpose of networking was to enable the regional stations to take simultaneous broadcasts of important London programmes such as talks or concerts.

At first the output of the regional stations fairly closely reflected the localities they served, while the relay stations were largely sustained by London; but Reith's centralized programming policy soon resulted in the elimination of genuinely local radio, which would not be heard again until 1967. By 1930 London was transmitting a service called the *National Programme* (until the 1970s the term 'programme' was used to mean 'network' as well as an individual broadcast that could be heard on a network – a usage that sometimes confuses the modern student). But an alternative *Regional Programme* was broadcast from centres serving the Midlands, North, South, West and Scotland, with Wales and Northern Ireland added later. Part of its programming was also supplied by London and part originated from the large and in most cases ill-defined areas the programme was intended to serve.

Radio listeners and wireless receivers

The country took to sound broadcasting with boundless enthusiasm: during the mid-1920s houses in towns and cities began to sprout aerials like a strange new vegetation. In 1923 the Post Office issued 80,000 licences, but in 1924 these jumped to 1 million, a figure which doubled over the next three years. By 1939 9 million wireless receivers were under licence. However, because there were anomalies and loopholes in the licensing system these figures represent only a fraction of the total listenership. At first there were three separate categories of licence: for ordinary listeners, experimenters and constructors. Though the company was entitled to royalties on ready-made wireless sets, many listeners bought and assembled their own from simple kits on which no royalties were payable, and then qualified for the much cheaper, experimental licence. Many more simply avoided paying any licence fee at all. It has therefore been estimated that in the early years of broadcasting there were five times as many unlicensed as licensed sets in use. The actual audiences were huge. After 1928 no programmes were heard by fewer than a million listeners and some attracted 15 million.

In 1923 the Postmaster General appointed a committee under Major General Sir Frederick Sykes to review the company's finances. Impressed even at this early stage by the quality of its programmes the committee declared that broadcasting was 'of great national importance as a medium for the performance of a valuable public service' (Sykes 1923:13) and rejected advertising as a possible source of revenue on the ground that it would lower standards. Instead the committee recommended a single licence fee of ten shillings, three quarters of which should go to the company. However, this proportion would be subject to a sliding scale as the number of licences increased, and royalty payments on wireless receivers should cease.

What were these receivers like? The very first were 'crystal sets', so called because they were based on the discovery that if certain kinds of crystal were touched in the right place with a fine wire known as a cat's whisker they could 'detect' radio waves and transform them into electric currents. The technology was unreliable, to say the least: because the signal would often fade and drift, the listener would spend much time tickling it back with the cat's whisker. But in the sense that listening was via headphones and thus a solitary activity the crystal set ironically prefigured that most sophisticated receiver of the 1980s, the personal stereo. It was easily assembled from kits or bought from the company ready-made and with two pairs of headphones for between two and four pounds.

However, the crystal set was soon followed by the valve wireless, whose much improved reception by way of a loudspeaker transformed listening into a group activity. The first valve sets cost £17 10s (£17.50) in 1923, but within two years mass production reduced the price to little more than five pounds, and by the 1930s they had virtually replaced crystal sets. Valve wirelesses also marked the transition from radio receivers as unsightly pieces of apparatus, the playthings of enthusiasts and eccentrics which had to be hidden in cupboards when not in use, to aesthetic objects – pieces of furniture in their own right. The first step in this process was to design receivers so that they could be passed off as something else – sewing boxes or cocktail cabinets. But as broadcasting grew in confidence and wove itself more closely into the fabric of domestic life their designs began to proclaim wireless sets for what they were.

These changes reflected something of a shift in the appeal of wireless from males to females. The earliest sets were largely a male preserve: it was mostly boys and men who rose to the technical challenge of building them and who, because the headphones severely limited the numbers of listeners, made up a large part of the first audience. But the development of loudspeaker sets enabled women to listen, too – and women, often housebound for much of the day, rapidly became a very important section of the wireless audience. Since they also assumed the main responsibility for 'making the home look nice' the manufacturers had a powerful spur to design aesthetically pleasing sets.

During the 1930s wirelesses could be bought for between five and six pounds, but this was still quite expensive for the less well-to-do. Many found an alternative in the *relay exchange*, a central receiver which was cabled to individual homes in return for a modest weekly rent and was therefore also known by the quaintly paradoxical term 'wired wireless'. Running costs could be shared among as many subscribers as could be connected to the exchange, but this meant that the system was viable only in densely populated areas. Furthermore, relay exchanges were opposed by the Post Office, the wireless manufacturers and the British Broadcasting Company. The Post Office disliked them because, although their subscribers each paid a licence fee in the normal way, it was obliged to give the relay operators another licence to pass messages over wires – something on which it otherwise enjoyed a statutory monopoly. The manufacturers disliked them because they enabled people to hire merely a loudspeaker instead of buying a full wireless set. And the BBC disliked them because they threatened its monopoly by carrying foreign stations as well as its own programmes.

The first of the relay exchanges opened in 1925; in 1929 there were thirty-four, and this number increased tenfold over the next six years. By 1939 they had attracted just over a million subscribers, and there was a further and rapid increase during the Second World War. But the arrival in 1944 of the widely affordable 'utility' set marked a turning-point, and thereafter the popularity of the wired wireless slowly declined.

Between the fire and the fire-brigade

For the financial ills of the British Broadcasting Company the Sykes Committee had found a palliative rather than a cure. Anomalies in the licensing system persisted, and in any case the Post Office was unwilling as a public body to collect fees on behalf of a private company, even though the proportion it retained more than covered its costs. For this and other reasons the wireless manufacturers were growing eager to abandon their offspring. Their need to compete ever more keenly with one another in order to sell wireless sets had cut their profits, and in a nearly saturated market there were few new buyers to be tempted by the company's programmes, however excellent these might be. Why not leave to someone else the trouble of making them? In 1925 the government therefore set up a new committee under the Earl of Crawford to consider the future of British broadcasting.

Despite the company's difficulties Reith maintained his belief in broadcasting as a public service, and one for which the public itself, rather than advertisers, should pay. He therefore convinced the Crawford Committee that the company should become a public corporation which would be free from commercial pressures by continuing to be funded by the licence fee, yet also free from close political control. The government of the time might well prove sympathetic: as we have seen, the institutional model that Reith and Crawford were proposing was a familiar and widely accepted one. But before the government could respond, a national crisis arose which posed a threat to Reith's hopes.

For some years labour relations within various major industries had been worsening. The Great War had been followed by economic problems which certain employers, notably the mine owners, sought to mitigate by imposing wage cuts on the workforce. The trade unions reacted by calling a general strike, which lasted from 3 to 12 May 1926 and paralysed the country's essential services. Since most of the press was affected the restrictions on the British Broadcasting Company's news coverage were temporarily lifted: it was allowed – indeed needed – to report the strike; and therein lay Reith's dilemma. If the company covered the strike in a way which the government felt was contrary to its interests, the old political fears about the seditious effects of the media would revive, prompting the government to turn the company into a mere mouthpiece or even to commandeer it altogether. Indeed, this was something one of its members, Winston Churchill, was already keen to do. And in the longer term the company's future would be not as an autonomous public corporation but a mere government department along the lines of the Post Office. If, on the other hand, the company were perceived by the strikers and the many who supported them as being simply pro-government, its editorial independence would be compromised and it would no longer command universal trust.

The company broadcast news of the strike in five daily bulletins – at 10 a.m. and 1, 4, 7 and 9.30 p.m. At the end of the crisis it had succeeded in walking the tightrope: though it sometimes lost balance it never quite fell. Absolute even-handedness was impossible because the government perceived the strike not simply as an industrial dispute but as a political and constitutional threat, and outlawed it. Consequently the company could only pre-empt interference in its news reportage by broadly reflecting the government's position and suppressing information which favoured the strikers or would encourage the strike to spread. It gave the unions' point of view but little else. It explained what was happening and what the citizen could do, but not why the strike came about. The company was twice humiliated by the government, first when its attempt to bring a union leader to the microphone was vetoed, and second when it was bullied into refusing to broadcast a peace formula devised by the Archbishop of Canterbury.

Nevertheless it achieved much. The tone in which it reported the strike was cheerful and conciliatory throughout. Furthermore its perspective on events was never wholly identified with the government's, prompting Churchill to attack Reith for his company's impartiality: 'I said he had no right to be impartial between the fire and the fire-brigade' (quoted in McIntyre 1993: 311). At the beginning of the strike there was a general assumption that the company would simply be a conduit for the views of its political overseers: by the end millions had come to depend on the accuracy of its information, many strikers among them.

Thus, however little it availed the disputants, the General Strike was good for the British Broadcasting Company. It enhanced its importance and eased that transition from private enterprise to public institution which Reith and Crawford desired. And the strike was good for broadcasting itself because it enabled even those who disapproved of the company as a biased news *source* to appreciate radio's power as a rapid news *medium*, despite the fact that more than ten years would pass before that power could be fully exercised. In one's own home one could not only read about the events of yesterday but be told about the events of the hour. As Asa Briggs (1961: 384) points out, broadcasting had become a major force in the nation's life: it could no longer be dismissed as a novelty for amateurs and enthusiasts. By the end of 1926 the government had accepted the recommendations of the Crawford Committee and John Reith had received a knighthood.

Sources/further reading

There are many useful accounts of early wireless technology. Winston (1998) and Briggs and Burke (2002) describe the development of telegraphy, telephony and broadcasting, Williams (1974) focuses on their political and social contexts, and Barnouw (1966, 1977) and Armes (1988) deal mainly with institutional developments. Gorham (1952), Paulu (1956, 1961, 1981) and Smith (1976) all offer concise descriptions of the beginnings of broadcasting in Britain. Golding (1974) includes a good chapter on the early history and development of the British media, while Briggs (1961) – the first of a classic five-volume history of broadcasting, much of which is condensed in Briggs (1985) – contains an account of the foundation and life-span of the British Broadcasting Company.

For Reith's own account of his early years at the company, including the problems posed by the General Strike, see Reith (1949) and Stuart (1975), which contains many of Reith's diary entries for this period. Tracey (2000) provides a clear perspective on the General Strike. Reith's broadcasting philosophy is set out in Reith (1924) and usefully summarized in McDonnell (1991). Two biographies of Reith which include helpful accounts of this period are Boyle (1972) and McIntyre (1993), and for a fuller discussion of the concept of public service broadcasting see Tracey (1998).

Smith (1974) contains extracts from key texts relating to early broadcasting history, and there is a number of helpful general accounts of this first era of broadcasting. Briggs (1981) combines 'scrapbook' material with a lively narrative; Curran and Seaton (1997) are concerned to set early broadcasting firmly within its institutional and political contexts; Pegg (1983) focuses on the social dimension; Scannell and Cardiff (1982, 1991) deal with the early development of the BBC as a public service broadcasting institution; Parker (1977) concentrates on early programmes and personalities rather than on institutions; and Black (1972a) offers his own reminiscences as a listener.

For programme genres, see Scannell (1996) on the way in which radio modified traditional forms of music and talk, and Gielgud (1957) for an account of the first years of radio drama and its migration from the theatre to the studio. Moores (1988) is a study of the early design of wireless sets and the way in which it reflected a change in the behaviour and profile of the audience.

Chapter 2

The BBC: from private company to national institution

27-47
76 - 93
172 - 183
244 - 260

The BBC: from private company to national institution

Regional, national, global

On 1 January 1927 the British Broadcasting Company became the *British Broadcasting Corporation*, a publicly funded yet quasi-autonomous organization whose constitution and statutory obligations have remained largely unchanged for seventy-five years. It was established by royal charter, with a board of governors to whom Sir John Reith was accountable as director general. Although the charter determines the corporation's structure, its activities are regulated by a 'licence and agreement' which are conferred by the government. It was, and is, obliged to inform, to educate and to entertain; to report the proceedings of Parliament; to provide a political balance; and in a national emergency to broadcast government messages. It may neither editorialize nor carry advertising. Its income is guaranteed from broadcast receiving licences and it strives to maintain a position of editorial independence.

However, it has never been entirely free from state pressure. Its licence to broadcast has always been granted for fixed periods, never in perpetuity; the state appoints its board of governors; and the state, not the BBC, determines the cost of the receiving licence, part of which it may withhold. Hence throughout its history the BBC's relations with governments of all political hues have been delicate and occasionally strained.

Soon after its foundation the corporation underwent a period of rapid expansion. In 1932 it moved its headquarters from Savoy Hill to the purpose-built Broadcasting House in Portland Place, an act which symbolized its coming-of-age as a national institution, and by this time both of its domestic networks, the National Programme and the Regional Programme, were accessible to most of its listeners. The National Programme originated mainly from London while the Regional Programme drew its material mostly from the regional centres but was also fed by a London sustaining service.

One network was not markedly different from the other: both broadcast *mixed programming*, which was at the heart of Reith's public service philosophy. Every day each network offered a variety of programmes – drama, sport, light and classical music, news, religion, talks, interviews and discussions, light entertainment. This meant that as many tastes as possible could be satisfied, and from time to time sections of the audience were explicitly targeted – children, women, business people, farmers, gardeners and so on. The first aim, then, was to provide 'something for everyone'.

But the second aim – the converse of the first – was perhaps even more important: to provide 'everything for someone'. It was not simply that each individual should seek and find her own interest and then switch off: the hope was that she would be enriched by exposure to the *full range* of the programming. Consequently, except in the case of news bulletins, regular or 'fixed point' scheduling – the practice of offering the same or similar programmes at the same times every day – was deliberately avoided. The high-minded intention was continually to renew the listener's alertness to the medium, not only to make her listen instead of merely hear but to 'surprise' her into an interest in a subject she had previously not known about or disliked, and at all times to give her 'something a little better than she thought she wanted'.

Essential to this varied diet was the maintenance of the BBC's monopoly, for if a competitor were allowed the fight for audiences would reduce programming simply to that which was known to be preferred by the largest number: minority-interest programmes, intellectually demanding programmes, even new kinds of programming which might *eventually* be popular, would all be sacrificed.

As well as providing two domestic networks the BBC inaugurated its *Empire Service* in 1932. This was the first of a series of external services, of whose history we here offer only the barest sketch before returning to domestic broadcasting, our main theme in this book. The Empire Service catered mostly to colonials of British origin; it did not set out to serve all the ethnic elements of the Empire. But by 1935 the BBC knew that an empire service of any sort was no longer enough. To counter the radio propaganda of Hitler's Germany and Mussolini's Italy the corporation would have to make overseas broadcasts in languages other than English, and these were started under the threat of war in 1938. In the following year the Empire Service became a part of the *Overseas and European Services*, which not only broadcast but gave invaluable help to the government by monitoring foreign stations. This was acknowledged in the fact that whereas until the war the cost of external broadcasting was met from the licence fee, it was funded thereafter by a parliamentary grant paid through the Foreign Office. Until recently the government determined the languages in which the BBC broadcast and the length of its transmissions, but the corporation has always kept editorial control.

In 1948, these services were renamed the *BBC External Services* and thenceforward reflected the vagaries of government policy and the national economy. In the 1950s they contracted, in the 1960s they expanded, and after the 1973 oil crisis they suffered cuts. By 1999 the *BBC World Service*, as they have been collectively known since 1965, was broadcasting in 44 languages with a combined output of 1,036 hours per week and to a total audience calculated at 143 million (Barnard 2000: 240). Its English language broadcasts alone are heard by over 100 million listeners. They run for twenty-four hours a day and consist half of news and half of mixed programming such as music, sport and drama. The World Service also offers a transcription facility of recordings and scripts for use by stations in other countries.

In 1991 the BBC hastened to exploit the arrival of TV as the major global mass medium by launching *World Service Television*, an operation which the Foreign Office decided not to fund. The corporation therefore took the momentous but little noticed decision to seek commercial funding for it, which was subsequently re-branded as *BBC World*. To reach a global TV audience the corporation must expand within satellite broadcasting, a pond with room for only a few big fish, and it has therefore sought alliances with other broadcasters, especially in America. In 1995 and in conjunction with the Pearson Group, it also launched *BBC Prime*, cable and satellite channels aimed at European audiences. What all this portends is a convergence of internal and external broadcasting – a situation in which major media institutions like the BBC will no longer make radical distinctions between their domestic and international strategies.

Growing pains

The expansion of its output during the early 1930s meant that as an institution the BBC had to undergo a fairly large and rapid growth. When it went to air in 1922 it had a staff of 31; by 1927, when it became a corporation, the staff numbered 773; and by 1938, the year of Reith's departure, there were nearly 5,000. This growth required organizational changes, and in an effort to maintain the corporate ethos Reith favoured a policy of unified control rather than devolved responsibility. At the same time he drew a distinction between a centralized administration, which he favoured, and a conformism of output, which he sought to avoid. For this reason he made an attempt during the early 1930s to separate administrative from creative staff. While the administrators developed a cost-effective, smoothly running organization, the producers and broadcasters could get on with the business of making programmes. In practice, however, the line between the administrative and the creative was often blurred and the concerns of the former usually seemed to prevail over those of the latter. It has therefore been said that before the corporation moved from Savoy Hill all was 'intimacy and harmony' whereas after all was 'bureaucracy and conflict'.

The Regional Programme neatly encapsulates the way in which administrative and technical considerations could override editorial, creative and even audience needs, sometimes producing successes but of a rather limited kind. As Maurice Gorham (1952: 78) points out, the Regional Programme destroyed the local basis of early broadcasting, which had drawn on local talent and catered to local needs. The new 'regions' were based not on any cultural or even geographical identity but on technical coverage and administrative convenience, and were to that extent arbitrary. The Black Country was thrown together with the Cotswolds, industrial Manchester with the agricultural North Riding, urbane Bristol with bucolic Cornwall. The result was that the distinctiveness of each region was not immediately and authentically expressed but only gradually and somewhat artificially achieved: the West Region pioneered agricultural programmes, the Midlands industrial documentaries and variety shows, the North 'features'.

Organizational problems went right to the top. Under the BBC's new constitution Reith was accountable to the board of governors. But a proud and sometimes prickly man who had already shaped the organization according to his own vision would never have found such accountability easy, and almost immediately he was at odds with one of its members, a Mrs Snowden, whom he regarded as officious and meddlesome. He also came to dislike the chair, Lord Clarendon, believing him to be weak and vacillating for his failure to restrain Mrs Snowden, and it was not until Clarendon's departure in 1930 that Reith's relations with the board began to improve.

Nevertheless he was by temperament an architect and builder rather than a caretaker, and as the 1930s wore on and the corporation became more systematic and settled in its ways, Reith grew bored. 'I am beginning to feel that I have organized and developed myself out of a job', he told his diary in 1935 (Stuart 1975: 169). In their different ways Reith and the corporation were outgrowing each other, but if during his last years in office he could not live comfortably within the BBC, the subsequent thirty-three years of his life were to show that he could not live comfortably without it. There is some dispute as to whether the chairman of the board of governors engineered his departure. What is certain is that his restlessness came to the notice of the government, by whom he was invited to take the chair at Imperial Airways. Yet even though his departure from the BBC was pretty well inevitable, not least because Reith himself appeared to want it, the manner of that departure was characteristically painful. Reith rightly felt that his new job would not be so central to the life of the nation; he was excluded from the deliberations as to who his successor at the BBC should be; and his hope of joining the board of governors was thwarted by some of its members on the reasonable ground that he would make life impossible for his successor. Thus it was in tearful bitterness that he returned his wireless and television sets to the corporation, and on 30 June 1938, the day of his resignation, made a symbolic trip to Droitwich to close down the high-power transmitter for the night.

Yet despite the organizational upheavals within the BBC, the 1930s were an era of continuing improvements in the quality and scope of its programmes, and as a result of the recommendations of the Ullswater Committee (1936) the government renewed the original ten-year charter for a further decade.

Developments in radio news

In its first years as a news medium, radio was obliged to declare that it was the prisoner of the press. 'This is London calling – 2LO calling,' the newsreader would intone – though not before 7 p.m. 'Here is the first general news bulletin, copyright by Reuters, Press Association, Exchange Telegraph and Central News.' There followed a dry, sedate bulletin of 20 or 25 minutes, with no interviews, features or actuality.

It was the General Strike which showed that sooner or later broadcasting's ability to deliver the latest news would not be denied, and the 1920s and 1930s saw the BBC gradually escape the stranglehold of the press. The 1927 charter recognized in principle the BBC's right to broadcast its own news, and thenceforth the corporation made a continuous effort to reduce its dependence on agency material and establish its own news-gathering facilities. But in order to protect the circulation of the papers restrictions remained upon the time that the news could be broadcast: it was not until the outbreak of the Second World War that bulletins were heard before 6 p.m. However in 1930 the BBC secured from Reuters the right to edit and write its own bulletins from the agency material on which it still largely relied, and was thus able to resume the attempt it had begun during the General Strike to transform news from something suited only to print into something that could comfortably be listened to.

To begin with, the production of the news was located within the large Department of Talks, but in 1934 a former economics professor, John Coatman, was appointed Chief News Editor and set about creating a separate news department. At first consisting of six people it had acquired a staff of thirty by 1939. At about the time of Coatman's appointment the news gained new impact with the arrival of portable sound-recording machines. Some of them made use of Blattner steel tape which had to be edited with metal clippers and welding instruments, the joints clattering through the machine like a train over points, but most recording was on nine-minute twelve-inch discs. It was also from about this time that the newspapers began to learn how to live with radio, realizing that although it had dented their circulation somewhat, they still possessed strengths in news reportage which the sound medium lacked. Becoming less concerned with the recency of the news, they began to exploit their special ability to amplify, contextualize, interpret and comment, an illustration of the point made in the introduction to Part I that old media are never entirely replaced by new ones: their roles may be altered, but they usually retain a distinctive and irreplaceable function. Because broadcast bulletins were briefer and sharper the newspapers reacted by reducing the amount of fine print, making bolder headlines, doubling columns, shortening sentences and paragraphs, and increasing the number of photographs.

Nevertheless, radio news had some unrivalled successes. The last illness of King George V in 1936, a saga which developed from moment to moment, could be much more vividly rendered by radio than by the press, with Reith himself coming to the microphone to announce the king's death. The royal funeral was also broadcast, and the abdication statement made eleven months later by the new king, Edward VIII, was much more compelling to listen to than to read. The BBC's first real scoop was the great fire which destroyed the exhibition centre at Crystal Palace in the same year. It occurred after the papers went to bed but before their morning appearance, thus emphasizing their relative inability to keep abreast of events. From the scene of the fire a young BBC reporter named Richard Dimbleby telephoned a live report which was accompanied by shouts, the roar of the flames and the clang of fire-bells.

Towards the end of the decade the press was still fighting a rearguard action against the BBC by getting certain news sources to embargo material as 'not for broadcasting', but it was the need to cover the 1938 Munich crisis by every means possible that finally enabled radio news to compete with the press on equal terms.

The cultural values of the BBC

Though widely admired, the BBC's output was not always enjoyed: indeed the corporation was often accused of being undemocratic and élitist in its programming policy. How could this be, when through mixed programming it set out to provide something for everyone?

Part of the answer lies in the shifting and paradoxical notions of 'democratic'. One notion, to which the BBC broadly subscribed, was that democracy consists of giving all the people what they want; but this is undemocratic in the sense that within a limited resource such as broadcasting then was, and because people have differing tastes, nobody gets *enough* of what they want. The second notion, to which many of the corporation's critics subscribed, was that democracy consists of giving the *majority* of the people what it wants – which is also undemocratic, positively despotic, in the sense that the minority gets nothing at all. The complaint against the BBC, then, was that the majority did not get enough of what it wanted – and a great deal of what it did *not* want.

Yet although, to take a hypothetical example, it might be 'undemocratic' that the great sport-loving majority was denied the amount of soccer commentary it wanted because from time to time minorities of farmers or business people had to be catered for, it was hardly élitist. The question of élitism arose, as we have seen, because the BBC's public service policy was to try to provide not just something for everyone, but the *best* of everything – and 'the best' is a notoriously difficult concept which is likely to cause controversy not simply about the merits of programmes within certain categories, but about where those categories should be drawn.

For instance, for all those listeners who liked music, what constituted 'the best'? Classical, as distinct from popular music? (After all, 'classical' is a value-judgment: 'serving as a standard of excellence', as well as a merely neutral description.) Or was there a separate category of popular music with its own distinctions of good and bad (as even within classical music there might be good or bad performances of the great works)? The same question applied to drama. Was 'the best' Shakespeare and Ibsen and 'the worst' music hall – or was the latter a separate category with its own qualitative differences?

From the number of programmes it devoted to them, the BBC evidently took the view that 'the best' works were the classical ones. This was especially true of music. Its Music Department dealt only with classical music, while popular music was seen merely as an adjunct of light entertainment and consigned to the Variety Department. The assumption was that if you liked music you could not be displeased with Bach or Beethoven, and that if you liked the theatre you could not be discontented with Shakespeare. But many listeners did not greatly care for these things and felt that the amount of airtime they occupied was not just undemocratic but élitist in the sense that unlike programmes about farming or sport, where 'the best' derived from other criteria programmes of classical music or drama simply reflected the values of those at the higher end of the social scale. The BBC, it was thought, regarded the likes of Bach and Shakespeare as the best only because they were preferred by the middle and upper classes.

The BBC's case was that Bach and Shakespeare were preferred by these classes only because they were the best. Certainly it reflected their judgments in the matter, but this was almost inevitable. Where else should judgments about artistic and intellectual merit come from, if not from the most highly educated, the most fully informed and the most widely travelled? And since these qualities generate wealth and are themselves sustained by it, where else would these people be found if not in the upper echelons of the social scale? But the corporation also held that there was no *inherent* connection between cultural values and social class. Given the opportunity, everyone – not just the élite – could appreciate Bach and Shakespeare, and this opportunity it was determined to provide. Hence the aim of public service broadcasting was to give to the public a 'better' service than it asked for. Reith himself was famously explicit on this. 'It is occasionally indicated to us that we are apparently setting out to give the public what we think they need – and not what they want,' he wrote, 'but few know what they want, and very few what they need' (1924: 34).

Such apparent arrogance must be seen in its historical context. In pre-war Britain universal education ended when children reached the age of about fourteen. Those temples of high art, the concert halls, opera-houses and theatres, were beyond the pockets of the great mass of people, and within the tiny minority who underwent higher education there was much more consensus than there is today about what in cultural terms was good, significant or worthwhile. Wireless was a new, and in terms of the number of frequencies available, a relatively scarce medium. Its potential was huge: in these early years nobody was sure what it could or could not do. To use it for less than those who were the fittest judges of these things acknowledged as 'the best' was a needless limitation – or as Reith put it more bluntly, a prostitution – of its powers.

Thus what Reith and the BBC were actually positing was a third notion of democracy which was concerned neither with majority nor universal *preferences* but with what they perceived as universal *needs*: for the aim was to open up to all those who had been denied them by a limited education, low social status and small income the great treasures of our culture. From a modern viewpoint 'treasures' perhaps begs the question, but they were regarded as such by those classes who embodied the prosperity and wisdom that set the standard for the other members of society. For the latter, Reith's BBC offered a chance of spiritual if not material enrichment, a policy which was surely less cynical than providing only what they would certainly have enjoyed, but which would neither have broadened their horizons nor raised their aspirations.

In practice, however, the BBC was rather more responsive to mass taste than Reith's words imply, for the logic of its cultural position would have been to broadcast no popular music, popular drama, light entertainment, or anything else which had a highbrow equivalent. It was aware that even with its virtual monopoly there were limits on how far it could edify or 'improve' listeners who might not wish to be improved: they could always switch off. The corporation therefore broadcast a fair amount of popular culture. For instance, according to figures it gave to the Ullswater Committee (1936: 31) it provided during 1934 nearly three times as much dance and light music as 'serious' music. Nevertheless it was always ready to discriminate on the listeners' behalf between 'the good' and 'the inferior' in popular culture – often on moral rather than aesthetic or intellectual grounds, as we shall shortly see in the case of jazz.

What would modify its cultural élitism was that, as the 1930s progressed, the political and indeed cultural tide in Britain ran ever more strongly in the direction of that notion of democracy which is based on the will of the majority; and Paddy Scannell and David Cardiff (1982) have detected a softening of the BBC's didactic approach during this period and an increasing sensitivity to popular taste.

Classical music programming

In the debate about cultural value and popular taste, music assumed a central position simply because a sound-only medium such as radio would almost inevitably transmit a great deal of it. On classical music the BBC's policy was twofold: to broadcast a wide range played to the highest standards, and to help the mass audience to understand and enjoy it. In its aim of combining quality and popularity it had been anticipated by Sir Henry Wood's annual Promenade Concerts, which ever since 1895 had provided London audiences with a cheap and informal blend of established works, adventurous new compositions and popular favourites. However in 1927 their sponsors, the music publishers Chappell, decided to pull out, and on the personal initiative of Reith the BBC took them over, and has ever since relayed them to the nation at large.

In 1930 the BBC founded its own symphony orchestra, and by the middle of the decade it was quite simply the most powerful music patron in the country – a huge concert-giving agency and the biggest employer of orchestral musicians. To ensure that the mass of its listeners would appreciate what they were hearing it engaged Percy Scholes and Sir Walford Davies to give talks on the rudiments and meaning of music – which they did clearly and without condescension. From 1927 to 1937 a fifteen-minute programme, *The Foundations of Music*, was broadcast five times a week, and some historians insist that the BBC succeeded in spreading a knowledge and enjoyment of classical music among those who were at the lower end of the social scale.

Nevertheless there was a sense in which its aim to broadcast the best performances of classical music was at odds with its aim to widen the public's access to it, because the former merged only too easily with its administrative policy of centralization. The BBC's cultural conservatism was typical of the time, in that broadly speaking it perceived the distinction between the good and the inferior as corresponding not only to the distinction between the preferences of the 'educated' and 'uneducated' or of those 'higher up' and 'lower down' the social scale, but to that which exists between 'capital city' and 'the regions'.

Something of this traditional association between culture and place can still be seen in words like *urbane* and *cosmopolitan*, which have the sense of 'cultured, educated'; for the former, like 'urban', comes from a word meaning 'belonging to the city', and the latter means 'a citizen of the world' in contrast to someone of merely local status or background. On the other hand, the words *parochial* and *provincial* can, in addition to their obvious meanings, imply ignorance and narrow-mindedness. Implicit in all these terms is the suggestion that since it draws from a variety of sources and not from any one place, great art or culture is a world-wide phenomenon, or at least characteristic of the city rather than the regions.

The BBC therefore believed that the best performances of classical music should, like those of any other art form, be transmitted from London, for as the capital city

London embodied the culture of the entire nation. However, its critics argued that at a fraction of the cost of hiring international artists to perform in the capital, the BBC should be encouraging music in the provinces – using the Regional Programme to introduce its listeners to their local orchestras and thus stimulate their attendance at local concerts.

Popular music

Rather less cosmopolitan than its view of the classics was the BBC's attitude to popular music, for much of the latter originated in America, specifically that sought-after negro music called jazz, and the corporation set itself against American influences as being vulgar in tendency. The question was not simply what 'the best' jazz was, but whether jazz had any merit at all, especially as it was widely denounced as 'jungle music', an unnatural sexual stimulant. Again, some knowledge of the historical context renders this view slightly less bizarre than it seems. Jazz had emerged only twenty or thirty years earlier from the brothels of New Orleans, the word itself deriving from negro slang 'to copulate'. Hence the music still seemed primitive and lewd. Only in the 1950s would it come to be regarded as 'high art', sanctified by old age, a decline in general popularity, and that growth of critical attention by which such decline is often accompanied.

In the early days the BBC's solution to what it saw as the problem of jazz was characteristic: it set out to 'improve' it, to make something decorously British out of this vigorous new art form. Though of unmistakably American provenance, jazz was mostly performed on air not by mere dance-bands but by smart hotel orchestras such as the Savoy Orpheans, and thus acquired something of the status and refinement of the native upper classes for whom they normally played. When the more authentically American or American-influenced 'hot jazz' was not actually banned, it was either filtered through the sedate presentation of the first disc-jockey, Christopher Stone, or broadcast not in 'jam sessions', where it might be merely enjoyable, but in 'recitals' of a solemnly educative nature.

Yet whether as jazz or in some other guise, popular music was given an enormous boost by radio, the latter soon surpassing gramophone records and local shows and dances as its main outlet. At the same time the balance of power within the music industry shifted from the publishers and music-hall impresarios to Broadcasting House. This shift was acknowledged by the BBC in 1933, when it instructed the producers of its dance programmes to deal directly with the bandleaders and no longer with the managers of the theatres from which they broadcast. For their part, the music publishers sought to turn the new medium to their advantage by paying bandleaders to play on air the songs they wished to promote from their lists, a practice known as 'plugging' and one which the BBC deplored as covert advertising. It therefore imposed a ban on the naming of songs so that the listeners would find them harder to identify, but the publishers' collecting agency, the Performing Right Society, responded by threatening to rescind its licensing agreement. The corporation was forced to back down, and plugging has ever since been a feature of music broadcasting.

At first it was not just the publishers and impresarios who felt threatened by radio; so, too, did the record companies – a rich irony in that records now make up virtually the whole of radio's output. Nevertheless, there seemed at the time to be good grounds for their anxiety. Records were a mass medium which had preceded broadcasting in the successful exploitation of popular music, but the ownership of wireless sets was becoming even more widespread than the ownership of gramophones and records. The companies feared that the BBC would simply use their products as a substitute for live music, thus relieving the public of the need to continue buying them, and in 1935 they charged the corporation several thousand pounds for the right to play records on the air.

What they perhaps underestimated was the durability of their products as against the evanescence of radio's, for broadcasting actually stimulated record sales. The BBC played relatively few records but it did broadcast live performances of many songs which, initially at least, were not available on disc. The companies were then able to offer contracts to the artists who performed them – and the public would buy their records on the strength of what they had heard on the air. Thus radio helped to create the record-based star system, for 'stardom' came to be defined not so much by popularity in the music halls or the sheet-music sales of songs as by popularity on the wireless and the sales of records. The BBC became a source of talent rather than a mere staging-post for it and the record companies grew to appreciate the promotional value of radio, even though they could not fully exploit it until the mid-1950s, when the more widely affordable cost of their products coincided so potently with the birth of rock music.

Of particular interest to the media student is the way in which broadcasting and records (whether discs, tapes, cassettes, CDs or minidiscs) have over the years wrought a change in the social consumption of music and in the status of popular musicians. When radio arrived, the traditional role of much popular music was as the setting or background for *dance*. People certainly bought the sheet versions of their favourite music-hall tunes to sing and play at home, but band music, especially under the growing influence of jazz, was primarily dance music, and in the early years many people used the wireless or gramophone as a kind of domestic dance band, rolling back the living-room carpet to do the waltz or the fox-trot. But although radio and records could domesticate music, for reasons of space they could less easily domesticate dance, the effect of which was, as Stephen Barnard (1989: 9) points out, that the music shifted from background to focus, the arrangements of the songs becoming steadily more elaborate to satisfy the inactive listening to which these media mostly gave rise. This in turn had the effect of raising the status of those bandleaders, popular singers and musicians who broadcast or made records to that which had long been enjoyed by classical virtuosi, and meant that they would mainly be watched and listened to even when audiences had the opportunity to dance to them.

This change in the consumption of popular music and the status of those who played it is well illustrated by the career of the early bandleader Jack Payne. In 1926 Payne got himself appointed as the BBC's Director of Dance Music , and in order to give the music a kind of corporate style he managed to form the BBC Dance Orchestra in 1928 – two years before an institution which was renowned for its cultural élitism created its first classical orchestra. His radio shows soon made Payne such a celebrity that in 1932 he left the BBC and took his orchestra on a national tour – not of dance-halls but theatres (Barnard 1989: 11–12).

The change from bands as dance accompanists to performers of interest in their own right is traceable through the wartime shows of the great Glenn Miller Band to the gargantuan rock and pop concerts of the last thirty years; and a measure of this change would be the presumptuousness of expecting any of the leading rock groups of our time to play at a mere dance. To repay our concentration on the music, their songs have become longer and more intricately arranged (the first rock songs of the 1950s lasted about two minutes whereas most are now between four and five minutes): and to heighten the visual appeal of the bands, there has been an increasing use of such accessories as light-shows, dry ice, moving rostrums, back projections, and onstage dancers to gyrate vicariously for the tightly packed spectators. Rock videos have gone yet further by posing bands in improbable locations far removed from dance- or even concert halls.

Light entertainment

During much of the 1920s and 1930s the BBC's producers continued to think of light entertainment in terms of its original habitat, the theatre and the music hall, and wireless merely as a means of relaying shows from that habitat or, at best, as a place to re-create it. Because stage shows had a chorus line so might the BBC, even in the shows it originated. Its 1925 revue *Radio Radiance* featured a troupe of dancing girls who were rendered audible by performing on boards! At first the BBC exploited the music hall fairly successfully, either by direct broadcasts of its shows or by using its stars, but not surprisingly it soon fell foul of the impresarios, notably the Society of West End Theatre Managers. Fearing a loss of custom, they periodically stopped shows from being heard on air and threatened to ban any performer who broadcast. The performers themselves were scarcely more enthusiastic. Radio simply devoured their material. The two or three routines which in the halls could last them a lifetime now vanished into the ether and could never be used again. By the early 1930s the live theatres were no longer a rich source for the BBC, for it had all but exhausted what material had not been denied to it by the managers.

In 1933 it therefore systematically began to develop its own material by creating a variety department under Eric Maschwitz. Nevertheless, it continued to regard light entertainment primarily as a creature of the theatre, in imitation of which it included a live studio audience. It was the latter to whom many of the performers sought to appeal, believing that if those in the studio were entertained the listeners at home would follow suit. On some radio shows during the 1930s the performers wore full costumes and make-up; in addition, the two co-stars of *Old Mother Riley*, which ran until 1948, insisted on learning their lines instead of reading from scripts (Foster and Furst 1996: 67).

The very titles of some of these shows were telling. Among the first, yet one which survived until 1952, was *Music Hall*, a blend of singing and comedy acts, but also for a time including more invisible tap-dancers, the Eight Step Sisters. Another with a title which betrayed its derivative nature was *Songs from the Shows*. But perhaps most extraordinary was the adaptation of a genre whose visual essence is expressed in its very name: black-face minstrelsy. *The White Coons' Concert Party* ran from 1932 until 1936, its theme-tune beginning with the exhortation 'Come on and listen to the gay white coons'. But even more popular was *The Kentucky Minstrels* (1933–50), later revamped for television as *The Black and White Minstrel Show*.

The early wireless entertainers fell into two main categories. The broader comedians and singers included Will Hay, Gracie Fields, Wee Georgie Wood and Elsie and Doris Waters, while a gentler, more sophisticated style was adopted by Gillie Potter, Ronald Frankau, Jack Hulbert and Beatrice Lillie, who incorporated into her act songs from cabaret and operetta.

Whether by inclination or necessity, the theatre impresarios and their artists gradually softened towards radio. The former came to appreciate the value of the publicity it gave to their shows, the latter to recognize that however greedily the medium swallowed their material it could, in a single show, provide them with an audience bigger than that acquired in a whole lifetime on the boards – and in any case, that if they declined to broadcast they would soon be eclipsed by the home-grown stars of the BBC. The evolving attitude of the music hall artists, along with that of the newspaper proprietors, theatre managers and owners of the record companies, illustrates a process which is a familiar feature of cultural history. Those who in some way control traditional media or genres begin by opposing a new medium, and then make an accommodation with it which often provides them with a new and profitable role, albeit one which is changed or reduced somewhat.

A final word on the broadcasting of sport. Before 1927 the BBC was unable to offer full running commentaries on sports events because the Newspaper Proprietors' Association had persuaded the government that these were another form of news reporting. The restriction was lifted when the company became a corporation, enabling it to cover such national events as the Derby, the Cup Final and the Boat Race.

Educational, features and documentary programmes

Most of the BBC's *educational* programmes were for schools and ranged from attempts at direct teaching – the giving of on-air lessons – to story-readings and dramatizations whose pedagogical aims were rather more oblique. They had begun in 1924, when they were received by 220 schools. By 1927 they were being heard in 3,000 schools, and in 1939 up to 10,000 schools were listening to 39 programmes a week.

Despite these figures schools broadcasting was attended by problems from which it has never altogether freed itself. Radio had already become so indelibly associated with leisure and entertainment that local education authorities could seldom be persuaded that it was an educational necessity and not a luxury. Second, in an era before off-air recording it was hard to integrate this time-based medium into individual school timetables and curricula: lessons had to be adjusted to wireless broadcasts and not vice versa. And third, the temporal dimension was a problem even within individual broadcasts because despite the reinforcement of their teachers, children sometimes found it hard to extract learning points from a constantly changing 'text'.

Its problems of blindness and evanescence mean that radio has always been more effective as an educative or informative than as a direct-teaching medium, and the BBC broadcast a wide range of educative talks. A measurable and gratifying effect of these was that in the shops and public libraries they would create an immediate demand for books on whatever subjects they were dealing with. The Talks Department was started in 1927 under Hilda Matheson and further developed from 1932 by Charles Siepmann, and among the distinguished speakers it used were the playwright George Bernard Shaw, the economist John Maynard Keynes, and the writers H. G. Wells and G. K. Chesterton.

Very different from educational and educative output was that strange category known as *features*, though as we shall see they tended to converge in a third category: documentaries. Features programmes, which date from 1928, occupied the large space between drama and current affairs and were often treated as a kind of broadcasting laboratory in which the aim was to test the limits of a sound-only medium. Many of them were montages of narrative, dramatic dialogue, music, verse, sound-effects and, later, sound actuality. Many were also blends of fact and fiction, and though 'features' is a term we still use, albeit in the rather different sense of a human interest story or investigation, these early wireless features seem to be distant ancestors of the modern TV docudrama. Certainly one important generic contribution of radio and television, with their use of actuality and 'real' locations, has been their ability to equivocate very effectively between real life and make-believe – a subject we shall return to later. In essaying vast themes such as *The Sea* or *Speed: a Tragi-Comic Fantasy of Gods and Mortals* (1928) some of these early features were ambitious failures, but as Paddy Scannell (1986: 7) points out, in the growing economic recession of the 1930s the programmes gradually acquired more social and political relevance, and were in this respect influenced by the contemporary cinema documentaries of Robert Flaherty and John Grierson. They thus became less easily distinguishable from the *documentary* genre.

The strength of the BBC's documentary output in the 1930s grew quite unexpectedly out of its organizational upheavals, in particular from Reith's desire for firm control at the centre and for radical and dissident members of the corporation to be dispersed to its fringes. One able features producer of left-wing views was A. E. Harding, whose *Crisis in Spain* (1931), which recounted the events that had recently led to the formation of the Spanish Republic, showed how much he had been influenced by the cinematic techniques of Grierson. It has been suggested that his political leanings were the cause of Harding's later removal to the Northern Region, and that the removal was ordered by Reith himself.

At its Manchester headquarters Harding gathered around him a talented team of writers and actors. His work included more poetic features such as *The March of the '45* (1936), a chronicle of the Jacobite Rebellion, but he also devised a strategy for making programmes which would evoke the characteristic spirit of the North. Harding and his team interviewed ordinary people, among them the unemployed, and encouraged them to relate their experiences in their own words. Their accounts would be worked up into scripts by such writers as D. G. Bridson and Crawford McNair, and then returned to them to rehearse and broadcast at the Manchester studio. Before the war, almost all broadcast utterances were scripted, partly because the BBC felt a need to maintain tight editorial control, but mainly because of poor recording and editing facilities. This meant that Harding's interviewees could never sound as spontaneous and authentic as those in a modern documentary, but at least they were reading out experiences which were both genuine and their own.

In the second half of the decade the Northern Region enjoyed a flowering of radio documentary. Harding's best-known creation was *Harry Hopeful*, a series which began in 1935. The eponymous character was an unemployed glass-blower's assistant played by Frank Nicolls, in real life a clock-mender from Irlam near Manchester. Its theme was that Harry Hopeful travelled through the North in search of work, meeting and talking to people in the places he visited – a blend of fiction and 'real life' which had been retained from earlier features programmes.

The BBC had gathered its first sound actuality in 1934, using a recording van which had been hired from a film company. It was incorporated into a documentary about cockneys hop-picking in Kent which was given the racy title *'Opping 'Oliday* to show that the BBC knew how such people talked. From 1937 Bridson was able to use a new but hugely unwieldy mobile recording unit to make such industrial features as *Steel* and *Coalface*, further blends of actuality, poetic narrative and music. Later, Olive Shapley also made use of actuality in her studies of lorry drivers, barge-people and other working-class folk.

As an informative genre, documentary could embrace both features programmes and talks on social, economic and political themes. During much of the 1930s Professor John Hilton spoke with chatty shrewdness, for the most part on economic matters but on a range of contemporary issues; and some talks embroiled the BBC in quarrels with politicians both inside and outside the government. Not surprisingly, the government feared the power of the new medium to disturb the *status quo*. In 1931 the Liberal peer Lord Beveridge was accused of left-wing bias after delivering a series of talks on unemployment, and in 1933 *SOS*, another series on the same subject, caused further controversy despite being given by the genteel S. P. B. Mais, a former public school master. In the same year Howard Marshall gave graphic reports of the poverty and squalor of the North in a series called *Other People's Houses*, and in 1934 even greater uproar attended a series called *Time to Spare*, in which the talks were delivered by the unemployed themselves. Fear of the subversive effects of the wireless perhaps reached its apogee in 1935, when the government forced the BBC to ban the communist Harry Pollitt and the fascist Sir Oswald Mosley from contributing to a series of talks it had planned on the British constitution. It was natural that politicians should fear that social unrest would follow such programmes. As Paddy Scannell (1980: 23–4) observes, their effects were potentially the more radical because they were not reports for the initiated or sermons to the converted but heard by the broadest cross-section of the public. What was perhaps less clear was the grim possibility that an accumulation of these programmes would not incite their listeners but inure them.

Constructing the listener: the need for audience research

Whether its aim was to improve or entertain, the BBC had a lively consciousness of the listener's 'presence', though not much idea of her or his precise identity. Such a consciousness was essential, for like most newspapers the new medium of broadcasting was received privately – by people in their homes. Yet whereas newspapers, which were targeted at particular socio-economic groups, could gauge their success in the finite terms of 'copies sold', broadcasting, which was aimed at everyone, could not. In *Broadcast over Britain* Reith manages to combine consciousness of the listener with a sense of the medium's indeterminacy when he writes of wireless entering both the rich person's mansion and the poor person's cottage, yet remaining freely available to the second however much it is used by the first.

In 1923 concern for the listener and for her or his needs was tangibly expressed in the launch of the *Radio Times*, which owed its existence to the newspapers' refusal to publish details of the BBC's programmes. As well as listing the programmes for the week ahead it contained articles and features, at first appearing under a deal with the publisher Newnes. Eventually the BBC took it over completely, and with its appeal to readers of all ages and its seven-day life, it became hugely popular and a very valuable medium for advertisers. By 1934 its circulation had climbed to 2 million, and it was especially important to listeners in the days before programming became routinized and hence more predictable.

But although the listener was provided for at this material level, the BBC remained largely in the dark as to her or his composite identity. In the absence of precise knowledge it was thus necessary to 'construct' the listener – and not surprisingly the BBC did so in its own image. Consistent with its conservative and élitist cultural perspective, it recruited most of its own staff from the educated middle class, and this provided the social background and moral values of the audience it constructed. Implicitly it promoted the idea that contemporary social arrangements were the best ones possible, that family togetherness was cemented by radio listening, and that in the context of our vast European cultural heritage the influence of America was for the most part a vulgar irrelevance. In matters of family morality, the standards the corporation set related not only to the nature of its output but the conduct of its employees: in 1929 Reith dismissed his much-valued chief engineer Peter Eckersley when the latter was cited in a divorce case.

Inasmuch as the BBC reflected what vast numbers of middle-class people were, and many working-class people aspired to be, its approach was successful. Inasmuch as it neglected or misrepresented what working-class people were, it was not. One should not exaggerate its failings. Much of its music and light entertainment was nothing if not populist, and many of the documentary and features programmes were attempts to express the problems and culture of working people. But it provided less than it might have done, for a number of reasons – social, geographical and cultural – which were mutually reinforcing.

In the first place the predominantly middle-class background of its administrative and production staff meant that within the corporation there was a widespread ignorance about the realities of working-class life. But this ignorance was not simply social; it had a geographical dimension, too. The main centres of education and affluence from which the BBC most readily recruited were in London and the south east, whereas the great mass of the industrial working class was in the midlands and the north. Moreover, middle-class ignorance of the latter was legitimated by the broad assumption we outlined above that what was culturally valuable or significant was not specific to regions or localities but urbane, cosmopolitan. In this respect, London, the capital city, did not count as a mere 'locality'. The Regional Programme was, of course, devised to temper metropolitan influence by expressing regional affairs and regional culture. But the artificial nature of its regions together with the sustaining service which London provided for it, and which its own programmes often had to make way for, showed where the BBC's real priorities lay. And to a large extent the limitations in regional programming were limitations in the programming that was provided for the working class. Folk songs and folk writings were given relatively little airtime, and according to Stephen Barnard (1989: 12) there were two working-class crazes of the 1920s and 1930s, accordion playing and community singing, which the BBC neglected altogether.

Some other aspects of working-class life were even more glaringly overlooked: Curran and Seaton (1997: 123) tartly observe that during 'a decade of hunger marches and "red united fighting fronts" the BBC regarded a succession of royal broadcasts as the triumph of outside broadcasting and actuality reporting'. This was not insensitivity pure and simple. Though the 1930s were a period of economic slump and severe unemployment, the corporation held the artless if well-meant belief that it could bring greater solace to working people by giving them a glimpse of the lives of their king and queen than by holding a mirror to their own. A similar belief presumably underlies the obsession of today's popular tabloids with the doings of the royal family, film stars, rock singers and other celebrities. But it should be added that for most people during the 1920s and 1930s the monarchy provided more than glamorous escapism. It symbolized a nation which despite its economic and political difficulties was one of the wealthiest and most powerful in the world – at the centre of a diverse and far-flung empire, yet ethnically and spiritually much more homogeneous than it is today. With whatever justification, many – though by no means all – working people felt they had as much reason as any other social group to be proud of the monarchy and of what it represented.

The BBC's preoccupation with royalty and its rituals, which now strike us as anachronisms that say much less about the health of the nation than those marches and movements it largely ignored, perhaps expressed another aspect of its cultural conservatism: a belief that the most valuable things are not only 'placeless' or cosmopolitan but timeless, and therefore that since current affairs are ephemeral there is a sense in which they are relatively unimportant. That the BBC inclined, at least intermittently, to this view seems less far fetched when we reflect that even today that conservative and highbrow network, Radio 3, carries almost no news or current affairs – 0.3 per cent of its total output, according to a recent calculation (Barnard 2000: 140).

Hence we can conclude that although working people did not necessarily feel excluded by programming which did not address their circumstances, they were clearly less well provided for than those who were higher up the social scale. However, from the early 1930s producers felt a growing need to identify rather than construct the national audience and discover just how effective their programmes were. By 1935 98 per cent of the population were within reach of at least one network, and 58 per cent could hear two. The other available figures, though broadly encouraging, were not very revealing. Homes with wireless sets rose from less than 4.5 million in 1931 to almost 8 million by 1939. But what did the myriad mute, invisible listeners think of what they were hearing? Was public service broadcasting effective? Were the serious programmes edifying and the lighter ones entertaining? Was the corporation overlooking anything which its listeners considered valuable?

Unfortunately, that more articulate section of the population whom we term the intelligentsia was of no help in these matters. In Gorham's (1952: 102) words, 'serious criticism of broadcasting was rare, mainly because serious people did not take broadcasting seriously'. Such people tend to be suspicious of new media because agreed critical standards for them have not yet emerged (later on, television was for many years dismissed as 'the idiots' lantern', while radio came to be regarded as a serious medium); and so in 1929 the BBC began *The Listener*, a periodical of essays and reviews for the more critically minded and analytical within the audience. The only things which were known about the identity and tastes of the listeners came from the casual letters they wrote to the BBC or the press. But these were not truly representative of the audience as a whole: they came from a tiny fraction of it and were written by untypically literate people with untypically strong views.

For a long time Reith resisted the demand for audience research. In pursuit of public service aims he did listen to the views of such bodies as the National Advisory Committee on Education and the Religious Advisory Committee, since both had been appointed to speak on the audience's behalf. But he knew that a comprehensive investigation of listener tastes would influence and eventually dictate broadcasting policy, and that worthwhile programmes for minorities would be sacrificed to the ratings. Nevertheless, the advocates of research eventually had their way, and in 1936 the Listener Research Section was set up within the Public Relations Department. Its first head was Robert Silvey, who conducted his research by a technique of random sampling and was soon gathering reassuring evidence that the BBC was being listened to by a broad cross-section of the population. This in itself suggests that the programmes could not have been wholly displeasing, but what, more precisely, did the listeners think of them? The general verdict seems to have been that they were substantial, reliable, sometimes highly enjoyable – but circumscribed. That many listeners did not get exactly what they wanted, or in sufficient measure, did not create frustration pure and simple. There was doubtless a measure of that, but just as we are apt to despise those who pander to our every whim and respect those who do not, there was a certain esteem for the BBC and pride in it as an august national institution. What the audience often had to take from it was rather like medicine: it was not altogether pleasurable but it sometimes made them feel better.

The converse of this is, of course, that a diet mainly of cakes and sweets can often result in disgust and nausea, but what made popular taste seem increasingly authoritative was the growing political status of that form of democracy which favours only the largest number. The most disquieting discovery of the audience researchers confirmed Reith's fears that the BBC could not withstand competition from populist, commercial stations. Such competition had been harrying it since the beginning of the 1930s, but that is a story for a later chapter.

Sources/further reading

This chapter owes a comprehensive debt to the three authorities on broadcasting in the 1930s: Asa Briggs, Paddy Scannell and David Cardiff. Briggs (1965) provides a general account of 'the extension and enrichment' of broadcasting between 1927 and 1939, and Scannell and Cardiff (1991) have written a history which is particularly illuminating on the social impact and cultural implications of broadcasting. A fascinating account of the unique social entity that was created with the establishment of the British Broadcasting Corporation in 1927 is provided by Burns (1977). For an excellent summary of the BBC's statutory position, its relations with government, and the mixed programming output of its first networks see also Scannell and Cardiff (1982). A defence of the BBC's monopoly and its public service policy is in Reith (1924).

A brief, illustrated history of BBC external broadcasting is Walker (1992). For the first ten years of the Empire Service see MacKenzie (1987), and for an account of external services up to the 1950s see Paulu (1956), which is extended to 1974 in Briggs (1995) and to 1980 in Paulu (1981). The standard history of the first fifty years of BBC external broadcasting is Mansell (1982).

Briggs (1965) and Scannell and Cardiff (1982) deal at some length with the early organizational problems of the BBC, and the latter summarizes the dilemmas of regional programming, on which Gorham (1952) is also illuminating. A useful sketch of the way in which regional expression was accommodated within the BBC's policy of centralization can be found in Harvey and Robins (1994). For various versions of the relations between Reith and the first board of governors, Reith's role in the BBC during the 1930s, and the events leading to his resignation, see Reith (1949), Boyle (1972), Stuart (1975) and McIntyre (1993).

Good general accounts of pre-war programming categories and individual programmes are to be found in the standard works of Briggs (1965) and Scannell and Cardiff (1982, 1991); also in Gorham (1952), Paulu (1956), Parker (1977), Briggs (1981), Gifford (1985) and Donovan (1992). In addition to all these, the following are illuminating on particular programme categories: Pegg (1983) on the impact of radio news on press news; Reith (1949) on radio coverage of the death of George V and the abdication crisis. Scannell (1981) provides an authoritative account of the BBC's pre-war policy on classical music. For similar accounts of its policy and practice on popular music, see Frith (1983) and Barnard (1989). Frith also covers contemporary light entertainment. General surveys of early radio comedy are in Took (1976) and Foster and Furst (1996), and Cardiff (1988) explores its origins and social basis. Pickering (1994, 1996) is useful on the origins and development of 'blackface' comedy on the radio.

In the field of educational talks and information presentation Cardiff (1980) detects a drift towards populism in the 1930s, but I argue (Crisell 1986, 1994) that radio is in any case of limited effectiveness as an educational and talks medium. For an understanding of early radio features, see Sieveking (1934). Bridson (1971) offers personal recollections of making features and documentaries for the Northern Region, and for a lucid and detailed account of pre-war features and documentaries see Scannell (1986). A transcript of some of John Hilton's 1930s talks is in Hilton (1938).

For the BBC's approach to the economic problems of the 1930s and the political controversies it provoked, see Scannell (1980). Curran and Seaton (1997) argue that as far as possible the BBC avoided contentious political issues during the 1930s as a way of consolidating itself as a national institution.

On the broadcasters' consciousness of the listener see Reith (1924). Pegg (1983) is especially useful on early listener reactions and on the birth of audience research. For the early methods and discoveries of audience research, see Silvey (1974).

Chapter 3

Keeping the sabbath, waging a war and building a pyramid

Keeping the sabbath, waging a war and building a pyramid

Breaches of the BBC's monopoly

As we have seen, the efforts of the corporation to inform, educate and edify would be ineffective if the audience had the option of ignoring it and tuning to stations which catered solely to popular taste. Since as a monopoly broadcaster the BBC did not depend for its survival on maximizing its audience it could maintain a varied and balanced diet of programmes and cater to minorities. But the arguments against monopoly were equally powerful. By any standards it was undemocratic, because even for those whose tastes were being met by the varied programming it was a denial of choice. Who was to say that the varied programming provided by a competitor might not delight them even more? Lack of choice was also a problem for those who had something to broadcast. If the BBC refused them access to the microphone – as it did to a Winston Churchill eager to denounce the government's policy of appeasing Hitler – no other outlet was available, and the audience might be worse off for not being able to hear what they had to say.

In the event the monopoly lasted less than ten years. Its demise was largely a result of the 'Reith Sunday', the grimmest of the corporation's attempts to 'improve' its listeners rather than provide the kinds of programmes that most of them wanted. Sunday was a day on which nearly everyone had the free time to listen to the radio, and after what was not uncommonly a working week of six days people felt especially in need of output which was lighthearted and relaxing. What Reith decreed they should get were programmes which did not begin until 12.30 p.m. and consisted entirely of religious services, serious talks and classical music. It must be acknowledged that during the 1920s and 1930s Britain was a more uniformly Christian country than it is today, and that among the faithful there was rather more observance of the sabbath, whether through churchgoing or in a fairly sedate and reflective life-style. Nevertheless, the Reith Sunday was a serious misjudgment of the national mood – or at best an indifference to it.

Inevitably, certain entrepreneurs found a profitable way of creating a service which the great bulk of the wireless audience would enjoy. Since under the agreement between the BBC and the Post Office no rival stations could be established in Britain itself, the solution was to beam programmes into it from stations located overseas. The entrepreneurs would make their money either by devising populist programmes which advertisers would pay for or by selling the advertisers airtime in which to broadcast programmes of their own.

One such entrepreneur, whose faith in the power of advertising was comically declared in his surname, was Captain Leonard Plugge, later a Conservative MP for the Medway towns. Running his International Broadcasting Company from an office in insolent proximity to Broadcasting House, Plugge bought airtime on several foreign stations within reach of Britain – Toulouse and Paris in France, Athlone in Ireland – and simply sold it as advertising space to British companies, leaving the actual programme content to be determined by the presenters he engaged. But in 1931 he also founded Radio Normandie, which broadcast from Fécamp on the northern coast of France and provided the clearest signal of all. Southern England was its main reception area, where listeners were regaled mostly by American-style dance music. Within twelve months twenty-one firms were sponsoring broadcasts, and by 1934 Normandie was reaping £400,000 a year in advertising.

On 4 June 1933 another station opened, the continentally owned Radio Luxembourg, broadcasting from the tiny principality of that name situated between France, Belgium and Germany. Ignoring the International Broadcasting Union, the body which had been set up to allocate wavelengths, it began by pirating a long-wave frequency and offered, like Normandie, output which was unashamedly populist. It declared its competitive intentions by at first broadcasting only on Sundays, and throughout its pre-war years it always reserved its strongest programmes for this day, featuring such major stars as George Formby and Gracie Fields. The BBC made strong representations to the IBU to get both Normandie and Luxembourg taken off the air but to no avail, and by 1934 ninety companies were advertising their products on the commercial stations.

Luxembourg was a highly professional enterprise, for shrewd commercial reasons exercising little control over its own output. It sold its airtime to advertisers on the basis that it was they, and not the station, who provided the programmes. This meant that Luxembourg gained revenue from the sale of airtime without having to spend money on providing entertainment. Its attitude was that those best qualified to make programmes were the advertising agencies, the biggest of which had their own radio production departments. The two main agencies were J. Walter Thompson and the London Press Exchange, which would find a programme format and a presenter to suit the brand image of each client. Since the Post Office's agreement with the BBC precluded it from supplying overseas lines for the agencies, they pre-recorded the programmes on disc and sent them out to Luxembourg for transmission. The quality of reception back in Britain was variable, but the station could be picked up nearly everywhere and was especially popular in the working-class areas of north-east England and south Wales. Its programmes consisted mostly of variety shows, dance-band half-hours and personality showcases in which the artists were closely associated with the products they advertised. Thus Joe Loss and his orchestra were heard thanks to Meltonian Shoe Polish, Geraldo and his by courtesy of Cadbury's Chocolates. One of Luxembourg's most successful pre-war shows was a children's programme sponsored by the makers of the malted drink Ovaltine, and punningly titled *The Ovaltineys' Concert Party*. As a by-product of the show a club called the League of Ovaltineys was formed in 1935, and by 1939 had enrolled some 5 million members.

What the BBC's audience researchers discovered in 1936 was that on Sundays a vast number of its listeners (its rivals put it as high as 82 per cent) were defecting to the commercial stations, and that of these Luxembourg had by far the largest single audience. Both Normandie and Luxembourg were eventually closed by the exigencies of the war, but the latter resumed in 1946. It is true that before 1939 the BBC was unable to compete with the commercial operators on altogether equal terms because its transmission hours were limited by the government – except during the General Strike it was never allowed to begin broadcasts before 10.15 a.m. But the real cause of its Sunday problem could not be disguised.

Nevertheless, the subtler change in listening habits which was taking place during the rest of the week was even more ominous, for the researchers found that even when the BBC's programme mixture included many lighter and brighter elements, a slowly growing number of people were abandoning it for the often weaker signals of its rivals. In his dour way Reith was right. If the listening public had a choice between continuous light programming and a mixture of serious and light programming it would gravitate towards the former, and his concept of public service broadcasting was therefore at risk from the moment the corporation's monopoly was broken.

Trimming some sails

It is possible to exaggerate the effects of competition on the BBC, especially before it initiated audience research in 1936: we saw in the last chapter that for much of the pre-war period it fashioned the listener very largely in its own image and planned its programmes accordingly. Nevertheless, Scannell and Cardiff (1982: 186–7) have detected a tendency during the second half of the decade towards popularization in its programmes, some acceptance of that notion of democracy which favours the majority. Not surprisingly it was a tendency which grew more marked after 1936 and gathered pace with the departure of Reith some two years later.

The earliest sign of a shift towards lighter programme content dates from about 1934. David Cardiff (1980: 29–47) argues that after the corporation's disputes with the government about their political content, its broadcast talks became generally less serious in subject matter and more entertaining in tone. Paddy Scannell suggests that from about the same time there was some falling away from the public service ideal in the sphere of classical music. We have already seen that there was a general policy within the Music Department to educate the mass audience into an appreciation of such music. However, the department came under growing pressure from the administrators not so much to raise popular taste to the level of the music as to 'jazz it up' – in effect to lower the music to the level of popular taste (Scannell 1981: 257).

The other signs of popularization were those which occurred in the *sequence* and *format* of the programmes, notably the development of routinized or 'fixed-point' scheduling. It will be remembered that one of the aims of Reith's concept of mixed programming was to combat lazy or routine listening. Frequently there were pauses between programmes to enable listeners to adjust to a change of stimulus or even to switch off. (The *Radio Times* urged them to 'give the wireless a rest' from time to time.) During the early 1930s fixed-point scheduling was generally avoided. Apart from news and special items like religious services and charity appeals the great bulk of the programmes dodged about from week to week, for we will recall that another of Reith's aims was to surprise the listener into new interests. Even popular series had only short runs and were replaced by something of quite different appeal. Programme under- or over-shoots were common and continuity was leisurely.

Reporting the inroads which were being made into the BBC's audience by the European stations, the Listener Research Section confirmed what by the late 1930s must have been the observations, if not the intuitions, of many programme producers: except at moments of national crisis, mourning or celebration, or during big sporting events, radio was treated by most people as little more than 'a cheerful noise in the background', a mere domestic utility. It is difficult to determine what influence listener research had upon the scheduling and format of the BBC's programmes, but these began to change at about the same time as it was making its findings. Scannell and Cardiff (1982: 181) observe that by 1937 there were as many as forty fixed points in the weekday output of each week. Just as significantly there was a growth in the number of series and serials, which strengthened continuity from one day's fixed point to that of the next, and in the case of soap operas (*The English Family Robinson* began in 1938) mirrored something of the domestic continuity of the listeners' own lives. Thus, because wireless broadcasts were received in the home, the scheduling, and even to some extent the content, of the programmes came increasingly to reflect daily routine rather than offering entertainment which broke with it, as the theatre and cinema did.

The series or serial format could of course characterize not only drama but talks, features, concerts, or almost any other kind of programme. But it had a further significance for the corporation. As Scannell and Cardiff (1991: 377) so shrewdly point out, it was the most efficient way of meeting the unrelenting demands of the daily programme schedule, providing a fixed structure which could accommodate changes of content, locating novelty and surprise within the familiar and predictable. Moreover, the problem of generating fresh material, a problem which was made harder by the disparate cultural backgrounds of the national audience, was alleviated by the shared culture that could be built up within the series itself, in the form of signature tunes, catch-phrases, stock characters and past themes. (In passing, we might add that programmes of all kinds could increasingly draw upon the wider culture which was developing within broadcasting: the common knowledge of other programmes and personalities and of the ethos and idiosyncrasies of the BBC.)

Of course, routinized and formatted programming was not an invariable sign of popularization: highbrow themes could also benefit from this treatment, and often did. But there is no doubt that it was especially suited to those kinds of output which did not require close attention or could be assimilated without too much effort, and which were therefore preferred by the great majority of listeners.

Two cheers for democracy

Those who condemn Reith for being arrogant and patronizing and for force-feeding the public with highbrow culture are just as likely to come back from other countries thankful that British television offers something more than an unvarying diet of populist entertainment: game shows, chat shows, soaps, sport, action movies, and news bulletins in which two presenters swap jokes in case the viewers are not finding the items exciting enough. Yet it is hardly an exaggeration to say that if in Britain we are aware that the media are capable of more than these things, it is thanks to the drag-anchor of Reith's influence – a man who quit broadcasting over sixty years ago.

In fact Reith's essentially conservative and élitist BBC was founded in a society whose commitment to democracy was already considerable and growing steadily. In 1918 all women over thirty were given the vote for the first time. In 1928 their minimum voting age was lowered to twenty-one, and here as in certain other countries the democratic ideal has prevailed ever since, sometimes shining the more brightly amid totalitarian regimes. In 1970 the franchise was widened yet further when the minimum voting age of both sexes was reduced to eighteen.

It was suggested in the last chapter that since Reith's policy of public service broadcasting strove to cater for each person's needs, it could be seen as in some sense democratic. But it was not a policy in which its beneficiaries were given any say. That more orthodox version of democracy which considers the individual herself to be the best judge of what is good or right has long roots which are traceable to the religious and political conflicts of the sixteenth and seventeenth centuries. The Protestant Reformation exalted private judgment over the received authority of the Catholic Church, which it held to be arbitrary and unnecessary, and in the gradual disentanglement of politics from religion we can see the Civil War as a secular development of this, since it was largely a struggle to establish parliamentary democracy.

The United States prides itself on being a nation which was founded in democracy. The first white settlers in America sought to escape the religious and civil persecutions of their native Europe, and at the end of the eighteenth century the American War of Independence, fought on the principle of 'no taxation without representation', was a struggle to escape a British political system which denied them suffrage. Indeed the furtherance of the democratic ideal – the emancipation of black slaves – was a major cause of the American Civil War, which was to take place in the middle of the following century.

Historians have commonly linked the rise of democracy with the rise of industrial capitalism and the development of a competitive, consumerist society, a common denominator being the sovereignty of individual taste or preference. We noted in the introduction to this first part of our history that a key feature of industrialization was mass production, and that printing – the mass production of writing – anticipated the main Industrial Revolution by several centuries. Mass production in general seems to encourage democratization because in needing mass markets its tendency is to make its products affordable to as many people as possible, and printing had democratic effects not only in helping to diffuse ideas of religious and civil democracy but by widening access to writing of all kinds.

The political ascendancy of Britain in the nineteenth century was based largely on industrialization, but the United States – which superseded it early in the twentieth – took the techniques of mass production much further. The Ford motor car, the Kodak camera and the McDonald's hamburger are only a few vivid instances of the American ability to create products for a mass market. But that ability also extended to the mass media of cinema, gramophone records, radio and television. The genius of the Hollywood system, for instance, 'was to take a model which was designed to ensure that each product was *exactly* like the other (like cars off a conveyor belt) and inject into it the unexpectedness of art' (Caughie 2000: 126); and the overall achievement of America was to use these mass media to hasten and extend that democratization of culture which began with printing but which printing had achieved only slowly because it pre-required from its audience the difficult 'decoding' skill of literacy:

American culture is built on quantities: on mass reproduction and consumption, on filling a vast space with a homogenous [*sic*] unity . . . [T]he great gift of

America to the cultural universe, the Hollywood movie, has, by and large, been the product of rigidly determined principles, guidelines and codes since its very inception. Yet Hollywood has taken over the world. And when the world is overrun without a shot having had to be fired, then you can be sure that the world wanted to be conquered. For the great point about American culture is that it forces one to take a side, pro- or anti-, on the issue of democracy. If you don't like American culture you had better ask yourself what it is you are precisely objecting to, and an honest answer to that is often an uncomfortable one.

(Lezard 2000: 3)

While Reith's BBC eagerly embraced the democratic medium of broadcasting – democratic in not only reaching millions of ordinary people but reaching them in the privacy of their homes – there is no doubt that it tried to resist the democratization of culture that came with it. The American media catered to the masses on their own terms, giving them what they wanted: the BBC sought to elevate and educate them.

Most of us, at one time or another, are thankful that we live in a democracy – a society which allows each of us to judge and choose for ourselves. Even those who are living under a government which did not receive their vote know that it nevertheless owes its existence to votes, to the principle of popular choice. And in our daily lives, within what are fairly broad limits if compared with those of other socio-political systems, we can live as we like, believe in what we like, say, read and watch what we like. Perhaps one of the healthiest features of democracy is scepticism: we can impugn or ignore received wisdom, expertise or values; we can come to our own conclusions. Indeed it is hard to resist the idea that the rise of democracy has owed something to scepticism and agnosticism, to an intellectual exhaustion after the futile religious and civil upheavals of several centuries; for the principle of one person–one vote seems to rest upon the assumption that one person's judgment is as good as another's, that there is no such thing as authority or expertise.

The conflict between the status of authority and the rights of the individual, between the fact that some people know more or better than others and the idea that each of us should be empowered or free to choose, is a central problem for political thinkers. Even though it should be wrong that the most sophisticated intellectual has no more than that single vote which is also the birthright of the ignoramus, in a democracy it seems right. The paradox troubled Reith, although he expressed it in terms which are characteristically moral as well as intellectual:

There must be some principle of ethics or economics to justify equality of electoral power to an intelligent, responsible, respectable citizen, a producer by hand or brain, contributor in large or small measure to the wellbeing and wealth of the State; and to another unintelligent, irresponsible, a lifelong charge on the State.

(Reith 1949: 170)

Thus, while democracy elevates individual judgment it also, in a sense, debases it. If one person's view is as good as another's, then they are equally worthless. And what if the views differ? The consequence in a democracy is that qualitative criteria are replaced by, or become identified with, a merely quantitative one. In matters of culture we might say that terms like 'excellent', 'superior', 'valuable' or 'worthwhile' are likely to be regarded either as meaningless or simply as synonymous with 'that which is preferred by most people'. Hence, as a consequence of democratization,

the public discourses of our society reflect an unease about the exercise of informed judgment. A broadly diffused but inconsistently held value relativism is at work here. People fear that judgment, the discrimination of better from worse in almost any sphere, is 'élitist', even snobbish, masking mere prejudice and in concrete cases sheer favouritism. By contrast measurement appears more palatable: it retains the aura of being impersonal, objective, open, even democratic. Measurement is thought of as a technical skill and therefore (it is falsely assumed) as value-neutral. Rational argument about one thing being more valuable or more worthwhile than another constantly threatens to be displaced by mere head-counting: when 'what people want' is sovereign, the pollster speaks with more authority than the philosopher.

(Collini 2000: 15)

There are a number of objections to according sovereignty to 'what people want'. The first is that what people want is not always what they think is the most valuable. When watching television most of us prefer game shows, soap operas, rock videos, and soft porn and action movies to serious discussions, documentaries, operas, ballets, classical dramas and symphony concerts. Sometimes we may also be willing to cite their greater popularity as proof that they are better than the programmes we have rejected. But often what people reject is what they regard more highly. As the Roman poet Ovid put it: 'I see better things and approve them: I incline towards the worse.' Indeed, among those who are keen to preserve highbrow television programmes are many who never watch them at all. What we avoid is often demanding and difficult, and what we watch is a soft option which we sense is less good for us, just as toffee may be sweeter but less nourishing than fresh fruit.

Yet it is also significant that even those people who feel unable to make up their own minds about cultural or artistic value will look to the critics rather than the opinion polls, for there seems to be a universal and irrepressible instinct to continue to regard value as an intellectual matter, as something to be determined by reason and argument rather than a counting of heads. Nobody, even among the most uninformed, is likely to be dissuaded from the judgments she makes merely by being told that 'the majority' disagree with her. While conceding that 'For some media theorists (e.g. Fiske, 1987) the very fact of popularity is a token of value in . . . cultural terms', Denis McQuail (2000: 43) demonstrates the difficulty of acquiescing in this notion. Reason and judgment keep creeping in, leading one to the conclusion that much media content is,

> variously, repetitive, undemanding, thematically limited and conformist. Many examples can be found of popular content that are ideologically tendentious, nasty and positively anti-intellectual. These judgements may be regarded as conventional and old-fashioned but it remains the case that most popular culture is produced by large corporations with an overriding view to their own profits rather than to enriching the cultural lives of the people. Audiences are viewed as consumer markets to be manipulated and managed. Popular formulas and products tend to be used until threadbare, then discarded when they cease to be popular . . . .
>
> (McQuail 2000: 104)

McQuail is not, of course, suggesting that popular culture is *necessarily* any of these things – that it is inferior merely by virtue of being popular. There are, on the contrary, many instances of popular culture for whose high quality a strong case can be made. His point is simply that popularity is not *of itself* a satisfactory indication of quality. And the overall purpose of this discussion has been to suggest that even though Reith's concept of public service broadcasting has been gradually eroded by the tides of democracy and the extension of individual choice, there is a sense in which nothing has changed, for people continue to determine cultural value not primarily by counting heads but by invoking reason and intellect. They thus make judgments which are, in their way, every bit as élitist as Reith's were.

The Home Service and the Forces Programme

The Second World War was the first total war in which Britain was involved: because of the Blitz, the bombardment of major cities by the German air force, British civilians, as much as the troops, were in the battle zone – and so, of course, was the BBC. It also heralded the use of propaganda to a greater extent than ever before, with a conflict of words in which radio played a greater part than did the medium of print. And besides these challenges the BBC had broadcasting duties which would be normal in any war: to provide an extensive and credible news service and to raise and maintain national morale with a varied diet of entertainment.

To adapt to its wartime role the corporation expanded rapidly. In 1939 it consisted of 4,000 personnel, but by the beginning of 1940 they had increased to 6,000, and by its end to 11,000.

During the war there was also an interesting development in the way that radio was listened to. Having been largely a domestic medium it became simultaneously domestic and public because there was a need to reach listeners in those collective situations that war required or created: workers in factories and canteens, officers in messes, soldiers in camps and barracks. When the war ended radio largely reverted to its domestic role, although it is still collectively listened to in many warehouses, shops and factories. It was also during the war that the BBC was forced for the first time to learn a great deal about its audience. Since the war effort depended so much on the workers in the factories, shipyards and mines, as well as upon thousands of ordinary servicemen and women, their tastes had to be discovered and catered for; and, as we shall see, the populist tendency within the output became so strong that when the war ended it was irreversible.

At the outbreak of hostilities in 1939 the BBC removed some of its operations to the provinces, notably Oxford, Evesham, Bristol, Bangor, Manchester and Glasgow, and combined its national and regional networks into a single *Home Service*. Broadcasting was certainly difficult while these organizational changes were being made, but at first the corporation seemed to think that because life was serious its programmes should be dull, and it offered a leaden routine of public announcements, concerts by Sandy Macpherson at the BBC theatre organ, ministerial pep talks and gramophone records. Even members of the government joined in the protests.

By contrast, the broadcasts of the pro-German radio propagandist William Joyce attracted a good deal of interest. He was first heard from Hamburg in 1939, in the droning, hyper-refined tones which earned him the nickname Lord Haw-Haw, and the British press gave him larger audiences than he would otherwise have gained by inviting their readers to tune in to him as a joke. But Joyce was less ludicrous, more plausible and sophisticated than the press implied, and the decline in his audience which set in as the war progressed has probably been exaggerated. Listeners were likely to return to him when they perceived some deficiencies in the BBC's news coverage (Doherty 2000: 90–2, 113, 120).

But by 1940 there was more worthwhile listening at home, for in that year the BBC launched a second network, the *Forces Programme*, which was intended to maintain the morale of the troops forming the British Expeditionary Force in France. Asa Briggs (1970: 310) observes that the theory behind the contrast between the Home Service and the Forces Programme was not so much that civilians' and soldiers' tastes differed as that their listening conditions did. Certainly the kinds of programmes which the new network carried – variety shows, dance music, talks and the occasional classical concert – were familiar enough: it was the relative narrowness of the mixture and the lightness with which it was presented that were new. What helped to shape the Forces Programme was pressure from the military authorities, who were hoping that a flow of entertaining and undemanding programmes would dissipate the boredom of the troops. Their hand was strengthened by a report on the troops' listening habits which was commissioned by the BBC from A. P. Ryan and entitled *Listening by the BEF*. Ryan observed that the great majority of service people lent a deaf ear to 'cultural' output, and he urged the corporation to stop broadcasting 'the more austere kind of programmes' and to build on the respect which it already commanded from the public in order to win its affection.

The Forces Programme was intended just for the troops and just for the duration of the war: it was assumed that the civilian population would maintain its allegiance to the more serious Home Service. But by 1942 the former was being listened to by even more civilians than service people and commanding a total audience 50 per cent higher than that of the Home. By late 1942 the BBC was also providing the *General Overseas Service* for troops stationed abroad, and in February 1944, when the invasion of France was imminent and the bulk of the armed forces would be moved overseas, it combined the two networks to form the *General Forces Programme*.

The significance of the forces networks was that they began a process of cultural streaming within the BBC's output which would conclude only with the reorganization of Radios 1 to 4 in 1970. Before the war Reith and his successor F. W. Ogilvie adhered to the full mixed programming concept, seeing it as vital to the cultural improvement of the nation. As we have seen, its justification was that if programmes were stratified within separate networks the individual listener would no longer be exposed to the full range and richness of the BBC's output. The forces networks were intended to be a temporary dilution, not an abandonment, of this concept – a dilution acceptable only in the peculiar conditions of wartime. They offered mixed programming of a sort, but the mixture was noticeably thinner. We have seen that there was less variety in their ingredients and a more uniform lightness of tone, but the assumption was that when the war ended there would be a return to the *status quo*. Yet it soon became clear that their popularity would allow no simple return to the old mixed programming networks, and the BBC would have to find some compromise between its public service ideals and the consistently lighter tastes of many of its listeners.

The sounds of war: news

During the war the BBC's relationship with the government inevitably became even more delicate than before. Since the General Strike governments had made fitful attempts to bring the corporation to heel, usually when they thought that those it invited to the microphone were politically too extreme, or that its treatment of such issues as unemployment was likely to provoke social unrest. The wartime government shared the general belief that in the present situation broadcasting would be a powerful, possibly a decisive, weapon of propaganda, and therefore decided that the BBC should be made firmly accountable to the Ministry of Information.

The BBC, however, had other ideas. At the outset of the war it took the policy decision to tell the truth, as far as the truth could be ascertained, rather than create propaganda – perhaps the wisest decision it has ever taken. In pursuit of this policy it maintained a measure of independence from the various government departments, though Curran and Seaton (1997: 142) suggest that this was in large part due to muddle and incompetence at the Ministry of Information. Nor was the independence absolute, for in 1942 the BBC was prevented by the government from reporting a disastrous raid on Dieppe in which more than half of the Anglo-Canadian assault force were killed or wounded.

It was thanks to the war that radio at last came into its own as a rapid news medium. The newspapers were handicapped by the shortage of newsprint, but at such a time the newness of the news was of paramount importance and this was something in which even a healthy press could never have competed with broad-casting. The BBC's 9 a.m. bulletin reached huge and hungry audiences calculated at between 43 and 50 per cent of the population, and the pressure of events combined with important advances in technology to create a revolution in the way the news was presented. Before the war, bulletins had consisted of little more than straight readings of a text, in which style was often given more attention than intelligibility. Now the priority was reversed: there was a new concern to use syntax and vocabulary which were more appropriate to the sound medium, and to find newsreaders whose accents were more broadly representative of the audience, less particularly associated with the privileged. One improbable recruit was Wilfred Pickles, who hailed unmistakably from Yorkshire. As the war progressed bulletins developed from simple readings into something richer. News-gathering became much more systematic and efficient, and from 1944 the BBC began to appoint its own correspondents. Moreover the bulletins were supplemented by extended news programmes like *Radio Newsreel*, which began in 1940. As we observed at the beginning of Part I, 'newsreel' was a term borrowed from film, and hints at the BBC's eagerness to incorporate actuality into news presentation. In order to do so it needed to adopt new production techniques, to combine newsreading, correspondents' reports, actuality and comment in ways which would lend the news depth and perspective.

The use of actuality would, of course, have been all but impossible without some improvement in the ponderous technology of sound recording that had characterized the pre-war years. But quite apart from its use in the battle zones, recording became important to the studio production of news and its associated material. From about 1941 it removed the need to bring broadcasters into studios which were threatened by air raids and provided reserve material if programming schedules were disrupted. Furthermore, it allowed producers to clear in advance any material which government ministries might regard as 'sensitive', and it facilitated both the export of material (known as 'bottled programmes') to the Empire and the United States and the monitoring of German and Italian broadcasts.

Nevertheless it was on the BBC correspondents' reports from the battle zones that improved recording technology had the most dramatic effect. The Germans had done most to develop it yet used it much less imaginatively than did the British. Reporters such as Richard Dimbleby and Wynford Vaughan-Thomas were put through the same battle training as the soldiers and equipped with 'portable' disc recorders. Weighing forty pounds and carrying twelve double-sided discs, they could be used to send back front-line dispatches which with skilful studio editing enabled commentary and actuality to be powerfully integrated. On D-Day, 6 June 1944, the BBC launched another extended news programme, *War Report*, which quickly commanded regular audiences of 10 to 15 million in Britain alone, as well as being heard in many other parts of the world.

The sounds of war: entertainment

As Stephen Barnard (1989: 17) points out, the war was the first time in which broadcast entertainment was used for ideological purposes: to cheer people up and bind them together. Perhaps no single programme contributed more to these purposes than a wartime comedy show with a superficially bizarre title: *ITMA*.

In the last chapter we observed that during the 1920s and most of the 1930s radio producers continued to think of comedy and the other forms of light entertainment in terms of the conventional stage. When they were no longer able to broadcast live relays from the theatres, they frequently re-created the conditions of the theatre within the broadcasting studio. The first realization that radio might be able to create its own distinctive kind of comedy came with the unpromisingly titled *Band Waggon*, which began in 1938. Though primarily conceived as a music show, it contained comic interludes featuring Arthur Askey and Richard Murdoch. These were a conventional blend of quickfire gags and sitcom – Askey and Murdoch were the occupants of an imaginary flat on top of Broadcasting House – but it lit the blindness of radio with a streak of surrealism. The flatmates were custodians of the pips in the Greenwich Time Signal, and on one occasion a grand piano was heard slipping down the back of their settee.

When *Band Waggon* ended in 1939, the Variety Department was keen to replace it with another show which would mine the radiogenic seam it had opened. The result, which was built round the comedian Tommy Handley, already a seasoned radio performer, was *It's That Man Again*, a title borrowed from a headline which was frequently used by the *Daily Express* to announce the latest activities of Adolf Hitler. Soon known by its acronym *ITMA*, the show began slowly but was given an enormous boost by the onset of war. In every episode Handley acted as master of ceremonies and was visited by a motley sequence of characters – Mrs Mopp the cleaning woman, Colonel Chinstrap, Funf the German spy, Ali Oop, and many others. A special feature of the show was a door which was fitted with a variety of handles, locks and bolts. Each character would make an audibly different entrance, exchange rapid comic dialogue with Handley, and then depart with a slam.

ITMA was peculiarly suited to radio because it exploited the speed, surprise and unstable reality that are the inherent properties of a blind medium. The characters came and went as fast as could be imagined, but faster than could be seen: driven by puns and sound effects, situations would take unpredictable turns. The formal innovation, catchphrases, word-play and surrealism were certainly popular, but what struck a universal chord were the jokes about the dreariness of wartime: the queues, the rationing (one character, a senior civil servant, was fittingly named Sir Short Supply), the black market, bureaucracy and bumbledom. At its peak *ITMA* was attracting audiences of 15 million a week, and although that figure must have included some repeat listeners (each show was broadcast three times) it amounts to almost 40 per cent of the entire population.

Though their timing and delivery are faultless *ITMA*'s jokes may now be so dated as to be scarcely comprehensible. It may also be true that during the war people were so desperate to laugh that they thought the shows funnier than they were. But when Handley died suddenly in 1949 he was mourned as someone who had brought mirth and joy to an otherwise dismal and tragic world, and he was the first comedian to be honoured by a memorial service in St Paul's Cathedral.

Radio comedy may have given particular enjoyment, but in terms of the amount of airtime it could fill it was clearly a less 'efficient' form of entertainment than music. Music, popular and classical, live and recorded, filled hour after hour, a banal yet comforting presence in millions of homes. The government and the BBC collaborated in certain quasi-scientific attempts to use music to raise morale and productivity. In June 1940 *Music While You Work*, a half-hour programme of band music which was broadcast twice a day, was launched for relay by loudspeakers in factories. Its aim was to keep mass production at a steady rate by broadcasting a non-stop sequence of jaunty, popular tunes, all of the same tempo. As Barnard (1989: 23) points out, it was an early acknowledgment from the BBC of the background function of radio music. By 1944 the programme was being heard in over 8,000 factories with a total workforce of more than 4.5 million.

Another programme whose aim was to boost morale and production was *Workers' Playtime*, launched in 1941. It was the brainchild of the Minister of Labour, Ernest Bevin, and brought variety acts and audience singalongs to munitions and other factories. What is interesting is that both these shows outlived their original objectives – and indeed outlasted the war – by many years. *Workers' Playtime* survived until 1964, while *Music While You Work* died only with the Light Programme in 1967.

Also beginning in 1941 was *Sincerely Yours*, a showcase for the singer Vera Lynn which was especially aimed at the men in the armed forces. Curran and Seaton (1997: 136) point out that the military authorities believed the show was a serious mistake because the unsexy persona of the singer and her sentimental songs would have an enervating effect on the fighting men. In fact, the idea of a homespun girl pining for her boy but proud that he was doing his duty provided just the antidote to the suggestions of German propaganda that back at home the soldiers' womenfolk were being unfaithful to them. Vera Lynn became the great icon of the Second World War, 'the forces' sweetheart'.

Not all entertainment was 'light'. From June 1940 the writer J. B. Priestley delivered a series of chats to a nation at war under the title of *Postscript*. Their determined, stoical tone exactly caught the national mood, but they were dropped in October after the Conservatives objected to Priestley's evident socialist sympathies, only to be reinstated for a short run in 1941. Even more stimulating was *The Brains Trust*, a highbrow discussion programme which considered questions that were sent in by the listeners, and was first heard in June 1941. The panel consisted of the philosopher C. E. M. Joad, the zoologist Julian Huxley and – a populist gesture this – Commander A. B. Campbell, a bluff naval officer with a penchant for tall stories. It is extraordinary to think that this programme, which wrestled with problems of philosophy, art and science, engrossed a third of the population. But perhaps because it reminds us of the fragility of our existence, war seemed to sharpen the appetite for everything – comedy and variety certainly, but also serious things: as well as *The Brains Trust*, traditional drama and classical music were regularly aired and listened to by large audiences.

One important feature of wartime entertainment was the growing influence of American culture, an influence which was felt in a number of spheres and in several ways. For popular music the BBC was obliged, for obvious reasons, to make increasing use of gramophone records. But as Stephen Barnard (1989: 28) points out, the shortage of raw materials meant that no British records were being made, and so most of the wartime releases were American. As the war progressed increasing numbers of US military personnel were stationed in Britain, and to cater for their needs the *American Forces Network* was set up in London in 1943 – the first, and temporary, domestically based breach of the BBC's monopoly. The low-power transmissions it beamed to the US bases were all but inaudible to more than 10 per cent of the native population, but it was to have an important indirect effect on British broadcasting. Removing the commercial breaks, the American Forces Network simply re-broadcast the most popular music and comedy shows of the

US domestic networks: it is not surprising that by comparison American service personnel had a low opinion of the BBC.

The AFN's slick, tight mode of presentation had an important influence on the British Forces Programme. From 1944 the latter was broadcasting not only at home but overseas, where its listeners would have no *Radio Times* but would still expect to hear their favourite programmes. It therefore developed a greater regularity of scheduling and sharpness of timing and fixed-point scheduling was strengthened not only on the Forces Programme but on the Home Service. It is interesting to note that on the Home the hugely popular *Saturday Night Theatre* had routine built into its very title. Moreover, it was at this stage that the continuity system – in which a single announcer is in charge of an entire evening's output, rather as a conductor is in charge of an orchestra – was introduced on both networks in order to eliminate pauses which during wartime could be alarming.

By 1944 American variety shows were being syndicated to the BBC, and British listeners became captivated by such stars as Bob Hope, Bing Crosby, Glenn Miller, Jack Benny, the Andrews Sisters and Frank Sinatra. It is perhaps at this point that British popular culture began to be dominated by that of America, a dominance whose end is not yet in sight.

Broadcasting in wartime: an assessment

The war years are of significance to our history partly because they were the occasion of particular achievements by the BBC and partly because they demonstrated the nature and capabilities of broadcasting in general. These two things are, of course, connected: it was largely because of what the BBC achieved that the nature and capabilities of broadcasting became clearer. But they were also directly illuminated by the war inasmuch as broadcasting proved much less vulnerable to its effects than did the other modes of mass communication.

Perhaps the BBC's greatest wartime success was to honour, for the most part, its original wise decision to tell the truth as far as it could rather than create propaganda. Because its sources of information were limited and because national security sometimes called for the suppression of certain facts, it could not tell the whole truth. But it consciously eschewed lies and distortions and thus gained an immeasurable advantage over the stations of the enemy. Since it told much bad news – there was nothing but bad news until the victory at El Alamein in November 1942 – its good news could also be believed, and it came to be depended on in much of occupied Europe, where the penalty for listening could be death, as well as in other parts of the world. But it was perhaps even more important that the BBC could be believed at home, because by telling the truth it matched the nation's concept of itself as fighting a just war, waging a moral crusade against evil and tyranny. Surveys suggested that by the end of the war people placed much more trust in wireless as a news medium, presumably because the BBC's willingness to tell unpleasant truths meant that it could not be as closely associated with the government as, fairly or unfairly, it had been in pre-war years.

What also increased the public's esteem for the BBC was the fact that whether it wished to or not it shared their experiences of fighting on the home front. Many of its operations were moved out to the provinces, but its core was still in London, and six of its employees were killed when Broadcasting House was bombed in 1940 – the explosion causing a slight pause in a news bulletin. The building was bombed again later, but the corporation soldiered on, radiating imperturbable good cheer from the thick of the Blitz. Hence the BBC helped to sustain the nation's morale not just by telling the truth, nor merely by setting an example of courage in the face of danger, but by the very steadiness and familiarity of its output, which, as Gorham (1952: 172) remarks, had a reassuring effect in an otherwise topsy-turvy world. However, more can be claimed for its output than mere familiarity, for as we have seen its news and light entertainment were highly appreciated. Moreover, they were increasingly conceived of in terms of the characteristics and resources of sound broadcasting itself: news was no longer seen as something that really belonged in the newspapers, nor comedy as something that had to be adapted from the stage.

The huge audiences for its programmes certainly did credit to the BBC, but also reflect the fact that radio was almost the only medium of information and entertainment which could thrive in wartime – and this, too, was thanks to those characteristics which set it apart from the other media. At the beginning of the war most of the cinemas, theatres, concert halls and sports stadiums were closed down in what George Bernard Shaw deplored as 'a masterstroke of unimaginative stupidity'. Although they soon reopened, people evidently felt safest in their homes, or at any rate preferred to be bombed there than elsewhere, and to rely for their news and entertainment mainly on those two domestic media, newspapers and radio. But aside from the hazards involved in distributing and delivering them, the papers were severely reduced in size by the shortage of newsprint. That left radio.

As Scannell and Cardiff (1991: 278) observe, radio located public within domestic life, probably more so than newspapers could ever have done, since it brought the *sounds* of the public sphere, not simply descriptions of it, into the privacy of the home. Moreover, because of the scarcity of the other media and the momentousness of wartime events, it gave the individual an unprecedented sense of himself as part of the larger community. He became aware that he was one of countless others, all listening to much the same thing. As Eric Hobsbawm (1994: 196) puts it, radio,

> though essentially centred on individual and family, created its own public sphere. For the first time in history people unknown to each other who met knew what each other had in all probability heard . . . the night before: the big game,

the favourite comedy show, Winston Churchill's speech, the contents of the news bulletin.

In this respect radio was very much like a party host who helps strangers to become friends by referring them to experiences they have in common. The point, then, is that when the BBC's role in uniting the nation and raising its morale has been freely admitted, there was something conducive to that end in the very nature of broadcasting.

The war was not an unalloyed success story for the BBC. As we have seen, it soon discovered that the full Reithian diet of mixed programming did not command the absolute support of its listeners, and that when the war was over it would have to find a new, more acceptable expression of its public service ideals.

Post-war reconstruction

In the light of its experiences with the Home Service and the Forces Programme the BBC formed its plan for post-war broadcasting in 1943, well before hostilities ended. This would consist of a new, tripartite system. The General Forces Programme would be replaced by a *Light Programme* which would resemble it in style and content. The *Home Service* would continue as in essence a London-based network, which a federation of regional services – Scottish, Northern, Midland, West, Welsh and Northern Irish – could draw upon. And there would also be a *Third Programme*, a highbrow network dedicated to the arts, philosophy, serious discussion and experimental programmes.

For several years after Reith's departure from the BBC those who followed him as Director General were undistinguished. Then in 1944 William Haley, a former editor of the *Manchester Guardian*, was appointed. Haley's first important task was to 'sell' the new tripartite system to the government on the one hand and the general public on the other, especially as the corporation's charter was due for renewal at the end of 1946. The influential sections of the nation, many of them in or close to the government, had largely accepted Reith's premise that broadcasting should be serious and improving. But the mass of the people inclined to the opposite view, and there were even demands in some quarters for a new inquiry to consider the introduction of competition.

The tripartite system was an attempt to respond to popular tastes and provide the listener with an element of choice without sacrificing the old Reithian seriousness of purpose. It was a continuing expression of his idea of public service broadcasting in the sense that it catered for the same full range of interests as BBC broadcasting always had. Like its predecessors it would provide 'something for everyone' – but across the *entirety* of its networks rather than within any one of them.

Yet the failure to cater for the full range of interests within any single network meant that the second and perhaps more important of Reith's original aims – to provide 'everything for someone' – was being dropped. Haley explained the problems it had raised:

> Before the war the system was to confront [the listener] with the necessity for pendulum-like leaps. [He] was deliberately plunged from one extreme to the other. The devotees of (Irving) Berlin were suddenly confronted with Bach. Many listeners were won for higher things in this way, but many were irretrievably lost. For the weakness of the system was that so many intolerances were set up.
>
> (quoted in Smith 1974: 83)

What Haley is regretting here as a 'weakness' is precisely that element of serendipity, of being exposed to valuable things by chance, that Reith envisaged as the strength of his system. Henceforth, thanks to stratified programming the listener would be exposed to no more surprises. In this respect the new plan was a significant dilution of Reith's original concept of public service. Indeed, it was in his sense of the word 'undemocratic', because in not automatically exposing the less educated listeners to at least some highbrow content it reinforced social and cultural divisions. Reith denounced it in his diary as 'an absolute abandonment of everything I stood for'.

Whatever the rights and wrongs of the matter, the addition of even a third network now made radio so abundant that the notion of providing a full range of programming on any one network was in practical terms unsustainable. The whole purpose of the new system was to provide the listener with *choice*, for which purpose the three networks were stratified or banded into highbrow (Third), middlebrow (Home) and populist (Light). As a way of sharpening that choice the Home and the Light, in particular, were expected to compete with each other.

Yet Haley's approving reference to pre-war listeners being 'won for higher things' illustrates the extent to which Reith's philosophy still held sway in broadcasting. To ensure that those listeners who never changed networks would be exposed to some cultural variety, a mixture of programming (albeit somewhat reduced) would be retained within each of them. But more than this, the listeners would be encouraged to work their way up through the tripartite system. The idea was that there would be a degree of overlap between the Light and the Home (indeed these differed more in tone than in substance), and between the Home and the Third, in order to give the overall system an edifying purpose. Haley perceived it as a 'cultural pyramid':

> This pyramid is served by three main Programmes, differentiated but broadly overlapping in levels and interest, each Programme leading on to the other, the listener being induced through the years increasingly to discriminate in favour

of the things that are more worth-while. Each Programme at any given moment must be ahead of its public, but not so much as to lose their confidence. The listener must be led from good to better by curiosity, liking, and a growth of understanding. As the standards of the education and culture of the country rise so should the programme pyramid rise as a whole.

(quoted in Smith 1974: 83)

Hence it would no longer be the BBC but the listener who would determine the extent to which she was exposed to the full range of its output, and this meant that she could *choose* to be 'improved' rather than having improvement thrust upon her. But, though diluted, the public service concept was far from being discarded, and the tripartite system heralded an Indian summer of sound broadcasting which would partly overlap with the rise of television in the 1950s.

On 29 July 1945 the General Forces Programme was replaced without a break by the very similar Light Programme. After the wartime discoveries of the audience researchers, it was here that the concern with listening figures was most acute, and perhaps best typified by the rise of the music request programme. *Forces' Favourites* was replaced by *Family Favourites*, and the latter was complemented by *Housewives' Choice* – a new vein of radio populism in that listeners determined programme content. The Third Programme was launched on 29 September 1946 and gave prompt and stern notice of its highbrow preoccupations. Amid much classical music its early listeners were treated to an eighty-three-part series on the ideas and beliefs of the Victorians and a six-part translation of Goethe's *Faust* by the poet Louis MacNeice. It was also on the Third Programme that Bertrand Russell was allowed to question the existence of God.

The new tripartite system not only settled the long-term future of sound broadcasting but secured the BBC's immediate objective. A new Labour government was elected in 1945, with many other and far graver problems to face than broadcasting. Mindful of the BBC's strong war record and that the newly completed network reforms would need some time to bed down, it renewed the corporation's charter without appointing a committee of inquiry, though for only five years instead of the usual ten.

Sources/further reading

For the circumstances leading to the foundation of Radios Normandie and Luxembourg and for their early development see Briggs (1965), Baron (1975), Barnard (1989) and Chapman (1992). A broadcaster's memories of pre-war commercial radio are in Plomley (1980). Gifford (1985) and Donovan (1992) provide vivid accounts of Luxembourg's programming, and Gifford also gives details of Normandie's. The importance to the commercial stations of the first attempts at audience research is stressed by Pegg (1983). For the impact of these stations on audiences and on the BBC's Sunday policy see Street (2000).

The trend towards popularization in BBC talks during the latter half of the 1930s is in Cardiff (1980), and Scannell (1981) traces a similar tendency in its approach to classical music. A more general account of the growth of popularization and of cultural and social streaming is given by Scannell and Cardiff (1982), who as well as Silvey (1974) outline the early findings of audience research which coincided with it. For the cultural significance of the development of fixed-point scheduling and of series and serial formats see Scannell and Cardiff (1982, 1991). The second of these explores the ways in which the early BBC expressed collective national life, but also explains why the American culture that the BBC tried to resist better expressed the new British democracy.

Briggs and Burke (2002) give a helpful account of the role of the media in the Enlightenment of the late eighteenth century, especially in the French revolutionary and American independence movements. For his meditations on the problem of reconciling democratic rights with intellectual and moral inequalities see Reith (1949). Lezard (2000) and Collini (2000) offer two different though equally challenging perspectives on élitism and popular culture. A potential critique of popular culture is offered by McQuail (2000), while Fiske (1987) inclines to the view that popularity is the main determinant of cultural value.

The standard history of wartime broadcasting is Briggs (1970), but for a brilliant résumé of the unprecedented nature of the Second World War and of the role of radio within it see Cardiff and Scannell (1981). The characteristic flavour of wartime programmes is captured in Black (1972a) and Parker (1977), with more factual descriptions in Gifford (1985) and Donovan (1992). Reid (1987) gives a vivid picture of Broadcasting House during the war years and Doherty (2000) assesses the overall impact of Lord Haw-Haw and Nazi wireless propaganda.

As well as giving a helpful general account of broadcasting and the Second World War, Curran and Seaton (1997) indicate how successfully the BBC's music and light-entertainment output expressed the popular mood. For the origins of radiogenic comedy see Cardiff (1988). A more general, theoretical discussion of its evolution is in Crisell (1986, 1994). Took (1976) describes *Band Waggon* and *ITMA*, and for a detailed account of the latter written by the show's producer, see Worsley (1948). An excellent account of the BBC's wartime music policy and of the growing American influence on British popular culture is in Barnard (1989). Another valuable account of programming during the war, including the American influence on the development of fixed-point scheduling and improved programme continuity in the British networks, is in Gorham (1952). That assimilation of public to domestic life which is a general feature of broadcasting but which became particularly significant during the war is acutely described in Scannell and Cardiff (1991) and in Hobsbawm (1994).

For particularly helpful accounts of the establishment of the BBC's tripartite network system at the end of the war see Barnard (1989) and Curran and Seaton (1997). The latter proposes the interesting argument that the social philosophy which underlay this system was essentially that which inspired the government's educational reforms of 1944. Haley's explanation of the cultural pyramid is quoted in Smith (1974), and Carpenter (1996) gives a full history of the Third Programme and its successor, Radio 3.

Chapter 4

The golden age of radio and the rise of television

The golden age of radio and the rise of television

Listeners' harvest

Between 1945 and about 1960 BBC radio enjoyed what was probably its greatest era, broadcasting distinguished programmes of every kind, many of them regional in origin, to audiences of several million. The pioneering *Radio Newsreel* continued into peacetime: one of its achievements was an eyewitness report of the assassination of Mahatma Gandhi in 1947. Among special interest programmes the long-running *Children's Hour* was joined soon after the war by *Woman's Hour* on the Light Programme and, since the BBC seemed to take horticulture more seriously than it took women, by *Gardeners' Question Time* on the more highbrow Home Service.

From 1948 *Any Questions?*, which was first heard on the West Region, complemented *The Brains Trust* as a discussion programme which managed to be both serious and popular. Features continued to thrive, and though they might just as easily have taken a turn in the direction of documentaries or current affairs, became closely associated with radio drama, examples of which regularly won the BBC the Italia Prize for Drama between 1947 and 1955. Radio drama included adaptations of classic stage plays, but also many plays which were especially written for the medium by such established authors as Giles Cooper and Henry Reed, some of them now widely regarded as part of the literary canon. Perhaps the three most famous of these made-for-radio plays are Louis MacNeice's *The Dark Tower* (Home Service, 1946), Dylan Thomas's *Under Milk Wood* (Third Programme, 1954) and Samuel Beckett's *All That Fall* (Third, 1957). But much drama was not highbrow. There were hugely popular serials on the Light – crime (*Dick Barton, Special Agent* began in 1947) and science fiction (*Journey into Space* blasted off in 1953) – as well as two enduring soap operas: from 1948 *Mrs Dale's Diary* and, three years later, *The Archers*, subtitled 'an everyday story of country folk' and still thriving on Radio 4.

We now hear and watch so many examples of soap opera that we are no longer aware of its formal and cultural originality, something it owes entirely to broadcasting. For the same reason we overlook the oddity, even obscurity, of its name. Since 'soap' refers to advertising it is clear that the genre came from America, where, because of their domestic themes, the early radio serials attracted the sponsorship of detergent makers. The facetious 'opera' was added presumably because these serials share opera's fondness for story-lines which are slow-moving yet somewhat melodramatic. Soap opera clearly has its roots in cultural forms which pre-date the age of broadcasting, notably the sentimental novel, serial magazine fiction and even serial films. Nevertheless, it is a genre peculiar to broadcasting, and we shall look at its original features when we come to consider the even greater popularity of soaps on television.

At the end of Chapter 3 we noted a new strain of programming which showed a greater awareness of the circumstances of the listener, and in some instances sought to give her more of a 'presence' on the medium. *Family Favourites* and *Housewives' Choice* began with the Light Programme, while *Music While You Work* and *Workers' Playtime* were carried over from the war. They were soon joined by *Have a Go!*, a quiz show which started in the North Region and under its Yorkshire compere Wilfred Pickles, whose heart was as warm as his accent was broad, travelled the length and breadth of the country 'presenting the people to the people'. Of all the BBC's attempts at demotic radio this was the most successful, attracting an audience during the 1950s which was estimated at 20 million. The 'ordinary folk' who came to the microphone were asked a few simple questions and their answers were always followed by Pickles's catchphrase, 'Give 'em the money, Barney!' – little more than a week's house-keeping but enough to make the programme a touchingly innocent forerunner of the big-prize shows on ITV.

As always, the BBC provided a vast amount of music of all kinds, but it was perhaps in the field of comedy that its greatest achievements lay. What is astonishing about this post-war period is not just the number and variety of comedy shows it developed but their durability: most lasted five, many ten years or more. In any one year of the 1950s the listener could enjoy episodes of not fewer than five different shows. In popularity the rival and immediate successor to *ITMA*, which ended in 1949, was *Much Binding in the Marsh* (1947–53), though it eschewed surrealism for a more conventional sitcom format. Other popular sitcoms were *Ray's a Laugh* (1949–61), starring the wise-cracking Liverpudlian Ted Ray; *Life with the Lyons* (1950–61), which featured a real-life American family; and the extraordinary *Educating Archie* (1950–60), in which the star, Archie Andrews, was a dummy and the sidekick his ventriloquist, Peter Brough. A topical blend of sketches, skits and songs, *Take It From Here* (1948–59), was the first creation of those prolific scriptwriters Frank Muir and Denis Norden, and featured Jimmy Edwards and Dick Bentley.

Within this galaxy two shows managed to outshine the rest, and between them neatly typified the two main strands of radio comedy which had developed in the medium's short history. The first was the highly surrealistic *Goon Show* (1952–9), a fusion of the crass and the clever, of naivety and knowingness, which is the essence of all great clowning. Peter Black shrewdly referred to its 'explosive and bloodless violence . . . in which childlike anarchy was overlaid with the whiff of something less innocent' (1972a: 193). One could also see it as an endless, consummate celebration of the power and limitations of radio itself. Whatever the source of its appeal, it convulsed millions, many of the younger listeners using its catchphrases as cultural passwords and attempting endless imitations of the characters created by Spike Milligan, Peter Sellers and Harry Secombe.

The other great show, a sitcom which had its roots in the conventional theatre and was therefore able to run concurrently on television from 1956, was *Hancock's Half Hour* (1954–61). But in its way *Hancock* was innovatory too, for its scriptwriters Alan Simpson and Ray Galton were interested not in creating a gag-show, but in using comic dialogue to explore and illuminate character. Its star, Tony Hancock, had previously had an undistinguished career in radio, but at different times supported by Sid James, Bill Kerr, Kenneth Williams and Hattie Jacques, now proved himself to be a great comic actor rather than a comedian. The lower-middle-class character he created was idle, pompous and tetchy, with aspirations to nobler things which were constantly thwarted by the earthiness of his companions. Peter Black (1972a: 191, 196) writes of his 'seedy grandiloquence and unavailing pretensions' and of a 'comedy of longing and failure' from which pathos was never far away.

What lends poignancy to this era is that even as radio was producing programmes of unprecedented range and quality fewer and fewer people were listening to it. By the second half of the 1950s it had already been supplanted as the major mass medium by a younger rival, whose birth and infancy we must now consider.

The early years of television

The search for ways of sending pictures over distances began almost as early as the efforts to transmit sound. The problem for scientists was to break down a sequence of images into units of information which could be transmitted by wireless, and the first attempts at a solution were mechanical – by the German, Paul Nipkow, and then by several others including the American Charles Francis Jenkins. In 1884 Nipkow created a revolving disc with perforations which were arranged in a spiral pattern. A beam of light shone through these perforations as the disc was turned, causing the light to 'scan' an image. This device formed the basis of television experiments for many years to come because it was seen as a means of transmitting images in the form of a sequence of dots. The other strand of research into the scanning of images was electronic. The cathode ray tube was developed by Karl Braun in 1897 and the photo-electric cell by Julius Elster and Hans Geitel in 1905. A major figure in this strand was Vladimir Zworykin, a refugee from the Russian Revolution who emigrated to the United States in the 1920s and worked for the Westinghouse Company, and then, when its research was transferred to RCA, for the latter. His discoveries were later combined with those of an unlikely genius in Philo Farnsworth, a farmer's boy from Idaho.

However, as Roy Armes (1988: 57) points out, romantic tales of lone inventors and brilliant eccentrics should not blind us to the mundane fact that the major developments in television were the result of well-funded and systematic research by the major communications companies such as Marconi and RCA. Indeed, the most romantic of the lone figures, the Scotsman John Logie Baird, pursued his ideas down a dead-end, persisting with the mechanical method of image scanning long after its limitations had become generally apparent. Nevertheless, Baird achieved one or two firsts and several publicity coups. He began demonstrations of his system at Selfridge's in 1925, televised moving images in the following year, and in 1928 sent the first intelligible TV signal across the Atlantic and began regular experimental transmissions in London. Yet much more productive were the 9 million dollars which RCA invested in research during the 1930s.

The BBC became involved in developing television from about 1929 and was pressed by the Post Office to provide the facility for Baird to continue his transmissions, the first of which was received by about thirty sets. Initially, sound and vision occupied a single wavelength: the speaker was first seen without being heard, then heard without being seen. However, in 1933 the BBC resolved to end Baird's experiments because the rival electronic technology seemed to be making more progress in the form of the American-originated EMI system.

In 1934 the government appointed the Selsdon Committee to consider the future of television broadcasting, and the latter recommended that a regular public television service should be operated by the BBC, using both the Baird and EMI systems on a weekly, alternating basis until the superiority of one or the other had been proved. It also recommended that the service should not carry advertising but be paid for out of the existing licence fee, although some form of sponsorship might be considered. The government accepted these recommendations and the BBC Television Service opened on 2 November 1936. According to Roy Armes (1988: 56–7) it was not the first regular TV service in the world: the Germans had begun theirs in March 1935. But since the latter was transmitting only 180-line pictures, the BBC could fairly claim credit for the first high-definition service. It transmitted from Alexandra Palace in north London and was received within a radius of 40 to 100 miles by a few thousand viewers in about 400 households.

Early broadcasts ran for two separate hours a day, excluding Sundays, and the weekly programme budget was £1,000. In the first week viewers were treated to a comedy featuring Ben Lyon and Bebe Daniels, excerpts from a West End play called *Marigold*, a demonstration of tap dancing, and a talk from a bus driver on how to build model boats.

The service sounded the knell of the Baird system, and perhaps of the man himself since he lived only a few years longer. While research into picture composition was at the level of 60 to 100 lines, Baird's system could hold its own. But the high-definition pictures proposed by Selsdon had a threshold of 240 lines, the uppermost limit for Baird. The EMI system, using all-electronic, mobile cameras, delivered a picture of 405 lines, and in February 1937 the Baird system was dropped.

By modern standards even the EMI picture was dim. It was, of course, mono-chrome, as all television pictures would be for the next thirty years or so. The average TV screen was about eight inches by ten, and the pictures lacked definition and detail and would often distort or roll. Brian Winston (1998: 113) identifies two factors which inhibited the pre-war sales of television sets: the limitedness of the transmission hours, and during the initial period that two transmitting systems were in operation, fears that one or the other type of receiver might be obsolescent. But cost must have been the biggest factor: receivers could cost up to £100, the price of a small car at that time, although the cheapest could be had for about £35. Nevertheless, even in the 1930s there were faint hints of the universal spell that the new medium would cast. By 1938 about 5,000 sets had been bought, and it is estimated that by the time the service closed 18,000 to 20,000 sets had been sold during the three years it had been running.

In this time of its infancy, television reflected the ambivalence which was felt towards it. On the one hand, because it was a new, expensive and not altogether reliable medium, there was a tendency to regard it as frivolous, a toy for the rich. As Stuart Hood (1980: 60) puts it:

> Pre-war television was aimed at a small and affluent audience in London and the Home Counties, which had not been affected by the depression and mass unemployment. In the South-East prosperity based on the boom in building and light industry and in consumer goods like refrigerators and radios and the car industry financed the purchase of sets. The programmes the viewers wanted were dominated by the concept of the West End show, of the revue and the kind of entertainment which was the middle class audience's idea of a night out.

In response to this the BBC included Noel Coward's *Hay Fever* and Brandon Thomas's *Charley's Aunt* among the two or three plays a week it was broadcasting by 1938. The lack of gravity was confirmed by the Gaumont-British and British

Movietone newsreels which the BBC offered instead of any news output of its own – exactly the same newsreels that were watched by cinema audiences. On the other hand, the service was a child of the BBC, and to that extent imbued with the same public service principles and obligations which John Reith had established in respect of radio. While television was new and there had to be more concern with its technical reliability than with its content, some lack of range and seriousness in the latter might be permissible. Even so, as well as light comedies, viewers were presented with plays by Beaumont and Fletcher, Shakespeare and George Bernard Shaw.

The major televised event of these pre-war years, and indeed television's first outside broadcast, was the coronation procession of George VI in May 1937. Coverage was provided by three fixed-point cameras at Hyde Park Corner: one viewed the procession as it approached, the second as it passed, the third as it receded. Despite poor weather the broadcast was accounted a great success and seen by between 10,000 and 50,000 viewers, some as far away as Ipswich and Brighton.

The approach of war brought fears that transmission masts would act as navigational aids to enemy aircraft – and, no doubt, the feeling that television was a dispensable luxury. With the outbreak of hostilities in September 1939 the service came to an abrupt end.

The BBC's post-war television service

Television transmissions resumed in 1946, initially to about 15,000 households. But bolstered by a new combined radio and TV licence, price £2, the service began to grow. In 1949 it was extended to the West Midlands, in 1951 to Manchester, and in the following year parts of Scotland, Wales and the West were covered. By 1954 the BBC was broadcasting about six hours of television a day, most of it live.

To a considerable extent television gave a renewed opportunity to those Reithian principles of public service which the corporation still espoused – something of an irony since it was a medium which Reith himself was inclined to despise. After the small yet significant compromises embodied by radio's cultural pyramid, the BBC Television Service, sole channel of a monopoly broadcaster, could pick up the torch of genuine mixed programming which enshrined the old principles of 'something for everyone' and 'everything for someone'. And, indeed, this is what it sought to do. But the service was beset with problems, not all of the corporation's making. There was the familiar opposition to a new medium from the controllers of old media and cultural genres. A boycott of television was variously imposed by the British film industry, the music halls, the West End theatre managers, and the controlling bodies of boxing and, except in respect of the Cup Final and certain international matches, of soccer. But the real problems were internal. For the next eight or ten years there was little understanding within the BBC of television's potential: indeed it is hard to avoid the conclusion that during this period the corporation was in two minds about the medium. On the one hand, it was the monopoly broadcaster and felt that it should naturally assume responsibility for what was a new kind of broadcasting. On the other hand, as a culturally conservative body the BBC did not warm to its task. Radio, an essentially verbal medium, was something that its staff, with their typically literate and literary backgrounds, could deal with comfortably. But television was pictures – and their suspicion that pictures were mindless and vulgar drew strength from the fact that cinema, a medium which was both new and popular, was widely regarded as lowbrow. Grace Wyndham Goldie (1977: 18–19) describes the broadcasters' dilemma thus:

> their speciality was the use of words; they had no knowledge of how to present either entertainment or information in vision, nor any experience of handling visual material. Moreover, most of them distrusted the visual; they associated vision with the movies and the music hall and were afraid that the high purposes of the Corporation would be trivialised by the influence of those concerned with what could be transmitted in visual terms.

The post-war Director General, William Haley, shared that misunderstanding and dislike of television of his great predecessor, John Reith. Just as before the war Reith had thought of 'integrating' radio and television (Briggs 1965: 608), Haley insisted in 1949 that television was merely 'an extension' of sound broadcasting and that TV and radio were 'parts of one whole' (Paulu 1981: 54). He seems to have had in mind a service in which television would be a mere adjunct to radio rather than one whose essence would be visual. In the case of drama, for instance, this would mean bringing cameras into a radio studio to film actors reading into microphones rather than shooting a 'television play' on purpose-built sets or in suitable locations.

What lent some respectability to this reductive view of television were the likely costs of a full-blooded service. In 1937 the BBC calculated that one hour of television was twelve times as expensive to produce as the costliest hour of radio, a ratio which has surely not diminished over the years. But it meant that after the war the service resumed not so much with the expectation that it would develop as that it would need to be curbed. Television programmes were the added responsibility of radio production departments, they were not produced from a separate source, and a rough indication of the funding they received is that in 1947–8 television accounted for less than one-tenth of total BBC expenditure. Even in 1950 the budget for television was only half that of the Home Service. This niggardliness prompted the resignation of two television controllers, the first in 1947 and his successor in 1950.

Nevertheless the BBC's brief monopoly of television was not without its achievements. Paddy Scannell (1979: 97–9) points out that in the realm of politics the corporation's radio and television coverage was limited. It saw politics as little more than a matter of politicians and Parliament, while its treatment of current affairs was distanced, non-committal, even non-political. But with *Special Enquiry* (1952) it made a first attempt to create documentary programming which was telegenic. By extreme contrast two frivolous yet durable TV shows originated at this time: *Come Dancing* in 1950 and *What's My Line?* in 1951, the latter a quiz game in which the winning contestants received not prizes but certificates. The first TV soap opera, *The Grove Family*, dates from early 1955. Perhaps the BBC's two most notable dramatic achievements were a science-fiction thriller, *The Quatermass Experiment* (1953), and a powerful adaptation of George Orwell's novel *1984* (1954), with Peter Cushing.

The BBC also achieved much in outside broadcasting. Those public events to which it was admitted – Wimbledon, the Test matches, the Lord Mayor's Show – it covered well. In August 1950 it forged the first live television link between two countries when it transmitted from Calais to Britain. This was not a truly international broadcast since because of different line-standards it was not seen in France; but the first real Eurovision link followed in July 1952.

Without doubt the corporation's greatest television triumph was its coverage of the coronation of Elizabeth II on 2 June 1953. This is widely regarded as having been the first ever 'media event', in the sense that although not created or prompted by television it seemed tailor-made for the medium, and was the first event to be watched and enjoyed in many parts of the world. It was recorded as it was televised, and the films were then flown for rapid re-broadcasting to Canada, the United States and elsewhere. The BBC's coverage, for which it gained permission only after delicate negotiations with both Church and state, was impressive even by today's standards. Transmission began at ten in the morning and continued till eleven-thirty at night. Beginning with the service in Westminster Abbey, on which a hushed, reverential commentary was supplied by Richard Dimbleby, it continued with the procession to Buckingham Palace, which was covered by cameras at every vantage-point along the way and by a further seven commentators. Some 56 per cent of the nation watched the service, 53 per cent the procession.

The coronation usefully symbolizes the point when television surpassed radio as the major mass medium. In itself it prompted a boom in the sales of TV sets, and 1953 was the first year in which more television than radio sets were manufactured, at an average unit price of about £85. But the coronation merely quickened a trend that had been apparent for some time, and the fact that television's ascendancy was established two full years before the arrival of commercial TV suggests that the nation did not find the BBC's programmes wholly unappealing. One or two figures outline the trend. In 1951 nearly three quarters of a million television licences were issued. In 1955 viewing began to exceed listening for the first time, and by 1958 9 million licences were held. Radio's figures are in their own sad way just as eloquent. The BBC's average evening audience in 1949 was almost 9 million; by 1958 it had shrunk to less than 3.5 million, three quarters of whom had no access to a television set.

Yet although the coronation trumpeted not only the power of television but at last the ability of the BBC to make television of high quality, the corporation's monopoly of the medium was about to end. This seems all the more surprising when we learn that only two years previously the monopoly had been approved by a government-appointed committee. What, from the corporation's point of view, had gone wrong?

The Beveridge Report and its aftermath

In 1949 the Labour government did what had become customary when the BBC's charter was shortly to expire: it appointed a committee to inquire into the present state of broadcasting and make recommendations for the future. Though wavelength scarcity applied as much to television as radio, there was room on the waveband for two national competitors for the BBC. Should it be allowed to continue as the sole domestic broadcaster? The chair of the committee was Lord Beveridge, who presented its bulky, thoughtful and well-reasoned report in January 1951. This was in some respects critical of the corporation and sensitive to the dangers of monopoly. Nevertheless, it recommended the continuance of the latter, though not unanimously and not without safeguards. It also opposed the introduction of advertising into the BBC's programmes. However, among its appendices was a minority report by the Conservative politician Selwyn Lloyd advocating competition in the form of a service paid for by advertising or, failing that, by some form of public funding.

The Beveridge Report was immediately made irrelevant by a general election and the return to power of the Conservatives, who extended the BBC's charter for a further six months (later renewed till 1962) so that they could take their own look at broadcasting's long-term future. But Curran and Seaton (1997: 162) point out that Beveridge was not a total waste of effort and paper: it was to have two marked effects on the commercial broadcasting it disfavoured. First, its alertness to the danger that advertising would influence programme content ensured that ITV would carry 'spot' commercials and not sponsorship. Second, its disapproval of what it termed the excessive 'Londonization' of the BBC provided the inspiration for ITV's regional structure.

Hence it was the Conservatives, or at any rate a well-organized minority thereof, who reopened the monopoly debate. But the monopoly had been safe under previous Conservative governments: why should it be questioned now? Three reasons suggest themselves. The first and most obvious was the inadequacy of the BBC's post-war television service, at least until about 1950, and the general feeling that it was being held back by radio. This feeling was confirmed by resignations among senior television staff, especially that of the controller of the service, Norman Collins, in 1950. Collins had argued within the corporation that television was the medium of the future, in competition with which radio was bound to decline in importance. Among those this argument failed to impress was Haley, who appointed to the new post of Chief Executive of Television not Collins but a candidate with a background in the Third Programme and speech output. In doing so Haley handed a piece of heavy artillery to the corporation's enemies. Collins promptly resigned and devoted himself to masterminding the campaign for commercial television, something he did with great skill.

A second threat to the monopoly grew out of changes occurring in the socio-political climate of the time. There was a renewal of the process of democratization that had been gathering pace before the war, of the campaign 'to let the people decide for themselves'. Asa Briggs (1979: 367) points out that in its evidence to Beveridge the Incorporated Society of Advertisers had suggested that it might be advisable to have a network which the public did not associate with a 'semi-official service'. He adds that this was to prove an immensely powerful argument in the Britain of the 1950s, when there was a reaction against the wartime system of managed information and bureaucratic paternalism. The BBC, in particular, was seen by many Tories as self-righteous and arrogant, and their party battle-cry 'set the people free' had certainly impressed the people at election time. Indeed, back in 1946 the BBC had been dealt a shrewd blow by one of its own former director generals, Sir Frederick Ogilvie. 'Freedom is choice,' he declared in a letter to *The Times*. 'And monopoly of broadcasting is inevitably the negation of freedom, no matter how efficiently it is run' (quoted in Smith 1974: 85). There was a growing democratic revulsion against 'someone else knowing best': people craved diversity and choice.

The third and least obvious challenge to the monopoly, yet perhaps the most powerful, was economic. After the hardships of the war and post-war years the nation was once again on the verge of prosperity. More goods were being made and there was more money to buy them with. By the early 1950s people were looking to replace a multiplicity of household objects which had had to last them through a long, lean period. Food rationing would end in 1954; new washing-machines and refrigerators would reduce the need for human effort and cool weather. Between 1951 and 1955 the manufacture of television sets leapt from 1 million to 5 million, the number of private cars from 2.25 million to 3.25 million. During the same period the ownership of telephones increased from 5 million to 6 million. The growth in production created a corresponding growth in the demand for advertising: newspapers and magazines experienced a bonanza. By 1954 there was a three-month waiting list for selling space in the quality journal *Vogue*. More outlets were needed, and the advertising potential of television, much greater than that of radio, was never more apparent. This largely explains why the monopoly debate focused on television rather than radio; although there was another reason for this, as we shall see shortly.

It is true that those for and against the continuance of the BBC's monopoly did not neatly divide along party lines. But since it was certain that the public would not support a large increase in the licence fee, the BBC's only conceivable rival would be commercial; and the reopening of the debate at this stage is attributable not only to the Conservatives' belief in individual choice but to the fact that, in general, they felt more enthusiasm than their opponents for the commercial principles of private enterprise and free competition.

The campaign for commercial television

The commercial TV lobby consisted of a relatively small group of Tory back-benchers and almost nobody in the cabinet: the party leadership was largely indifferent, if not actively hostile, to its aims. The leaders agreed to support the campaign only if it was directed at television, for they felt that the BBC's performance in radio had been so good, especially during the war, that its monopoly therein should be left alone. The party chair, Lord Woolton, believed in any case that radio was by far the more important of the two media. However, the BBC had no ally in the Prime Minister, Winston Churchill. His wartime speeches on BBC radio were highly successful and he was generally contemptuous of television, 'that tuppenny Punch and Judy show'. But he held a grudge against the corporation. He and Reith had always disliked each other, and Churchill had been so outraged by what he regarded as the BBC's 'soft' attitude to the strikers during the events of 1926 that he had urged the government to commandeer it. In the 1930s he had been denied the opportunity to broadcast his opposition to the government's appeasement of Hitler, and he also believed that the BBC had contributed to his defeat in the 1945 general election.

The commercial TV campaign was orchestrated from outside Parliament by Norman Collins, and enjoyed strong backing from business – among others, Pye Radio, the West End theatre managers and the advertising agency J. Walter Thompson – as well as the support of the *Daily Mirror* and the *Financial Times*. Bernard Sendall (1982: 17) suggests that the campaigners were concerned not so much with television content as with its *distribution*: many wished to be able to offer their services to more than one broadcasting organization. Calling themselves the Popular Television Association, they included performers and scriptwriters, manufacturers of equipment, advertisers and market researchers, pragmatic politicians and some journalists. Their opponents were more concerned with *content*. Led by the Labour MP and BBC broadcaster Christopher Mayhew, they were known as the National Television Council, and among their number were churchmen, educators, moralists, ideological politicians and, again, some journalists. They also enjoyed the less principled backing of most of the main newspapers, who were fearful that commercial TV would steal their advertising revenue.

The opponents of commercial television argued that it was only as a monopoly broadcaster that the BBC could continue to operate a comprehensive public service – to provide 'something for everyone' – for if faced with a competitor it would be forced to fight for the lion's share of the total audience in order to justify its claim to a universal licence fee; and it could do this only by abandoning the programmes it made for minorities. As a monopoly it could still apply broadcasting to the most serious purposes, cooperating with such civilizing forces as the schools and universities. And it could maintain editorial independence, since it was a creature of neither government nor commerce. This distrust of commerce seems to have struck a chord with the public since it was part of an anti-American feeling that was quite widely shared at this time. Stephen Barnard (1989: 29) shrewdly observes that

Behind [it] lay a sense of national economic inferiority, exacerbated by Britain's dependence on American finance for post-war reconstruction, and a feeling that Britain's cultural 'superiority' over the United States (and the values reflected in its history and traditions) was under threat.

The campaigners for commercial TV insisted that the BBC's monopoly discouraged efficiency and denied choice, and that in a democracy broadcasting should be as unrestricted as possible. Why should it differ from the press, where competition produced diversity and prevented the concentration of power in a single organization? Even in a competitive system many minorities would be large enough to target, so the BBC could continue to provide programmes for them just as an open and competitive press continued to provide for those readers who wanted specialist newspapers and magazines. It was, of course, true that such programmes would no longer be experienced by those who did *not* want them, that the BBC's educative policy of 'everything for someone' could not be sustained. But in an increasingly democratic climate it was surely right that the responsibility for extending their cultural horizons should be shifted from broadcaster to audiences – a principle the BBC had already conceded in its cultural pyramid, which allowed the radio listener to opt out of highbrow content, if she wished, and hear nothing but populist programmes.

Between 1952 and 1954 the fortunes of battle favoured first one side and then the other. The anti-commercial campaigners scored a great victory with the coronation, partly because the BBC covered it so well as to suggest that its standards in television were now no lower than its standards in radio; and partly because the public was horrified to hear that when the coronation was re-broadcast in the United

States, NBC had interrupted the service in Westminster Abbey with commercials for deodorant, tea (sold by J. Fred Muggs, a performing chimpanzee) and Pepperell's Bed Sheets. On the other hand, the pro-commercial campaigners won ground when they convinced many waverers that commercial broadcasting did not have to mean advertisers controlling programme content through sponsorship – a practice which had a notorious and American reputation. Editorial integrity could be safeguarded through separate, 'spot' advertising – a practice which was subsequently adopted.

It seems true to say that despite occasional setbacks, the inherent advantage lay with the pro-commercialists since their opponents were arguing a case which was, on the face of it, anti-democratic. Hence, when the debate finally reached the Commons, that forum of democracy, the result was never really in doubt. The harder the champions of the BBC argued for the retention of its monopoly, the more priggish and patronizing they sounded. As the beneficiaries of democratic choice how could Christopher Mayhew and his parliamentary allies deplore such choice when it was applied to broadcasting? In the Lord Chancellor's words: 'Must we not give people what they want because they might want something that is not good for them?' (Hood 1980: 65). For those who believed in democracy such an outcome was unthinkable.

But in the Upper House there was one man before whom people of all views would pause and listen with respect. Lord Reith, stout old Canute to the last, got to his feet, and in its likely effects on civilization compared commercial television to dog-racing, smallpox and bubonic plague. With voting broadly though not exactly on party lines the Television Bill was carried in 1954. Nevertheless, in order to placate its opponents and critics, who were by no means united in their objections to it, the plans for commercial television underwent many revisions, and the system that emerged was a practical compromise between those who wished merely to break the BBC's monopoly, those who sought new sources of profit, and those who feared the worst excesses of American television.

Sources/further reading

General details of the BBC's post-war radio programmes are in Parker (1977), Gifford (1985) and Donovan (1992). Drakakis (1981) contains academic studies of some of the major radio dramatists of the 1940s and 1950s. For a discussion of the relationship of radio drama to the mainstream of English literature see Lewis (1981). Fink (1981) is useful on popular radio drama, including soap opera. Black (1972a) and Took (1976) include accounts of post-war radio comedy and light entertainment, while Crisell (1986, 1994) attempts a close analysis of the *Goon Show*. For an account of the American influences on BBC post-war radio broadcasting see Camporesi (1994).

For the early development of television see Barnouw (1977), Winston (1998) and Briggs and Burke (2002). To brief accounts of this development, Gorham (1952), Briggs (1965) and Armes (1988) add a description of the establishment of the BBC's pre-war television service, the blueprint for which is in Selsdon (1935). Hood (1980) offers some discussion of the economic and cultural background of the first viewers, and information about the programmes is in Davis (1976) and Day-Lewis (1992). Various descriptions of the BBC's post-war television service are in Gorham (1952), Briggs (1979) and Paulu (1981). Illuminating accounts of the particular economic, administrative and creative problems it had to deal with can be found in Goldie (1977), Hood (1980) and Curran and Seaton (1997). Its achievements in entertainment are outlined by Day-Lewis (1992), in current affairs by Scannell (1979), and in international and outside broadcasting by Davis (1976). The devastating impact of post-war television on radio listening is summarized in Paulu (1961) and Briggs (1979).

For the findings of the Beveridge Committee and the minority report of Selwyn Lloyd see Beveridge (1951). A summary account of the development of the BBC during the 1950s and the establishment of ITV is in Paulu (1981). Curran and Seaton (1997) provide a perceptive discussion of the political issues raised by the Beveridge Report, the problems of the monopoly television service, and the factors behind the introduction of commercial television. Smith (1974) quotes from the contemporary debate on the BBC's monopoly, and Seymour-Ure (1996) contains a brief but useful discussion of the issues of public service, monopoly and competition in broadcasting.

The general political and economic background to the campaign for commercial TV can be gleaned from Briggs (1979), Hood (1980) and Gable (1980). For the particular events which triggered the campaign, some of them occurring within the BBC, see Black (1972b) and Sendall (1982). Together with Briggs (1979), these also contain the best accounts of the campaign itself and of the parliamentary debates which led to the establishment of Independent Television.

Television: the first years of competition

Chapter 5

Television: the first years of competition

The structure of commercial television

Commercial television began, with suitable fanfares, on 22 September 1955. Agog, viewers watched, among many other offerings, the first-ever British TV advert, for Gibbs SR toothpaste, and the evening was generally judged a success although somewhat upstaged by the BBC. In that day's episode of its radio soap opera *The Archers*, the much-loved Grace Archer was killed in a stable fire. Competition had got off to a flying start.

It is a measure of the strength of the Reithian values which still pervaded broadcasting, and perhaps of a more general distrust of unfettered money-making, that commercial television was set up as an extension of the public service concept. It was to be supervised by the Independent Television Authority (ITA), a public body constituted rather like the BBC's board of governors. The government retained the power of appointment over its members – its first chairman was Sir Kenneth, later Lord, Clark and its first director general Sir Robert Fraser – and the 1954 Television Act gave it an initial life of ten years.

Though it owned and operated the television transmitters, the ITA did not itself make programmes but allocated a number of regional franchises on a fixed-term basis – initially nine years – to various programme-making companies ('the contractors'). The regional concept was an interesting though not wholly practicable response to Beveridge's complaint about what, in the hands of the BBC, was the excessive 'Londonization' of broadcasting.

The ITA required the contractors to inform, educate and entertain – to produce programmes of balance, quality and variety in accordance with the promises of performance they had made in their competitive bids for the franchises. The contractors were also responsible for selling airtime to the advertisers and for supporting the ITA through a levy raised on their revenue. However, the nature and quality of advertising were strictly controlled by the authority, and programme sponsorship was forbidden. Advertisers could only buy time within different 'slots' situated within and between programmes. The slots varied in price according to their place in the daily schedule, but there could be no more than an average of six minutes of advertising in any one hour.

This rigid separation of advertising from programme content was designed to prevent commercial interference in the latter, thus allaying another of Beveridge's fears. It was widely regarded as one of the great virtues of British commercial television: 'The model followed was the press, in which news and editorial material are kept entirely separate from advertising copy, rather than American commercial broadcasting, in which advertisers often provide programmes, or at least participate in their development' (Paulu 1981: 63).

The term 'independent', said to have been thought up by Norman Collins, was a mischievously clever one. It damaged the BBC, Collins's former employer and sworn enemy, since if ITV was so called because it was independent of government control the implication was that the BBC was not. In practice, too, 'independent' became a handy euphemism for 'commercial', which had connotations of greed and vulgarity.

The original plan for ITV was that there should be three franchise regions, London, the Midlands and the North, which would each be occupied by more than one contractor. Hence there was to be competition *between* contractors, as well as between the whole ITV system and the BBC. But because of the government's failure to allocate enough frequencies to enable this to happen the ITA adopted another plan. In order to maximize the number of contractors and create as much competition as it could the authority split franchises on a weekday/weekend basis. The first franchises were allocated thus:

Region	Weekdays	Weekends
LONDON	Associated-Rediffusion	Associated Television
MIDLANDS	Associated Television	ABC Television
NORTH	Granada	ABC Television

For its first few months ITV could be seen only in the London area, but it spread quite rapidly. Broadcasts began in the Midlands in February 1956, in the North in May, and after the establishment of the four original contractors further regional franchises were allocated – in Wales, Scotland, Northern Ireland and the Channel Islands, together with other regions of England. By 1962 the system was complete, but the main population areas were connected before 1960.

However, it became clear well before the end of the 1950s that the system could not survive without networking, since on their own most of the regions could not deliver big enough audiences to the advertisers. Hence a cost-sharing carve-up swiftly developed in which the four contractors who held between them the three original and most profitable franchises were guaranteed access to the network for agreed amounts of their programmes. This meant that the only real competition was between all the contractors and the BBC. It should be added that under the contractors' joint ownership the ITA also set up a separate organization, ITN, Independent Television News.

Where did the contractors' programme-making expertise and financial backing come from, and what experience did they have which was relevant to the unprecedented business of running a television company? Many of their programme-makers were lured away from the BBC; unsurprisingly, the salaries of TV production staff in both the public and commercial sectors soared during this period. And a source of both finance and management experience was the entertainment industry: theatre and cinema (two notable examples of shareholders with show-business connections were Lew Grade at ATV and Sidney Bernstein at Granada). Another, as in the case of Associated-Rediffusion, was the radio and TV rental business. A third and rather more controversial source of money was the press, and other financial backing came in the usual way from banks, pension funds and investors on the stock market. Press interest was controversial because while it was reasonable that one mass medium might seek to protect itself by investing in another, a Conservative-dominated press could thereby lead to a Conservative-dominated television industry, and in any event to media outlets which were concentrated in too few hands. Somewhat surprisingly, however, it was the pro-Labour Mirror Group which until 1990 was the largest single newspaper conglomerate to be continuously associated with ITV.

A dissection of the complicated structures of the different ITV contractors would take up too much space in a book of this kind, and perhaps leave the reader scarcely the wiser. Suffice to say that the contractors were highly miscellaneous groups of businesses – perhaps more accurately, business coalitions. One random example might be Associated-Rediffusion, first holder of the London weekday franchise. Rediffusion, formerly Broadcast Relay Service Ltd, was a company founded in the 1920s to operate the wireless relay exchanges. In 1947 it became a division of British Electric Traction, a vehicle manufacturing group, and later expanded its radio and TV rental business. Before making its bid for one of the franchises Rediffusion had agreed to form a partnership with Lord Rothermere's Associated Newspapers, owners of the *Daily Mail*, which explains the name of the contractor. To complicate matters further, the contractors used their television profits to diversify into other businesses, a prudent course of action since there was no guarantee that the ITA would renew their nine-year franchises. Granada, for example, had interests in book and music publishing, bingo halls, motorway services, cinemas, property and TV rentals, while ATV was involved in feature films, theatres, cinemas, music publishing, record companies and property.

In the red, then in the pink

ITV got off to a shaky start. In order to receive it, viewers needed to fit a special aerial and either to buy a new television or have their existing set adapted. Since in the first franchise areas only 33 per cent of households had taken these measures, the medium was not especially attractive to advertisers in terms of cost per thousand. Understandably, they remained cagey.

The first contractors were not allowed to broadcast more than fifty hours per week, but their rental charge was considerable. It was fixed by the ITA at about ten pence per head of the *total* population within their respective franchise areas. Nevertheless, in order to attract new viewers and advertising, they were obliged to spend big money on programmes. The start-up and running costs were, in a word, enormous, and there was an early panic that the first programmes were insufficiently populist and that the entire system might fail. Among the contractors, the Programme Controller of Associated-Rediffusion expressed a common view:

> Let's face it once and for all. The public likes girls, wrestling, bright musicals, quiz-shows and real-life drama. We gave them the Hallé orchestra, Foreign Press Club . . . and visits to the local fire station. Well, we've learned. From now on, what the public wants, it's going to get.
>
> (quoted in Sendall 1982: 328)

ITV was soon seen, not altogether accurately, as consisting of little other than quiz games, known as 'give-away shows' because of the big and rather easily won prizes they offered, variety spectaculars, soap operas and American film series, and described by its apologists as 'people's television' (another artful term).

By the second half of 1956, barely a year after it started, the tide began to turn. Whereas in September 1955 only 188,000 homes had been equipped to receive ITV, the number in September 1956 was 1.5 million. During the autumn and winter of 1956 viewers were rising by 50,000 a week, networking among the contractors was helping to cut production costs, and advertisers were having to queue for airtime. But not everyone's nerve held. Between 1955 and 1957 Associated-Rediffusion, holder of the London weekday franchise, lost nearly £3 million. One of its key shareholders, Associated Newspapers, decided to sell out. Two years later Rediffusion began to turn annual profits of £5 million. In 1958 the number of homes which could receive ITV had reached 5.25 million and by 1960 that number had almost doubled. However, it was not merely that many homes could receive the channel: millions of viewers were glued to it. As recently as 1953 the status of the BBC as the national broadcasting institution, a status it had acquired during the General Strike back in 1926, seemed to have been confirmed by its television coverage of the coronation. Now, the audience, especially its working-class segment, was deserting it in droves. By July 1957 the BBC was admitting that in homes with a choice, three adults watched ITV for every two who stayed with the corporation. Two months later the Chairman of the ITA, Sir Kenneth Clark, claimed a 79:21 ratio in favour of ITV.

As we shall see, the BBC's programming was by no means weak: indeed most of the memorable programmes which date from this era are the corporation's. Part of the problem lay in the way they were scheduled. Under Director General Sir Ian Jacob the policy was partly to compete with ITV, to match like with like, but true to its old public service philosophy of providing range and catering for minorities, the BBC also tried to offer contrast by scheduling some of its more serious output at peak viewing hours – with predictable results. Unsurprisingly, morale within the corporation sank. Its creative staff either felt disgust at the public's lack of taste and discernment or formed the belief that the lack of popularity of its programmes implied a lack of quality. But the BBC had to adjust to a changed world. The public could no longer be patronized: through programme promotion, shrewder scheduling and a change in styles of presentation, it had to be courted.

Technological developments in television

We might define a live communication act as one in which the reception of a message occurs instantaneously with its transmission. A slight complication occurs when the message which is being transmitted has already been recorded – that is, stored for a delayed reception. But this act of transmission is still 'live' in the sense that the recording is received by the viewers in the instant that the broadcaster sends it. The first kind of live communication would be the viewers' instantaneous reception of a soccer match which is being transmitted as it is happening. The second kind would be their instantaneous reception of a feature film which was made for and shown in the cinema many years before its present transmission on television.

The most important technological developments in television during the 1940s and 1950s all pertained to *recording* – to the medium's ability both to transmit the recorded material of the cinema and to record its own material either before or during the time of its transmission.

Television was at first thought of as an exclusively live medium – that is, as devoid of any recorded content of its own and therefore dealing wholly in ephemera – and any recordings it used as borrowed, as material which essentially belonged to another medium. Why? First, because during the pre- and immediate post-war years television was unable to record its own material, and, second, because it had difficulty in transmitting cinema films. Its electronic image consisted of 25 frames per second, whereas cinema film's was 24, the disparity appearing as a series of black bars on the TV screen (Winston 1998: 268). Yet despite its almost total reliance on live programming, the visual (and moreover domestic) nature of television hit post-war cinema audiences hard, and as the custodian of an older medium the motion picture industry fought that rearguard action against a clever new upstart which is by now familiar to us. Even as the problem of televising cinema film was being solved, the Cinematograph Exhibitors' Association refused to sell any of its movies to television, and in the late 1940s the only celluloid stock the BBC possessed was some European films and a few scientific documentaries (Jacobs 2000: 80).

From 1947 it became possible for broadcasters to record or pre-record the content of television itself, a practice known during the 1950s as 'telerecording'. Yet doubtless because recordings had at first been unavailable to it, and also because unlike cinema it was daily, continuous and hence 'banal', television continued to be regarded primarily as a medium which dealt in non-recorded output. Even telerecording was conceived not so much in order to preserve programmes for archival or artistic purposes as simply to free up studio space and time and save the expense of live repeats. And the arrival of video technology over ten years later did little to alter the perception of television content as essentially ephemeral, for in both the BBC and ITV videotapes were routinely wiped and re-used because they were thought to be more valuable than the programmes they contained (Jacobs 2000: 11).

Nevertheless television's eventual ability to screen cinema films and to record its own material began to change the way in which the medium was perceived. The major studios and distributors in America came to accept that if television could not be resisted it should be worked with, and after 1955 they made their film libraries available to the TV stations. Moreover, the contraction of the cinema which television had caused left the film studios with surplus capacity, and this allowed companies such as Warner to do deals with the TV networks to produce whole series of films exclusively for television. By 1957 over 100 such series were running on the US networks: cops-and-robbers and detective stories like *Highway Patrol* and *Dragnet,* spy and war dramas, and most of all westerns, of which *Cheyenne* and *Rawhide* were the most popular. They were cheap to make, predictable in structure, and bought in bulk by the ITV contractors, who used them as a heavy weapon in the battle for audiences. Though it relied on them less, the BBC soon followed suit. Despite strong resistance from the British film industry, the BBC also bought its first old cinema movies in 1957, 100 of them from RKO. In 1959 it acquired a further twenty-four, this batch from the Selznick Corporation.

Hence, from the beginning of the 1950s an increasing proportion of the material that television was transmitting was pre-recorded, in the form of either cinema films or home-produced programmes, and this had a number of consequences which would in one way or another transform the experience of the viewer. First, the successful screening of cinema films greatly increased the amount of material that television was able to broadcast and vividly illustrates the ability of one medium to exploit the content of another. Though by no means alone in this respect, television is perhaps more obviously parasitic than most other media. Second, the ability of television to record its own material meant that in many respects television aesthetics grew closer to those of the cinema. Instead of being performed in a single sequence as they would be in a theatre, plays could be shot in the manner of movies – discontinuously and in a number of takes from which a final version would be assembled and edited. They also became like the movies in making greater use of locations rather than being confined to not wholly believable studio sets. (We might add at this point that despite the formal enmity between the cinema and television industries, there was some fruitful interchange between their employees. Several cinema directors got into television, and one or two TV directors, such as John Schlesinger and Ken Russell, made highly successful moves to cinema.)

Television's ability to record also 'encouraged the economic development of the programme factory. Recording was exploited because it offered management the maximum use of scarce resources' (Bakewell and Garnham 1970: 14). It enabled programmes of all kinds to be stockpiled for future transmission and, with respect to drama, favoured the production of series and serials over single plays. Like the made-for-TV movies which were being imported from America, these series and serials were often formulaic, providing a blend of familiarity and surprise (at its most obvious in the soap opera) which gave new satisfactions to the audience.

Telerecording had two further and related consequences, one aesthetic and one economic. The transformation of television broadcasts from mere ephemera into physical objects meant that they could not only be stored for future use but used over and over again. Programmes began to acquire the definitiveness and fixity that we normally expect from 'works of art' and repeats of viewers' favourites came to occupy a significant part of the schedule. But, as a result of this, recorded programmes also acquired the status of commodities or 'tradeable goods' (Caughie 2000: 54; Jacobs 2000: 12–13). It was not just that the old movie studios could sell tailor-made films to television: TV broadcasters could buy and sell programmes among themselves, something else which helped to broaden the programme base of British television.

Though the practice of telerecording increased throughout the 1950s, it was the arrival in Britain of magnetic recording technology which gave it real impetus. The first Ampex videotape machine was imported from America by Rediffusion in June 1958, and others arrived at the BBC soon after (Briggs 1995: 837). The long-term consequence of the video revolution is that the great majority of TV programmes are now pre-recorded. Yet at this point it is important to remind ourselves that television remains essentially *live* in the sense that reception is instantaneous with the transmission even of pre-recorded content. Indeed, we may feel that the programmes which best express the real nature of the medium are those which are least susceptible to pre-recording, whose value depends on their up-to-dateness or topicality: news (even though it usually contains filmed inserts), current affairs and outside broadcasts, especially of sport. Moreover, the great irony about video technology is that it was first wanted not so much as a new means of pre-recording television output but as a way of enhancing *non-pre-recorded* transmissions – those which are televised as they are happening. For editing on video was all but impossible. Cutting and splicing were dangerously imprecise, and since tapes were about £100 each and not re-usable the cost of failure was high. But since what it could offer instead was an instant playback facility, video was used to review some recent event in a transmission so that the viewers could appreciate its drama, complexity, ambiguity or whatever, and then to allow a rapid return to the events as they were happening.

As we might expect, the Ampex machines were especially in demand for sport, and are yet another instance of the way in which the viewer's experience of television was transformed by recording technology. Video not only enhanced sport as a spectacle but improved the viewers' knowledge and understanding of it, especially when slow-motion replay was developed. It also enabled the decisions of referees and umpires to be questioned. As Asa Briggs (1995: 838) pertinently remarks, 'Through technology as much as through ideology, authority in sport, as in politics, was becoming more open to doubt.'

News and current affairs

One field in which the BBC's failure to match ITV was a matter of quality rather than mere scheduling was the news. As noted in the last chapter, a major reason why the corporation's television monopoly was unsatisfactory was that its production staff were more comfortable with words than with images, which they tended to distrust. Their faith in the former was embodied in a department of 'Television Talks', which had been created as a kind of catch-all for everything not fitting into such traditional programme categories as drama, sport and light entertainment. As Stuart Hood (1975: 40) puts it:

> The name continued in use for a very long time and is an indication of how difficult the BBC found it to come to terms with the fundamental difference between radio and television, how many of the concepts of radio were taken over and imposed on television and how little the top echelons of the television service understood the new medium.

This mentality seems to have persisted longer in news than in other kinds of programming, for TV news continued to be presented in a way which was much more appropriate to sound broadcasting. Hence it was in this field that the BBC would be hit hardest by the competition. Funded by the contractors, Independent Television News was a networked organization which was concerned with the news to the exclusion of all else, and whose approach to it was entirely uncluttered by preconceptions carried over from radio. It could be argued that in the form of ITN, independent television's greatest contribution to the history of broadcasting was to make TV news into something truly televisual.

The BBC's backwardness in this field has been attributed to the New Zealander Tahu Hole, who was head of news throughout most of the 1940s and 1950s. Hole held a view of the news which was impossibly purist. He deplored the fact that in contrast to the apparently authorless and objective medium of print, broadcast news was unavoidably 'tainted' by the personality of a reader. But if the evil of conveying the news through a human voice could not be avoided in broadcasting, the worse evil of conveying it through a visible presenter most certainly could. Between 1946 and 1954 the BBC offered no television news as such, merely a late evening relay of the radio news during which viewers were obliged to stare at a single photograph of Big Ben. Apart from this there was only a ten-minute newsreel five evenings a week, whose format – a sequence of items accompanied by a voice-over – exactly resembled that of its counterpart in the cinema. In 1954 a new combined daily bulletin and newsreel was launched, the former using film and still photographs with captions or voiceovers. But the newsreaders remained in purdah, coyly concealed behind the caption cards: there was no visible reader on BBC news until three weeks before ITV went to air.

ITN had been set up in May 1955 under the editorship of Aidan Crawley, a journalist and former MP. This made a much more appropriate use of the medium. Crawley recognized that if the element of personality could not be eliminated from television, it should be used to best effect. The ITN presenters, Robin Day, Christopher Chataway and Barbara Mandell, were more than merely visible. They were authoritative and journalistic and known not by that rather passive term 'newsreaders' but as news*casters*, which implied – accurately – that they had something to say in their own right. They helped to gather and select the news and wrote the scripts to suit their own style of delivery.

ITN's mission was 'to make significant news more interesting, more comprehensible and more acceptable'. It used an unprecedented quantity of film in its bulletins and incorporated as much informed comment as possible to give viewers a better perspective. Like a newspaper it also set out to get scoops and exclusives. It managed to send back the only film – shots of Port Said – from the 1956 Suez War, and in the following year gained an exclusive interview in Cairo with Britain's arch-enemy, President Nasser. On the frequent occasions when the importance of the news justified it, the ITN bulletins would overrun. Its news-gathering units used lighter film cameras, for whose lack of studio quality the dramatic impact of their location shots more than compensated. As a former politician himself Crawley encouraged a persistent questioning of public figures which contrasted with the deferential style of BBC interviewers perhaps overmindful of who fixed the licence fee. ITN also favoured the spontaneity and human interest of 'vox pops', informal interviews with people in the street which were then assembled into a tightly edited package.

Two episodes serve to illustrate the much more televisual approach of ITN. At an open-air meeting of the boilermakers' union, reporter Reginald Bosanquet climbed on to a platform to question the leader Ted Hill against a background of three thousand shouting strikers; and during a 'Keep death off the roads' campaign the Minister of Transport was interviewed beside a main road to the coast just before the Whitsun Holiday rush. Crawley's early resignation in January 1956, on the ground that the contractors were seeking to curb ITN's budget, served only to strengthen the organization he had helped to set up. Renewed backing for it was extracted from the Chairman of the ITA, Lord Clark, during a tough televised interview on the day Crawley resigned. But even ITV's local news held an advantage over its rival's, since unlike the more centralized and metropolitan BBC, the contractors were regionally based.

In both ITV and the BBC current affairs were organizationally separate from news, although the former were strongly influenced by the presentation of the latter. At ITV current affairs were the responsibility of the contractors, not of ITN, and because BBC current affairs occupied a department of their own they were able to respond to ITV news more promptly than the corporation's news department did. Part of their response had its origins in the demise, at the end of 1956, of the 'toddlers' truce', an extraordinary instance of Reithian paternalism which had been conceived by the BBC. This was a total shutdown of television between 6 p.m. and 7 p.m. so that parents could put their younger children to bed and persuade the older ones to do their homework. Only too aware that this period was valuable in advertising terms, the ITA argued that the responsibility for children lay not with broadcasters but parents – and it and now the BBC both realized that whichever captured the viewers during this period had a fair chance of holding them for the rest of the evening. From 1957 the six to seven slot therefore saw the fiercest competition of the entire schedule.

For five nights a week the BBC filled it with the *Tonight* programme, a current affairs magazine which by 1960 was commanding an average audience of 9 million. Its items varying in mood, pace and style, yet each lasting no more than a few minutes, *Tonight* offered an original blend of political and current affairs with light entertainment. Yet underlying it was a serious philosophy: the programme was meant to be 'on the side of the viewer'. Using Cliff Michelmore as the presenter, and as interviewers and reporters the former print journalists Fyfe Robertson, Trevor Philpott and Alan Whicker, who adapted very well to their new medium, producer Donald Baverstock encouraged a style of questioning which was more incisive than the bland and often obsequious approach that had been common hitherto. *Tonight* aimed, in Grace Wyndham Goldie's (1977: 216) words, to show that 'It was not always necessary to be respectful; experts were not invariably right; the opinions of those in high places did not have to be accepted.' Its approach chimed well with an informal, sceptical, even irreverent *zeitgeist* which was beginning to develop during the second half of the decade. This was perhaps a manifestation of that broader democratizing trend that was mentioned earlier – more certainly an effect of the familiarizing, demystifying effects of television itself, on whose innate iconoclastic tendencies we shall have more to say later. For the BBC at any rate, *Tonight* was a beneficial consequence of competition in the sense that the casually authoritative style of ITN allowed it to treat current affairs in a way which might have seemed too flippant in a monopoly broadcaster.

Whereas *Tonight* was lightly sceptical, the BBC's other major current affairs programme, the weekly *Panorama*, seemed more serious and weighty. Presented by the magisterial Richard Dimbleby, it had started in 1953 as a mainly arts and cultural programme, but from about 1957 its concerns became more exclusively political. Its contributors included Woodrow Wyatt, Ludovic Kennedy, John Freeman and Robert Kee, and Christopher Chataway and Robin Day were later lured from ITN. *Panorama* attracted some early competition from Associated-Rediffusion's *This Week*, which had an approach to current affairs that has been described as 'tabloid but serious'.

In 1958 Tahu Hole was replaced as head of news by Stuart Hood, who formed a team of presenters including Robert Dougall, Richard Baker, Kenneth Kendall and Michael Aspel. Thereafter news on BBC television was able to stand comparison with that of ITN and with the corporation's own current affairs output. But what finally established television, both BBC and ITV, as the main news medium was the Cuban missile crisis of 1962. With the world on the brink of war, only radio and television could keep people fully abreast of events – and only television could show the pictures taken by US reconnaissance planes of the Soviet missiles on freighter decks. Whereas in 1957 out of every hundred people in Britain 30 chose newspapers as their main news source, 46 chose radio and 24 chose television, by 1962 52 per cent were treating television as their main news source, with only 31 per cent opting for newspapers and 17 per cent for radio.

Some other programming milestones

In other kinds of programmes – notably drama, comedy and light entertainment, pop music shows and sport – the impact of competition was highly variable. Much depended on the foresight of the BBC's individual heads of department and the energy and originality of their commercial rivals.

In drama the BBC persisted long after the arrival of ITV with a policy which one might expect of a public service broadcaster. It tried to be as eclectic as possible, offering classic plays, adaptations of great novels, original series and serials, and single plays by modern authors. Its head of drama, Michael Barry, prided himself on an ability to encourage talented new playwrights such as N. F. Simpson, John Mortimer and Johnny Speight. The BBC also offered much popular drama – science fiction and detective stories (its outstanding adaptation of *Maigret* began in 1960), and, of course, soap opera. But though the BBC was first in this field, the earliest successes were ITV's: the hospital soap *Emergency – Ward Ten* (ATV) lasted for ten years from 1957 and Granada's *Coronation Street*, launched in 1960, is still running.

At first most plays were broadcast live, but as we saw earlier the increased use of recording moved them away from the ambit of the theatre and closer to that of the cinema, since it gave TV producers some of the flexibility of the film director. By the end of the 1950s plays written especially for television at last began to outnumber those which were adapted from the stage (Jacobs 2000: 76). But commendable as the BBC's drama policy was, it perforce became more sharply focused when in the late 1950s ABC introduced a Sunday night series shrewdly entitled *Armchair Theatre*: all the delights of a vivid public experience brought to you in the comfort of your sitting-room. The series was soon entrusted to a Canadian director, Sydney Newman, who saw contemporary British drama and society with a fresh eye. He realized that the theatre was a largely middle-class sphere which failed to reach a working-class and regional audience. He therefore concentrated on plays of social realism, many of them reflecting a changing Britain.

After 1958 Newman was able to stockpile plays with the aid of the new video technology. The series format, which recording made easier, had an obvious economic appeal to broadcasting institutions. But it also commanded audience loyalty, and by the end of the decade *Armchair Theatre* could boast 12 million viewers. Moreover, the series was a success with the critics, and when its own head of drama resigned in 1962 the BBC brought in Newman as his replacement – its first appointment of a senior figure from ITV and thus its first, if tacit, admission that it had a competitor.

In the field of comedy and light entertainment ITV mounted a formidable challenge by exploiting the showbiz connections of Lew Grade and Sidney Bernstein. It did particularly well with such variety spectaculars as *Sunday Night at the London Palladium*, but the BBC held its own in straight comedy shows, many of which proved more enduring than ITV's. The BBC's head of light entertainment, Eric Maschwitz, ascribed this to a recognition that the strength of comedy, even television comedy, lies in the writing: that however important its visual elements they must grow out of the dialogue. Yet he also stressed that the shows were written for television, not for the theatre: they respected and made use of the intimacy of the medium rather than striving for big visual effects.

The force of these arguments becomes apparent when recalling the early ITV variety shows. Largely theatrical in concept (many were relayed from theatres), they seemed in some respects too vast, too detailed, for the small screen. The very term 'spectacular' reveals their predominantly theatrical concerns, and as the theatre has existed far longer than television there seemed to be something oddly old-fashioned about them, which is not to deny that they were hugely popular with the TV audience. In this respect, then, the BBC's concentration on comedy series was more progressive, more telegenic. The excellent *Hancock's Half Hour* transferred from radio in 1956 to reveal an artist whose facial expressions and physical posture were just as variously expressive as his voice. Moreover the show was one of the first to use Ampex videotape, its producer realizing that if Hancock could be freed of the strain of a live performance, and if the show were recorded in discontinuous segments, the range of shots (especially of Hancock's comic reactions) could be extended, and the overall pace and finish of the programmes improved (Goddard 1991: 84–5).

Asa Briggs (1995: 143) has made another important point about the television comedy of this period, whether on ITV or BBC: although both imported US shows (the former offered *I Love Lucy*, the latter *The Phil Silvers Show*), the bulk of it was British – neither American nor Americanized. The BBC featured not only Tony Hancock but Michael Bentine, Billy Cotton, Charlie Drake, Jimmy Edwards and Benny Hill, while ITV's hugely popular sitcom *The Army Game* focused on a very British experience: national service.

In the field of light entertainment, ITV had another and yet heavier weapon than the variety spectacular: the competition show offering big prizes of cash or consumer durables such as fridges and TV sets. ATV provided two of the most popular: *Double Your Money* (1955–68), featuring the ersatz sincerity of quizmaster Hughie Green and a top prize of £1,000; and *Take Your Pick*, presented by Michael Miles, who in the words of one TV critic looked like a public schoolboy gone wrong. The shows were banal and trite, but had the virtue of being cheap – cheaper than than full variety shows – and of pulling in big audiences. Moreover, as ITV realized, these were all the bigger for the fact that give-away shows were a kind of programming in which the BBC, inhibited by the anti-materialistic nature of its public service ethos if not by the letter of its charter, would decline to compete.

Pop music shows began only with the era of competition, because pop music as we now know it did not exist before the birth of rock 'n' roll in the mid-1950s. Today's pop music is the recognizable descendant of rock 'n' roll, just as rock music was a recognizable relative of the jazz-based popular music which preceded it. Like 'jazz' its name was a sexual euphemism. But the kinship of rock to jazz was more like that of niece or nephew than offspring: the change of musical direction in the 1950s was abrupt, and the extraordinary popularity of the new music quite unforeseeable. Rock's own parents were black rhythm and blues and white country music, and its novelty, as the name suggests, lay in a heavy, plangent beat.

Yet the simple, rural background of rock 'n' roll was deceptive. Whereas the vehicle of jazz had been the old labour-intensive orchestra or big band, its driving-force the human breath of trumpet and saxophone, rock was performed by a modern, labour-saving 'group', its driving-force the electricity of guitar and bass. Within twenty years rock music had been eagerly adopted far beyond America and the English-speaking world. In its modern form it is an accompaniment to activities both public and private, pervading everyday life in a way which is barely noticed. It is a staple of both radio and television; and with its panoply of stars, bands, singles and album charts, videos, vast concerts and unending tours, it has become a major preoccupation of people all over the globe.

As we shall see, it was radio which played the major part in spreading rock music, but television also made early if faltering attempts to feature it – attempts which would reach their apotheosis some thirty years later with MTV. The records of the first great rock stars, Bill Haley and the Comets and Elvis Presley, reached Britain in 1955–6, and Associated-Rediffusion was the first to present rock music on television with *Cool for Cats* (1956–9). The BBC followed in January 1957 with *Six-Five Special*, which replaced the toddlers' truce on Saturdays. But while it tried to target teenagers, the main fans of the new music, the show was hampered by a residual public service impulse to appeal to everybody else. Consequently there were interludes for sport, comedy and even classical music.

One important aim of pop music shows on both channels was to develop British versions of the American rock stars: Cliff Richard made his début on ABC's *Oh Boy!* (1958–9). But there was also an expectation that when the young rock 'n' roll idol 'grew up' he would develop into something called an all-round entertainer – a fate which, to universal relief, soon befell Tommy Steele. In its early years rock music was so potent that it was hugely popular on television even though producers had not yet succeeded in making it televisual. The BBC's *Juke Box Jury*, for instance, which ran from 1959 to 1967, showed nothing more than a panel of celebrities listening to new releases and voting on whether they would be 'hits' or 'misses'. As Asa Briggs (1995: 208) observes, the popularity of the show was a means by which figures from rock culture were assimilated into mainstream entertainment. Nevertheless, by the mid-1960s rock music, in all its rebellious and anti-social posturing, had *become* mainstream. To their great credit, swaggering, devil-may-care bands like the Rolling Stones have never felt the need to develop into 'all-round entertainers'.

In its television coverage of sport the BBC had already reached high standards which its new rival was unable to match until the next decade. This was thanks to a rare act of foresight by the corporation. At the start of ITV it retained its head of sport, Peter Dymock, by increasing his salary, and Dymock then secured all its most important sporting contracts for the next five to seven years. Until 1958 the BBC's main offering in this field was *Sportsview*. For Saturday afternoons it then launched the hugely successful *Grandstand*, whose title well evoked the privileged perspective of the viewers. However, Dymock had his struggles within the corporation. He had to fight hard for modern cameras, for the use of the expensive new video equipment, even for priority over children's programmes so that *Grandstand* would not be superseded at that climactic point when the afternoon's results were coming in. The BBC's great achievement under Dymock was to exploit the dramatic possibilities of sport, and in so doing bring it nearer to other, more conventionally theatrical kinds of entertainment.

With respect to programme innovation, whether in the form of new genres or of new developments to old genres, the BBC took most of the honours, which is perhaps to be expected of an organization not solely concerned with maximizing its audience. In 1959 it launched *Monitor*, a fortnightly arts programme presented with infectious enthusiasm by Huw Wheldon. Sir Brian Horrocks brought a similar quality to his accounts of the battles of the Second World War. No modern TV producer would risk such a series with the meagre visual aids available to Horrocks: enthralled by the power of his narrative, no viewer felt the slightest need of them. Also dating from this period were the pioneering nature series *Zoo Quest*, and, from 1959 to 1962, *Face to Face*, a series of interviews of public figures tactfully yet searchingly conducted by John Freeman. Among his thirty-five guests were Evelyn Waugh, Bertrand Russell, John Osborne, Tony Hancock and Lord Reith.

It would be fair to conclude that after five years of competition the BBC and ITV shared the honours fairly evenly. By persevering in its duty to provide something for everyone the BBC created many programmes which were critical successes – applauded by those who took a serious analytical interest in television. But there is no doubt that most of the populist successes were ITV's. Its televisual news coverage, its widely accessible drama in the form of soaps and American made-for-TV series, and its give-away shows and variety spectaculars were devastating weapons in the ratings war. Noting the vast range of programming that the rivals were providing between them, the government decided to increase transmission from fifty to sixty hours a week – a move which gave ITV extra revenue from more advertising time but brought the BBC only extra expense.

Television and advertising

It is now difficult to understand the nervous excitement that the first TV advertisements created in a nation largely unused to commercials, even on the radio. The public felt deeply ambivalent about them. Adverts were associated with the glamour and prestige of America, whose way of life seemed a triumphant vindication of business enterprise and sales promotion. On the other hand, the decade was marked by widespread if rather naive fears of 'brainwashing', mainly as a result of the traumatized state some fifty Allied prisoners were found to be in after their communist captors had tried to indoctrinate them during the Korean War. Could TV adverts be a form of brainwashing? After watching them, would we all be reduced to automatons, helplessly buying toilet rolls and pots of jam by the gross?

For their part, the creative and production staff of ITV could draw upon no received wisdom in order to cope with the 'commercial breaks', as the advertising slots were called – many of them within as well as between programmes. Writers of documentaries and plays were likely to be the most frustrated by them. Suspense points had to be devised just before the breaks in order to hold the viewers until the programme could resume. On the other hand, the breaks might fatally halt a narrative or drama as it hastened towards its climax. The impact of commercial breaks on artistic and narrative structures in television is a fascinating subject that has hardly been explored.

Technical staff also faced a challenge. They had to 'package' commercial breaks in a way which would render them neither too similar to nor too incongruous with the adjacent programme content. One unhappy instance of accidental continuity dates from the earliest days of ITV when a boxing match was being screened. A commercial break between rounds concluded with the shot of a man downing a glass of Watney's beer. Viewers then cut straight to one of the boxers spitting copiously into a bucket.

After an initial uncertainty, commercials became enormously popular. Viewers gleefully quoted advertising jingles and slogans at one another, using them as cultural passwords. For young and old alike they provided a whole new treasury of nursery rhymes:

You'll wonder where the yellow went
When you clean your teeth with Pepsodent . . .

Esso sign means happy motoring . . .

Murraymints, Murraymints,
The too-good-to-hurry mints . . .

Oxo gives a meal man-appeal . . .

Carpets at prices you can afford
From Cyril Lord!

For the advertisers themselves, TV was a much more attractive medium than street hoardings, cinemas, stadiums or public transport because, like newspapers, it was essentially domestic. But sound and moving pictures gave it obvious advantages over the latter. In 1957, a mere two years after the launch of ITV, £13.7 million was spent on television advertising, and by the following year ITV's total advertising revenue had already surpassed that of the press. The commonest products to be advertised were soaps and detergents, soft drinks, beer, petrol and lubricants, sweets and toothpaste. In theory, advertisers could not buy into a programme but only into time-slots which were more or less expensive according to their proximity to peak viewing periods. In practice, however, the contractors sold many advertisers slots in or next to programmes which were appropriate to their products. This is why children's television has always been punctuated by commercials for toys, games, soft drinks and snacks.

Though extraneous to programme content, commercials can be seen as 'distilled television' not only because in needing to make their point – in a matter of seconds and often through a complete dramatic narrative – they are a compendium of shooting and editing techniques, but because they constitute a magpie genre, borrowing freely from TV programmes in the form of pastiche and parody. Even our awareness of their similar borrowings from cinema films derives largely from seeing those films on television. But in their techniques of shooting and editing, commercials have influenced other genres, notably the travelogue, the pop video and certain kinds of full-length drama.

We might take TV advertising's continuing popularity with viewers as proof of its infallible power to increase sales and change behaviour. In many cases this has certainly happened. After a television campaign in 1960 sales of Kennomeat dog-food rose by 53 per cent in nine months. TV commercials for toothpaste have been credited with the vast improvement in dental hygiene which has occurred over the last forty years or so. In 1959, when ITV was still an infant, only two out of every five households owned a toothbrush. Yet despite those early fears of brainwashing there are evident limits to the power of TV advertising. One reason for its popularity is, of course, negative: the commercial breaks give us the chance to make a cup of tea or answer a call of nature without missing any of the programme we are watching. But even when we sit through them we might enjoy the commercials without feeling impelled to buy the products they feature, or even being able to recall their brand-names. Of itself TV advertising is power-less to reverse certain social trends. Some products which were once intensively advertised have all but disappeared. Among them was starch, which since the middle of the 1960s has succumbed to collar stiffeners, new fabrics and the fashion for more casual clothes. Another was shoe polish, whose sales have declined as leather has yielded to synthetic materials that require less care.

As all this might suggest, the real interest of TV commercials to the media historian lies in the keyhole view they offer into the social conditions of a particular era. In the late 1950s, for instance, a fierce advertising war broke out between the two main detergent manufacturers, Procter and Gamble and Lever Brothers, a war from which ITV derived one quarter of its entire advertising revenue. Their new or newly promoted products, with brand-names like Omo, Surf, Persil, Oxydol, Daz, Tide and Fairy Snow, combined soap with grease-dissolving agents. But what explains the number of brands that were marketed, and the intensity of the competition? Automatic washing-machines were beginning to sell during this period, but for the majority of housewives laundry was the most burdensome of all the domestic chores. Many families lived in houses which lacked a permanent hot-water supply. Water had to be specially heated and with the aid of soap powder clothes were washed by hand, with the additional use of bar soap for heavy stains. White clothes and linen had to be bleached. The weekly wash could occupy a whole day, and that was if the weather was good enough for outside drying. Ironing and putting away could occupy much of another, and in wet weather the house would be festooned with drying clothes for the best part of a week. Any product which would lighten this burden was likely to sell well. One such, fashioned from the new 'man-made' fibres and frequently advertised on television, was the drip-dry, non-iron Rael-Brook shirt. But even more crucial were the new detergents, which were depicted, in Jo Gable's (1980: 58) words, 'like laundering Sir Galahads come to free the housewife from wash-day tyranny'. Even in an era of near-universal ownership of washing-machines the TV soap war has rumbled on, brandishing newer weapons with names like Ariel, Bold and Radion. Other and more recent commercials which offer similar social clues have been for foreign package holidays, computers, cars, mobile phones, and, reflecting the greater competitiveness in financial services, banks, building societies and insurance companies.

The history of television advertising also reflects the changes that have occurred in public morals and mores. The 1954 Television Act carefully defined those products and services which could not be advertised, and though many prohibitions have remained constant, some have been lifted and fresh ones imposed. The Act forbade advertising with a political or religious aim, or on any public question on which there could be more than one opinion, such as abortion or capital punishment. No commercials could be broadcast for money-lenders, matrimonial agencies or fortune-tellers. On the ground that they might offend public taste there could be no adverts for condoms or, until the late 1970s, for female sanitary products. Before 1971 no woman could be seen modelling underwear except in silhouette, yet cigarette commercials were not banned until August 1965.

Since 1955 two important changes have occurred which pertain not to commercials for individual products but to the overall relationship between advertising and programme content. The first was the early abolition of what were called 'ad-mags', fifteen-minute sequences of dialogue set in shops or pubs, whose purpose was to promote a whole range of products. The most notable ad-mag was *Jim's Inn*, which began in 1957. The problem posed by ad-mags was that the more interesting they were made to seem the more they came to resemble straight programmes, thus threatening the principle that advertising and programming should remain absolutely separate. Moreover they clearly exceeded the amount of advertising per hour which had been permitted by the Television Act. They disappeared in 1963, at the behest of the Pilkington Committee. Of an opposite tendency was the relaxation in 1988 of the rules governing sponsorship, for it eroded that acclaimed distinction between advertising and programming which had been maintained for over thirty years. News and current affairs were among the few genres to which this relaxation did not apply, and viewers soon learned that they were to be grateful to Croft's Port for *Rumpole of the Bailey* and to PowerGen for disclosing the secrets of the next day's weather.

'A licence to print your own money'

The major shareholder of Scottish Television, the biggest ITV contractor north of the border, was the Canadian news magnate and businessman Roy Thomson. At its launch in August 1957 he announced, in a famously indiscreet phrase, that owning a commercial TV franchise in Britain was 'like having a licence to print your own money'. Uttered less than two years after ITV started, it is a measure of the speed with which the service turned its fortunes round. Yet its very success would render it vulnerable. By 1959 questions about the size of the contractors' profits were being put to the ITA by members of the Commons Public Accounts Committee, doubtless with Thomson's words ringing in their ears. And two years later the government introduced an 11 per cent excise duty on television advertising, payable by the contractors. Had their profits accrued from a programme diet of opera, ballet, documentaries and discussions, they might well have been ignored or even applauded. But the contractors were seen as having made their pile from nothing but 'wiggle dances, give-aways, panels and light entertainment' (quoted in Briggs 1995: 16).

This was not altogether fair, but as was noted earlier the contractors' initial financial problems certainly pushed them further along the populist road, a move the ITA could block only by risking the future of the whole system. When their fortunes improved the authority pressed the contractors to produce more serious programming, but not with total success. In January 1957, for example, the ITV network was running no less than ten give-away shows a week. The consequence was that by 1960 it was easily winning the ratings war, but losing the battle for the support of the nation's opinion-formers – the Members of Parliament and the press, those in academia and the arts. In these circles there was anxiety about cultural standards, the erosion of 'British civilization', and the lack of a public service ethos on ITV. More specifically, its programmes were seen as mostly trite, the game shows – along with the commercials, which were attacked for being too frequent and often misleading – as encouraging crassly acquisitive attitudes. Above all, there was dismay that such a programme diet could attract and hold a great majority of the viewing public.

These strictures helped to place ITV and the BBC on much more of an equal footing. Commercial television had won the lion's share of the audience, but the BBC retained a moral and cultural superiority – and the rivals still had much to play for. The BBC's charter was now due for renewal in 1964, the same year in which under the terms of the Television Act of 1954 the progress of ITV would be reviewed. In 1960 the Conservative government therefore set up a committee under the industrialist Sir Harry Pilkington to appraise the performance of both organizations and to consider the future of British broadcasting. The government also intended to authorize a third television channel and there was every chance that it would be awarded to the organization that Pilkington preferred.

The BBC believed that it simply had to win this third channel. Its claim to a universal licence fee had been weakened by the fact that in competition with just one ITV channel it had already lost over half the viewing public. How much weaker would its claim be if it had to compete for that public against two? Under Director General Sir Hugh Greene, who had succeeded Sir Ian Jacob on 1 January 1960, the corporation therefore strove to increase its audience share to 50:50 by 1962, the year the committee was to report. One of Greene's first acts was to revamp the news and encourage the new Controller of Television, Stuart Hood, to reschedule the BBC's programmes in order to meet the challenge of ITV head on. But Greene was also an astute public relations man and a clever political lobbyist, and while ITV counted its profits the corporation carefully assembled the case it would put to Pilkington.

Sources/further reading

The standard history of the birth and early years of commercial television is Sendall (1982, 1983), but useful summary accounts of the establishment and structure of ITV and of the birth of competition are in Paulu (1981) and Tunstall (1983). The political and cultural implications of competition are explored by Curran and Seaton (1997). Seymour-Ure (1996) is generally useful on broadcasting during this period and, along with Hood (1980), particularly illuminating on the economic composition and overall business interests of the ITV contractors. For the first years of competition I am generally indebted to Briggs (1995), which is brilliantly researched and highly detailed, though primarily written from the perspective of the BBC. For another, more compact, more journalistic yet also enlightening account of this period, written primarily from the perspective of ITV, see Black (1972b).

On technological developments in television Armes (1988) and Winston (1998) are invaluable, especially on the historical relationship between live and pre-recorded television content. Bakewell and Garnham (1970), Jacobs (2000) and Caughie (2000) are illuminating on the ways in which the economics and aesthetics of television production were affected by recording technology. Ward (1989) gives a useful account of how the US movie industry offset its own contraction by making films for television, many of which were soon sold on to ITV. Comparing British reactions unfavourably with those of the Americans, Buscombe (1991) describes the ways in which the motion picture industry tried to cope with the rise of television.

For the deficiencies of early television news on the BBC, see Hood (1975). Detailed accounts of the early years of ITN are in Sendall (1982) and Davis (1976), who also covers current affairs. The best characterization of the *Tonight* programme is in Goldie (1977).

In his editorial introduction to a useful collection of essays on other programme genres of this period, Corner (1991) gives an excellent synoptic account of television and British society during the 1950s. A briefer survey of the programmes of this time is in Day-Lewis (1992).

Caughie (1991, 2000) helpfully traces the transition of television drama from relay and rival of conventional live theatre to a genre whose nature and aesthetics more closely resembled those of film, one consequence of which was that TV plays became a kind of commodity. For a fascinating account of early television drama, arguing that it quickly developed an aesthetic independent of both theatre and cinema, see Jacobs (2000). Goddard (1991) is illuminating on the way in which the new technology of Ampex videotape transformed the production of *Hancock's Half Hour*; Sendall (1982) on the give-away shows; Hill (1991) on early pop music television; and Whannel (1991) on TV coverage of sport during the first period of competition.

Gable (1980) offers a full account of television's first years as an advertising medium, but my remarks on the aesthetics of TV commercials have been inspired by Corner (1995). For a perspective on the more recent history of television advertising, see Brierley (1998). The factors which led up to the appointment of the Pilkington Committee are described in Sendall (1983) and Briggs (1995).

Chapter 6

Pilkington and after

Pilkington and after

Sir Hugh Greene: character and achievements

Sir Hugh Greene, whose period of office spanned the 1960s, is reckoned by many to have been the greatest Director General of the BBC since John Reith. However the two men, who managed only a brief and uneasy friendship, were cast in very different moulds. Whereas Reith had stamped himself upon the corporation, Greene commanded the loyalty of his staff by being relaxed and liberal, affording freedom and flexibility to programme-makers and performers. He had his weaknesses, including a flippant, mischievous streak which prevented him from taking certain matters as seriously as his high office required: he fell out with Reith because he was unable to agree with the latter's assertion that dignity was the greatest quality to which humans could aspire. He could be contemptuous of his opponents, some of whom were influential, and he was rather more interested in news and current affairs than in other kinds of programming. But he was also tough and decisive, and a shrewd and unfailing champion of the corporation.

Probably his greatest achievements date from the early years of his tenure. By the time the Pilkington Committee reported in 1962 Greene had raised the BBC's audience share to 50:50 for the first time since competition began. Under him the corporation succeeded in justifying itself to Pilkington, in thoroughly discrediting the achievements of ITV, and in capturing the third channel. It also ensured that it would be regarded for many years to come as, in Pilkington's (1962: 288) fulsome phrase, 'the main instrument of broadcasting in the United Kingdom'. Indeed the enormity of its success was almost embarrassing: 'The BBC know good broadcasting,' the committee concluded, as if with a nod and a wink, 'by and large they are providing it' (Pilkington 1962: 46).

Having had military experience of psychological warfare Greene was an adroit propagandist, and under him the BBC presented a much more painstaking and persuasive case than its competitors did. The ITA and the contractors mistook winning the war of the ratings for winning the war of words, and their approach to the committee was complacent, sloppy and uncoordinated. But if credit must be given to Greene and the BBC it has to be said that the Pilkington Committee was predisposed in their favour. From the start many of its members held a severely Reithian view of broadcasting and were altogether reluctant to grant legitimacy to any other. Though Pilkington himself was an industrialist its dominant member seems to have been Professor Richard Hoggart, a working-class beneficiary of higher education and celebrated historian of popular culture. Hoggart was inclined to be critical of the cultural standards of ITV, believing that it confined itself to entertaining people when it should also be improving and educating them. The committee as a whole was highly sensitive to the enormous profits which were being made by the ITV contractors; the acquisitive attitudes encouraged by the big money prizes of the ITV give-away shows; the possible effects on young people of the frequent depictions of violence in TV films (ITV was also perceived as mainly responsible for these); and, more generally, to the possibility, at a time when TV sets were being bought in huge numbers, that television had become the most influential force in modern society.

Public service broadcasting in an age of competition

As the ITV system expanded through the regions and captured the majority of viewers in each, one question grew ever more insistent: Could public service broadcasting survive in a competitive environment?

It will be remembered that the latter was dedicated to two aims: to provide 'something for everyone' and 'everything for someone'. But when the listeners and viewers were given a choice of networks the second of these aims – to expose each of them, as it were forcibly, to the fullest range of programming within a single channel or network – was no longer achievable. And this was true whether the choice was between networks within the BBC's monopoly (radio's 'cultural pyramid' was established in 1945–6) or between the BBC and an external rival (ITV began in 1955). Within each network of the cultural pyramid some variety of programming might combine with the listener's inertia to introduce her to a topic she might not have chosen for herself; but she could still choose to switch to another network. On the single channel of the BBC television service the twin aims of 'something for everyone' and 'everything for someone' could be maintained for a few years longer. But with the gradual spread of ITV and thus the gradual extension of choice among the viewing public, the latter aim ceased to be achievable in television, too. The consequence was that from about the time of Pilkington the rationale of public service was moving from a Reithian to a post-Reithian phase: universal provision – 'something for everyone' – remained the avowed aim, but universal provision on a single channel or network – 'everything for someone' – was less and less proclaimed as its necessary accompaniment.

In the post-Reithian era, how would the aim of providing something for everyone be realized? In the virtual monopoly which it held in radio the BBC could, as we have seen, spread the provision over several networks, and in the (relatively limited) competitive environment of television it could still aim to provide this service on a single network, even if viewers might sometimes choose to ignore it. The problem was that the original Reithian principles of public service were so interconnected that the abandonment of one made the others seem increasingly vulnerable. Why?

In order to justify themselves the various networks even of the BBC's radio monopoly needed to be banded or diversified in some way, almost inevitably along the lines of majority and minority interests. It then became clearer to the individual listener which of those services she was not using but nevertheless having to pay for through the licence fee. The Third Programme, for instance, was a relatively expensive network which never captured more than 2 per cent of the total listenership. Hence, even in the lofty realms of monopoly public service, audience size came to matter. And it mattered even more in the truly competitive world of television, especially if the BBC were to find itself facing not just one but two rival networks. In such a case the majority of the total viewing audience might be permanently captured by the commercial stations and keenly resent paying the licence fee for the one network it never watched. This explains why the BBC was so desperate to acquire the third channel.

So the end of monopoly and the arrival of audience choice not only meant the end of 'everything for someone' but threatened the principles of 'something for everyone' and the universal licence fee. Why pay for what you don't use? But it was not simply that the majority became more aware that they were having to pay for the pro-grammes of minorities: the commercial system showed that they could enjoy their own majority programmes *without paying anything at all*. Affluent minorities might even enjoy a similar privilege since advertisers would find them worth targeting. But failing that, it was surely right that minorities should pay for their programmes through some form of subscription system rather than leeching off the majority.

Quite aside from the fact that some minorities are neither big enough nor rich enough to attract advertisers or a subscription service (Garnham 1994: 17), and that the encryption and revenue collection that subscription involves pose technical difficulties (Franklin 1997: 184), such minorities would be catered for only in proportion to the revenue they generated. On the other hand, because the licence-fee system buries individual programme costs it can provide amply funded, high-quality programmes for minorities who are small and poor as well as large and rich.

Yet the question remains: Why should the majority pay for what is consumed by, or of importance to, only a minority? This question is in essence about the difference between individualism ('I wish to pay only for what I consume') and mutualism ('I'll sometimes pay more than I need to in order to give my fellow citizens what they otherwise couldn't have – on the basis that in different circumstances they will do the same for me'). Those who adopt the latter approach would probably regard broadcasting as the expression of deeper social and political values. At this level, mutualism is unavoidable – the glue that holds a society together. As a taxpayer each of us funds at least some services which we do not use or benefit from, on the principle that those we do use will be better and more affordable because they are likewise partly paid for by those who do not use them. In public service broadcasting, programmes for one interest group are part-financed by others. But just as our physical needs may change over time – today while I was as fit as a fiddle I helped to pay for the doctor to treat your bunions, but next year you will help to fund my heart bypass operation and lengthy stay in hospital – so our broadcasting interests may do likewise: yesterday's Radio 1 fan is tomorrow's disciple of Radio 4. Moreover at any one time each of us is likely to hold some interests which are of a minority nature as well as others which are not.

Those who take the individualist view of broadcasting – and who would probably deny that broadcasting has any deeper social or political significance – see it as an *audience-focused* activity. Programme costs are tied to audience size so that majority programmes get the lion's share of funding while programmes for minorities will be less frequently and more cheaply made, and in some cases not made at all. They perceive broadcasting as primarily a medium of populist entertainment. Those who take a mutualist (public service) view regard broadcasting as *programme-focused*. Programme costs are not tied to audience size, which means that programmes – if need be, expensive ones – can be made for small audiences. They perceive broadcasting as the fullest cultural expression of society as a whole. And notwithstanding the reputation of the BBC, theirs is less élitist than the other view in the sense that it does not discount certain interests or tastes merely because they are shared by a small number of people. Yet in catering for those interests this view also acknowledges the possibility that there is some other, presumably intellectual, way in which value or 'quality' might be determined. As suggested in Chapter 3, it is a belief which most of us instinctively incline to at one time or another but which can be difficult to defend in a democratic society.

The BBC's case to Pilkington

In an increasingly competitive environment, then, the only realistic way that the BBC could continue with its central aim of providing something for everyone – and in so doing secure the future of its licence funding – would be to do in television as it had done in radio: spread its service over more than one channel and offer a degree of specialist programming. Yet the case it made to Pilkington owed its success to the skill with which it equivocated between the older and newer notions of 'public service' – between the Reithian idea of universal provision on a single channel and the post-Reithian idea of universal provision over several channels (and thus an end to 'everything for someone').

In order to discredit ITV the BBC pointed to the Reithian variety of the programmes it had continued to offer since its rival's launch. But to make too much of this variety might cause Pilkington to question its need for an extra channel. Hence the BBC also claimed that the presence of ITV had forced it to schedule competitively – a situation in which serious and minority programmes were the first casualties. The award of a second channel would therefore provide it with the opportunity to complement its present service with programmes of a more diverse, distinctive or experimental nature. This looked like the blueprint for a minority, special-interest channel. Yet presumably in order to placate the great licence-paying majority who felt that they should not be expected to fund a channel which held nothing of interest to them, and indeed to encourage them to acquire it, the corporation insisted that it would also carry popular programming. According to Asa Briggs (1995: 403), Greene disapproved of the idea of BBC 2 as a narrowcast or specifically educational service, and Pilkington was duly persuaded to recommend that the third channel should not be specialized but carry a range of programming.

As well as, or perhaps as part of, its preoccupation with public service, the BBC professed concern about the social and moral effects of broadcasting, especially television. This further endeared it to Pilkington since the committee happened to believe that the audiences' domestic situation made them peculiarly susceptible to television's messages. The report began by accepting the premise that 'television is and will be a main factor in influencing the values and moral standards of our society' (Pilkington 1962: 15).

The ITA took the opposite view. It believed that, despite the popularity and pervasiveness of television, its effects had been exaggerated, that it was much more of a mirror of than an influence on society. This, perhaps more than anything, damned the commercial network before the committee. 'The Authority's working assumption is that television has little effect. This is, in our view, a mistake,' it announced tersely. 'Our general appraisal is that the Authority have too negative a conception of the purposes of broadcasting. In discounting the influence of the medium they scale down their responsibilities' (Pilkington 1962: 53–4).

The Pilkington Report: immediate impact and long-term effects

When the report was published in June 1962 the BBC was vindicated and ITV blamed. Pilkington retained its pristine objections to commercial television, judging it by Reithian standards and refusing to allow it any of its own. Its undeniable popularity was simply perceived as vulgarity and used against it. Claiming that the public service aims enshrined in the 1954 Television Act had never been fulfilled, the report proposed that ITV should start all over again, with the ITA planning the programming and selling the advertising time, and buying its programmes from the contractors for inclusion in the schedules it planned. The committee felt that the maximum prizes in the give-away shows should be greatly reduced. And, most important of all, it recommended that the third channel should go to the BBC.

Among the ITV contractors, some sections of the press and many Conservative MPs the report caused outrage. As Bernard Sendall (1983: 91) points out, it appeared to judge the achievements of the two services on unrepresentative evidence – on the basis of complaints received rather than the satisfactions implicit in the viewing figures. *The Economist* attacked its 'compulsive nannying' of British audiences, while the *Daily Telegraph* averred that 'this amazing document' was 'saturated by a haughty conviction that whatever is popular must be bad' (quoted in Sendall 1983: 137). Indeed, the real reason for Pilkington's disapproval had perhaps been identified some two years before by the Director General of the ITA, Sir Robert Fraser. His relaxed and humane view of the mass TV audience certainly makes a refreshing contrast to the weighty, moralistic pronouncements of the committee:

If you decide to have a system of people's television, then people's television you must expect it to be, and it will reflect their likes and dislikes, their tastes and aversions, what they can comprehend and what is beyond them. Every person of common sense knows that people of superior mental constitution are bound to find much of television intellectually beneath them. If such innately fortunate people cannot realise this gently and considerately and with good manners, if in their hearts they despise popular pleasures and interests, then of course they will be angrily dissatisfied with television. But it is not really television with which they are dissatisfied. It is with people.

(quoted in Potter 1989: 85–6)

Still, the supporters of ITV had no fundamental reason to worry. Politically the Pilkington Report was a dinosaur. No government of any colour would attempt radical reforms to a service as popular with the electorate as ITV was, and the present Conservative administration, with its faith in commercial enterprise, was broadly unsympathetic to the report. In a new Television Act it awarded the third channel to the BBC on 625 lines UHF, a standard to which all channels were to change, and it extended the corporation's charter from 1964 to 1976. It also empowered the ITA to take firmer control over the contractors and it imposed a levy on their advertising revenue. But the other proposals were ignored. Indeed, like Beveridge before it and Annan later, the Pilkington Report was significant not so much for the substantive changes it wrought as for its broader role in shaping the values which would suffuse broadcasting in the years to follow. As Sendall (1983: 256) points out, the term 'people's television' rapidly became pejorative, and by 1967 an aspiring contractor could impress the ITA with talk of 'producer's television'. It is significant, too, that when the authority renewed Scottish Television's contract in 1968 its price was that Roy Thomson, author of the famous remark about a franchise being a licence to print money, should relinquish control. His shareholding was to be reduced from 55 to 25 per cent. Yet Thomson had the last laugh. He sold out at the height of the boom. A year later ITV was hit by recession and STV's survival was in doubt.

What Pilkington did above all by insisting on the public service responsibilities of ITV was to strengthen the non-competitive aspects of the British system of television. During the 1960s and 1970s the extent to which it was a duopoly became much clearer than it had been during its first five years. The BBC and ITV continued to compete for audiences, but as Ralph Negrine (1994: 85) observes, neither had an absolute incentive to destroy the other because each had its own source of revenue. Clearly if ITV lost too many viewers it lost advertisers; and if the BBC lost too many its case for a compulsory licence fee was weakened. But a split of up to 60:40 was acceptable to both. Hence an almost accidental virtue of the system was that while it kept both broadcasters on their toes the competition was not so cut-throat as to rule out all programmes which were experimental or of special interest rather than merely audience-chasing. As Colin Seymour-Ure (1996: 67) so happily puts it, the system looked increasingly like 'an expression of the British genius for making practical contraptions which then turn into beautiful machines'.

As a result of Pilkington, then, ITV's programming over the next two decades became more like the BBC's. The Television Act of 1964 allowed the ITA to 'mandate' certain serious kinds of programmes and to require all the contractors to show them at prescribed times in the schedule. In the late 1960s, for instance, all contractors had to broadcast *News at Ten*, one weekday play, one weekend play, and two weekly current affairs programmes. *News at Ten* began in 1967 and epitomized for many ITV's renewed dominance in the field of news and current affairs. In using two newscasters, Alastair Burnet and Andrew Gardner, it followed an American practice which provided variation for the viewers and the opportunity to give fresh briefings to whichever newscaster was out of shot. It also used interviews within the programme not only to comment on news stories but to develop or even create them. It deliberately blurred the old distinctions between newscasters, interviewers and journalists, and it made greater use of on-screen graphics and of special reports and features. Some of the contractors also won fresh acclaim for their current affairs programmes. Rediffusion's *This Week*, which was later continued by Thames Television, was joined in 1963 by Granada's *World in Action*, whose refusal to pull its punches gave the ITA as well as its targets a severe headache.

The contractors renewed their efforts at high-quality drama, and, according to Curran and Seaton (1997: 183), the 26 per cent of ITV programming which was 'serious' in 1959 had risen to 36 per cent by 1965, a figure that was maintained.

But convergence was not solely the effect of Pilkington. Despite the latter's praise for its serious output, the BBC had been badly shaken by the loss of its audiences during the late 1950s, and its programming now grew more like ITV's in the sense of becoming more populist. Game shows and US imports, including soap operas, were every bit as likely to be encountered on the BBC as on ITV. For ITV, then, convergence meant moving 'up-market' – becoming less competitive, more duopolistic: for the BBC it meant going 'down-market' – becoming more competitive and less duopolistic. The extent to which the organizations operated both in competition and as a duopoly was reflected in their various types of programming. Their bids for Hollywood movies and major sporting events such as the Olympic Games and Football League matches were fiercely competitive, a reminder that one negative feature of rivalry is its inflationary effect on programme costs.

In certain other fields, such as educational and religious programming, there were more or less firm agreements to offer complementary coverage. And in others, notably party political broadcasts, general elections and state occasions, duplication was acceptable and even enforced by legislation. The only element of competition here might be in style of coverage. Sometimes too, the ITA pressed the contractors to create duplication through their programme schedules, albeit in a way which bore a semblance of competition. For those viewers in search of light entertainment, for instance, it could hardly be said that the scheduling of *This Week* against *Panorama* was an enlargement of choice. The question it raised was whether such scheduling was in the public interest or just an excess of paternalism.

The cultural convergence of the organizations was reflected in the movements of their top personnel. In 1967 Lord Hill, a former Conservative MP and typical champion of commercial broadcasting, was transferred from the chair of the ITA, which he had occupied since 1963, to that of the BBC's board of governors. At the ITA he was succeeded by Lord Aylestone, the Labour government's former chief whip, who in 1975 would be followed by another Labour Party member, Lady Plowden, previously a vice-chair of the BBC. It was also typical of the new *gravitas* of the ITA that when its director general, Sir Robert Fraser, retired in 1970 he should be replaced by an educationalist and intellectual, Sir Brian Young.

The birth and infancy of BBC 2

By the mid-1960s the morale of the BBC was, not surprisingly, high. The sale of TV sets had been growing steadily, and the government was prompted by the findings of Pilkington to raise the licence fee to a realistic level it had not attained for some years. But the corporation's biggest reward for impressing Pilkington was the third channel: BBC 2 was launched on 20 April 1964.

In all the rhetoric about what the new network would offer there was a strong practical reason why its special-interest, experimental flavour could not be over-emphasized, why it should have some 'mixed, popular appeal' and not be 'an intellectual ghetto' (Briggs 1995: 405). The government as well as the BBC intended that the network should be used as a test-bed for new technologies, and in order to receive it viewers would have to purchase new television sets. These were needed because BBC 2 broadcast not on VHF with 405 lines but on UHF with 625 lines, a higher-definition picture that would become the standard for all British television channels. Hence it was only on 625 lines UHF that colour would be introduced some three years later. But although viewers would eventually be unable to receive any of the networks on the old 405-line sets, few would be in a hurry to purchase new ones if BBC 2 were merely to offer programmes for minorities. (In the event, the change to the new standard was to take just over twenty years: the manufacture of VHF sets ended in 1975, by which time UHF was available to 95 per cent of the population, and VHF transmissions were phased out by both the BBC and ITV between 1982 and 1985.)

Hence the programming strategy was to leaven the generally serious output with a sprinkling of populist items (*Match of the Day* made its début on BBC 2). Yet, notwithstanding Greene's professed aims and the subsequent recommendations of Pilkington, BBC 2 did mark the hesitant beginning of television narrowcasting. There was a variety of programmes, but many of them – and their overall packaging and presentation – wore a rather more sedate and thoughtful air than those of BBC 1. They were not exactly recherché, but nor were they likely to win the ratings war. Indeed, the way in which a difference of tone between the two channels belied a degree of programming overlap was reminiscent of the relationship between the Light and the Home or between the Home and the Third that characterized the cultural pyramid of radio.

Because BBC 2 was at first available only in the south east of England, and further restricted to the few who had bought 625-line televisions, it took some time to make its mark. Nor was it helped by a catastrophic opening night during which it was deprived of a significant part of its tiny audience by a huge power failure in central and west London. Its early programmes attracted some very low viewing figures. After six months about 1.25 million people could receive it, though by 1966 it was within reach of nearly two-thirds of the population should they choose to buy the appropriate receivers. At first it broadcast for a mere four hours per evening, and even in 1974 was on air only 60 per cent as much as BBC 1. Eventually the typical viewing percentages for the three channels were ITV: 49, BBC 1: 39, BBC 2: 12.

Despite its modest start the new network managed some early successes both in traditional programme genres and in its experiments with new kinds of programming. At first it tried to liberate television from the straitjacket of the conventional programme schedule by having occasional 'themed' evenings – perhaps an extended debate on a major political issue or the celebration of a particular film genre. Unfortunately the idea was abandoned within three months, partly because the sustained coverage of a single theme made programme 'junctions' with BBC 1 difficult to achieve, and thus deterred viewers from switching into the new channel; and partly because viewers who were in any case uninterested in the theme were lost to the network for a whole evening.

The biggest triumph of its opening year was undoubtedly *The Great War*, an archive compilation in twenty-six parts of immense interest to both professional historian and uninitiated viewer. Before this series the technical limitations of old ciné film had caused its subjects to move about at a frenetic, unintentionally comical pace, but BBC production staff now found a way to screen the contemporary footage of the war at a natural speed. With *Late Night Line-Up*, presented by Joan Bakewell, BBC 2 also pioneered the 'talk show' – less vapid than the celebrity-based 'chat show' of a later era, more relaxed and wide ranging than the old-fashioned studio discussion. Its aim was to provide an open-ended critical review of the current output of BBC television.

From 1965 Johnny Speight's sitcom *Till Death Us Do Part* brought us the jingoistic cockney character Alf Garnett, who gave great pleasure not only to those who regarded him as a caricature of prejudice and ignorance but those who admired him as the last champion of traditional British values. He was thus an interesting though not unique instance of the way in which irony can rebound upon the ironist, yet make him popular with everyone.

In 1966 the channel began a magnificent twenty-six-part adaptation of *The Forsyte Saga*, the series of novels by John Galsworthy. Its significance was twofold. It was the first notable example of the way in which television could give serious literature a renewed and indeed unprecedented popularity, not only in its screenings thereof but by stimulating sales and readings of the original texts: and it was the last major television serial to be shot in black and white.

BBC 2 began regular colour transmissions on 1 July 1967, the first British – and European – network to do so. By no means all of its programmes were in colour, but their proportion steadily increased. Like the introduction of 625 lines UHF, they were part of the BBC's dual policy of using the network, with its relatively low audiences, as a test-bed for new technology, and using a new technology which would eventually become a standard feature of television to lure more viewers to the network. The United States had had colour TV since 1953, but British engineers had preferred to wait for a system which would offer subtler tones and a wider range. Nevertheless, whether because of teething troubles in the technology itself or because it was difficult to fine-tune the first colour receivers, many early pictures revealed people with unhealthily green skins and soccer strips whose reds and oranges showed a menacing tendency to shimmer and flare. Nor were these receivers cheap. Their average cost was £350 – several thousand pounds at today's values. However, by the time colour was extended to the other two channels in November 1969 its quality seemed to be consistently better. At the same time the cost of sets fell and there was a dramatic surge in sales. The obvious effect of colour was to make the medium of television immensely more vivid and picturesque: costume dramas and natural history programmes were only two of its more obvious beneficiaries. But there were also negative implications. Those who worried about the social impact of television were not slow to point out that in its representations of violence, whether real or simulated, the blood would now run red.

There were several other fine monuments to the serious and educative intentions of BBC 2, notably three documentary series with almost encyclopedic ambitions. In 1969 *Civilisation*, a thirteen-part history of art presented by the scholar and former chair of ITA Lord Clark, fully exploited the new colour pictures. Three years later, in *Alistair Cooke's America*, a veteran broadcaster brought shrewd insights to a historical and political account of the United States. But perhaps most ambitious of all was *The Ascent of Man* (1972–3), a thirteen-part history of scientific discovery and a philosophy of human nature presented by the eminent scientist Dr Jacob Bronowski. In pushing television to its intellectual limits this series marked an important moment in the history of the medium, when it was of sufficient technical maturity to provide high picture and sound quality, yet still young enough to command concentration from its audiences. In daring to put that moment to its fullest use, BBC 2, and British television generally, can take a certain pride.

Three programme landmarks of the 1960s

There is probably less agreement among historians than among geographers about what constitutes a landmark. Nevertheless, I have selected three programmes, all on BBC, which in their different ways broadened the range of TV output and caught the spirit of the age: *That Was the Week That Was* (or *TW3* for short); *Z Cars*; and, at its very end, *Monty Python's Flying Circus*.

In an attempt to evoke its carefree hedonism the decade was known, even in its own time, as 'the swinging sixties'. Its driving force seems to have been the new economic and cultural power of young people, those in their late teens and early twenties. For them more than any other social group, post-war austerity had yielded to full employment and an affluence largely free of domestic or family liabilities. They thus had a considerable amount of money to spend on such things as clothes, records (by now a burgeoning industry), cars and the cinema. Hence the pre-occupations of youth, all of which were interrelated, became the fashionable preoccupations, and during the 1960s Britain was seen throughout the world as a trend-setter in those fields where the spending power of young people was a significant factor. One such area was the arts and entertainment, especially pop music: the Beatles became famous in 1963 and were the first of many British bands to storm the American charts. Another was design: the millionth Mini, a hugely popular car developed by the British Motor Corporation, rolled off the assembly-line in 1965 and gave a prefix to the mini-skirt, one of the era's great icons. And a third was fashion, symbolized by London's Carnaby Street, where young Britons donned ceremonial military tunics and bought accessories covered in Union Jack motifs, partly to recall but mainly to ridicule their country's former imperial greatness.

The economic and cultural power of the young was also a manifestation of the general rise in educational standards which had resulted from the 1944 Education Act. More teenagers were going on to higher education, and it was during the 1960s that the universities underwent the first of their enormous expansions. Thus the natural tendency of young people to question 'the received wisdom' and get impatient with the pretensions of established authority was reinforced in some by the sceptical habits of study and learning. For one or two university students it was but a short step from scepticism to satire. The vastly successful Oxbridge stage revue *Beyond the Fringe* (1961) and the fortnightly magazine *Private Eye*, launched in the same year and also the work of Oxbridge graduates, seemed to set the tone of the time.

In a curious way this general trend was strengthened by television, a medium which the 1960s generation was the first to have grown up with. As was suggested in the last chapter, programmes like *Tonight* showed that a certain spirit of scepticism and irreverence was developing at the end of the 1950s; but even more important was the fact that there was something almost iconoclastic in the medium itself. Largely because written words obscure their object and sounds and photographs are limited, newspapers and radio represent public figures in ways that are unavoidably 'distant' or incomplete; and distance lends enchantment, a lack of familiarity breeds respect. But television showed people in close-up, 'warts and all'. It revealed every mannerism, uncertainty and hesitation. Mystique evaporated. The great and the good – aristocrats, statesmen, 'authorities' and experts – turned out to be people like the rest of us, their average physical blemishes and peculiarities implying average fallibility. Thus, despite the élitist tendency of Reith's broad-casting philosophy, there was a sense in which television was a leveller, an inherently democratizing medium. Like that great democratic process which has been continuing over several centuries and which was outlined in Chapter 3, it seemed to call into question the ideas of status, authority and expertise.

Since during the 1960s it was the young who were in the vanguard of this questioning and often debunking tendency, and since the young are naturally preoccupied with sexual matters, it was here that scepticism of traditional values seemed at its strongest. With the wider availability of reliable contraception (the Pill was on sale from 1961), there was a new concern with 'permissiveness'. The previous connections between sex and fertility and between sex and marriage were no longer as necessary as they had once seemed. It was not surprising that a libertarian spirit was developing, though for many, perhaps, it was more a matter of images and dreams than of solid fact.

The characteristic trends and concerns of the time were caught by the Saturday night show *That Was the Week That Was*, launched in November 1962. Fronted by David Frost and including Millicent Martin, William Rushton and Bernard Levin, it had its roots in the gently flippant *Tonight* programme, but was the brain-child of Sir Hugh Greene: 'I had the idea that it was a good time in history to have a programme that would do something to prick the pomposity of public figures.' *TW3* thus became the first satire show to be seen on British television. That it was broadcast by the BBC, that a publicly funded institution should at the prompting of its own director general see it as part of its role to 'prick the pomposity of public figures', was remarkable – and most likely possible only because the corporation was no longer the sole broadcaster. Since *TW3*'s content was highly topical and the show had to be put together in great haste, often with last-minute additions and alterations, it had a freshness and informality which was quite new to television. The studio from which it was broadcast was largely bare, using obviously improvised sets and props and with the cameras themselves sometimes in shot. But the show was so popular that its absence of style became a kind of style in itself and was imitated by other programmes. One effect of its irreverence and the obvious relish of the studio audience was, as Grace Wyndham Goldie (1977: 234–5) points out, to make it less like a conventional television programme than a private party, at which the viewer was nevertheless welcome.

At its peak 10 million people were watching *TW3*, meaning that for the first time in its history satire had become a genuinely popular art form. It marked television's coming-of-age in the sense that many of its jokes and references depended for their effect on the audience's knowledge of a culture which had largely been created, or at least disseminated, by the medium itself. That such knowledge could be assumed is a measure of the extent to which television had embedded itself in the national consciousness. However, in running to only two series, the show had a short life. It always provoked angry complaints, and the second series suffered some loss of quality. But it remained popular, and few were convinced by the reasons which were given for its sudden demise in December 1963.

The police drama series *Z Cars*, which also began in 1962, was another programme which seemed to capture the contemporary mood. Set in Merseyside, it responded to the interest in provincial, especially northern, life which, as Asa Briggs (1995: 428) points out, was a feature of the late 1950s and early 1960s and was expressed in several cinema films such as *Saturday Night and Sunday Morning*, *A Taste of Honey* and *This Sporting Life*, as well as in the celebrated TV soap opera *Coronation Street*. In order to achieve a factual, documentary effect, *Z Cars* used the narrative techniques which television had borrowed from film. Briggs has perceptively brought out the extent of its originality by comparing it with an example of the traditional police series *Dixon of Dock Green*. The latter had been running since 1955 and was the BBC's most popular programme of this kind. It was set in an old-fashioned east London community where its hero walked the beat. His domestic life was idealized, and every episode moved to a neat ending in which the villains were apprehended and the moral was spelt out by Dixon himself in an address straight to camera. *Z Cars*, on the other hand, was set in the wilderness of a modern housing estate which could be patrolled only in vehicles. Its policemen were human beings who lost their temper, might even quarrel with their wives, and were often outwitted by the villains. Its atmosphere was gritty and unsentimental, though there was sometimes pathos; and while every episode was morally suggestive, there were few neat endings. Within a year *Z Cars* was attracting an audience of 16.5 million to *Dixon*'s 13.5 million and had the effect of making subsequent episodes of the latter slightly tougher and less cosy. But while *Z Cars* in its original form ended in 1965, *Dixon* comfortably outlasted it, perhaps proving T. S. Eliot's maxim that 'human kind cannot bear very much reality'. Both the series and its hero staggered on until 1976, by which time Jack Warner, the actor who played Dixon, was eighty years old.

By the late 1960s soldier-boy tunics and Union Jacks had yielded to hippies and flower power, and, perhaps assisted by soft drugs, to a more knowing and self-absorbed mood. This self-absorption permeated the mass media as much as any other area of life, and helps to explain the popularity of a surreal comedy show named *Monty Python's Flying Circus*. The show made an unpromising début at the very end of the decade as the replacement for a late-night religious programme on BBC 2, yet became the only one of our three landmark programmes to be enjoyed around the globe. Featuring John Cleese, Michael Palin, Terry Jones, Graham Chapman and Eric Idle, it continued into the mid-1970s – a sequence of fragmented, anarchic sketches and disconcerting animated drawings which is of interest to the media student not simply because it was vastly popular and often explosively funny, but because it consciously followed *The Goon Show* in deriving much of its humour from broadcasting itself: in this case, television.

In drama and comedy, television, like radio before it, had vacillated between merely relaying or simulating the traditional forms of the theatre and seeing itself as the locus of new and distinctive forms. *Monty Python* was the first comedy show to think wholly in terms of television; whereas *TW3* could be said merely to have marked the medium's age of majority, *Python* celebrated its maturity. It took as the material for many of its jokes not just the culture and content of television, as *TW3* had done several years before, but its very 'grammar': the forms, codes and conventions of the medium. These things are rather less consciously absorbed by viewers than the content they express, but they are still delightedly recognized when parodied, and it is small wonder that *Python* struck a universal chord.

Other developments in programmes and technology

In our more general review of programmes it seems appropriate to remain a little longer with comedy, since (on the BBC especially) the 1960s were a continuation of that golden age which had begun in the previous decade. From the creators of *Hancock's Half Hour* came *Steptoe and Son* (1962–74), in which the relationship between Hancock and Sid James was transposed to that between a dreaming, idealistic rag-and-bone man and his crude, manipulative father, yet broadened to take in farce at one extreme and something approaching pathos at the other. From 1965 viewers had the pleasurable company of *The Likely Lads* and its sequel *Whatever Happened to the Likely Lads?*, starring James Bolam and Rodney Bewes; and from 1968 until 1977 a delightful gallery of characters made up *Dad's Army*, tales of the wartime Home Guard.

ITV's strength lay less in sitcoms than in the straight comedy showcase, but by the end of the 1950s the old variety spectacular with its teeming, ornate stage had evolved into something better suited to television: a programme built round a single star or act. Moreover, many of the stars now owed their fame to television itself rather than TV's exploitation of earlier stage success. As Jeremy Potter (1990: 231) puts it:

> For the viewers the magic illusion which had to be created was no longer that of a seat in the stalls but of the studio as an extension of their living room. The most popular entertainers, like Benny Hill in *The Benny Hill Show* (Thames), were those who adjusted their timing and projection to this more intimate relationship with an invisible audience.

Among the other stars around whom ITV created special shows were Stanley Baxter, Tommy Cooper, Les Dawson, Bruce Forsyth, Rolf Harris, Morecambe and Wise, and Jimmy Tarbuck.

Drama continued to flourish along a broad front. Under Sydney Newman the BBC's *Wednesday Play* commanded a regular audience of between 10 and 12 million. Typically, its productions tackled contemporary social issues in a realistic, uncompromising way – or, if you agreed with the 'Clean Up TV' campaigner Mary Whitehouse, offered nothing but 'dirt, doubt and disbelief'. The most famous play was *Cathy Come Home* (1966), directed by Ken Loach and credited with leading to the founding of the homeless persons' charity, Shelter, and with persuading the government to change its housing policy. In 1967 the aims of the series were rather better expressed in a new title: *Play for Today*.

In adventure series and serials honours were evenly shared between the BBC and ITV. From 1963 the former offered the long-running *Dr Who*, which soon became a cult with science-fiction enthusiasts, while ABC gave us the chic detectives of

The Avengers. But it was still ITV alone which held the lead in soap operas, though not altogether a qualitative one. The redoubtable *Coronation Street* was joined in 1964 by ATV's *Crossroads* ('hugely popular and irredeemably shoddy' (Day-Lewis 1992: 17)) – a saga which was set in a motel and has recently been revived. Its production values were so poor that despite its massive following the ITA stepped in to prevent the public from having too much of what it enjoyed by ordering ATV to reduce the episodes from four to three a week, as compulsive an act of nannying as anything in Pilkington.

Sport was an area in which its regional structure of ITV left ITV at something of a disadvantage. In 1968 its Saturday afternoon programme *World of Sport*, which had been launched by ABC with ATV in 1964, was taken over by London Weekend Television in order to give it a firmer metropolitan base. But in *Grandstand* the BBC maintained its exclusive long-term contracts with the governing bodies of a number of popular sports: athletics, swimming, cricket, rugby. ITV's strategy was therefore to broaden the range of sports it covered as a supplement to the main diet of soccer and horse-racing. Since the great majority of soccer matches could not be broadcast live it was a strategy which was largely adopted by the BBC too, and meant that many sports like hockey, badminton, basketball, ice-skating and motorcycle scrambling gained an unprecedented if sometimes short-lived boost from television. However, certain others were permanently transformed by the medium, many viewers coming to enjoy sports like show-jumping, snooker and darts which they had previously known little of.

The sport which benefited most was probably snooker. Before the 1960s it had largely been confined to working men's clubs. But it caught the attention of television once the medium had acquired colour – and then its popularity soared. By 1985 the World Championship Final was able to hold a TV audience of 18.5 million until after midnight, and snooker is now so commercialized that its humble pedigree has been all but forgotten. With American football and Japanese sumo wrestling, television's popularization of sports which were little known in Britain was to continue into later decades. However, television has also encouraged 'para-sports', blends of sport and show-business such as its recent hit *The Gladiators* (Blain and Boyle 1998: 366). Perhaps the first example of this hybridization, and one in which ITV held a hugely popular monopoly, was professional wrestling. In the tussle between sport and showbiz it was the latter which generally came out on top: among some of the combatants the acting was as bad as anything seen on *Crossroads*.

We have already seen that both networks created good programmes which seemed to be *sui generis* as well as adding good programmes to the traditional categories. But they also achieved some original variations within the latter. A sample from each must suffice. In 1962 Granada introduced yet another game show, but one which featured competitors of supposedly above-average intelligence and education, tested real knowledge and skills, and offered a trophy, not TV sets, to the winners. *University Challenge* was an ideal concept for people's television in an era of the Pilkington Report and the Open University, of mass education and individual self-betterment. It was a bright if modest instance of edifying programming, and one which drew big audiences. A BBC programme which offered something different within an established format was *Nationwide*, born in 1966 and another offspring of the fertile *Tonight* programme. Like *Tonight*, whose tea-time slot it filled and which it resembled in style and structure, it aimed to capture the bulk of the audience for the rest of the evening. But it had a novel element: after a networked opening the programme divided into several versions, each providing twenty-five minutes of news and current affairs within a different BBC region. These regions then reunited with London to contribute local angles and views on national issues, and thus reach a wider audience. The programme was devised partly to counter criticisms that the BBC was still excessively metropolitan. As its title implies it was an attempt to match the regional strengths of ITV yet remain of national interest.

We must now turn to what, notwithstanding the arrival of colour TV, was the most momentous technological development of the 1960s: satellite broadcasting. The Soviet Union had inaugurated the space age in October 1957 with its rocket-launched satellite, Sputnik, but it was the Americans who most quickly exploited the broadcasting potential of satellite technology. Thanks to Telstar, the first transatlantic transmission took place in July 1962, when viewers in sixteen European countries saw live pictures from Washington, Chicago and Ontario; the first two-way TV link between the continents followed soon after. Since Telstar was an orbiting satellite, the transmission 'windows' were relatively brief and did not always coincide with popular viewing times, but in 1963 longer transmissions became possible when the Americans launched a geostationary satellite, Syncom II. Its first extended transmission, in November 1963, marked a melancholy occasion, the state funeral of the recently assassinated President Kennedy.

From April 1965 the Intelsat series of satellites made transmissions possible for eighteen hours a day. The first live global television event was the Mexico Olympics of 1968. In July 1969 live pictures of the American moon landings provided a fitting climax both to the space race and to the global satellite broadcasts which had been developing over the past decade. Twelve million watched on BBC, 14.5 million on ITV. Yet there are other and more dramatic figures: the global audience was 600 million, one-fifth of the world's population. Whereas in 1965 40 channel hours of international television had been transmitted, the number of hours in 1970 would be 1,214 and rising rapidly. Thanks to satellites television could now provide live pictures of everything that the human race was capable of seeing, whether on this planet or any other, and it could capture a single audience of unparalleled size. Yet as a mass medium it was barely thirty-five years old.

Educational television

The first years of television, like those of radio, were attended by the very reasonable and powerful feeling that since the medium can reach so many, span such vast distances, and bring such new and varied impressions and experiences to its audience, it is not only educative in itself but should be put to the services of formal education. Yet in practice it has been difficult to integrate both media to the structured courses of the latter. Though partly offset by advances in audio and video recording, there are three main reasons for this. The first is the difficulty of adjusting the dates and times of programmes to individual school or college curricula and timetables. Second, there is the problem of extracting learning points from a constantly evolving and – in television at least – a highly detailed and unavoidably ambiguous 'text'. And the third is the students' abiding perception of the broad-cast media as primarily intended for entertainment and leisure, and therefore to be consumed only passively. These problems can be overstated: they are less serious in some subjects than in others, and there have been notable successes at both school and tertiary level. But even the Open University, which has its own production facilities and takes great care to tailor programmes to individual courses, does not expect audio and television to take up more than about 10 per cent of its students' time. Thus, while not belittling the important contribution which broad-casting has made to education, the account of it in this section is necessarily summary.

It is perhaps surprising that the first regular TV series for schools – which reached about 100 institutions – was provided not by the BBC but by Rediffusion in 1957. With a tendency to specialize in different areas of the curriculum, other ITV contractors soon followed, but their output was particularly enriched by the arrival of Yorkshire Television in 1968. By the late 1970s ITV schools programmes were at some point reaching 22,000 primary and 3,800 secondary institutions, about 76 per cent of the total. The authority allowed no commercials to be screened in or around these programmes. By 1961 the BBC had eliminated ITV's early lead, and over the subsequent years showed, as one might expect, a more consistent commitment to educational broadcasting at all levels. In 1969 it launched the pre-school *Watch with Mother* on BBC 1 and *Playschool* on BBC 2. At the same level *Rainbow* began on Thames in 1972, and the American import *Sesame Street* has graced Channel 4 for many years. In 1987 Channel 4 became the main ITV outlet for the few educational programmes still made by the contractors and by one or two independent producers.

At the other end of the educational spectrum the future Prime Minister, Harold Wilson, mooted the idea of a 'university of the air' in 1963 – an idea which was of a piece with the expansion of the traditional universities that was taking place at that time, and which also chimed nicely with the edifying impulse behind the Pilkington

Report. When Labour came to power it announced that the Open University, as it was eventually to be called, would broadcast on BBC 2. The university admitted its first students in 1971 and in that year collaborated with the BBC to make no fewer than 300 television programmes for four foundation courses. The Open University has, of course, marked a significant stage in the liberalization of Britain's system of higher education. Many regard it as the greatest single achievement of Harold Wilson's premiership, and it is to the credit of British television, specifically the BBC, that it has played a significant role in that achievement.

The ITV franchise awards, 1964 and 1967

The original ITV contracts ran for nine years, which meant that the franchises would be open to new or renewed bids in 1964. However, the next contracts would run for only three years because there was uncertainty as to whether ITV would gain a second channel, when it would be required to convert to a UHF 625-line signal, and at what stage it would be able to switch to colour. All the existing contractors reapplied in 1964 and all were reappointed, not so much because the ITA felt that their performances could not be bettered as that it would have been unfair to offer any new contractor a franchise which might last no longer than three years.

The 1967 contracts were to be awarded for six years in the first instance, though quite unforeseeably they ultimately lasted for more than thirteen. However, in allocating these, the ITA wielded the surgeon's knife, causing howls of anguish and fury, and there were many who felt that the commercial television service emerged from the operation in worse shape than it had entered it. For the new round of contracts the authority determined that it would increase the number of franchise holders and end the weekday/weekend split, except in London. In the North it therefore rolled Granada back to the west of the Pennines but extended its broadcasting time to seven days a week. The new franchise to the east of the Pennines went to Yorkshire Television, though its area – a large one – was not coterminous with the county itself. Associated Television, which had previously held the Midland weekday and London weekend franchises was now confined to the Midlands, but like Granada's its airtime was extended to the full week.

It was in London and the West that blood was shed. The London weekday contractor, Rediffusion, had an excellent record. As well as having a good portfolio of general programmes it had been first in the field of schools broadcasting. It had also pioneered the use of Ampex videotape in Britain. But in its renewal bid it struck the authority as a shade complacent. It was prepared to argue, for instance, that public service broadcasting merely consists of giving the majority of the public what it wants, a view which after the strictures of Pilkington could hardly find favour with the ITA. At the same time the authority was bedazzled by a star-studded consortium including Aidan Crawley and David Frost which was bidding for the

London weekend franchise, and which said exactly the right things about the need to educate and elevate popular taste even while satisfying it. One attractive feature of this group was that it signalled a new era in ITV management, in the sense that its membership did not consist wholly of novices in the industry – businessmen, pioneers or moneyed amateurs – but included people who had already made careers in television. These were either home grown or, like Michael Peacock and Jeremy Isaacs, from the BBC: they could stand on their records as programme-makers or performers.

The authority's new dispensation for London was to grant the weekend franchise to the star-studded consortium, London Weekend Television (LWT), and the weekday franchise to a new contractor, Thames Television, which it created from a forced marriage between ABC Television and Rediffusion, with the latter as junior partner. Further west, however, one contractor was axed altogether – merely, many thought, to demonstrate that an ITV contract was not perpetual. It was true that the sacrificial victim, Television Wales and the West (TWW), had an undistinguished record. But it had managed to maintain an awkward franchise which shackled Bristol and the near South-west of England to a nation whose advocates of a separate native-language service raised a clamour out of all proportion to their number. When the axe fell the cold fury of TWW's chairman, Lord Derby, prompted a hand-wringing apologia from the head of ITA, Lord Hill: 'if promise is never to be preferred to performance, then every television company will go on for ever'. TWW spurned an ITA offer of a 40 per cent interest in its successor, Harlech Television, and threw back its franchise four months early.

As a condition of the 1967 contracts the ITA required the new contractors to accept a single programme journal which would bear comparison with the BBC's *Radio Times*. Hitherto there had been several journals published by, or on behalf of, the individual contractors. As a result of the new requirement the *TV Times* was launched and soon became hugely profitable, attracting the largest readership in Britain (12 million adults, 2 million children). During the 1970s the *TV Times* and the *Radio Times* became the two largest-selling magazines in the country, far outstripping the more specialist women's magazines and delivering an unusually wide readership to their eager advertisers.

From swinging sixties to sombre seventies

The 1967 franchise awards had damaging consequences for ITV. LWT, the new contractor whose lucrative metropolitan franchise was the cornerstone of the entire commercial system, lacked experience of its hard realities and in its efforts to elevate public taste got off to a disastrous start. Its business people had little understanding of television and its television people knew little of business. Its programming strengths – in current affairs, the arts and children's TV – were ill suited to a weekend franchise, and it was hammered in the ratings by what was now the much more populist output of BBC 1. Nor could the company count on goodwill and support within the ITV system, for in making its distinctively up-market bid to the ITA it had disparaged the programmes of the other contractors.

But problems were not confined to LWT. The introduction of a fifth major contractor, Yorkshire Television, raised the cost of the whole system in facilities and staff while reducing the role – and revenue – of the other four. Moreover, the franchise upheavals had left production and technical staff insecure and resentful. In August 1968 one of the unions, the Association of Cinematographic and Television Technicians, called a two-week national strike. Programme schedules were disrupted, production halted, future projects shelved or dropped. Audiences plummeted and advertisers grew restive.

Yet even without the problems caused by the franchise awards, ITV would have faced difficulties. Its two principal growth factors during the first half of the 1960s had now disappeared. Since the ownership of television sets had just about reached saturation point, the audience was no longer increasing. Nor could ITV hope to take a larger share of the existing audience – indeed its share decreased – because it was now competing against two BBC networks instead of one. On the other hand, ITV was faced with increased capital expenditure. The introduction of UHF 625 lines and of colour committed all the contractors to re-equipping their studios and post-production facilities. And whereas the BBC benefited when viewers switched from monochrome to colour because the colour licence was more expensive, the change-over brought no extra revenue to ITV.

When at Pilkington's prompting the government imposed a levy on ITV's revenue – a heavier imposition than a tax on profits – it had not foreseen that ITV could be affected by a recession. Indeed it increased the levy in 1969, the very year that revenue began to fall. By 1970 revenue had declined by 12 per cent in real terms and successive governments were obliged to reduce the levy in that year and 1971. Despite this, several contractors faced financial collapse, notably Scottish TV, Harlech Television and Tyne-Tees TV. To ensure the latter's survival the ITA had to allow it to affiliate with Yorkshire TV under a joint management company named Trident Television. But unsurprisingly it was LWT which threatened to become the most spectacular casualty, until at the end of 1970 Rupert Murdoch's News of the World organization offered to buy into it and put it on a more businesslike footing. The ITA vetoed Murdoch as chair of the company because of his press interests, but it had little choice than to approve his bid – not the only occasion on which it would allow a contractor to stay afloat by throwing its weightier programme promises overboard. LWT was duly restructured and successfully relaunched in 1971.

Meanwhile life had not been altogether rosy for the BBC. It had launched its second channel and was competing directly and very successfully with ITV on its first. But its finances, like those of its rival, deteriorated during the second half of the decade, and for similar reasons. The launch of a second service and the conversions to UHF 625 lines and colour all imposed extra costs, but its income from licences levelled off because the ownership of TV sets had reached saturation point and the initial take-up of colour was slow. Indeed with a sudden rise in inflation, its real income declined.

But if media institutions could suffer occasional bouts of sickness, the medium itself was unmistakably healthy. In January 1972 the government would lift all restrictions on broadcasting hours – an acknowledgment that television had passed the stage of being novel or exotic and had inextricably woven itself into the fabric of modern life. This liberalization was not wholly welcome to the BBC. Whereas extra airtime could mean more advertising revenue for ITV, it merely meant extra expense for the corporation, which was already burdened with a second network. But it was a portent that could not be ignored. Within twenty years viewers would be able to watch television round the clock.

Sources/further reading

The standard histories of this period, to which I owe general and particular debts, are Briggs (1995) of the BBC and Sendall (1983) and Potter (1989, 1990) of ITV. The biography of Sir Hugh Greene by Tracey (1983) contains an account of Greene's years as Director General of the BBC.

Wide-ranging discussions of public service broadcasting are in MacCabe and Stewart (1986) and Tracey (1998), while McDonnell (1991) charts its historical development through the deliberations of the various broadcasting committees. The problem of how to determine 'quality' in broadcasting is discussed at length by Mulgan (1990), Corner, Harvey and Lury (1994) and Corner (1995), and though all of these discussions are in the context of broadcasting in the 1990s their relevance to the 1950s debate shows how perennial and complex the problem is.

The Pilkington Report (1962) makes interesting reading: as a conservative view of broadcasting it is elegantly and eloquently written. Curran and Seaton (1997) usefully summarize its overall philosophy and its impact on subsequent broadcasting. Other accounts of its attitudes and findings are in Hood (1980) and Black (1972b), who also describes the public reactions to it. Seymour-Ure (1996) and Negrine (1994) both contain shrewd comments on the partly competitive, partly duopolistic relationship between the BBC and ITV, and Hood and O'Leary (1990) point out that Pilkington created buoyancy at the BBC and tighter controls over ITV. Within a concise account of the fortunes of both the BBC and ITV during this period, Lambert (1982) outlines the case for the third channel which the BBC made to Pilkington. Briggs (1995) provides an excellent description of the birth and early years of BBC 2 and of the introduction of colour transmissions.

For helpful attempts to characterize the spirit of the 'swinging sixties' see Booker (1970) and Levin (1972). There are analyses of *That Was the Week That Was* in Goldie (1977), Wilmut (1980), Sherrin (1983) and Crisell (1991). On *Z Cars* see Laing (1991). For the comparison of *Z Cars* with *Dixon of Dock Green* I am heavily indebted to Briggs (1995). Wilmut (1980) outlines the genesis and evolution of *Monty Python's Flying Circus*, and there are remarks on its telegenic nature in Nathan (1971). A general survey of the TV programmes of this period is provided by Day-Lewis (1992) and an illuminating discussion of television forms of light entertainment by Dyer (1973). Blain and Boyle (1998) give a useful overview of the relationship between television and sport. Brunsdon and Morley (1978) is a detailed analysis of *Nationwide*. News and current affairs programming is treated in Davis (1976), which also gives a useful account of early satellite transmissions. For an assessment of the strengths and weaknesses of broadcasting as an educational resource see Bates (1984) and Crisell (1986).

Within a helpful outline of broadcasting during this period, Tunstall (1983) describes the ITV franchise reallocations, as does Potter (1989), who also provides a detailed account of the subsequent difficulties which the service encountered.

The fall and rise of radio

Chapter 7

The fall and rise of radio

The BBC's dwindling audience

Despite maintaining the high quality of its radio programmes the BBC continued to lose listeners throughout the 1960s. Only the statutory limit which the government had imposed on television's transmission hours prevented radio from being hit even harder. It was in the evenings, TV's peak period, that the older medium suffered most, though its audiences were never negligible.

Yet if TV was the main cause of radio's woes (BBC expenditure on vision began to exceed expenditure on sound in 1958–9), there were also problems within its network structure – that cultural pyramid with the Light Programme at its base, the Home Service in the middle and the Third Programme at its apex. The reader will recall that in order to give the structure an edifying aim – to retain an element of serendipity and, in Haley's words, to lead the listener 'from good to better' (quoted in Smith 1974: 83) – there was a deliberate element of overlap between Light and Home and between Home and Third. However, the overlap was such that the networks were not sufficiently distinctive to command listener loyalty. This was a particular problem for the Light and the Home. Some serious programming existed even on the Light. On the other hand, the comedy show *ITMA* had been on the Home Service, while some of its other programmes would not have seemed out of place on the Third. In search of a certain kind of output, a listener might find herself scanning the schedules of two or even all three networks. Since programmes on the Third were unwaveringly serious it commanded the strongest loyalty – but of a tiny number. Even before 1951, when television had yet to make its impact, the network never gained more than 2 per cent of the total radio audience. In order to boost its following, surgery – or more accurately dismemberment – was performed in 1957. Its output was cut from five and a half to three and a half hours a day and confined to the evenings, while the other two hours were devoted to an educational concept, mostly consisting of instructive talks, called Network Three. This attracted even fewer listeners than the Third. On Sundays the daytime service was re-named the Music Programme, which from 1965 was extended to weekdays, and was followed in the early evenings by Study Session (Sport Service on Saturdays) and later by the curtailed Third Programme. Thus, over several years the BBC adopted the extraordinary measure of offering two and then three separate services on a single wavelength, the inevitable effect of which was to blur the identity of the old Third Programme and strain the loyalty of what few adherents it had previously possessed. But it was not simply the case that the Third Programme and its associated services were too serious and demanding for the great majority of radio listeners: for many, so were the Home and even the Light. Radio Luxembourg, which had reopened after the war, was again eating into the BBC's audience.

Despite all this, television remained radio's greatest enemy, and 1964 perhaps marked the nadir of BBC sound broadcasting. This was the year in which it yielded several kinds of programmes to television and in which the latter, confident in its ascendancy, launched a third network. *Children's Hour* had already been axed in 1961, but now *For the Young* was also discontinued, bringing to an end all regular sound broadcasts for children. The year 1964 also saw the death of the charismatic head of radio features, Laurence Gilliam, who knew that his department would not long outlast him. Back in the 1920s and 1930s features had been radio's programme laboratory, the place in which it had tried to create its own unique genre. Its closure seemed to have dark implications for the medium in general.

Technological developments in radio

However, the melancholy events of the 1960s had been preceded by three developments in radio technology, two of which would help to secure the medium's future.

Perhaps the least important, though rewarding to the suitably equipped listener, was *stereophony*, a system by which sound is split into and reproduced by two separate channels in order to create a spatial effect. The first test transmissions took place in 1958, the first regular broadcasts in 1966. Stereo meant that, despite television, radio was to remain for many years the medium to which people turned when sound quality was paramount. It also prompted the development of 'simulcasts', television programmes, especially music concerts and operas, which were simultaneously carried by radio in order to provide a standard of sound commensurate with what viewers could see. It was only with the arrival of stereo TV sets in the 1980s that simulcasts died out.

Much more important was the development of *very high frequency* or VHF transmissions. The first two VHF transmitters were opened in 1955 at Wrotham in Kent, one of them also providing *frequency modulation* (FM), which gave freedom from interference. There was little public demand for VHF/FM: in 1972 about 60 per cent of radio listeners were still unequipped to receive it. But its long-term significance was considerable. First, it offered much better sound quality than the medium and long waves, and by the 1990s all of the four traditional BBC networks had moved to the VHF waveband. Second, it greatly increased the number of stations which could broadcast, since its low-power transmissions allowed stations that were a reasonable distance apart to occupy neighbouring or even identical wavelengths. VHF was therefore the technology which facilitated the expansion of local radio during the 1970s and 1980s – something of a return to the very first pattern of sound broadcasting which John Reith had abandoned during the late 1920s in favour of a centralized, national service.

However, the most important of the three technical innovations was the first to be developed, the *transistor*. It ensured that even in a television age radio would continue to be used by significant numbers of people. Developed in the United States in 1947, the transistor was a tiny semi-conductor device which replaced the wireless valve. The latter, somewhat like a light-bulb in appearance, was large, costly and fragile. It also consumed a lot of electricity, which meant that a battery-powered wireless was hardly an economical proposition. The new transistor radios could make use of batteries since they consumed much less power. They were more reliable and cheap enough for almost everyone to buy. And they were so much lighter and smaller than the old wireless sets that they were genuinely portable. They were first marketed in America in 1953, and in 1956 the annual sale of portable sets reached 3.1 million, double that of the previous year. At about this time transistor sets also appeared in Britain, but it was from the beginning of the 1960s that ownership increased dramatically, and for some years radio receivers became generically known, especially among the young, as 'trannies'.

By the end of the 1970s the transistor meant that nearly 70 per cent of radios were either portable or, since it had also stimulated the growth of car radios, 'mobile'. In 1960 radios were fitted in only 4 per cent of cars on the road. By the end of the 1980s they were standard equipment in all new cars and could be found in 85 per cent of cars of any age. But the importance of the transistor was not simply that it enabled more people than ever before to own a radio set: along with television it caused a revolution in the way the medium was used.

As well as sitting and listening to the wireless, audiences had always used their large, immovable receivers in a secondary way, as a background to other activities. This was especially true during the working day, which was spent by many women in the home and by many men in the factory or workshop. But during leisure periods, and particularly in the evenings, the emphasis was often reversed: instead of using the wireless as an accompaniment to other activities, people would engage only in those activities which allowed them to listen to the wireless. However, from the 1950s onwards, more and more people were devoting their leisure to watching television. This meant that from about this time many of them only *ever* experienced radio as a background medium, as entirely secondary. What the transistor did was to greatly expand the range of situations in which radio could be so used. A receiver was no longer tied by a wire and its own weight to the sitting-room, kitchen or workshop. Thanks to its cheapness and portability it could be heard anywhere in the house, in the garage or in the countryside, at the beach or in the car. As Frank Gillard (1964: 8) pointed out: 'Radio is no longer something to which you necessarily have to go. Radio goes with you.' The sound medium had insinuated itself into the daily routine in a way that television could never do, because aside from the fact that portable TV had not yet arrived, it was in this respect handicapped by its own visuality.

Thus at the very moment when radio's blindness seemed to have condemned it to extinction, it discovered, thanks to the transistor, a new and impregnable advantage in that blindness, in the fact that it was 'secondary'. But the advantage was ambiguous: the transistor ensured not only that radio would undergo a revival but that the revival would be limited. The medium would be heard in many more places and situations than before, but for this very reason listened to rather less – treated simply as a background noise and sometimes ignored altogether.

In these circumstances the BBC's cultural pyramid, with its banded varieties of programming, made less and less sense because it assumed devout listeners instead of casual hearers. We noted that even before the arrival of the transistor, the generality of the BBC's output was regarded as too serious and demanding by many people, who were again turning to Radio Luxembourg. By 1955 the latter was once more winning the Sunday ratings battle and claiming that its weekday evening audience outstripped the Home's. In encouraging casual, background listening the likely effect of the transistor was simply to strengthen this drift towards Luxembourg. Since, like the BBC, Luxembourg had been forced to yield much of its programming to television, the range of background listening it could offer was limited. For many years it had combined music programmes consisting of record requests and tunes from the hit parade with quiz shows and talent contests, but in 1955 the latter were lost to ITV, leaving it with nothing but music.

However, although we shall see later that certain kinds of 'spoken word' output were suitable for the new listening habits, it is hardly surprising that music, especially of the kind which Luxembourg broadcast, was ideal for them. Music was essentially non-visual (TV had not yet learnt how to exploit it); it was generally easier to assimilate than spoken word; and light or popular music was even better than other kinds since its short and simple tunes were more suited than symphonies or concertos to the intermittent or 'shallow' nature of the new listening. The other characteristic of this music was that it was almost invariably *recorded*. Why?

Radio, records and rock

It will be recalled from Chapter 2 that the record companies soon learnt to use radio as a source of talent and material, and to appreciate its promotional value to them. But they also felt an anxiety, which lingers to this day, that it would discourage the public from buying records.

The BBC's initial attitude to the use of records typified that of most broadcasting institutions: it was reluctant to play music which the listener could purchase for herself. Since they were already publicly available, records were as far as possible treated on the radio as an 'understudy' to the uniqueness of a live performance – and although this attitude was softened by a necessarily greater dependence on records during the war, it persisted till the end of the 1940s.

The first radio institutions to rely almost totally on gramophone records were in the United States. Why? Until the mid-1940s the great majority of its several hundred local stations were affiliated to one or other of the main broadcasting networks, from which they obtained a substantial amount of programming. But at the end of the Second World War the networks turned their energies to television, and those radio stations which were unaffiliated to a network rose from 18 per cent of the total in 1946 to 47 per cent by 1952. Even the affiliated stations were now expected to originate more of their own output. How were they to fill the empty hours? Given the increasing use of radio as a background medium, thanks first to TV and then to the transistor, music was the obvious answer; above all *recorded* music, because records were cheap and enabled the stations to dispense with their own musicians.

What were at first regarded as a poor dead substitute for live music soon came to seem in certain respects superior to it. Records benefited radio in two important ways. First, the richness and variety of sound that they could provide would have needed a multitude of live bands and orchestras quite beyond the studio space, let alone the budgets, of most radio stations. And second, each tune represented the best performance that an artist or band was capable of, for in the process of recording mistakes could be eliminated and the best version chosen from a number of takes. Records also meant that listeners' favourites could be played repeatedly without any variation in musical quality.

This perfect marriage of records and radio perhaps led to the premature shelving of an interesting philosophical question about the purpose of broadcasting: Should broadcasting simply act as 'the common carrier' of any material which is of interest to its audiences, including that which they can obtain by commercial means, or should it confine itself to material or performances of material which are not available in any other medium? Broadcasting had never, of course, wholly succeeded in the latter aim, though it had largely done so. Now, however, it was offering popular music which was almost entirely in 'the public domain'. A similar tendency has occurred in television, which often screens as 'a live event' a feature film that many viewers have already seen not only in the cinema but on video, and may even own on cassette – a tendency which darkly hints at the potential redundancy of much broadcasting.

But if records benefited radio, it was equally true that radio benefited records. Despite continuing misgivings among record companies and musicians, radio stimulated sales rather than depressed them, the evanescence of the medium tempting millions of listeners to go out and capture their favourite tunes on disc. This was helped by the fact that recent technological developments and the general growth of affluence in America and Britain made the products of the recording industry much more attractive to the public. By the end of the 1940s the wind-up gramophone, with its huge and heavy pick-up and endless need for needles, was giving way to the electrically powered record-player, with a lightweight pick-up and long-lasting stylus. The old graphite record, which contained one tune on each side and was played at 78 r.p.m., was heavy, scratchy, soon worn out, and easily broken. Its successor was the 45 r.p.m. disc, which was developed by RCA Victor in 1949, and was usually a 'single' (one tune on each side) but might also be an EP or 'extended play', with two tunes a side. It was small, easily handled, and made of vinylite, which was much tougher than graphite. Constructed from the same material was the LP or 'long play' record, which had been developed by Columbia in 1948, and playing at 33⅓ r.p.m. was able to carry six or even eight tunes per side.

What sealed the alliance of radio and records was the sudden and explosive popularity of rock 'n' roll in the mid-1950s. As Roy Armes (1988: 81) points out, rock 'became the first form of popular music for which the record is the key element – the "original" as it were'. The launching pad of such new performers as Elvis Presley and Jerry Lee Lewis was not the ballroom or concert hall but the recording studio. So perfect was the marriage of records and radio that it is difficult to make a claim for the achievements of one without acknowledging the crucial contribution of the other. If records were the key to the success of the new stars and their music, it was radio which enabled them to find their enormous markets. The sales of records rocketed. Between 1954 and 1957 they more than doubled in the United States, from $213 million to $460 million, and, continuing their upward flight, reached $4 billion in 1980. Though recording technology evolved after the 1960s, with vinyl discs yielding first to cassettes and then to CDs, the highly profitable relationship between the record industry and broadcasting changed little, except in being strengthened during the 1980s by a larger contribution from television.

The reliance of radio on records and *vice versa* is indicated by an example of realpolitik from the 1950s. Radio Luxembourg lay outside the reach of Phonographic Performance Limited (PPL), the organization which acted on behalf of the record companies and in league with the Musicians' Union to impose 'needle-time' agreements on broadcasters – limits on the number of records they could play. Yet in spite of the fact that the station was conveniently located where it could avoid the limits that the record companies sought to impose, Decca and EMI made extensive use of Luxembourg to promote their latest releases. The station focused increasingly on rock, for rock was young people's music, and it was the young, as we have seen, who had most money to spend on records.

Luxembourg, however, was not fully able to exploit its lead in this field because its programmes in English were restricted to the evenings, and in many parts of Britain its signal was weak. Still, for many young rock addicts it was the main source of supply for nearly ten years, until the initiative was suddenly snatched from it.

Pirates ahoy!

In 1964 an Irish entrepreneur named Ronan O'Rahilly found a more effective way than Luxembourg's to circumvent the BBC's monopoly of sound broadcasting. He converted a trawler into a radio station which he called Radio Caroline, moored it just off the Essex coast, and on Easter Sunday, 29 March, began beaming all-day pop music on to the mainland. Its success soon attracted rivals. In December a second ship, broadcasting as Radio London, dropped anchor near by, and by 1967 no fewer than nine stations were broadcasting on pirated wavelengths from ships and offshore forts around Britain.

Of all these pirates, Caroline and London were the most professional. Commissioning their own call-signs from a radio station in Texas ('Sounds fine, it's Caroline!', 'Wonderful Big L!') they developed coherent marketing strategies, broadcasting almost round the clock and directing their signals at the Home Counties, and thus at the largest and most affluent segment of the population. But wherever they could be heard, the impact of the pirates was sensational. In cocking a snook at authority and reflecting the obsession with pop music which had been fuelled by the Beatles and Rolling Stones, they were a perfect expression of the swinging sixties. As early as 1965 their daily audience was estimated at between 10 and 15 million, and by 1966 they were attracting nearly £2 million worth of advertising a year – some of it from government-funded bodies like the Egg Marketing Board!

The pirates were certainly inspired by Radio Luxembourg, but even more by American radio, in that the Top 40 was the nucleus around which their programming revolved. The concept of the hit parade, a ranking of the current most popular songs based on sales figures, was well known in Britain long before rock and modern pop music developed. It had originated in the United States during the war as 'The Lucky Strike Hit Parade', a product of market research, and during the 1950s the two leading British record manufacturers, Decca and EMI, had promoted their own versions of the hit parade on Luxembourg. However, the pirates' innovation was to use the hit parade not just as an incidental feature of their output but as its focus, an idea which had also come from the United States. In 1949 the owner of the Mid Continent Broadcasting Company, Todd Storz, observed the choices of records which customers made from jukeboxes. These coin-operated record-players had been mass produced from 1934, and for many years before they appeared in Britain were an important medium for promoting records in the States. From the fifty or sixty records that the jukebox suppliers changed weekly, Storz noticed that the customers selected the same few current favourites. He then adopted a similar selection at his radio station, making his presenters play only the most popular (that is, the best-selling and fastest-rising) records repeatedly, right round the clock. As the practice spread to other US stations the sequence of records (and, of course, commercials) was gradually enriched with other ear-catching elements – time checks, weather reports, golden oldies, station call-signs, trailers, traffic information, news summaries – to make up what became the standard Top 40 format. Competitions and merchandising were elements that were added later.

Though pre-dating rock music, the format was ideally suited to it, and quite apart from their stronger signals gave the pirates two significant advantages over Luxembourg. First, their versions of the Top 40 seemed to be more authentic than Luxembourg's hit parades. On Luxembourg, Decca and EMI continued to offer their own, proprietorial versions of the hit parade, for their shows were basically sales-pitches – extended commercials in which each company tried to pretend that all the hits were entirely from its own labels. Second, the pirates seemed keener to entertain the listener than simply sell her something, for they played each record in full, whereas the Luxembourg shows often faded them early in order to tease the listener into buying them.

Though the great majority broadcast pop, one or two of the pirates explored the market for other kinds of music. King Radio, later known as Radio 390, specialized in 'sweet music' and offered daytime programming described as 'Eve, the woman's magazine of the air'.

There is no doubt that the pirate phenomenon caught the BBC unawares. Its Audience Research Department quickly discovered that in that part of the country where both could be received, Caroline captured an audience one-third the size of the Light Programme's. About 70 per cent of Caroline's listeners were under the age of thirty and treated its output as background listening. Yet the Light's audience did not decline in this period, meaning that the pirates must have tapped into a large listenership which the BBC had ignored. Thanks to rock 'n' roll, the new popular music, radio suddenly became a young persons' medium, and it has largely remained such even though the audience for rock music has since fragmented. In the BBC's defence it has to be said that the corporation could not easily have competed with the pirates, even had it been minded to do so. Its longstanding public service obligations did not allow it the option of abandoning the mixed programming even of the populist Light Programme in order to provide a continuous stream of pop music. And in any case its use of records was severely limited by the expensive needle-time agreement it had made with PPL. Its rivals, on the other hand, were not called pirates just because they usurped their frequencies. They observed no restrictions on their use of records, paid no royalties, acknowledged no copyright or performance laws.

For their part, the pirates at first hoped that the Conservative government, naturally sympathetic to business initiative and enterprise, would bow to the enormous popular demand they had identified and legalize them. But the Conservatives were defeated in the 1964 general election, and the Labour Party was ideologically hostile to what it regarded as their unscrupulous commercial opportunism. It was determined to close them down. To do so, however, would incur the wrath of that large portion of the electorate whom the pirates had won over, so before acting the new government instructed the BBC to prepare a similar service of continuous pop music. In August 1967 the Marine Broadcasting (Offences) Act was passed, and, though it was intermittently defied in subsequent years, succeeded in forcing the pirates off the air. Their crumb of comfort was that although they had quickly been scuttled, their impact was permanent. British sound broadcasting would never be the same again.

The Beeb strikes back

A month after the Act was passed the BBC launched its first-ever network to be dedicated not to mixed programming but to a single kind of output. Radio 1, broadcasting nothing but pop music, took over one of the frequencies previously occupied by the Light Programme, which was itself re-named Radio 2. At the same time the Third Programme and its associated services became Radio 3, and the Home Service was henceforth known as Radio 4.

As a result of being handed on a plate several million listeners of whose existence it had scarcely known before the pirates had identified them, the BBC enlarged its audience by 14 per cent. But Radio 1 was not the perfect equivalent of the pirates and in open competition would surely have fared badly against them. It aped their presentational gimmicks and jingles and even recruited many of their presenters, or 'disc jockeys', such as Tony Blackburn, John Peel and Simon Dee. But from the Light Programme it also acquired one or two presenters of incongruous maturity, such as Jimmy Young and Pete Murray, and its start-up budget was only £200,000. Moreover, since it had been able to extract from PPL only two extra hours of needle-time per day, the disc jockeys ('Hollow men – electronic lice', the writer Anthony Burgess called them) needed to have a 'gift of the gab' in order to eke out the supply of records. These were also supplemented by live cover versions of current hits, in which with sometimes embarrassing results old-fashioned session musicians tried to imitate the quite different idiom of the rock groups. Even with the padding, Radio 1 could not manage more than about five and a half hours of its own output per day, and for the rest of the time was reabsorbed by Radio 2. Some years would elapse before the network acquired the clear-cut identity and professionalism of a respectable pop music channel. Moreover, with regard to its radio operations as a whole, the BBC had still not learnt all the lessons. Despite the pirates, television, sourly described by one executive as 'radio's autistic younger brother', remained the arch enemy – and as if to confirm this, colour transmissions began in the very year that the pirates were scuppered.

Although TV's impact was strongly felt, the corporation still seemed unwilling to shape radio to withstand it. Radios 2, 3 and 4 were new in name only: they continued to offer the same kinds of mixed programming as before. While there were many for whom sound was still a medium to be listened to and not merely overheard, there were not enough to sustain three separate networks of this kind. The fact that radio was no longer the main mass medium would have to be confronted, and in the networks as a whole the old Reithian pattern of varied and self-contained programmes would have to be cut back.

But for its dwindling band of close listeners, there was no decline in the quality of radio during the 1960s, even if its range was eroded somewhat. Durable comedy persisted in the form of *The Clitheroe Kid* (1958–72), regularly listened to by over 10 million people in the middle of the decade, and *The Men from the Ministry* (1962–77). The humour of *I'm Sorry I'll Read That Again* (1964–8) had a kind of frenetic wit which anticipated *Monty Python*. The most celebrated comedy shows of the era were *Beyond Our Ken* (1958–64) and its successor *Round the Horne* (1965–9), written by Barry Took and Marty Feldman and starring Kenneth Horne, Kenneth Williams, Hugh Paddick, Betty Marsden and Bill Pertwee. These were radiogenic in the sense that their magazine format, with Kenneth Horne as the compere, mimicked the increasingly popular news and current affairs magazines of radio and television, each with its own anchor-man such as Richard Dimbleby or William Hardcastle. Within this format were sketches which also parodied broadcasting genres – plays, movies, documentaries. Moreover, the shows aptly expressed the swinging sixties in their exploitation of the double entendre, a device which carries a particular resonance in a non-visual medium and which was almost personified in the hilarious camp couple, Julian and Sandy. As Derek Parker (1977: 139–40) puts it, the shows generated 'a whirlpool of outrageous suggestiveness never before tolerated at Broadcasting House'.

Among the hardy survivors from an earlier era were *Desert Island Discs,* in which a celebrity imagined life as a castaway and chose the eight gramophone records he would take with him; the audience-focused programmes *Housewives' Choice, Family Favourites* and *Down Your Way*; and panel games like *Round Britain Quiz* and *Twenty Questions*, which were joined in 1967 by *Just a Minute*. In 1962 the soap opera *Mrs Dale's Diary* was re-named *The Dales,* and thus rejuvenated, managed to last until the end of the decade.

The news and current affairs magazine was a significant development in BBC radio during this period because it was among the few types of programme which took some account of the intermittent and variable nature of the new listening patterns. Held together by a presenter it typically consisted of a string of items, such as bulletins, interviews, debates, reports, short talks, weather and traffic announcements, each lasting only a few minutes and some of them repeated at intervals. Though we have seen that music was perhaps ideal for the new listening, these informative 'bites' or segments were also well suited to it. They have subsequently helped to create a sense of news and information as being part of radio's irreducible repertoire or programming 'rump', since unlike the news items of the press or television they can be absorbed by the audience even while it is otherwise occupied. This also helps to explain why news output seems to have assumed a more dominant position on BBC radio since the rise of television.

The earliest notable example of the current affairs magazine was the breakfast programme *Today*, which began on the Home Service in 1957 and became popular under presenter Jack De Manio. It was the brain-child of former ITN newscaster Robin Day, who showed a still rare insight into the new role of radio by pointing out that it could supply to those people driving to work 'the comment and description that the rail or 'bus traveller can read in his newspaper' (Donovan 1997: 3). At first dealing more in topics of general interest it subsequently became harder and newsier, and for the last quarter-century its interview slots have been much coveted by all politicians who are seeking publicity. Indeed, some of them have been keen to use the programme to *create* news, in the sense of treating it as a place to make important announcements on matters of policy (Donovan 1997: 196–7). *Today* was followed in 1965 by the lunchtime magazine *The World at One*, which, with its celebrated presenter William Hardcastle, found a crazy echo in *Round the Horne*.

The launch of local radio

We noted earlier that the arrival of VHF in the 1950s facilitated the development of local radio since it created much more room on the waveband. But two questions remained. Was there a public demand for local radio? And, if so, what broadcasting institution or institutions should be allowed to run it?

Asa Briggs (1995: 638) observes that there is no evidence that there was a substantial demand for local radio. Nevertheless, the pirate phenomenon and contemporary political thinking combined to make the concept fashionable. The pirates were relevant because they were, in a loose sense, local. Few broadcast over an area bigger than the Home Counties, many of them promoted local events, and some appealed to local loyalties by taking such names as Radio Essex and Radio Kent. Moreover, although they offered no broadcasting access to the public they broke the BBC's virtual radio monopoly to answer a huge demand which the corporation had ignored, and so in that sense they assumed a public voice. It was in this respect that piracy converged with mainstream politics, for among politicians there was a desire to stimulate local democracy and make the mass media not only more responsive to public opinion but a more efficient conduit for it.

Under a Labour government it was almost inevitable that local radio would be run by the BBC, especially as Pilkington had favoured this. After a successful experiment in 1963–4 the corporation opened its first local station at Leicester in 1967 and followed up with many others during the 1970s and 1980s. Part of their purpose was to replace regional radio, which was discontinued in 1983. Though some of the stations were also given medium-wave frequencies to attract larger audiences, their prime mode of delivery was VHF, and they thus led the network conversion to VHF/FM which began at the end of the 1980s. Moreover, part of their 'democratic' achievement was to make radio something of a two-way medium by using the phone-in as a staple of their output. The phone-in was first heard on BBC Radio Nottingham in 1968 and was a genuinely new broadcasting development in the sense that it enabled the ordinary listener to become a broadcaster, not because she was a guest of the radio station, an expert or an interviewee, but simply because she chose to initiate the broadcast from her own private environment. It could almost be claimed, then, that the phone-in was the first *interactive* form of mass communication. It has also, of course, been adopted on network radio and even television, but is perhaps used to best effect at the local level.

The BBC has always seen news-gathering as the primary asset of the local radio system, its purpose not just to serve the immediate community but to feed the networks in the way that the old regions had. Its output typically consists of local news, chat, phone-ins, programmes on local themes and educative features. However, Lewis and Booth (1989: 95–6) express disappointment in the achievements of BBC local radio, pointing to financial starvation (including a restricted needle-time allowance) and excessive control from London. As long as it was a BBC monopoly it certainly kept a low profile, most stations managing only between six and twelve hours of output a day before opting into one of the networks, usually Radio 2.

Broadcasting in the Seventies

It was not until the end of the 1960s that the BBC was forced to grasp the nettle of network radio – and, as is so often the case, the spur was financial. At the end of the last chapter we mentioned that the corporation's income was declining in the second half of the decade, yet to its two TV channels and four sound networks had been added the burden of local radio. Nevertheless, the government would allow no further increase in the licence fee and so the BBC hired management consultants to investigate its structure and use of resources. Retrenchment was their predictable remedy.

This forced a hard look at radio as the less popular of the two broadcasting media, and the consequence was *Broadcasting in the Seventies*, a BBC policy document published in July 1969 and announcing a radical new plan for network radio. It acknowledged that television had now replaced sound as the primary leisure medium: 'The millions who once listened to "In Town Tonight" and "Itma" now watch television' (BBC 1969a: 2) – and in a lecture given at about the same time the Managing Director of Radio, Ian Trethowan, developed the point:

> few [listeners] today use radio as the staple diet of family entertainment in the evening. Most of them use it as individuals, mostly during the day, often casually, while they're doing something else. We may not like it: we may wish that everyone was listening intently, but these are listening habits we cannot ignore.
>
> (Trethowan 1970: 5)

Radio was now recognized as a personal possession rather than a domestic fixture. It was no longer consumed collectively, as a primary source of entertainment, but individually – mostly as a background to other activities. Consequently, as Trethowan (1970: 6) pointed out, 'the old concept of "mixed programming" no longer applies in radio and . . . what listeners seek is the convenience of predictable networks'. This is an echo of *Broadcasting in the Seventies*: 'experience . . . suggests that many listeners now expect radio to be based on a different principle – that of the specialised network, offering a continuous stream of one particular type of programme, meeting one particular interest' (BBC 1969a: 3).

Streamed or 'strip' programming, now typical of so much radio output, was an important development. If the output was all of one kind, then programme divisions became less important – indeed virtually non-existent. On the pirate stations, for instance, which had led the way in streaming, they were merely marked by changes of presenter: the music remained much the same throughout the day. But the idea of a 'stream' or 'strip' of output is misleading if it implies an *entire* absence of divisions, something which becomes more obvious if we recall that news and informational content is almost as well suited to it as music. The real point of such output is that its significant unit is not the *programme*, which listeners have to adjust to, but the *segment* or 'bite' – a pop record, news bulletin, commercial, interview, or whatever; for the segment adjusts to the situation and attention span of the modern listener. Moreover, the aggregation of these segments is an indefinite sequence because in general it lacks the progression, the internal causal or logical connections, which would characterize the traditional 'built' programme. The sequence can therefore be of any length. The whole point of it is that the listener can 'get into' and 'out of' it at will without feeling that she has missed, or will miss, anything of importance.

This kind of sound broadcasting later became known as 'format' radio – somewhat misleadingly so since it is not the only kind which is as artfully structured as the word suggests. News, talk and various types of music have on different stations all been adapted to the segmented yet streamed character of format. Yet, thanks to the relative brevity of its tunes, pop music clearly fits comfortably into it, as does commercial radio since the duration of its advertising breaks can be assimilated to that of the programming segments within which they are interspersed.

With *Broadcasting in the Seventies* the BBC took its first steps in the direction of format radio, and in April 1970 the old Reithian concept of tempting the listener to a diversity of programmes was largely laid to rest, though not without much public debate and fierce opposition within the corporation. Radio 2 matched Radio 1's pop format with continuous 'middle-of-the-road' music, alternatively known as 'easy listening'. Radio 3 lost many of its speech programmes to Radio 4 and became mostly a classical music network, although it kept a modicum of serious drama and vestiges of other types of programmes such as sport. Radio 4 survived in something like its old form and is still the nearest thing to a traditional mixed programme network that the BBC offers. Yet even here there is some specialization in spoken word and informational output – mostly news and current affairs, with some drama and light entertainment, but very little music.

In summary, the mixed (albeit banded) programming which had been retained under the old cultural pyramid was now all but eliminated. To a greater extent even than before, BBC radio could be perceived as a 'public service' – as providing 'something for everyone' – only across the totality of its four networks and not within any one of them. But in any case radio had largely yielded to television as the main focus of debate about public service broadcasting.

It should be added that these network changes, which brought large financial savings, were forced on the BBC not just by the ascendancy of television but by the new technological sophistication of radio. Thanks to the transistor, radio receivers had now become so numerous and portable that the Post Office, still the collector of the licence fee, could no longer keep track of those who owned them. Acknowledging the millions who avoided payment, the government abolished the radio-only licence in 1971. But within the corporation this weakened the position of radio with respect to television because there was no longer a sum of money raised specifically for it, and it was therefore parasitic upon its more popular rival.

The largely specialized pattern of BBC network radio has continued ever since. Audiences accept it and are not greatly enthused by attempts to revive mixed programming, as the launch of Radio 5 was to show some twenty years later.

Sources/further reading

On the developing problems within the BBC's tripartite network structure, see Paulu (1956, 1961) and Briggs (1979). These also deal with the general shift from serious to 'lighter' radio listening and with the post-war resurgence of Radio Luxembourg. Silvey (1974) considers the decline of overall radio use between 1948 and 1960, while Snagge and Barsley (1972) lament the end of radio features.

Briggs (1979, 1995) offers the fullest general account of the technological developments in sound broadcasting, though the nature and origins of transistor technology are usefully sketched in Goldhamer (1971), together with its revolutionary impact on the radio receiver. For a contemporary and farsighted view of the new transistor radios and the differences in listening – and hence programming – that they would give rise to, see Gillard (1964).

There are good accounts of the relationship between rock music, records and radio in Barnard (1989) and Turow (1999), while Armes (1988) offers an excellent historical summary of recording technology and its importance to rock music. For the origins of pop music radio Chapman (1992) is also useful, while Fornatale and Mills (1980) stress the closeness of the early relationship between radio and rock music in the United States and outline the development of format radio there. The phenomenon of the pirates has attracted much attention, since it is seen by many as the most romantic episode in British radio history. Harris (1970), Baron (1975) and Chapman (1992) are among the best-known studies, and there is a summary of the pirates' impact in Paulu (1981). Barnard (1989) also offers some thoughtful analysis of the pirates and their adoption of the Top 40 format, though he takes the view that they had less influence on the history of radio than is commonly supposed. Silvey (1974) recalls the BBC survey of Radio Caroline's audience and explores its implications.

The lukewarm beginnings of Radio 1 are anecdotally described in Garfield (1998), more systematically so in Briggs (1995). The views of its first controller on the new listening demands created by the transistor, and on the inadequacy of the old networks in meeting them, are in Scott (1967). The *BBC Handbook 1968* (1967) explains what the new network is seeking to achieve, while the major radio programmes which the other three networks offered during the 1960s are concisely described by Parker (1977), Donovan (1992) and Briggs (1995). For a focus on the comedy shows of the period see Foster and Furst (1996) and for an historical account of the *Today* programme see Donovan (1997).

The standard study of local radio is Lewis and Booth (1989). It includes an account of the genesis of BBC local radio and explains why it has been less successful than was hoped. Briggs (1995) is also enlightening on local radio, especially on its political and technological background. Smith (1974) points out that interest in local radio was largely stimulated by the pirates, since it was they who prompted the BBC to be more responsive to the listeners' voice. For an exploration of the nature and significance of the phone-in, a new programming element which would be especially important in local radio, and also for an analysis of the segmented output that would characterize so much format radio, see Crisell (1994).

Broadcasting in the Seventies (1969a) summarizes the reasons for streaming the BBC networks, details of which are also contained in the *BBC Handbook 1970* (1969b). A further rationale of the network changes is in Trethowan (1970), and the way in which they were carried through, as well as the debate and opposition they fomented, are in Briggs (1995).

Chapter 8

Modern television (1): some characteristics and tendencies

Modern television (1): some characteristics and tendencies

Open the box

We can identify 19 January 1972, the day when all restrictions on broadcasting hours were lifted, as the beginning of the era of modern television. It is an era in which not merely every home but almost every individual has come to own a set, and in which the search for broadcastable material has grown so relentless that there is scarcely a subject it has not covered. From 1972 there would be a steady growth in daytime as well as evening viewing, a growth which reflected more flexible patterns of work and an amount of leisure which was not always welcome. Unemployment increased during the 1970s with the quickening decline of the old labour-intensive industries such as coal-mining and shipbuilding. The expansion of transmission hours had the overdue effect of helping people to see television as something of a utility and not just a source of entertainment, and the decade marked a rise in output of an ostensibly informative or instructive nature which was partly a response to the problems of the unemployed. In addition to the rise in unemployment, the country was racked by inflation and strikes, and there were civil upheavals in Northern Ireland, acts of terrorism both in Britain and abroad (themselves fuelled by the publicity which television gave them), and an international oil crisis.

Yet despite these difficulties it was also a period of rising living standards, which explains the soaring sales of colour TV sets. Even for those who could barely afford one, the volume of spectacle, entertainment and information that television provided gave a value for money absolutely unprecedented in cultural history. Up to 1970 a mere 775,000 colour TVs had been bought; by 1973 the number had leapt to 6 million; and in 1977 there were more homes with a colour set than with a telephone. In this turbulent decade the cheapness and domestic convenience of a TV set brought great solace – a point well made by Jeremy Potter:

The average citizen could do little in the face of economic recession, industrial unrest and sometimes capricious public services, but he and she had a comfortable retreat at home where they could amuse themselves inexpensively through ITV or BBC channels. The more dire the state of the economy, the less other amusements could be afforded and the greater the nation's dependence on the box in its sitting room.

(Potter 1989: 12)

Between 1961 and 1986 average weekly viewing doubled from 13.5 to 26 hours. By the latter date nearly 80 per cent of people watched television at some point during the day, for it had become the main leisure activity. Mr and Mrs Briton were now Mr and Mrs Viewer.

We have thus reached a stage in our history when it seems appropriate to consider one or two inherent features and characteristic tendencies of the television medium and something of its social impact. To do so we shall not observe chronological sequence but range back and forth in time. TV's choice of themes and the conventions its programmes adopt are to some extent determined by fashion: but they are at all times subject to the limitations imposed by television's technology. To speak of limitations is important. Because TV is 'modern', because it provides both sound and moving vision which enter our domestic and private worlds and take relatively little effort to absorb, there is a common assumption that it has rendered all older media obsolete – that it is more truthful, more sophisticated, than print, photography or sound broadcasting. We thus need to remind ourselves that it has its crudities and deficiencies just like any other medium, and indeed some that certain other media, notably print, do not have. In this chapter and the next we shall look at its strengths and limitations and try to assess its effects on various social activities and institutions – as well as on its audiences – before moving into the last thirty years or so of its history.

Words and pictures

It is not surprising that 80 per cent of the population get their news from television and regard it as the most credible news source. Pictures seem more real and powerful than words. Whereas different languages signify a dog differently, a picture of a dog is universally recognizable. Hence television's pictures seem incapable of lying. Moreover, they exist within a frame which serves to intensify them. When we perceive the world through TV, vision seems to dominate over sound to an even greater extent than our faculty of sight dominates over our hearing when we perceive the world directly. The circumscribed nature of television's pictures, their brightness and the fact that their movements do not correspond to those which might occur in the vicinity of the set, act as a magnet for even the most reluctant eye. Whenever I

153

meet a friend in a pub we never sit within sight of a TV set, even if its sound is inaudible: conversation would succumb to watching.

Yet pictures are seldom self-explanatory: for their full impact they need words. Try watching soundless television for a while. One channel, perhaps, shows crowds of people advancing down a broad urban avenue. Are they on their way to a pop concert or a sporting event or are they part of a political uprising? Another channel shows what is unmistakably a soccer match. But where is it taking place, who are the teams, and is it a cup or a league match? Only words can answer these questions, either on the soundtrack or as a visible text.

Words, on the other hand, have little need for pictures. Books and even newspapers can get by without them: radio must do without them altogether. Words are a very effective substitute, even a shorthand, for pictures. The word 'house' encapsulates not just a particular house that a picture can only convey in some detail, but unlike the house in a picture – which necessarily excludes every other house – it serves as a label for *all* buildings designated as places of habitation or storage. But more than this, words can express abstract conceptual things like 'bankruptcy' or 'integrity' and also the relationships between things, whether concrete or abstract, that pictures on their own struggle to convey.

When it is presenting situations of a primarily concrete, visual nature and with a relatively uncomplicated conceptual background, television is a hugely effective medium. Quite simply, it enables us to see more things, and to see them better, than we ever could with the naked eye or from natural viewpoints. It has shown us not simply those things which are normally unseeable, such as the moon's surface, the ocean depths, animals inside their burrows or the internal organs of the human body, but seeable things and places which are nevertheless so remote and exotic that few of us are likely to see them with our own eyes. But perhaps most remarkable are the unfamiliar views which TV offers us of *familiar* things – cricket from micro-cameras fixed to the stumps, soccer from cameras attached to the stanchions of the goals. Most obviously in its coverage of sport, television's use of angles, close-ups, long views and slow-motion replays has enormously enhanced our understanding of what we are watching – to such an extent that attendance at games can seem a paltry experience by comparison. To remedy this, many stadiums and arenas provide giant TV screens to give those present a better view, a timely reminder that it was television and not computers which first taught us the joys of virtual reality! But to describe this as a 'virtual' experience is in a sense unfair, for it is an experience which is *preferable* to the real thing, not an inferior substitute for it.

Yet certain other benefits which television brings are more serious and substantial than these. For years there had been newspaper accounts of famine in Africa, but when TV showed pictures of the starving people of Ethiopia in 1984–5 audiences all over the world were galvanized. Live Aid and an enormous relief operation rapidly followed. In this instance the physical fact that people were suffering was what mattered above all, and television was very good at showing it. One can think of other situations in which its focus on the physical and the visible is, or would have been, beneficial. Its 'real time' coverage of wars can, and does, powerfully influence public opinion in ways which might embarrass governments, but rightly so. The colossal tragedy of the First World War would surely have been averted, or at least curtailed, if like that of Vietnam it had been seen on television. Where television can observe them, an increasing number of nations must find solutions to their disputes which are more generally acceptable than a use of force.

In yet another sense, then, television is a strongly democratizing medium. We have already seen how it acts as a leveller in demystifying expertise, rank and authority. It also, of course, puts politicians under the critical gaze of the voters. And in the broader context, thanks to satellite technology, it now seems to be creating a global pressure towards open government, democracy and fair play. Television's pictures of the students and tanks in Tiananmen Square in 1989 and of the attempted political coup in Moscow in 1991 powerfully illustrate that with everyone watching everyone else it is becoming harder for nations to conceal their misdeeds.

Words *versus* pictures

In all these instances relatively few words were needed, whether in the form of commentary, interviews or captions, to support and complement the pictures. Though their full meaning is seldom apparent without the help of words, it seems fair to say that on the whole pictures have a more powerful, immediate and emotional effect than words alone. They seem to be a direct expression of reality, whereas words – a human invention – interpose themselves between reality and us, perhaps filtering or even distorting the former. Pictures show; words merely represent, and have to be 'decoded' by their audience – a process which itself dissipates the emotional force of what they convey. The newspaper and radio reports of the Ethiopian famine were no doubt affecting, but it was the pictures shown by television which horrified the world and prompted the relief operation. Nevertheless, one major reason why we feel a need for words is our awareness that there is always more to reality than we can see at any one time – more, indeed, than is ever visible. As is implied by some of their functions that were outlined above – their ability to qualify, question, dissect, rearrange, abstract and generalize from the visible world – part of the purpose of words is to *reject* what we can see (Postman 1986: 73). As the old sayings have it, there is more to this than meets the eye; don't judge by appearances. And that is why the statue of Justice, personifying a process whose purpose is to discover the truth and whose currency is words – the words of witnesses, advocates, judge and jury – almost always wears a blindfold.

In any medium which makes use of pictures there is thus a need to include enough words to explain and contextualize them, a need which the print media of books and newspapers can meet without too much difficulty. The need can be acute in the case of television, because it must always have pictures yet must sometimes cover complex, abstract items or stories which either do not lend themselves to pictorial treatment or in which the pictures are only one, not necessarily representative, element. But television finds it rather harder than books and newspapers to provide an adequate verbal context for its pictures. Why? Unlike the latter, which exist in space, television is a *temporal* medium: its pictures and words exist in time. And within any period of time there is a severe limit to the number of words that can be spoken to an audience in comparison with the number of words that that audience could read for itself. (It is, of course, true that not all of television's words have to be spoken since it can also carry visible text; but again, there are evident limits to both the duration and quantity of that text.) John Whale (1969: 21) instances a twenty-five-minute TV programme in the 1960s about the Bank of France, arguing that a newspaper article on the same theme could have been read in five minutes and would have left a clearer impression. It has been estimated that a TV news programme which broadcast the total contents of a single edition of *The Times* would last for between two and four days (Davis 1976: 141).

Hence, although the distinctive achievement of television is to bring reality in the form of moving pictures into our private spaces, the only way we can make sense of that reality is through words, and as a time-based medium its words are much less plentiful than those of old-fashioned print. This prompts Robert Hughes's ironic lament that in the primitive days before television people had to make do with books: 'those portable, low-energy, high-density information storage and retrieval systems' (Hughes 1995: 6). His adoption of computer-speak provides a bracing antidote to our infatuation with new technology, especially when we recall that printed books, an extremely efficient form of 'information system' which television and computers do not entirely emulate, have been available for more than five centuries.

Since sustained and complex reasoning, argument and explanation are much easier to conduct in the spatial medium of print than in a time-based medium, newspapers and journals have reacted to the rise of broadcasting by developing their strength of 'news in depth', backgrounding and contextualizing the major stories. Despite the best efforts of certain broadcasting institutions, TV news seems by comparison to be desultory and superficial. Ralph Negrine (1994: 31) observes that although its account of events is sometimes lengthy, it never seems quite adequate. While television's coverage of the Ethiopian famine was hugely vivid and influential, characteristically the medium was not very effective in explaining its causes. Even a big story will run on television for no more than a few weeks before being superseded by another. (This is also true of newspapers, but at least the extensive backgrounding of the broadsheets affords some reservoir of knowledge to their readers.) The story will not be revived until a fresh crisis breaks, offering the medium something specific and tangible to point its cameras at. Thus news on television is essentially a series of discrete events: the medium hops from the tip of one iceberg to the next. Television news is naive news.

But a time-based medium whose words must mostly be spoken rather than printed poses another, more elementary problem. Television's pictures are constantly changing, but the spoken words that accompany them are of even shorter duration. Not only are there relatively few of them, they are *evanescent* – that is, they cease to be heard as soon as they have been uttered, and this makes their meaning harder to assimilate than words on a page. Radio's words have the same problem, except that its audience is not distracted by pictures. What often seems to happen on television is that once words have outlined the meaning of the pictures, the latter overwhelm any further words which qualify, amplify or contextualize them. This can happen in various ways. In some news stories, for instance, the picture is not always the key element: we may see a business correspondent standing outside the Bank of England, perhaps, but the subject of her story is 'invisible' – the state of the country's economy. Yet it seems to be the case that if for any length of time the words which accompany the picture are not fairly closely related to it they are imperfectly absorbed by the viewers and the picture tends to prevail. After noting that inflation is once again rising we might lose the subsequent intricacies of the correspondent's report and concentrate instead on the cut of her hair or her choice of neckscarf. Hence the TV producers' precept: always speak 'to' the pictures, because if words and pictures refer to different things the pictures will invariably win.

Even when the pictures are the key element of the story they can, once identified, have such a powerful impact that any subsequent attempt to qualify them will fail. In both instances the impression formed is that appearance and reality – what can be seen and what is true or significant – are much the same thing, or at least that through pictures we can gain an adequate account of reality. In 1995 a series of TV news bulletins carried pictures of cattle lorries, in the back of which velvety heads and soft bovine eyes could be glimpsed. Once the pictures had been identified – the lorries were part of the export of British veal calves to the continent – they drowned any further explanation, discussion or mitigation and there was an immediate outcry against the trade, lending weight to Robert Hughes's (1995: 7) complaint that 'tv teaches the people to scorn complexity and to feel, not think'. Certain sections of the public were so outraged that they immediately began to blockade the ports and chain themselves to the lorries. One protester was killed, becoming a martyr to the cause, and before long few ports would handle the trade.

For many this was another straightforward instance of television's power to do good. Thanks to its haunting images, an evil activity was stopped and the consequent financial losses to exporters, their employees and the port authorities were a price worth paying. But what others found disquieting was that the protesters' actions forestalled rational consideration of a trade which, given the hard fact that all cattle are eventually slaughtered, might conceivably have been less evil than it looked. Whether evil or not, the trade was lawful, and it was perhaps an even bigger cause for concern that the processes of democracy could be so easily supplanted by the actions of an unelected pressure group.

Let us summarize our argument, then. Pictures often need words to render them intelligible, but once this has happened they generally have a more powerful, often emotional, effect than words alone. But provided they exist in sufficient quantity and/or fixity, words may also *dilute* or *qualify* that effect since a major function of words is not only to describe the world of appearances but to question and transcend it. Nevertheless, since the words of television are relatively limited in number and, even more crucially, evanescent and difficult to absorb, its pictures tend to dominate, giving the impression that reality is explicable wholly in terms of appearances. While this may be appropriate for some themes or news stories it would seem to be less so for those of a more complex or conceptual nature.

Pictures rule OK!

As was seen in the case of the veal trade, television's pictures can have palpable social effects. But as well as prompting people to respond directly to what they perceive as a specific evil, its pictures can lead them to believe that the evil is far more widespread than it really is. We noted earlier that pictures are unable to generalize: the image of a particular house contains detail that precludes every other house. But certain pictures on television, frequently shown and accompanied by simplified or selectively absorbed words, can lead the audience to make generalizations: every Afghan is a terrorist; one televised fight on a terrace means that every soccer stadium is a battlefield; a single bomb in Belfast suggests a province exploding from end to end. Somewhat disingenuously, we accuse television rather than ourselves of creating mere stereotypes and we acknowledge their deceptiveness. Yet television's images do influence attitudes and behaviour. The isolated bombings in Northern Ireland have badly affected tourism and foreign investment, and there were countless men in the 1980s and 1990s who were deterred by TV footage of crowd violence from taking their wives and children to soccer matches.

Like the outraged response to the veal trade these are conceivably symptoms of 'moral panic', a media-generated public anxiety about certain problems which is far greater than their seriousness would justify. The press has always been able to create moral panics without the help of television, but the pictorial power of the latter has undeniably added to their frequency, scale and intensity. And however irrational they may be, politicians ignore them at their peril. Ralph Negrine (1994:

12) recalls events at the end of the 1970s, when television's pictures of picket lines and uncollected refuse in the streets suggested an entire nation ravaged by strikes and social unrest. The Prime Minister James Callaghan flew back from the Caribbean intending to steady the nation with his knowledge of a larger and less frightening reality. 'Crisis? What crisis?' he is said to have asked waiting journalists. But the millions who had seen the turmoil on television would not be denied the evidence of their eyes and regarded the Prime Minister's reaction as unforgivably complacent. His government fell at the next election.

On the other hand the partial evidence of TV can hurry politicians into measures which with hindsight can seem ill-judged. In 1990 television showed pictures of certain ferocious dogs called pit-bull terriers and the horribly injured children they had attacked. Parliament promptly passed the Dangerous Dogs Act, which required all 10,000 specimens of the breed to be either neutered or destroyed, three consequences of which were that certain quite docile pit-bulls faced a bleak future; other breeds which might be just as vicious remained legal; and dogs which might or might not have been cross-bred from pit-bulls gave insoluble problems to the courts.

But perhaps the most notable moral panic of recent years, in which television's heart-rending pictures of the animal and human victims played a key part, was caused by the outbreak of 'mad cow disease' (BSE) in 1996 and the subsequent suspicion that it had spread to humans in the form of variant Creutzfeldt-Jakob disease (vCJD), a fatal illness for which there is no cure. The consequences for British agriculture were disastrous – a ban on the domestic sale of certain cuts of meat and on the export of beef to the rest of the European Union – and all this despite the fact that vCJD remained an extremely rare disease whose link with the consumption of beef was as yet unproven. By the beginning of 1998 fewer than twenty people were believed to have died of vCJD and even though the death rate rose to just over 100 by 2001 it still needs to be seen in context. In an average year some 3,000 Britons die in road accidents, 70,000 of smoking-related diseases, and 90,000 from the effects of alcohol consumption (McNair 1998: 53).

Thanks to television's desultory treatment of many of its stories the moral panics that they generate are often as brief as they are intense: pit-bull terriers and veal calves have long since faded from public consciousness. But instead of seeking, when appropriate, to mitigate the impact of pictures in the interests of a deeper, fuller truth, the practitioners of modern television seem intent on exploiting its visuality to the full. This can sometimes mean favouring news stories which lend themselves to pictures over conceivably more important stories which do not. 'Unemployment, pollution, malnutrition, disease and political oppression are . . . slow-acting, if far-reaching, developments, but lack the visual punch of an earthquake or a rocket exploding and so tend to have a lower priority on television bulletins' (McQueen 1998: 102). Sometimes editors will even help to manufacture a story in order to get pictures, staging 'photo-opportunities' and meet-the-people routines for politicians and other public figures; or they will represent a non-news item as if it were genuine news because they have pictures of it which are certain to arouse strong feelings in the audience.

One evening in the early 1990s ITN treated as its lead story the funeral service of James Bulger, a little boy who had been abducted and killed by two other boys. But this was not news because as its association with 'novelty' implies, news is concerned with the unexpected or with that which materially advances or alters an existing course of events. Whatever its emotive effects, it is essentially a factual or intellectual matter. James's funeral did not tell us anything about the Bulger case which we did not already know or could not reasonably infer – and it was passed off as news only because television could present it in a number of poignant images, including that of James's teddy bear sitting in the church.

The importance which TV practitioners ascribe to pictures is demonstrated by the extraordinary, almost risible lengths to which they will go in order to present in a visual way certain stories that lack visual content but are too important to be omitted. In 2001 many of the BBC's main evening bulletins included coverage of a national epidemic of foot-and-mouth disease. One contained a live interview by the newsreader with a correspondent who was standing in front of a building which the newsreader identified as the Ministry of Agriculture. The building was in darkness and clearly closed for business. No fresh information was likely to emerge from it so the reason for conducting a location interview was presumably to establish the authenticity of the correspondent's information. But what was behind him was not self-evidently the Ministry: it could have been any building. Hence the image used to authenticate the correspondent's words itself needed to be authenticated by the words of the newsreader – and even if any viewers were able to recognize the Ministry in its darkened guise, the correspondent's report might still have been fabricated. In other words, the report he delivered on location was no more authentic or illuminating than if he had delivered it in the studio or given it to the newsreader to deliver on his behalf.

At about the same time another BBC bulletin contained a correspondent's report on the problem of asylum seekers. The only 'pictorial interest' it could manage was a shot of the correspondent addressing us half inaudibly from the noisy interior of a helicopter, through whose portholes was a distant aerial view of a building we were told was an asylum seekers' detention centre. Such a thumping insistence on pictures tends to cast doubt on the truthfulness or efficiency of the words. It is as though the news staff are saying, 'If we cannot show it to you, don't believe us. Judge, above all, by appearances. What is invisible is either insignificant, untrue or non-existent.'

In 1995 the BBC broadcast a documentary about euthanasia entitled *Death on Request*. This might reasonably have consisted of a studio discussion on the ethical and social dimensions of humane killing between, say, a doctor, a theologian, a philosopher and a social worker. But instead, and with television's usual confidence that pictures bring enlightenment, it showed us an act of euthanasia. An elderly, terminally ill man and his wife were visited by a doctor in their quiet, softly lit flat in Amsterdam. At a point entirely determined by the patient the doctor administered an injection, and the former, comforted by his wife, slipped into a final unconsciousness. As a viewing experience this was undoubtedly powerful, disturbing even. But as a documentary it was unsatisfactory since it told us nothing new: it merely illustrated what we already understood by the word *euthanasia* – from the Greek, meaning 'easy death'. The option of a studio discussion – mere faces talking about things we cannot see – was presumably rejected because it lacked visual interest, but it would have been much likelier to yield moral insights. Television embodies an old paradox: often the more we see the less we learn, the less we see the more we learn.

Television and theatre

Our assumption that reality can be reliably inferred from appearances is doubtless a consequence of the fact that sight is our primary cognitive faculty, the means by which we get to know of the existence of most (though not all) things. The primacy of this faculty may also explain why for most of us the mere *act* of looking is pleasurable – and this in turn helps to explain why television practitioners exploit rather than mitigate the visuality of the medium. 'Scopophilia', as the pleasure of looking is sometimes called, seems integral to television whatever its subject matter. Indeed, it would not be too cynical to suggest that the aim of *Death on Request* was not only to imply that we can arrive at moral insights into a phenomenon merely by observing it but to give us the simple, voyeuristic thrill of seeing someone being put to death.

Watching factual as well as fictional television is thus akin to the experience of being at the theatre. Both make the assumption – which is not shared by newspapers or the print medium in general – that the world they portray is largely explicable in terms of appearances. In the theatre that assumption is made for the purposes of entertainment. In television entertainment is very often an effect, even if not always the purpose, of the assumption. But if theatre, like television, is a time-based medium, using spoken words which are relatively few and constantly dissolving, does this mean that it shares television's difficulty in handling complex or conceptual themes? And if so, how can we explain the achievements of a Shakespeare or an Ibsen? *Hamlet* and *King Lear* are among the most complex, intellectual artefacts of any kind. Why are their words not overwhelmed by spectacle, as I have argued that words often are on factual television?

Part of the answer is that theatrical plays are usually much longer than individual television items or even whole programmes. Their scenery also tends to be less detailed and 'busy' than television's pictures and to change less often – all of which gives the dramatist a fuller opportunity to integrate what is heard with what is seen, perhaps through subtle repetition in the dialogue. Even so, much conceptual or intellectual drama is preoccupied with the fact that appearances – 'pictures' – are, indeed, a poor guide to reality. The problem for those who write it is that even that deeper, normally invisible reality must be represented in the at least partly visual conditions of the theatre. Hence the dissimulations of Shakespeare's characters are expressed either by physical, often transvestite, disguises or by the improbable device of the monologue, which enables a highly secretive Iago, Hamlet or Richard of Gloucester to disclose his real nature to the audience. Moreover, it is at least arguable that the intellectual depth and complexity of Shakespeare and certain other dramatists have become fully apparent only since their plays have been studied in printed form – as literature – rather than treated merely as theatrical spectacles.

Even so, the spectacle is paramount. Playwrights may be as intellectual as they wish, but only to subserve their primary duty to give us the pleasure, the entertainment, of something *to look at*. Certain forms of theatre, such as ice-shows, dance displays, circuses and military tattoos, provide almost nothing else: they are devoid of dialogue, plot or intellectual content. But even intellectual forms of theatre must satisfy by means of costume, scenery, lighting, choreography, acrobatics, fights, explosions, murders, slapstick, lovemaking or other forms of erotic behaviour, its audience's primary craving for spectacle. Shakespeare himself is no exception: even his uncompromisingly intellectual *King Lear* enables excited theatregoers to watch one character having his eyes gouged out.

The ubiquity of television seems to have led to an unprecedented theatricalization of public life. Theatre has always, of course, been used to enhance the mystique and symbolize the power of those in authority (the ritualized activities of Louis XIV of France were a notable example). But because they are now under almost continuous observation, public figures, whether politicians, social and religious leaders or celebrities in the worlds of the arts, sport and entertainment, have needed more than ever to be premeditated and self-conscious in their behaviour, even when 'off duty' and in ostensibly private situations such as family holidays. Moreover, the ambiguous motives of the observers mean that those of the observed may be equally mixed. Insofar as the former seek a reliable guide to reality in appearances the latter will behave in a self-conscious, and in that sense 'theatrical', way so as to affirm what is (or what they take to be) the truth about themselves. Actors and actresses have traditionally been ridiculed for behaving even offstage in the exaggerated manner of those who are used to being observed. Yet it is perhaps not too fanciful to suggest that one diffuse effect of television has been to make the public behaviour even of private individuals more demonstrative than it once was, on the basis that if feelings are not apparent their existence may be doubted. Some years ago the mother of a woman who was believed to have been abducted and murdered fell under suspicion because she did not show enough grief before the TV cameras.

Yet insofar as the observers are motivated by the sheer pleasure of watching, those who are being observed may feel it incumbent on them to behave in a way which justifies the observers' interest – a way which is in some sense 'entertaining'. There may even be a not wholly misplaced feeling among the observed that if their behaviour is sufficiently entertaining it will also be regarded as authentic and truthful. Let us return to the veal trade. Those who had concluded from the pictures of cattle lorries that the trade was evil at once realized that if they were to explain their view in verbal, purely intellectual terms it would hardly be noticed by television, let alone seem convincing, for as we saw in the case of *Death on Request*, television is uneasy with the intellectual and the abstract. In order to win the general public over to their point of view they would have to show how passionately they held it by providing a spectacle which matched that of the trade itself. Of course, the passion with which a view is held is one thing and the reasonableness of it is another. But to display one's passion on television is at least half the battle, because since its pictures cannot in themselves 'show' a logical case its audience will be tempted to assume that a view so deeply held must have some basis in reason or fact. Argument is transformed into theatrical spectacle – and like all theatre it is irresistibly entertaining.

The reader may feel that I am in danger of emphasizing 'spectacle' to the exclusion of all else, of suggesting that as long as theatre provides us with something to look at we are not greatly concerned about its content. And I have, indeed, argued that some theatre consists only of spectacle, doubtless as a consequence of our instinctive scopophilia – of the simple pleasure we derive from gazing out of the window (as I frequently do when I should be writing this book) or watching fish in an aquarium. Hence to justify their existence the theatrical media – cinema, TV and the traditional stage – must do one of two things. Either they must provide pictures which are more 'spectacular' than those of ordinary life (though not by much, perhaps: I shall be arguing shortly that round-the-clock multi-channel television, not to mention web-cam TV, has introduced new levels of banality into mass viewing); or they must extend or substantiate their pictures by incorporating narrative elements – 'plots' – and moral issues whose only precondition is that they can be expressed in a medium which is based on the premise that, with a little help from what we hear, what we can see is a fair guide to the truth.

Hence, even though the aim of the veal protesters was not merely to be seen but to convince the viewing public of the strength, and by implication the rightfulness, of their beliefs, it was inevitable that the actions they adopted would remind us of the other things we frequently encounter in the theatre. Robert Hughes (1995: 7) is in no doubt about the theatricality of television when he claims that the basic message of much of it is that 'human life tends to the condition of drama. Conflict. Goodies and baddies. Moral absolutes.' And the veal episode had some stock theatrical ingredients: confrontations, struggles, pursuits and other physical business; anger, suffering, even tragedy; and the moral simplifications and certainties that much theatre, with its need to render most things in physical, visible terms, tends towards. The goodies were of course the protesters (and the innocents were the calves); the baddies were the exporters and their minions, the police. The protesters no doubt hoped that viewers would generalize from the images of direct action and assume that the hostility to the trade was not only reasonable but almost universal. Their hope was probably well founded.

To sum up, then. In its assumption that (albeit with the assistance of words) truth or reality can be expressed in visual terms, factual television resembles the conventional theatre. As a consequence of this, people who appear on it – or who wish to appear on it – are often obliged to behave in theatrical ways, some of which may have powerful social effects. And while factual TV does not make this assumption (as theatre does) for the purposes of entertainment, such is our pleasure in watching that entertainment is an almost inevitable consequence. The gratifications which we gain from watching news or documentaries seem not to be very different from those derived from watching plays, sport, pop concerts, comedy shows, and so on. This helps to explain why in spite of the serious and factual nature of so much of its output television is associated, *above all*, with entertainment. And because of the sheer universality of the medium, its importance in the lives of so many, 'it has made entertainment itself the natural format for the representation of all experience' (Postman 1986: 87). TV is for most people the main source of culture and general knowledge. Consequently the way in which it imparts these things tends to become the norm for other, more specialized branches of knowledge. And whether through television or some other medium, politics, religion, the law, business and education have in more or less subtle ways sought to pass themselves off as forms of entertainment, as affording the emotional gratifications of a film, play or TV show. Many in the teaching profession will have heard visiting inspectors commend a course of study as 'exciting', on the assumption that students will find it hard to learn unless the experience is enjoyable or diverting. To teachers of quadratic equations or irregular verbs this poses a stern challenge.

Television and genre

We now need to re-focus our terms somewhat. We have associated theatre with 'spectacle' – with anything which satisfies our scopophilia (though much, like Shakespeare, does so in highly sophisticated ways) – but not necessarily with 'fiction'. Indeed *Death on Request* holds a theatrical fascination for us precisely because the killing is actual and not make-believe. Nevertheless, theatre has always seemed to tend towards the fictional, probably because (before the advent of television, at least) there was not enough in ordinary existence to satisfy our scopophilia for very long. Spectacles have to be contrived which are either interesting *per se* or made interesting by a narrative, and we have already noted the paradox that in order to affirm a truth about themselves people who are being watched by a large audience often behave in an artificially premeditated and in that sense 'theatrical' way. But since, as we saw earlier in this chapter, television is also perceived to be a highly realistic medium, we should hardly be surprised that its most original and interesting contributions to cultural genre are those which explore, or attempt to straddle, the indestructible boundary between truth and make-believe, real life on the one hand and, in its more usual fictional sense, 'theatre' on the other.

Television's realness seems self-evident. It is an iconic medium – it shows things as they are – and its other characteristics reinforce its verisimilitude. Its liveness, its continuousness and its frequently domestic mode of reception render it 'true to life', sometimes to the point of banality. But we have also seen how, even in the attempt to be truthful, it can gravitate towards theatrical fiction by encouraging performative behaviour in those whom it observes and a tendency to impose on life the elements of conflict, causality and climax we commonly witness on the stage. On the other hand much television drama is highly realistic, partly as a result of its cinematic heritage. It is not located on a stage, where pieces of painted hardboard signify trees or the wall of a house, but in an actual location, where trees or the wall of a house are signified by the things themselves. A car crash will be signified by nothing less than a car crash, not by off-stage noises or by wooden replicas or miming actors. Sometimes too, TV plays will be intercut with actual news footage. In both cinema and television actors behave much more naturalistically than they do on the conventional stage; but unlike in the cinema, where the actors are physically much larger than life, we seem to be as close to the actors on television as we are to those people with whom we interact in the real world.

The seeming reality of cinema and television can have bizarre and unsettling effects. Because for theatrical purposes they have so successfully simulated the conditions of *ordinary* life, we have no difficulty in believing the *extraordinary* life which they can extrapolate from these conditions. Most of us have never seen an actual train crash, but one which is staged for a movie or a TV drama seems entirely credible. Yet so used to these staged versions have we become that when we finally see the real thing part of us cannot believe it. Reared on a diet of vivid action movies like *Towering Inferno*, we baulked at the pictures of the terrorist aeroplane attacks on the World Trade Centre, New York, in 2001. Artifice had for so long looked lifelike that life suddenly looked artificial.

(In a brief digression it is worth noting that our familiarity with digitized images, whether on a computer or a TV screen, can further blur our sense of the difference between reality and make-believe, but for a contrary reason. They are a reminder that while the predominant mode of television is realism, it also shows much that is patently fictional: cartoons and graphics of various kinds. And just as we were inclined to disbelieve the terrorist attacks because they looked like a Hollywood action movie, so we are tempted to detach ourselves from the digitized pictures of bombs hitting targets in the Gulf, Serbia or Afghanistan because they resemble the artificial images of a Nintendo game (Dahlgren 1995: 68; Poster 1995: 159).)

Among television's attempts to represent theatrical fiction as real life, the *soap opera* is without doubt the most distinctive and interesting. It is, as we have seen, a child of radio but one which has thrived even more lustily in the newer medium. Among the best known are *Coronation Street*, *Emergency – Ward Ten*, *Crossroads*; the American soaps *Dallas* and *Dynasty*, which were popular during the 1980s; and more recently *EastEnders*, *Brookside* and the Australian imports *Neighbours* and *Home and Away*. The most remarkable, though as we shall see not the only, innovation of the soap opera was its lack of an ending, for unlike all previous narratives it never reaches an ultimate climax, denouement and point of closure or completion. These features were traditionally thought to be essential to a narrative in providing its readers or audience with the motivation to begin it, and in constituting the main characteristic which distinguishes fiction from the endless nature of life itself. In fact, in the daily and unending nature of its content and in its typically domestic setting the genre seems to embody the essence of both television and radio. It is a kind of fragmented version of the 'sequence' programming discussed with reference to radio in Chapter 7 since the viewer can step into or out of it at any stage without feeling that she has missed, or will miss, anything of crucial significance. But soap opera also differs from traditional stories in being presented from rapidly changing points of view. It has no narrative 'centre' nor does it merely revolve around a single hero (Livingstone 1990: 76).

In an excellent discussion of the genre John Fiske (1987: 144–50, 179–223) points out some other distinctive features: its huge casts consisting of forty or more characters and as many as twelve protagonists; 'real time' chronology, which implies that the action continues whether we can view it or not; and stars whose celebrity depends not on the usual qualities of distance and mystique but on their familiarity. All of this suggests a genre which is closer to daily reality than are most traditional art forms.

As well as television's attempts to represent theatre as life we must consider its efforts to represent life as theatre. *Docudrama*, variously known as drama documentary, documentary drama, dramatized documentary, dramadoc and faction (a blend of 'fact' and 'fiction'), attempts imaginative reconstructions of significant social or political events, though latterly it has also extended to dramatizations of real-life interactions within groups of 'ordinary people'. Before video and film equipment became better and more portable in the early 1960s many conventional TV documentaries contained dramatized elements whose 'fabricated' nature was made clear to the viewers. What docudrama sought to do was to blend fact and fiction much more subtly, to exploit that paradox by which artistic licence can come closer than known fact to an essential moral truth. On the other hand, ethical problems have arisen when, as is often the case, viewers could have no way of distinguishing between literal fact and fictional licence. Unsurprisingly, many of the best-known docudramas have had repercussions in the real world, some of them beneficial but most causing controversy. Among those which have explored contemporary social issues, *Cathy Come Home* (BBC, 1966), about the problems of the homeless, was credited with a change in government housing policy, but *The War Game*, a 'preconstruction' of nuclear war which was made at about the same time, was considered too frightening and banned until 1985. In the next decade the BBC's docudrama *Law and Order* was felt to be so unfairly critical of the penal system that the Prison Officers' Association stopped the corporation from filming inside gaols for a year.

Other docudramas have focused on specific individuals and events rather than on broader issues. The BBC's *Monocled Mutineer* (1986), attempting 'a greater truth' about the First World War, was another which attracted censure, but perhaps the most controversial was *Death of a Princess* (ATV, 1980), which dealt with the execution of an Arab princess for alleged adultery and provoked a diplomatic row between Britain and Saudi Arabia. On the other hand, *Hillsborough* (Granada, 1996), about the 1989 FA Cup semi-final in which ninety-seven people were crushed to death, is believed to have persuaded the government to agree to a fresh inquiry into the disaster (Paget 1998: 207).

However, even from its early years docudrama has gone through a number of developments and divergencies. One form of it attempts dramatic reconstructions of certain events but with a specific practical purpose: the prevention of crime or accidents. The best-known example is *Crimewatch UK* (BBC 1, from 1984) which has not only gained high viewing figures but encouraged the public to assist the police in their fight against crime and has resulted in numerous arrests and convictions.

Instead of using a formal script which seeks to re-create events in the past, another kind of docudrama attempts an unscripted investigation of contemporary social phenomena without necessarily focusing on widely known individuals. Among the earliest of these was *The Family* (BBC, 1974), a twelve-week 'fly-on-the-wall' series looking at the daily lives of the Wilkins family of Reading. This was perhaps more of a straight documentary than a docudrama except that the interactions of the various members of the family were an irresistible reminder of the plot dynamics of soap opera and, notwithstanding its sociological pretensions, afforded many of the same gratifications to the viewers. By the mid-1990s ever more manageable cameras and recording equipment enabled such docudramas to be made easily and cheaply, and viewers were being regaled with other fly-on-the-wall series about airports, hotels, cruise-liners, motorway service areas, hospitals, veterinary practices, and police and coastguard stations.

More recently the docudrama has undergone a move away from reconstructing past events or passively reflecting contemporary ones to making events happen – a move in which social or psychological investigation has all but yielded to the entertainment imperative. The elements of docudrama are created by throwing a group of people together in a restricted space – a sealed house, an island or a patch of jungle – and then providing round-the-clock television coverage of the way in which they interact. Called 'reality TV' or 'Big Brother TV' after the all-seeing dictator in George Orwell's novel *1984*, the genre has included *Big Brother* itself (Channel 4, 2000), *Castaway* (BBC1, 2000) and *Survivor* (ITV, 2001). In the more frankly titillating *Temptation Island* (Channel 4, 2001) a number of couples are deposited on an island where attractive men and women seek to lure them apart. Reality TV is often blended with other genres, notably the game-show. As a particular programme develops viewers may be encouraged to vote by telephone to expel members of the group one by one. The last remaining person then receives a substantial cash prize. This kind of docudrama could thus be seen as an attempt by television to get reality to stage its own soap opera. Not only are the characters auditioned for their telegenic qualities but the competitive element maximizes their incentive to put on a good show for the cameras. They are in any case likely to be exhibitionists who believe that they are undeservedly obscure (Persaud 2000: 6–7) – and the reward for all of them is at least a moment's celebrity.

The institutional implications of the reality show are interesting and its audience gratifications complex. Although the traditional television networks will normally show only recorded highlights which are contextualized by a narrator, continuous 'real time' coverage is often provided on the digital channels, such as E4, and on internet or 'web' TV. Inevitably, much of it is fairly uneventful. Hence it may be the case that the phenomenon of television has become so ubiquitous and so banal that we must now expect it even as an organized mass medium to be no more concerned for the gratifications of its viewers than is closed-circuit TV in a shopping mall or on a motorway. On the other hand, a division of function may develop whereby these 'raw' transmissions will be viewable only on web TV, while the traditional networks carry the edited and more interesting version.

What do the viewers get from reality TV? Clearly some of them gain gratification even from its uneventfulness, which is, at least, a kind of *guarantee* of its authenticity. Such gratification seems explicable only in terms of the scopophilia which we mentioned earlier and which can often be satisfied relatively modestly. However, they are always in hopes of seeing something a bit out of the ordinary, such as fights and confrontations, and, bearing in mind that cameras are installed even in bedrooms and bathrooms, 'voyeurism' may be a better description of their behaviour.

Sources/further reading

For an excellent survey of the social and political background to the growth of TV viewing during the 1970s see Potter (1989). The realism and domesticity of television are neatly described in Alvarado, Gutch and Wollen (1987). To Postman (1986) I owe a general debt for his excellent critique of TV and for his insight into the contrasting functions of imagery and language.

For a brief yet scintillating polemic on the limitations of television see Hughes (1995). Whale (1969) argues that television is a crude medium for the presentation of news and politics, since pictures cannot be used to 'explain'. He and Davis (1976) also stress its quantitative limitations. For perceptive remarks on the desultory, deracinated and often dramatized character of television news, see Negrine (1994) and Bourdieu (1998). Further discussion of the genre can be found in McNair (1998) along with some trenchant insights into the causes and character of 'moral panics'. There is a critique of television as a medium of knowledge in Corner (1999).

On the elements of performance and spectacle in modern life and on the image as a primary means of conceptualization, see Chaney (1993). Postman (1986) argues cogently that television has made entertainment the model for almost all other kinds of discourse, and in an impressive analysis of the medium Corner (1995) acknowledges its 'overall dramatic character' in relation to both fictional and non-fictional output. There are some interesting remarks on television aesthetics in Mulgan (1990).

In the context of soap opera the traditional view that narrative structures are informed by the sense of an ending is set out in Kermode (1967). Selby and Cowdery (1995) provide a useful historical sketch of the genre, and Geraghty (1996), Fiske (1987) and Mepham (1990) are excellent on its general characteristics. Three specialized studies of soap opera are Hobson (1982) on *Crossroads*, Ang (1985) on *Dallas*, and Buckingham (1996) on *EastEnders*. Further insights into the genre can be found in Abercrombie (1996).

Corner (1995, 1996) provides a fascinating account of the historical development of the documentary genre in cinema, radio and TV, together with analysis of the conventions of both documentary and docudrama. Kerr (1990) and Paget (1998) are also informative on the historical development of docudrama, and for some sharp insights into the gratifications afforded by 'reality TV' see Persaud (2000).

Chapter 9

Modern television (2): social impacts and influences

Modern television (2): social impacts and influences

From hatstand to arbiter

Although an important aim of this and the previous chapter is to chart the extraordinary rise in the popularity and significance of television, we must not forget that it has always been part of a much broader media landscape. The word 'media' is used as a singular by many people (among them media studies students, who ought to know better) and often as a synonym for 'television'; but television is not the only medium, nor even the only medium of broadcasting.

As with most newcomers its arrival began a process of displacement while its predecessors – radio, cinema and newspapers – made room for it, mostly with an ill grace. The latter were largely obliged to surrender to television what television did best and concentrate on their own unrivalled strengths. Whereas in current affairs, for instance, TV (and still radio) were best equipped to focus on concrete facts and events, provide the very latest news, and deal in certain kinds of actuality, cinema eventually had to quit this field altogether, while the newspapers not only increased news backgrounding but expanded into 'softer' news, features and 'life-style' topics, thus displacing a number of magazines and periodicals. Among the latter, those which cater for specialist interests have stood the best chance of survival.

But if the other media have been displaced and in some instances diminished by television, they have been able to get their revenge by living off it: television and its content have provided them with a great deal of subject matter. This is especially true of the newspapers, which contain daily reviews and previews of TV programmes, listings, and gossip about TV personalities and even about the characters in the soaps. Hence, as seems always to be the case in media history, the initial period of displacement has given way to a fairly close if often unacknowledged collaboration between all the media, especially in the business of setting the news and cultural agendas. In this respect I have more than once been fooled by some item on BBC Radio 4's *Today* programme, which in dealing with an obscure yet important issue has made me applaud the alertness and diligence of its news staff. It is only when I open my newspaper that I discover the item has been lifted from that day's edition of the *Independent* or *Guardian*.

A more obvious instance of the way in which the media will perpetuate a story by batting it about among themselves, rather as the flippers and studs of a pinball machine can be used to keep the ball in play, was an episode in the decline of the marriage of Prince Charles and Princess Diana. It began with a *book* – Jonathan Dimbleby's biography of Charles, which included disclosures about his relationship with his wife. The book was then serialized in a *newspaper*, the *Sunday Times*, but also covered in other papers and on *radio* and *television*, the latter two breathing fresh life into the story by question-begging references to 'the continuing controversy' about the royal marriage. Though doubtless a story that was popular with the public, it was hard to resist the impression that those whom it excited most were the broadcasters and journalists themselves.

Nevertheless, while television has undoubtedly had an enormous impact on the media ecology, it is the history of its effects on social institutions and audiences with which we are primarily concerned. We will begin with sport because this offers perhaps the most vivid illustration of a progression which if not already familiar to us will soon become so. After at first being barred from many sports events because of its likely impact on crowd attendances, and then admitted only on the strictest conditions, television has gradually begun to take them over, in some instances adapting them to its own particular requirements by changing the way in which they are played. It has been able to compensate them for the overall drop in their live attendances with huge sums of money in screening rights and with vastly bigger 'home gates'. And although this is of course very much a matter of media economics and the politics of media ownership, we should be clear that its precondition is the nature of television itself. Some of the changes it has caused are perhaps subconscious, like the theatrical head-clutchings of soccer players when they miss a goal or lose a game, but others are premeditated. Ostensibly superficial, though even more spectacular, are the changes in 'packaging': in sports kit, which has become much more colourful and often includes sponsors' logos, and in the proliferation of stadium and trackside advertising. (In motor racing advertisers prefer television to cover circuits with tight bends because these force the cars to slow down and thus make the trackside hoardings more legible to the viewers.) Professional boxing provides perhaps the most striking example of the growth of packaging. Before televised title fights there are now prolonged fanfares, the play of spotlights in a darkened arena, pounding music, and colourful processions to a ring which often boasts advertisers' logos on its corner posts and canvas. The boxers wear garishly patterned shorts, and between the rounds scantily clad women circle the ring displaying the number of the next round.

However, some changes have been more fundamental and are likely to increase in the future. Despite the effect on the players, many matches of the 1994 Soccer World Cup, which was staged in the United States, were played in the fierce midday heat so that they could be broadcast live during peak evening viewing times in Europe. As the precondition of its deal with the English Rugby League BSkyB insisted that for the convenience of its own scheduling the league should switch from a winter to a summer season and that for promotional purposes it should thenceforth be known as the Super League. But so far it has been on cricket, that most sedate and conservative of games, that television has made its biggest impact. It was in 1977 that the Australian media magnate Kerry Packer launched his 'cricket circus', and with it a new era of floodlit games, players in coloured pyjamas instead of the traditional whites, and stumps with logos. Limited-over cricket was largely a consequence of television, and further changes have been mooted. In order to accommodate its commercial breaks BSkyB wants longer intervals between overs but much shorter breaks for lunch and tea. There has even been talk of one-hour, eight-a-side matches in which each player would both bowl and bat.

More than any other sport cricket has also used television evidence to assist umpires in making their decisions. Although the new rugby Super League led the way by using a video referee who displays his close-try decisions on a big screen, cricket now includes a third umpire to rule on run-outs and on whether a ball has touched a boundary rope. Although it is not used for lbw decisions, Channel 4's new videographic 'hawk-eye' device would seem to show conclusively whether the ball would have carried on to hit the stumps.

We shall shortly see that sport is only one area in which television has graduated from modest onlooker to a mighty arbiter whom the world cannot oppose and whose gaze it often courts. Colin Seymour-Ure reviews its post-war progress as follows:

As TV poured over the surface of everyday life its programmes made fewer and fewer concessions to pre-existing forms, institutions, media, manners. TV made plays, told the news, taught school, increasingly on its own terms, not as a parasite, imitator, or tolerated intruder concealed as a hat-stand . . . [It] responded to popular taste, observing new taboos about racism and sexism, just as it helped to demolish old ones of sexual modesty or obscene language. But common to all programming, on any channel, was an eventual confidence in the distinctive value of the TV medium. Well before 1995, TV did not need to make excuses for itself.

(Seymour-Ure 1996: 163)

The historical relationship between television and politics typifies that which has existed between television and most institutions of public life. Television begins as a loftily patronized messenger boy or barely tolerated guest, and ends up largely dictating how these institutions should present and even conduct their business.

For the genesis of its relationship with politics we have to go back to the days of sound broadcasting. In the early years of radio the BBC's political coverage was fairly limited. Reith himself was largely uninterested in politics, thinking it less significant than other cultural matters such as religion, drama, education and the arts. Moreover, it was an inherently controversial field in which the controversy could involve not just the political parties but the BBC itself. Hence political discussions were seldom broadcast, gingerly handled, and often contentious in their effects, especially during the 1930s. And until the end of the 1950s it was mainly the politicians who determined what issues radio and television would cover and the way in which they should cover them.

The broadcasting of politics was shaped by two notable principles. The first was that the coverage of the views of the different political parties should be 'balanced'. This principle was in any case implicit in the BBC's public service tenet that it should be independent of pressure groups and sectional interests and was made part of its statutory duties in 1927. It was later applied to ITV too, and is still sometimes invoked. When, as often happens, one or other institution is accused of bias by *all* of the main parties it will take this as a comforting sign that it is managing a fair measure of balance. In practice, balance has always been an impossible concept and therefore a constant bone of contention. How can balance be defined or quantified? Is two minutes of soaring eloquence by the politician of one party 'balanced' by two minutes of stumbling prevarication by the politician of another? Should the party spokespersons be chosen by the programme producers or by the parties themselves? – an important question since it is often wayward politicians who make the best or most interesting broadcasters. Does balance mean affording equal coverage to all shades of political opinion or coverage which is proportionate to the numbers of seats which the parties occupy in Parliament?

In the day-to-day coverage of politics balance has generally meant an even-handedness between the three main parties, but it has not extended to views which do not have significant parliamentary representation – views which would be, almost by definition, eccentric or 'extreme'. Moreover, there have certainly been times when even this degree of even-handedness has been sacrificed to a practical need (usually the BBC's) to appease the party in power. However, with reference to party political and party election broadcasts, 'balance' has meant coverage proportionate to the parliamentary strength of the main parties. The principle might equally be used to justify coverage which was *inversely* proportionate to it: that is, one could argue that if a party has few seats, it should be entitled to more coverage in order to bring its views before a wider public – but this notion of balance has only logic, not realpolitik, in its favour.

Ministerial broadcasts have always been especially contentious. Ministers could not demand airtime since this would make a nonsense of the BBC's independence. They might therefore seek an invitation. But if they did, could the BBC withhold it? And if not, should it extend a similar invitation to the opposition? In 1947 an agreement between the government and the BBC established four categories of political broadcast. The first was the straight ministerial broadcast to be given usually at times of emergency and always 'in the national interest'. Since there could be no dispute about the national interest this category was uncontroversial and allowed the opposition no right of reply. The second was the controversial ministerial broadcast, to which the opposition was entitled to reply. The third was the party political broadcast, produced by the political parties themselves, with the government and opposition allocated equal numbers of broadcasts and the smaller parties – the Liberals and nationalists – fewer, proportionate to their parliamentary strength. The fourth category was the controversial discussion.

Apart from placing the BBC in an invidious position between government and opposition the 1947 agreement achieved little. The opposition claimed, quite reasonably, that the definition of an 'uncontroversial' ministerial broadcast was itself controversial, and so the distinction between the first two categories all but collapsed. Moreover, there were constant squabbles between the parties about the number of broadcasts to which each was entitled under the third category, with the corporation used as a common whipping-boy. However acrimonious, these squabbles were usually settled informally and away from the public view, but a judicial element was introduced as recently as 1995 when opposition MPs sought an injunction against the BBC to prevent it from showing in Scotland an interview with the Prime Minister just before that country's local elections. Their action was successful because the opposition was to be denied equal coverage.

Before the arrival of ITV political television mostly consisted of party election broadcasts. In the broader field of politics the BBC and ITV have seldom been so naive as to believe that the principle of balance or even-handedness has applied to conflicts between Britain and her external enemies, though during the Falklands and Gulf wars there were complaints among certain sections of the public that the Argentinian and Iraqi cases had been insufficiently explained. However, the question of balance between the unionist and republican positions on Northern Ireland, both of which have sometimes been expressed through acts of terrorism, has always been a peculiarly thorny one and tackled by the broadcasters with varying temerity. The BBC's attempt to reflect the republican point of view in *Real Lives: At the Edge of the Union* (1985) caused predictable outrage, while a *This Week* documentary called *Death on the Rock* (1988), which investigated the killing of certain IRA activists by the SAS in Gibraltar, was shown by ITV despite government pressure.

Balance and neutrality are not just matters of apportioning equal coverage to all shades of political opinion but of refraining from endorsing any of those opinions or expressing opinions of one's own. Under its charter the BBC was forbidden to editorialize and this prohibition has extended to all the other major broadcasting institutions. Unlike the newspapers, they may not express an opinion on political issues or urge their audiences to vote for a particular party. When radio and TV differed from newspapers in being limited by the shortage of frequencies it seemed proper that each broadcasting institution should reflect the widest range of opinion rather than one point of view. But now that digital technology is able to provide an almost limitless number of channels it could be argued that the only broadcaster whom we should henceforth expect to be balanced and neutral is the BBC, since it is directly funded by a public which reflects the whole range of political opinion.

The second principle which shaped the early broadcasting of politics was that a broadcasting institution should not pre-empt or prejudice discussions which were due to be conducted in Parliament by the country's elected representatives. This was somewhat analogous to the *sub judice* rule in courts of law, which forbids public pronouncements about innocence or guilt before the conclusion of a trial so that the verdict shall not be improperly influenced. The principle was enshrined in an informal understanding reached in 1944 between the BBC and the political parties and became known as the 'fourteen-day rule': there could be no broadcast coverage of any issue which was due to be debated in Parliament within the following fortnight. Though it was the BBC, not the parties, which had proposed the rule, it soon formed the view that parliamentary discussion was likely to be informed and stimulated rather than prejudiced by any preceding broadcast coverage. In 1955 it therefore asked the government to revoke the rule, but the government's response was to make it formal and binding on the BBC and ITV alike.

Nevertheless, by this time the tide was beginning to turn in the relationship between broadcasters and politicians. The latter could deal confidently with radio, having been used to it since the early 1930s, but the new medium of television was less easy to handle. It could show politicians in pitiless close-up, exposing not only physical blemishes but idiosyncrasies of character. Broadcasters, too, were growing more aware of their power, particularly with the arrival of ITV, whose commercial source of income meant that it was not beholden to politicians in the way that the BBC was. Its new generation of interviewers such as Robin Day were more journalistic, less deferential. But in this respect competition strengthened the BBC too, because if its political broadcasting grew more incisive so as to match ITV's, the politicians could complain only by admitting that in the old days the BBC had been partly under their thumb.

It was the Suez crisis of 1956 which marked the beginning of the end of the old relationship between politicians and broadcasters. In July of that year President Nasser of Egypt nationalized the Anglo-French-controlled Suez Canal Company, as a consequence of which British, French and Israeli forces bombed and occupied the Canal zone. This colonialist adventure split the country from top to bottom as well as incurring the displeasure not only of the Soviet Union but of Britain's main ally, the United States. Paddy Scannell (1979: 100) points out that before 1956 the BBC's political broadcasts focused on foreign affairs because it was here, in the twilight of empire and with the Soviet Union as everybody's *bête noire*, that controversy could be avoided and party consensus lay. But consensus collapsed with Suez, and as Asa Briggs (1995: 76) observes, Suez threatened the BBC because for the first time in the history of broadcasting the corporation was obliged to reflect a deep rift over foreign policy and report a large body of domestic opinion which was strongly critical of the government on a matter of great national importance. One consequence was that the BBC incurred the deep hostility of the Prime Minister, Sir Anthony Eden. When Eden or one of his ministers broadcast, the opposition demanded a right of reply. But Eden's view was that this was a national crisis which transcended party politics, and therefore that the BBC was obliged not to be even-handed between government and opposition but to support the government. This was in accordance with the 1947 agreement between the government and the corporation, but, as the Labour politician Clement Attlee had remarked in 1934,

> The control of the BBC by the State in an emergency is obviously necessary, but there is a point where it is difficult to decide whether the emergency is really that of the State or of the Government as representing the political party in power.
>
> (quoted in McDonnell 1991: 17)

Was Suez a crisis for the nation – or merely for the government? The BBC certainly saw it as the government's and its relations with the latter sank to a new depth.

Nevertheless, broadcasting in general, and the BBC in particular, ended the year 1956 with its power enhanced rather than diminished. First, under the pressure of events in the Middle East and elsewhere, the government indefinitely suspended the fourteen-day rule in return for assurances from the broadcasters which were as insincerely given as they were unrealistically demanded. The rule could hardly survive because ITV was much less vulnerable to government threats and pressures than was the BBC, and if the independence of its editorial line on Suez could be praised, as it was by many people, to criticize the BBC's would involve the admission, unthinkable in a democracy, that the latter was a creature of the government. The BBC was also able to maintain its independence precisely because there was no general agreement, even within the ruling Conservative Party, as to where 'the national interest' lay. Finally, and only a few months after the Suez crisis began, a mass uprising broke out in Hungary against the Soviet Union. In Britain (as elsewhere in the West) there was almost unanimous support for Hungary and a general agreement, endorsed by many Hungarians themselves, that the BBC's coverage of the uprising was excellent. The corporation was thus able to restore its fair standing with the government.

Thenceforward both ITV and the BBC took steps to raise the quality of their political broadcasting, though as was noted in Chapter 5 the former had already taken the lead with the launch of ITN. It is perhaps unsurprising, then, that an ITV contractor, Granada, was the first to offer in-depth TV coverage of a by-election campaign. This took place at Rochdale in February and March of 1958, and programmes included a live discussion of the election issues between all the candidates and interviews of the latter by three experienced journalists.

Television and politics since 1959

The general election of 1959 was the first in which television could be said to have played a major role in the electoral process and the point at which the broadcasters seized the initiative from the politicians. Sir Hugh Greene, the overall head of BBC news and soon to be Director General, announced that the corporation would cover the election on 'news values' rather than according to literalistic notions of balance: in effect that broadcasters rather than politicians would set the agenda. The sheer scale of the BBC's coverage was unprecedented, with fifty-seven cameras in the field, some of them moving on election night from one constituency to another.

Since 1959 television has increasingly dictated the terms on which election campaigns have been conducted – and, indeed, on which politics in general can be publicized. From 1985 it was allowed into the House of Lords (radio had been relaying the proceedings of both Houses since 1976) and from 1989 into the Commons. It is for the individual to decide whether TV has altered the behaviour of politicians for better or for worse, or had no discernible effect.

But of equal interest is the way in which, thanks largely to the medium itself, the general understanding of what 'politics' consists of has broadened beyond the traditional and well-defined realms of cabinet, Parliament and party warfare. The year 1958 marked television's importance in terms of the conventional political processes: it covered the Rochdale by-election and for the first time the State Opening of Parliament, but it also covered politics of an unconventional but no less significant kind: the first of the Aldermaston marches organized by the Campaign for Nuclear Disarmament (CND) and an example *par excellence* of pressure-group publicity. On the nation's screens appeared an astonishing, motley procession of people: bearded students in duffel coats; young couples with placard-bearing infants in pushchairs; leading public figures – radical clergymen, aquiline intellectuals like

Bertrand Russell, and personalities from the arts; and accompanying the spectacle the sounds of skiffle groups, jazz bands and oratory. This was a new kind of 'visual politics' which television had largely brought into being and which would reach its apotheosis in the great anti-Vietnam and civil rights marches of the 1960s and 1970s. It is still with us in the publicity coups of Greenpeace and anti-road protesters.

As Ralph Negrine (1994: 139–40) points out and as was noted in the last chapter, such campaigners and protesters have always made an emotive and moralistic appeal on single issues, which are represented as straightforward clashes between good and evil. And they have always attracted TV coverage not only because of their deliberate theatricality, but because in cutting across the lines of conventional party politics they can be seen as in a sense non-political. The broadcasting institutions can therefore televise them without having to worry about 'balance' or accusations of being politically partisan. But television has had a theatrical effect on politics *in general* (indeed, we saw earlier that it is liable to theatricalize almost every sphere of activity). It often replaces thoughtful discussions of abstract issues with 'personalities' and confrontations, and concocts phoney news items like photo-opportunities and walkabouts. Yet, thanks to TV, some news items have managed the sinister feat of being both 'concocted' and genuine: the IRA set its bombs to explode in the late afternoon so that the effects could appear on the early evening bulletins.

Just as television has made us see politics as a broader matter of social issues and problems that are often expressed through campaigns, direct action and demonstrations, so since the 1960s it has added to the arenas in which even traditional politics is conducted: Downing Street, the Houses of Parliament and the election hustings. As the tribune of the people TV felt more and more justified in setting its own political agenda – not only in *Panorama* and *News at Ten* but *Question Time* and *World in Action* – for which it often succeeded in luring the politicians away from their habitat and into its own: the studio. One could even argue that the TV studio has replaced the House of Commons as the main arena of political debate. And where TV leads, even the broadsheets will follow. Newspaper coverage of Commons speeches has decreased sharply in recent years, one arguable effect of which is that Parliament has seemed less important in relation to other sources of power: the judiciary, utility regulators, European institutions and even market forces (Riddell 1998: 8–14).

Whether they wish to or not, politicians are obliged to adjust their demeanour to the needs of the small screen. Harold Macmillan, who was Prime Minister from 1957 to 1963, was quite adept at this, combining a reassuring patrician image with a hint of self-parody. Before he submitted to a television interview with the American Ed Murrow, only 37 per cent of the electorate thought that Macmillan was doing a good job; afterwards the number rose to 50 per cent. But Harold Wilson, who was Prime Minister from 1964 to 1970 and from 1974 to 1976, was the first to make a careful study of television, and with his pipe and mackintosh projected the image of a canny man of the people. Nevertheless he was discomfited by the BBC in much the same way as Sir Anthony Eden had been many years before. In 1966 he used television to explain his 'National Plan' for Britain's economic recovery. In spite of the rhetoric the BBC declined to regard it as any more than a matter of party politics and allowed the opposition a right of reply. It thus incurred Wilson's undying hostility, the episode proving that dealing with the media, and with television especially, is like riding a tiger. Woe betide those who think it will serve only the purposes they want it to serve!

But the adjustment of politics to television has been much more fundamental than this. It is not just appearances but political events and whole election campaigns which have had to be tailored to the medium and its news schedules. Indeed, television is itself a part of politics in the sense that almost every political decision will include some calculation as to the effect it will have on the viewing electorate. Moreover, the medium is even more pervasive than has so far been suggested. We mentioned that it has enticed politicians out of their traditional habitats and into its own. But the world, not just the studio, is television's oyster and politicians may find themselves being accosted on airport runways, answering questions in a shopping precinct, giving in-flight or on-train interviews. For many years there have been permanent TV studios at Heathrow as well as at Westminster. In sum it could be said that the relationship between television and politics, though punctuated by rows and crises over Suez, the Falklands, Northern Ireland and so on, is so close that they can scarcely be disentangled from each other.

Colin Seymour-Ure (1996: 202) has discerned three main effects that the media, with television pre-eminent among them, have had upon the role of the premiership. First, the Prime Minister must give more time and thought to dealing with the media. Second, she or he is more often drawn away from the power bases of the office: Downing Street and the House of Commons. Third, and predictably in view of television's requirements, the Prime Minister must be more of a 'personality', an 'opinion leader' or mobilizer: in a word, more like an American President. Since the concerns of politics themselves have broadened it is hardly surprising that the Prime Minister and even his senior colleagues are now expected to have a view on almost everything. In 2000, for instance, the Chancellor of the Exchequer, Gordon Brown, was happy to pontificate on the 'élitist' nature of Oxford University's admissions policy.

But the fact that television and the other media encourage politicians to be opinion leaders serves to remind us that power does not lie wholly with the former. Politicians need television for exposure, but television needs politicians for views and information. And if politicians dislike the way they are treated, they can always, in a world of competing networks, threaten to take their business elsewhere (Gaber 1998: 266). As they rediscovered their value to television the political parties and individual politicians strove to bend it to their own purposes by employing image consultants and publicists – 'spin-doctors' who feed news to the media in which achievements are emphasized and failures disguised. These people also help to stage slick, telegenic party conferences which deal in short, memorable quotes ('sound-bites') rather than the genuine debates which might reflect internal divisions (McNair 1998: 152). Moreover, it is largely due to their influence that election campaigns are now 'managed events more akin to advertising, public relations and marketing than traditional politics' (McQuail 2000: 472).

We must conclude with some brief remarks about the government's formal policy on broadcasting. In the paradoxical impression it gives of not being subject to special legislation yet being closely monitored by a number of public agencies, television (and radio) reflects the ambivalence which society feels towards it. We believe that as guardians of democracy, arenas of public debate and the guarantors of freedom of information, the media should be as free from political interference as possible – especially from the government, whose deeds (and misdeeds) they report to us. It is also noticeable that when the government seeks to regulate the media it is usually those media which deal with news and politics – newspapers, radio and television – rather than those which do not, such as films, books and compact discs (Seymour-Ure 1996: 236). Hence, to allay public fears of state control, governments have traditionally professed a 'non-policy' towards broadcasting. There is no 'Department of Communication' (the Postmaster-General's regulatory responsibility for the electronic media disappeared in 1969), and such statutory provisions as exist are piecemeal and of makeshift origins – intended, as Seymour-Ure (1996: 228) points out, to serve broad objectives like 'freedom of speech', 'freedom of information', 'public service' and 'balance'. Legislation affects aspects of broadcasting and its audiences (for example, the TV licence), but in other respects television and radio are regarded as 'nothing special' – subject to those ordinary laws of obscenity, blasphemy, copyright, defamation and official secrets which affect many other spheres in addition to broadcasting.

On the other hand, we dislike the idea that the media can exert too much influence over people or become 'a law unto themselves', and for this reason both the BBC and the commercial sector are carefully if discreetly policed by publicly appointed boards. Moreover, certain government departments such as the Treasury and the Foreign Office take an oblique interest in broadcasting (by fixing the TV licence, financing the World Service and so on); and media legislation has established various self-regulatory bodies such as the Broadcasting Complaints Commission and the Advertising Standards Authority. It has been calculated that by the end of the 1970s some thirty organizations were involved in controlling or in some way shaping British television and radio output.

Television and the royal family

The history of television's dealings with royalty is very similar to the history of its dealings with politics and sport. At the 1937 coronation it was a mere spectator in the crowd. At the 1953 coronation it was a humble supplicant, knocking at the door of Westminster Abbey and being allowed in to watch discreetly from the loft, though there was a part of the ceremony from which it was excluded. By the 1990s it was a monstrous potentate before whom a prince and princess would come to justify their private lives.

Until the 1970s the royal family retained a fair degree of mystique and was held in some reverence. It is true that there had been a scandal and a constitutional crisis back in 1936, when after the death of George V it gradually emerged that his son and successor, Edward VIII, intended to marry the twice-divorced Mrs Wallis Simpson. But the crisis was well managed. Television scarcely existed, and the BBC and the Newspaper Proprietors' Association, with their instinctive respect for rank and authority, joined in a conspiracy to keep the news from the wider public. When the King decided that he would rather renounce the throne than Mrs Simpson he explained the decision in a radio broadcast which ensured both sympathy for himself and support for his successor and younger brother, George VI.

It was not until 1969 that royalty decided to make some concession to the democratizing effects of the new medium of television by allowing itself to be seen in a more intimate and less formal light. The result was Richard Cawston's documentary *The Royal Family* (both BBC and ITV), in which the Queen appeared in a happy domestic setting and thus inaugurated a honeymoon period in royalty's relations with television. The royal family still maintained much of its dignity and detachment through televised events like the investiture of Charles as Prince of Wales in the same year, and his marriage to Lady Diana Spencer in 1981; but the images of family picnics and bustling corgis lingered in the nation's mind. The royals were likeably human – at bottom, 'just like the rest of us'.

However, the three decades since the screening of Cawston's programme have shown that television is always a dangerous guest to admit because it ends up hosting the party. As members of the royal family were seen more and more often on TV, their magic began to wane and popular reverence to diminish. They came to seem unremarkable, even a little dull. An attempt by its younger members to show that they could laugh at themselves by taking part in a game-show, *It's a Royal Knockout* (BBC 1, 1987), seriously dented their dignity: the nation was not amused. And finally, with the revelations of matrimonial breakdowns and sexual adventures, notably those of Prince Charles and Princess Diana, royalty began to acquire a negative, more tawdry kind of glamour.

It has to be said that television was not the only, perhaps not even the primary, cause of this change. Its news programmes simply echoed stories which had invariably begun in the tabloids – and even then only when they had become so sensational that they could no longer be ignored. But television clearly gave them a wider currency, and its pictures fleshed out and made us all too familiar with those about whom they were written. Yet instead of shunning TV on the reasonable assumption that a measure of retirement, an interval of oblivion, might restore their standing, first Charles and then Diana seemed to solicit the medium to put his or her case, vainly seeking yet another, this time favourable, dose of publicity to counter the damaging effects of the last. The interviews of Charles and Diana – the former on ITV in the summer of 1995, the latter on BBC 1 in November of the same year – were extraordinary instances of the power of television. Each broadcast was a curious mixture of intimacy and exhibitionism, a series of confidences which implied the acceptance of millions of prurient viewers as confessors and even judges. But while Prince and Princess were seeking to justify themselves and restore their reputations, what television revealed above all was their ordinariness, their merely average weaknesses – that at close quarters, royals, like everybody else, are anything but royal. Even the Queen, to whom no wisp of scandal attaches, has been damaged. In 1984 her Christmas message was heard by 28 million; by the mid-1990s the number had dropped to 14.5 million.

It is of course true that as well as destroying mystique and exposing the ordinariness of those in power and authority, television is able to take people who are already 'ordinary' and elevate or idealize them. These tend to be pop or film stars, who are generally allowed to use the medium on *their* terms precisely because they deal in fantasy and entertainment rather than in 'real world' matters. The bulk of their TV appearances consists of soft-focus movies and videos, and the few close interviews they give are carefully stage-managed. But provided the medium is subsequently given the sort of spectacle around which fantasy might be woven, that destruction of mystique which it can also cause is by no means irreversible – a fact which was illustrated by the later history of Princess Diana, even if it took a tragic finale to complete her apotheosis. Although Diana was frequently vexed by intrusions into her privacy, as when photographed while exercising at the gym or dallying with her boyfriends, she also became adept at turning the media to her advantage. As the intrusions imply, she had attractions that the other royals lacked: youth and beauty. But through press and TV interviews she was able to represent herself as a royal outcast – rejected by a family who had already sunk in the public's esteem. Since she could now never be the Queen of England, she coyly expressed a shrewd ambition to become another and more egalitarian kind of monarch – 'the queen of people's hearts' – and did so by making highly publicized visits to the sick, the starving and the poor in various parts of the globe. Hence this young and beautiful woman was not simply a princess (with some famous showbiz friends), but one who was both victim and comforter – a blend of glamour, vulnerability and kindness whose potency would only later become clear.

It must again be stressed that the popular press gave much more prominence to Diana than television did. But without TV's pictures of her cuddling maimed and starving infants or holding the hands of emaciated AIDS victims it is inconceivable that she could have attracted such world-wide interest. Her charitable activities were neither full time nor of a long overall duration. But when in August 1997 she was killed with her latest boyfriend in a car crash in Paris, apparently fleeing some photographers whose attentions were on this occasion unwelcome, the international reaction was astonishing. An outpouring of grief – as theatrical as the events that had caused it – came not only from the famous but the general public, above all from those who knew her only from press and TV coverage, and she was instantly elevated from mere celebrity to near sainthood. The royal family came under attack for not showing enough grief, even though she had criticized them and her marriage to Charles had ended. Nor would any of the media, including the broadsheet newspapers, allow space to those who might wish to call into question either the character of Diana herself or the appropriateness of the reaction to her death. The orgy of emotional kitsch culminated in a funeral service in Westminster Abbey which was televised to a world audience of 2.5 billion.

However, these events were attended by a hint of irony. Shortly after Diana's death, but before her funeral, there died another famous champion of the down-trodden: Mother Teresa, a small, wizened nun who conceivably had a better claim on the world's grief since she had devoted most of her life to the care of Calcutta's poor. But for the TV-dominated media Mother Teresa suffered from a fatal flaw: she was elderly, unworldly – in a word, not telegenic – and her death was reported as if a slightly irritating distraction from the main event.

The Diana episode is chiefly of interest in showing how television encourages people to regard mere appearances as a reliable guide to the truth, perhaps because they are also in some sense 'entertaining', and to react to them in emotionally disproportionate ways.

Television and audiences

As the number of TV channels has increased, and with it the kinds of content they offer, the television audience has divided along class lines just as it did with the proliferation of radio networks after the war. Since ITV was launched with a need to deliver the biggest possible audience to its advertisers, we noticed that it attracted a large number of working-class viewers, while most of the middle class stayed with the BBC. With the arrival of BBC 2 in 1964 and the first move towards narrowcasting, further divisions became apparent: the working class stayed with ITV and BBC 1; the middle class divided its viewing between BBC 1 and BBC 2 and later extended its interest to Channel 4. With similar motivation to ITV, satellite and cable television are seeking and capturing a strong working-class audience.

Knowledge of this demographic information is clearly vital to broadcasting researchers, who need to keep advertisers and programme planners well informed as to who is watching what and in what numbers. But the answers to certain other questions they ask, though just as desirable, are much more elusive. What effect do programmes have on people? What do they think of them? How far do programmes influence their views and behaviour? As the reader will appreciate, our earlier discussion of the characteristics of television was in many respects inseparable from a discussion of its likely effects on the viewer, but we must now try to take a more systematic and empirical look at audience effects and influences.

For the first twenty-five years of competition the BBC and ITV were incapable of coordinating their audience researches. While the BBC depended on its own broadcasting research department, the individual ITV contractors engaged companies like Television Audience Measurement and A. C. Nielsen to do theirs. The BBC had one system of measurement, ITV had another: they were incompatible, and unsurprisingly each system tended to favour the organization which used it. In the early years of television it was assumed by virtually everyone that the social and moral effects and influences of the medium were considerable – a view fervently espoused by the Pilkington Committee, who penalized the ITA for being among the few who doubted it. After Pilkington there was a flowering of interest in this field which we may broadly divide into industry based, audience based and academic.

ITV was quick to atone for the heresy it had uttered. In 1964 it coordinated its research efforts under the Joint Industry Committee for Television Advertising Research (JICTAR), though it was another seventeen years before the BBC and ITV set up, at the behest of the Annan Committee, a joint company, the Broadcasters' Audience Research Board (BARB), with a single system of audience research. Among audiences themselves the interest in television's effects took the form of campaigning rather than investigation, since they were already convinced that they knew what those effects were, or should be. Most audience groups were interested in television as either a moral or an educational force. The most publicized (because of its opposition to 'permissiveness') was Mrs Mary Whitehouse's National Viewers' and Listeners' Association. Others included the more libertarian Television and Radio Committee, under the leadership of Professor Richard Hoggart, and a group with a special interest in educational broadcasting, the Television Viewers' Council. But British television (and, to a much lesser extent, radio) was also beginning to attract the attention of academics. The key date is 1959, when Joseph Trenaman left the BBC's Further Education Unit to become the first holder of the Granada Research Fellowship in Television at Leeds University. Soon after, the Centre for Mass Communication Research was founded at Leicester University, and degree programmes in media studies began to sprout at polytechnics and at other universities during the 1970s and 1980s. Since then a substantial amount of empirical work has been done by researchers like David Morley and Roger Silverstone on the identity, behaviour and tastes of television audiences. It has been established, for instance, that whereas women incline towards comedies, soap operas, dramas, romantic movies and quiz shows, men prefer news and current affairs, science and documentary programmes, action and adventure movies and sport. But Morley (1992: 146) also observes that whereas for men the home is primarily a place of relaxation and leisure, it is a sphere of work for women, even those who have jobs outside it. This means that while men watch television in a continuous and attentive way, women's viewing is often intermittent and informed by a sense of guilt; and because it is less premeditated than men's, women do not make nearly as much use of the VCR to record television output.

In spite of the early optimism of academics, the questions which have been raised by audience research have proved impossibly difficult, yielding few certain answers. For this reason I do not intend to offer an historical account of a field which Colin Seymour-Ure (1996: xii) with his usual metaphorical flair describes as 'too much like an ancient map of the world: large wastes of conjecture punctuated by occasional islands of knowledge'. I shall merely sketch some of the problems it raises before suggesting the ways in which TV *seems* to be an influential medium and the ways in which it does not.

Although a major challenge is to identify influences and effects, it is by no means a straightforward matter even to identify the audience:

> If a valid comparison might be made with the theatre audience – where a specifiable group of people are gathered together in one place to give their attention to a live performance – the parallel with watching television or listening to the radio becomes less clear. Here, consumption is geographically dispersed across a multitude of settings and frequently in competition with other practices as a consequence of its embedding in day-to-day social life. It becomes harder to specify exactly where media audiences begin and end. The conditions and boundaries of audiencehood are inherently unstable.
>
> (Moores 1993: 2)

The difficulty of identifying an audience is particularly acute in the case of radio since radio listening is almost always secondary to some other activity. How far are the listeners paying attention, and does the strength of radio's influence on them bear any relation to the degree of their attentiveness (Crisell 1994: 221–3)?

But even if we can agree on what we mean by a television audience, the question of influences and effects is altogether more complex. It is almost impossible to separate the effects of TV from those of the other media, which is why it makes more sense to talk about 'media' rather than 'television' effects. But then it is equally difficult to distinguish media effects from those of other social phenomena such as personal relationships, education and general life experiences. Moreover, media material is not homogeneous: while some of it has originated in the media much of it is merely a reflection of what has come from society (McQuail 2000: 416). In other words, what we may take to be an instance of the media's influence on us may actually be an instance of our influence on the media.

Yet even if we could be sure that we had clearly identified a 'television influence', how could we measure it? An individual programme such as a play or political debate might be highly influential yet have different influences on different viewers because it embraces different, even conflicting, values. If we could assume that the viewers were able to describe these influences, how could their differing subjective judgments be compared? Influences on the one hand and viewers' needs and motives on the other are in any case likely to be multi-layered. Beneath the wish for news and entertainment lie deeper needs – for companionship, escape, excitement, romantic or erotic pleasure. The enormous difficulties they face mean that audience studies have tended to oscillate between a focus on 'powerful media' on the one hand – their content and the 'dominant' meanings they impose; and 'powerful audiences' on the other – their autonomy and activeness and their 'oppositional', or at least critically alert, interpretations of media content (Livingstone 1990: 8; Abercrombie 1996: 201–4).

So just how influential might television be? Although the medium is our main concern here, and although it probably commands the most enthusiasm and attention from the public, we need to remember that TV acts in concert with several other media – radio, books, newspapers, magazines, cinema films, CDs and tapes, videos – and that it is therefore more useful to speak of media effects as a whole. In some ways the media seem hugely influential:

We dress for the weather as forecast, buy something because of an advertisement, go to a film mentioned in a newspaper, react in countless ways to media news, to films, to music on the radio, and so on. There are many reported cases of negative media publicity concerning, for instance, food contamination or adulteration, leading to significant changes in food consumption behaviour, sometimes with large economic impact. Acts of violence or suicide appear to be copied or stimulated by media portrayals. Much policy and regulation is directed at preventing the media from causing harm.

Our minds are full of media-dominated information and impressions. We live in a world saturated by media sounds and images, where politics, government and business operate on the assumption that we know what is going on in the wider world. Few of us cannot think of some personal instance of gaining significant information or of forming an opinion because of the media.

(McQuail 2000: 416)

Moreover, in spite of the recent resurgence of nationalism in the world and the renewed emphasis on local distinctions, we are everywhere watching the same programmes, and thanks largely to the life-styles promoted by such programmes and by TV commercials, eating the same food, singing the same songs, and wearing the same clothes. And though we must always remember that the media follow as well as set trends, it is clear that we are highly susceptible to those media messages we like: to new fashions in clothes, to the fantasies offered or implied by much advertising, to new slang and speech patterns (usually American), to pop music, and changes in sexual mores. But we may also be highly susceptible to messages we do *not* like. We are easily incensed by veal exports or new motorways, and the emotive images of television can quickly implant in us 'moral panics' about violence, public order, education, diet or disease. Yet in many other ways media influences seem trivial, transient, even non-existent. Most individual programmes appear to have negligible effects, not least because they are rapidly superseded by others, day after day and over umpteen channels. Even moral panics are often as fleeting as they are intense, for the restless, roving eye of TV constantly throws up fresh concerns, relatively few of which effect a permanent change in behaviour. Moreover, TV and the other media may tell us a great deal about commercial products or politicians, for instance, but unless we are already inclined to, they are unlikely to make us buy the former or vote for the latter. And despite its largely good intentions, constant TV exposure has demystified the royal family and others who occupy positions of status or authority, making us hold them in rather less respect than before. While this is not, perhaps, the *intended* influence of television it is still an influence of sorts.

If familiarity with public figures has meant that we regard them with a certain lack of respect, familiarity with television has also bred a kind of contempt for the medium itself. The way in which we watch it has probably changed from the early years of rapt viewing to varying degrees of passivity and fitfulness – a tendency which was strengthened by the arrival of the remote controller, since this allows the easy 'zapping' of uninteresting material and the practice of 'channel surfing'. These newer viewing patterns must surely make the medium less influential than it was, or at least less influential than it might be.

On the other hand, it is possible that we underestimate media effects merely because they are not discernible over short periods of time. In the last thirty years or so there has been a veritable sea change in certain social attitudes, to which television and the other media have surely contributed: attitudes to the environment, to women and sexual issues, to race and ethnicity. We might describe this as the 'drip, drip' effect of the mass media. One recent theory of media influences is that whereas they may be reduced or even negated by 'personal meaning structures' they are likely to be stronger with respect to matters which are generally outside our experience, such as wars and famine – that is, where the media are our *sole* sources of information (McQuail 2000: 420–2). But so ambiguous is the evidence about influences and effects that the only safe conclusion we can reach was formulated more than fifty years ago: 'some kinds of communication, on some kinds of issues, brought to the attention of some kinds of people, under some kinds of conditions, have some kinds of effects' (McQueen 1998: 189).

It was suggested earlier that much TV output consists of entertainment – in effect if not in intention – and that one apparent consequence of this has been an extension of the 'entertainment imperative' into other spheres of activity such as news, education, even religious worship. There seems to be a common if tacit belief that it is almost impossible to inform, teach or edify without at the same time providing amusement or diversion of some kind. Since TV is often entertaining whether it wishes to be or not, the early fears that viewing would encroach on children's study-time and result in them reading fewer books – part of the rationale behind the 'toddlers' truce' – were probably well founded. A recent study by the Organization for Economic Cooperation and Development found that Britain has more television addicts than any other country in the developed world, yet is lagging badly in advanced literacy – and that these facts are related (Ezard 2000: 3). Some teachers are certainly worried that even for older pupils reading is a difficult and by no means habitual or congenial activity. If television could supply all the benefits of the print medium this would matter little, but print is able to perform certain vital intellectual tasks which are beyond TV.

Sources/further reading

For much material in this chapter I must acknowledge a substantial debt to Seymour-Ure (1996). He is illuminating on the interrelationship of the mass media, even more so on the comprehensive way in which television has invaded many areas of modern life and often modified them to suit its own requirements. See Whannel (1990) and Blain and Boyle (1998) for some helpful remarks on the way in which television interacts with sport.

There is a thoughtful account of the first forty years of broadcasting and politics in Goldie (1977), and Scannell (1979) is enlightening on TV and politics before 1956. A comprehensive account of the relationship between the mass media and the political process is in Golding, Murdock and Schlesinger (1986). Barendt (1998) is helpful on broadcasting and the notion of impartiality. Among the many other works on the media and politics Tunstall (1983) is brightly written and perceptive, and Negrine (1994) is also useful – particularly on the question of balance and on the nature and behaviour of political pressure groups. Riddell (1998) suggests that decreasing media interest in the proceedings of Parliament has led to its apparent decline in importance, while Gaber (1998) insists that politicians rather than the media continue to set the political agenda. Both Wernick (1991) and McNair (1998) consider the promotional aspect of the political process.

For an account of the fourteen-day rule and of TV's role in the Rochdale by-election see Sendall (1982). A full discussion of the Suez crisis and the other events of 1956 can be found in Briggs (1995). Schlesinger (1978) is still the authoritative work on the BBC's news production and is particularly illuminating on its coverage of the conflict in Northern Ireland. I must again cite Seymour-Ure (1996) for a concise and lucid perspective on the more recent relationship between television and politics – an account which manages to be balanced, yet colourful and witty. Pimlott (1998) outlines the relationships between royalty and the media, while Russell (1999) offers a brief discussion of the 'Diana phenomenon'.

An informative account of BBC radio and TV audience research up to the end of the 1960s can be found in Silvey (1974). Potter (1989) discusses the historical development of audience research, and for an account of audience campaign groups see Sendall (1983) and Briggs (1995). Morley (1992) is a highly sophisticated discussion of television audiences which includes a critical history of audience research, an examination of theoretical frameworks, and an exploration of the nature and impact of influences. Another theory of the television audience is offered by Silverstone (1994). Moores (1993, 2000) is helpful on the nature and behaviour of media audiences, as is McQuail (2000), who also outlines the range and complexity of the possible influences on them. Corner (1995) points to some of the problems involved in audience analysis, and Cumberbatch and Howitt (1989) and Lewis (1990) indicate the difficulties of measuring media influences and effects. For an account of the OECD study of the relationship between TV viewing and levels of literacy see Ezard (2000).

Chapter 10

A growth of sights and sounds

A growth of sights and sounds

'A peevish decade'

During the 1970s the mood which had characterized the 1960s seemed to darken. There remained that scepticism of authority and of traditional values and institutions which television had almost certainly helped to create. But it was now less genial and relaxed, more serious and militant – a change which was doubtless both a cause and a consequence of the economic and political crises that were developing in many parts of the world. There were new variations on, and additions to, the longstanding antagonism between commmunist East and capitalist West. Politics became more radical, resulting in a leftward shift of the entire spectrum of opinion, and there seemed to be a much greater preoccupation with class conflict and the rights of minorities than with social cohesiveness and interdependence.

The horrific drama of Vietnam continued to play before the TV cameras, and there were many other wars, too. There was also an upsurge in political assassinations, kidnappings and terrorist attacks. There seemed to be developing an unprecedented though by no means universal acceptance that extreme or violent measures were the only ways in which certain causes could be advanced.

Britain had its own generous share of strikes, sit-ins, lock-outs, occupations, demonstrations, pressure and splinter groups, and acts of terrorism – most of the last emanating from a conflict in Northern Ireland whose roots went down through centuries. But on top of all this, the country experienced deep economic difficulties in the late 1960s and throughout the 1970s: industrial stoppages were so common-place and inflation so rampant that Britain became known as 'the sick man of Europe'. In October 1973 Egypt and Syria suddenly made war on Israel and were just as suddenly defeated. The Arab oil-producing states took revenge on the world economy, and by the end of 1974 the price of oil had quadrupled. As Britain struggled to cope with this crisis, the National Union of Mineworkers called a strike. In February 1974 the Conservative government introduced public expenditure cuts, together with a three-day week to save electricity and a 50 m.p.h. speed limit to save petrol. To escape being held to ransom, it called an election for the end of that month on the issue 'Who governs Britain?'. But the public was less sure of the answer than the government had hoped, especially when that magisterial renegade Enoch Powell attacked Britain's membership of the European Economic Community (it had joined on 1 January 1973), condemned its policy on Northern Ireland, and exhorted the electorate to vote Labour.

The broadcasting organizations, and the BBC especially, were in an invidious position between the government and its many opponents and critics. Labour won the election, but by a whisker, scarcely consolidating its position when it held another in October of the same year. Nor were its answers to the problems of the time much better than the Tories'. Prices continued to rise: overall they trebled during the 1970s. In 1977 alone, 1 million working days were lost in strikes. In 1979 a 'dirty jobs' dispute disrupted schools, hospitals and ambulances, closed mortuaries and put a stop to refuse collection. Although, as we shall see shortly, both broadcasters produced surprisingly good programmes in such a troubled era, they were inevitably afflicted by the same difficulties as everybody else. The BBC's economic state was a microcosm of the nation's. Inflation devoured its licence fee, necessitating cuts in transmission hours and new programme projects. In reflecting contemporary issues it was always more vulnerable to the main political parties than ITV was, and managed to fall foul of both opposition and government. In June 1971 its current affairs magazine *Twenty-four Hours* broadcast a special feature entitled *Yesterday's Men*, which explored what it had been like for members of the Labour government to lose high office so unexpectedly in the 1970 general election. By using music and cartoons the feature injudiciously blended documentary with satire. The following evening insult was added to injury in the form of a programme called *Mr Heath's Quiet Revolution*, a sober and entirely respectful assessment of the Conservative government's first year in office. The Labour opposition was incensed. However, in January 1972 the government was offended when the BBC ignored its advice to withhold a documentary on *The Question of Ulster*. The programme reached, and mostly impressed, 7.5 million viewers.

On the other hand, the corporation did not greatly fear internal labour disputes because strikes saved it money. Not so the ITV contractors, who were confronted by strong trade unions. For ITV, stoppages meant an instant loss of advertising revenue. Moreover, in dealing with disputes the contractors were unable to play a long game because their franchises were scheduled to last for only a few years, with no guarantee of a renewal. Indeed, a renewal was unlikely if strikes took them off air for long spells during their existing franchise period. The worst strike in ITV's history blacked out the entire network for eleven weeks, from 10 August to

19 October 1979. As was usually the case, the cause was a rejected wage claim, but the strike itself cost the contractors £100 million and the huge pay rise which settled it was a victory for the unions. Yet the golden goose was already looking sickly, for by slimming the contractors' workforces and creating more freelance and casual labour, the arrival of new technologies and the growth of independent production houses would soon help to loosen the unions' hold.

The launch of independent local radio

To the surprise of the opinion pollsters the Conservatives regained power in the 1970 general election, and the new government was keen to give commercial interests the opportunity to exploit radio just as they had been able to exploit television since 1955. It saw three main merits in a system of commercial radio: first, it would enlarge audience choice; second, it would be 'free' to the listener; third, it would provide an economic stimulus by allowing business to run stations, and advertisers a new medium through which to promote their products. Hence in 1972 the Sound Broadcasting Act established a system of independent local radio (ILR) which would run pretty much in parallel with that of ITV. The ITA was renamed the Independent Broadcasting Authority (IBA) and appointed to regulate both. But why was it a system of *local* radio?

Although some medium-wave frequencies were allocated to help launch ILR, the modern technology of VHF/FM would allow a large number of stations on to the spectrum, every one of them offering good reception. Thus not only was the system a bow towards the political fashion for 'localism', it maximized the broadcasting opportunities for aspiring station operators and advertisers. Moreover, it provided direct competition against BBC local radio, which had already opened about twenty stations.

The ILR stations operated under similar statutory controls to the ITV contractors. The IBA selected the companies (which could be part owned by newspapers, but not by the ITV contractors within their respective areas); it owned the transmitters, for which the companies paid a rent; and it enforced acceptable standards of content and balance. As with ITV it drew an absolute distinction between programme content and advertising: sponsorship was not allowed.

The first two ILR stations opened in London in October 1973: Capital Radio, which has always been among the most successful, and LBC, which adopted a news-and-talk format. LBC also provided a news service, Independent Radio News, to the other ILR stations. The ILR system spread through the United Kingdom fairly rapidly. By 1977 there were nineteen stations, by 1983 forty-three stations covering more than 80 per cent of the population. It was anticipated that they would be very profitable, but for the first two decades of their existence they were not. There were even some mergers and closures. Why?

Three main reasons suggest themselves. First, the stations' launch coincided with a major economic recession which lasted until the early 1980s, thus depressing advertising revenue. Second, it coincided with stiffening competition from other media. Even the growing market in audio-cassettes was something of a threat because many receivers were now radio-cassette players, making it just as easy for the aspiring listener to turn on a tape as to switch on the radio. News updates had long been one of radio's strengths, but from 1974 the audience could get these when it required them and not when radio was ready to provide them – by turning on teletext. Breakfast was always one of radio's peak listening times, but from 1983 breakfast television could be watched instead.

The third reason was the most serious. The ILR stations were too tightly regulated by the IBA, which was itself constrained by a government that had still not grasped the fact that radio was no longer used in the way it had been before the arrival of television and transistors. Only a tiny number of listeners now expected the medium to provide the varied range of programmes that characterized TV: most merely sought music and news as secondary listening. Yet under the Sound Broadcasting Act the IBA required from each station a 'balance of programming' (including the provision of substantial – and inevitably costly – news bulletins) which was a vestige of the old public service ideal. If there was not to be old-fashioned mixed programming, there must at any rate be 'cross-community appeal' – if appropriate, access, or at least output, for ethnic minorities. Thus, as Stephen Barnard (1989: 75) observes: 'In effect, each of the ILR stations outside London had to provide the full range of BBC services within a smaller, localized framework, and entirely from commercial resources.' Moreover, with the arguable exception of Radio 4, not one of the traditional BBC networks now attempted to provide such a range of services.

As a result of the duties which were placed on it, ILR acquired an assortment of listeners of different backgrounds and tastes, but no individual group of sufficient size to attract much advertising interest. As Barnard (1989: 80) again points out, the very terms of the IBA franchise precluded the ILR stations from targeting those groups most sought by advertisers. To try to get round this problem the stations couched their public service material in the form of interviews, announcements, bulletins and short features which were sprinkled within the overall music-and-entertainment format of the sequence programme, but the strategy was not wholly successful. Barnard also observes that the IBA's regulatory zeal tended to vary with the government in office. Under the Labour regime of 1974–9 it got tough with stations who put profit before public service, and in 1979 awarded franchises to two community-based consortia, Cardiff Broadcasting and Midlands Community Radio (Coventry). Neither survived in that form.

Programme pageant

The de-restriction of television broadcasting hours in 1972 took both ITV and the BBC by surprise, and they proceeded cautiously. Yet despite – perhaps even because of – the economic and political gloom of the decade, they produced some excellent programmes of all types. According to Jeremy Potter (1989: 82), serious programming on ITV increased both absolutely and relatively during the 1970s.

One form of serious programming which was vitally important to both broadcasters was, of course, news – and for foreign news the decade was particularly eventful and turbulent. There were wars in the Middle East, Bangladesh, Cyprus, Vietnam (culminating in the US withdrawal); there was the American presidential scandal of Watergate; there were hijackings and political kidnappings; the overthrow of the Shah of Iran and the resurgence of Islam; a peripatetic papacy; conflict between Iran and Iraq, and between the Soviet Union and Afghanistan. Fortunately new technology arrived to cover these events more effectively, and the 1973 Yom Kippur War marked the point when television could end the press's lingering dominance in foreign news by providing up-to-date pictures. ITN obtained film of the earliest fighting and beamed it to London via the satellite station at Tel Aviv so that it could be shown on the same day's edition of *News at Ten*.

From the second half of the decade electronic news-gathering (ENG) made TV's news coverage even quicker and more flexible. ENG units were small cameras which used magnetic tape instead of conventional film. No processing was needed, editing was simple and the technical quality was better than film's. By the mid-1980s ITN would have its first transportable ground satellite station, and the increasing miniaturization of cameras and other equipment allowed editing and dubbing on site. Live two-way updates with the newscaster in the studio would also become possible (Bonner with Aston 1998: 221).

In the equally serious categories of arts programmes and documentaries the BBC maintained a steady output but ITV could also boast some great achievements. *The World at War*, a major series on the Second World War, was launched by Thames in 1973, and in that year Yorkshire TV showed *Too Long a Winter*, a moving documentary about Hannah Hauxwell, a lone subsistence farmer living high in the Pennines. From 1978 LWT's *The South Bank Show*, which was fronted by Melvyn Bragg, consistently achieved the difficult feat of presenting the arts in a way which was both serious and 'accessible'.

Drama and comedy seem to be a good measure of the health of broadcasting because although less 'serious' than news and current affairs they are often less ephemeral, too. In this respect the 1970s bear comparison with any other decade in the history of television, and from a historical perspective series and serials are always more conspicuous than single plays or shows. Period dramas opened the decade: the BBC gave us *The Six Wives of Henry VIII*, while Granada portrayed

A Family at War, and from 1971 to 1977 *Upstairs Downstairs* (LWT) explored life among the servants of an aristocratic Edwardian household. A little later in the decade *When the Boat Comes In* (BBC) showed scenes of Geordie hardship during the inter-war years, and Yorkshire TV launched its first soap opera, *Emmerdale Farm*. Not long after, some tough battles were fought by the hard-nosed cops and robbers of *The Sweeney* (ATV). In mid-decade three serials were marked by high ambitions, albeit of very different kinds. The first was Yorkshire TV's *South Riding* (1974), a sensitive and highly praised adaptation of Winifred Holtby's novel of Yorkshire life. The second was *A Bouquet of Barbed Wire* (LWT, 1976) by Andrea Newman – as Sean Day-Lewis (1992: 35) puts it, 'the first of her televisual explorations of sexuality that gave the pleasures as much space as the tears that follow'. And the third was the BBC's dramatization of Robert Graves's historical novel *I, Claudius* (1976), which included a phenomenal performance by Derek Jacobi as the eponymous Roman Emperor. A very different yet even more popular adaptation was *All Creatures Great and Small* (BBC, 1977) – from James Herriot's stories of a veterinary surgeon working in the Yorkshire Dales. High standards were maintained to the end of the decade with *Edward and Mrs Simpson*, starring Edward Fox, John Mortimer's *Rumpole of the Bailey* (both Thames, 1978), and an extraordinary serial, *Pennies from Heaven* (BBC, 1978), which was set in the 1930s and written by Dennis Potter. This was a popular and highly original blend of allegory, parable, autobiography, and musical sequences mimed to the popular songs of the period – a rare and successful attempt to break away from the tyrannous naturalism of television drama.

We should note two important trends which occurred in TV drama during the 1970s. The first was the development of co-productions between one or other of the British broadcasting organizations and a foreign partner. Their obvious advantages were that they could be more ambitious and lavish because they could raise more funding and find bigger audiences. The international television market was now growing rapidly, creating an unprecedented demand for quality programmes. Co-productions provoked an interesting debate within the BBC. Aubrey Singer, the Controller of BBC 2, thought them a straightforwardly beneficial way of cutting costs and expanding markets, whereas the Managing Director of Television, Huw Wheldon, believed that they compromised the integrity and editorial independence of a non-commercial organization which continued to regard itself as the only genuine public service broadcaster.

The second and more disquieting trend was the decline of the single play. For obvious reasons drama is one of the most expensive forms of television programming, and as we noted in Chapter 5 new recording technologies and the cinematic mode of production they allowed could offset costs by enabling several episodes of a series or serial to be shot together. During the 1970s, an era of high inflation, the cost of a single play became almost prohibitive. It was also a high-risk venture because many viewers were now unused to the conventional theatre and therefore to the need to absorb plot, situation and character fairly rapidly. Finally, and a consideration of increasing importance at this time, the single play was difficult to package and sell in the export market.

The single play posed a problem for both broadcasters, but as one might expect it was greater for ITV, whose need to win a large audience and keep costs down was more acute. One compromise it tried was to 'anthologize' the single play – to make it part of a themed series such as *Love Story* or *Tales of the Unexpected*. One triumphant example of a play which was not part of a series was Philip Mackie's *The Naked Civil Servant* (Thames, 1975), a brilliantly witty portrait of the famous homosexual Quentin Crisp. But there was no disguising its growing rarity. In 1969–70 ITV screened 112 single plays; in 1979–80 it showed 13.

The BBC fought a stronger rearguard action against the trend, featuring works by Alan Bennett, Trevor Griffiths, John Mortimer, Peter Nichols, Dennis Potter and William Trevor – a small yet striking instance of what could be regarded as a public service. There were two strong reasons why the single play could not be allowed to disappear from television. The first was that it was a form which made intellectual demands on the audience and created aesthetic satisfactions that could not be derived from the series or serial. Though many of the latter were undoubtedly serious and ambitious in nature, their forms, in allowing the audience rather longer to assimilate plot, situation and character, were potentially less disciplined and liable to admit what were at certain levels less challenging kinds of drama. The single play was a concentrated form of expression in which the dramatist was obliged to make his artistic statement within a single 'sitting' – a statement which the audience took a special pleasure in seeking to understand. The second reason for preserving the single play was that it was the only form which drama took in the traditional theatre, where the series and serial were unknown. To abandon it would therefore be to deny the television audience access to all the major dramatists of the past – Euripides, Shakespeare, Ibsen, Chekhov and so on – not to mention those of the present, like Alan Ayckbourn, Alan Bennett and Tom Stoppard, who also wished to write single plays. Hence, even though the series and the serial were much more cost-effective, and even though they had in certain respects enlarged and enriched the traditional perception of drama, the loss of the single play would mean a real impoverishment of television content.

There was also an abundance of excellent comic drama, notably *The Good Life*, *Fawlty Towers* and *Porridge* (all BBC) and *Rising Damp* (Yorkshire TV). The year 1979 marked the beginning of outstanding comedy series on both BBC and ITV. *Minder* (Thames) was about the relationship between Arthur Daley, an endearing spiv played by George Cole, and his gullible bodyguard, Terry McCann (Dennis Waterman). Critics might now look back on it as an ironic prologue to the frenziedly entrepreneurial Thatcher years. *Yes, Minister* (BBC), by Anthony Jay and Jonathan

Lynn, concerned the manipulation of cabinet ministers by self-interested civil servants, and was enriched by the viewers' suspicion that what they were watching was unhealthily close to real life.

In addition to these first-rate comedy dramas there was much good comedy which was not dramatic in form. On the BBC, *The Two Ronnies* – Barker and Corbett – delighted audiences from 1971, while from 1973 *That's Life*, presented by Esther Rantzen, offered an original mixture of serious consumerism and comic features. ATV scored a huge success with *The Muppet Show* (1976), and two years later graduate humour was brought to a large BBC audience in *Not the Nine O'Clock News*. During the long ITV strike of 1979 the BBC was able to use two quiz shows, *The Generation Game* and *Blankety Blank*, to secure especially large audiences.

The Annan Committee

Ever since the BBC had been awarded the third channel, there had been a general understanding that the government would soon allocate a fourth – and a further assumption, most consistently made by the Conservatives, that once it had put its house in order after the strictures of Pilkington, the ITA would run the channel in symmetrical continuance of the duopoly.

That assumption was much less common on the parliamentary Left, where there was talk of giving the channel to the BBC to transmit programmes for the proposed Open University; and it was Labour who came to power in 1964. However, in 1966 the government announced that because of other priorities it would defer the allocation of a fourth channel until 1969. In that year the allocation was again deferred because of the financial difficulties of ITV, which had to be regarded as at least a contender for such a channel. The following year, retaining its natural suspicion of commercial television, the Labour government decided that the whole future of broadcasting in the United Kingdom merited a committee of inquiry and appointed Lord Annan as its head.

Annan was certainly not predisposed to give the channel to ITV, believing that this would simply intensify competition for the mass audience and result in a neglect of minorities. However, 1970 was also the year of a general election and before his committee could be appointed the Conservatives were returned to power. Seeing no need of Annan and his committee they adjourned it indefinitely, resolving to open up sound broadcasting to commercial competition before settling the question of the fourth TV channel. But before they could do so, the country was once more in crisis, there was another election, and Labour resumed office in 1974. The Annan Committee was promptly reconvened by the Home Secretary Roy Jenkins and began work in March of that year. While its report was awaited and then debated, the life of the IBA and its contractors was prolonged to 1976 – and then it and the BBC's charter were extended to 1979, and finally to 1981.

However, the climate had changed since 1970. To Labour's distrust of ITV was added, after the affair of *Yesterday's Men*, a distrust of the BBC. And outside Parliament there were strident attacks on both broadcasters, mostly though not entirely from the political Left. ITV was a predictable target of ideologues, whether students, academic media theorists or trade unionists, not so much for the quality of its programmes as for its connections with big business, the size of its profits, its preoccupation with ratings, the evils of its advertising, and for the concentration of media ownership into the hands of a few large companies. But the BBC also came under fire for its arrogance and its social and cultural élitism.

The mood of the 1970s was typified by the various radical pressure groups: the Free Communications Group, the 76 Group (some disaffected BBC and ITV producers), and the Standing Conference on Broadcasting. All had ostensibly democratic aims: to widen public access to the production side of broadcasting (in an astute public relations move the BBC formed its Community Programmes Unit in 1972); and/or to increase the public accountability of broadcasters. In the latter aim they were joined by an unlikely ally from the Right: Mrs Whitehouse's National Viewers' and Listeners' Association, which attacked both broadcasters, but especially the BBC for its 'permissive' programming and contempt for the moral majority. Despite their differing perspectives, then, the one thing on which all these groups were agreed was that the broadcasters were out of control, answerable neither to the people nor even to their elected representatives – and therefore that the fourth channel should go neither to ITV nor the BBC. The duopoly should be broken, especially as the imminent technologies of cable and satellite could provide a range of choice and specialization which would bring broadcasting somewhat closer to the less restricted world of newspaper and magazine publishing.

With these views Annan was largely in sympathy. The extent and vehemence of the broadcasting debate made it clear that from now on only a modified version of public service broadcasting would be sustainable: the provision of 'something for everyone' over a range of channels. It will be recalled that from about the time of the Pilkington Report, with two TV networks already in existence and a third one promised, the complementary notion of 'everything for someone', of universal programme provision on a single radio or television network, was quietly abandoned. But this modified notion of public service was not simply a response to technology, to a growth in the number of channels. It was based on society's changing perception of itself in the 1960s and 1970s, just as Reith's original theory had been based on how society perceived itself in the 1920s. Reith could scarcely have formed his theory had he not shared the prevalent view of a coherent if stratified society imbued with a certain sense of mutual obligation and a consensual idea of cultural and artistic value which emanated from its élite. The new notion, on the other hand, posited a more heterogeneous society (in part a product of the different ethnic influxes of the post-war decades), each of whose elements had its own view of the world and its own concept of what was culturally significant. ('Multi-culturalism' was a word which would soon gain wide currency.) Annan believed that the role of public service broadcasting was to embody all these views:

> Our society's culture is now multi-racial and pluralist: that is to say, people adhere to different views of the nature and purpose of life and expect their own view to be expressed in some form or other. The structure of broadcasting should reflect this variety.
>
> (Annan 1977: 30)

It was no longer for broadcasters merely to relay an élitist view of cultural value or to seek to expose the audience to the whole range of output. 'We do not accept that it is part of the broadcasters' function to act as arbiters of morals or manners, or set themselves up as social engineers' (Annan quoted in McDonnell 1991: 68). Their duty was simply to cater for as many tastes and interests as possible. How far the viewer chose to indulge her particular interests to the exclusion of others and how far she chose to lay herself open to the full range of output was entirely a matter for her. Hence, in one sense public service broadcasting was the same as before – a matter of universal provision, of something for everyone. But after Annan its ideological underpinning would be very different from, indeed the opposite of, Reith's. For the latter it was social cement; for the former a reflection of social differences.

The committee sat for three years and presented its report in March 1977. There was a widespread feeling that its deliberations were better than its recommendations, all 174 of them. *The Times* described the report as 'a fair audit but a weak blueprint'. Part of the problem was that the committee seems to have reflected the spirit of the time in being riven by internal disagreements. Consequently its recommendations bore the marks of compromise and were not always consistent with its findings or conclusions. The heart of its difficulty was that its two main aims – to extend and diversify broadcasting services and to provide for greater public control and access – were ultimately conflicting. In order to liberate broadcasting from the straitjacket of duopoly it merely proposed an increase in the number of bureaucracies which would control it. Its main recommendations were as follows:

- The existing ITV system should not be awarded a second channel and its governing body, the IBA, should be renamed the Regional Television Authority.
- The new fourth channel should be a network catering for interests and minorities presently ill served by television.
- It should be supervised by an Open Broadcasting Authority which would be modelled along lines suggested by Anthony Smith, an academic and former BBC producer.

- It would not make programmes but be a publisher and commissioner of programmes made by others, and its funding would come from a variety of sources: the Open University, the Arts Council, charities, the Trades Union Congress, the Confederation of British Industry, advertising.
- The duopoly of the BBC and the IBA would also be broken at local level. A Local Broadcasting Authority, partly financed by advertising, would control all local radio, together with the new field of cable TV.
- There should be further regulatory bodies: a Public Enquiry Board, a Broadcasting Complaints Commission, a Telecommunications Advisory Committee.

To 'open up' broadcasting the Annan Report was thus proposing a veritable thicket of authorities, commissions and committees. It nevertheless met with the broad approval of those who had called for it. In 1978 the government announced its intention to allocate a fourth channel, and in the following year that the channel would begin broadcasting in November 1982 and be administered by an Open Broadcasting Authority. Nevertheless, Labour lost the 1979 election to the Conservatives, and as so often happens with public committees, the recommendations of Annan, so lengthily and laboriously arrived at, were lightly set aside by the politicians. The Tories simply placed the fourth channel in the hands of the IBA; though, as we shall see, under an arrangement which reflected Annan's general concern to diversify both the sources of programme production and the kinds of programmes viewers could hope to watch.

New ITV franchises and the arrival of breakfast television

After the Annan Report had been published and discussed, the ITV franchises fell due for renewal in 1980. The previous period, which had quite unexpectedly run for an unprecedented thirteen and a half years, had been one of very mixed fortunes for the companies. The lack of contractual upheavals, which was partly thanks to the delay in appointing Annan's committee, gave ITV a healthy continuity that was expressed in many programmes of high quality. On the other hand, it suffered recurrent and often damaging industrial disputes and from a chronic inflation which was only partly offset when in 1974 the government switched its levy from ITV's income to its profits.

The new contracts would run until the end of 1989 (in 1981 the BBC's charter was renewed for another ten years) and the changes which were made in 1980 were as much determined by the technicalities of shareholding and the contractors' sources of investment as by programme quality, which would remain fairly consistent during the next ten years or so. In the Midlands ATV disappeared into a new contractor, Central Television, while TV South replaced Southern Television and Television South West replaced Westward. Tyne Tees and Yorkshire TV were once again split into two strictly separate companies.

However, the 1980 franchise round contained one novelty. Ever since 1972, when restrictions on transmission hours were lifted, breakfast television had been blocked by the broadcasting unions' demand for 'golden payments'. The IBA now decided to offer a separate contract for a national service, 'primarily of news, information and current affairs' (Potter 1990: 328), to be transmitted between six and nine-fifteen every morning of the week. It attracted no less than eight different bids, and in an extraordinary re-run of events which had occurred in the previous franchise round, the contract went to a group named TV-AM.

Like LWT back in 1968, TV-AM was a consortium of stars which included David Frost. Its others were Peter Jay, Robert Kee, Angela Rippon, Michael Parkinson and Anna Ford. As LWT had, it bewitched the authority not only with the calibre of its personnel but with the seriousness of its programming ambitions. It believed that programme-makers, not financial institutions, should drive the new service, and it brought to news and current affairs 'a mission to explain'. Like LWT, it was quickly damaged by populist competition from the BBC – and again like LWT, it had to be rescued by an Australian businessman whose programming instincts were surer than those of the 'professionals'.

Jeremy Potter asserts that the IBA should have seen the danger signs in TV-AM: an over-intellectual approach to breakfast programming, no named chief executive, and too many stars with a say in company policy. It was two years before the company went to air – on 1 February 1983 – and even then it was trumped by the BBC, which launched its own much lighter breakfast service a fortnight earlier. TV-AM's failure to win an audience brought it by way of the usual sequence of dismissals, recriminations and resignations to the brink of bankruptcy, at which point it was bailed out not by Rupert Murdoch this time but by his compatriot Kerry Packer.

Ultimately a rat saved the sinking ship, for as his chief executive Packer installed Bruce Gyngell, and as his major star Gyngell installed Roland Rat, a puppet. The new company was hugely successful, but as Potter (1990: 335) ruefully remarks, one to which the IBA in its search for a serious and informative service would never have awarded a contract in 1980. The re-launch resulted in an enduring impression of breakfast television as a blend of the bland and the trite, its central symbol the sofa on which the presenters sat simpering at the cameras, their guests and each other.

However, breakfast TV was significant for two reasons. First it marked a further assimilation of television to the daily routines of the public, and thus contributed to that weakening of the distinction between work and leisure which, thanks to new technologies and their impact on the nature and patterns of employment, has become an important feature of modern life. Whether watched by those preparing to go to work or those who were unemployed or on part-time or shift work, breakfast TV was an acknowledgment that leisure was no longer a clearly demarcated period in the evening but a state which might occupy any part of the day. Second, the new service ate into radio audiences at what was traditionally a peak listening time. It was estimated that in 1983–4 radio's early morning audience declined by 10 per cent.

The launch of Channel 4

In different ways Channel 4 marked the end of one broadcasting era and the beginning of another. As Brian Wenham (1982: 15) points out, it was the last terrestrial channel to be established before the arrival of cable and satellite during the 1980s. Stephen Lambert (1982: 2) observes that it was also the first terrestrial channel whose birth did not require new viewing hardware because the facility to receive it had been included in all TV sets made since the late 1960s. When it went to air on 2 November 1982 it was already within reach of 87 per cent of the population. This meant that debate about the channel could focus on what purpose it should serve, who should run it, and how it should be funded.

The IBA had always argued that the fourth channel should be integrated with the existing ITV network, and in 1979 it neatly adapted Annan's recommendations to its own purposes by proposing that it rather than a new 'Open Broadcasting Authority' should run the fourth channel. The incoming Conservative government agreed and simply handed it to the IBA. However, an unforeseen difficulty was raised by pressure groups who campaigned for a separate channel for Wales, threatening civil disobedience and hunger strikes if they failed to get their way. The government capitulated, setting up a separate Welsh authority, S4C – Sianel Pedwar Cymru – which would be supplied with programmes not only from the IBA but, if S4C so desired, from the BBC.

In spite of these divergencies from the report, Channel 4 was to embody some of Annan's key ideas. It would be commercially funded yet offer its own version of 'public service', and to this end a radically new structure was devised for it which would herald a new era of television broadcasting. The channel would sell no advertising of its own, but be funded by subscriptions from the ITV contractors commensurate with their rental payments. However, each contractor would sell Channel 4's advertising within its own region and keep the proceeds.

It must be remembered that commercial television, and not just the BBC, has in theory always been bound by public service principles, especially since Pilkington. Yet while ITV has from time to time managed to produce serious, high-quality programmes, notably in drama and current affairs, it has generally been recognized that the range of its output will always be restricted by its likely popularity with the audience – a much more vital consideration for commercial than for licence-funded broadcasting. This explains why most discussions about 'public service', in this book as elsewhere, have tended to focus on the BBC.

However, what Channel 4 represented was a first attempt to apply a modified version of the public service concept to the commercial model of broadcasting.

Before Pilkington, public service had consisted of the provision of a full range of programmes on a *single* network. By Annan the concept had been modified to the provision of a full range of programmes over *two or more* networks (for example across BBCs 1 and 2 or Radios 1 to 4). With Channel 4 it would now be modified yet further to the provision not of a full range of programmes but of programmes primarily for *minorities*. Its policy statement announced that the new channel would have 'as a particular charge the service of special interests and concerns for which television has until now lacked adequate time' (McDonnell 1991: 71). This was a much more open declaration of narrowcast intentions than had been made for BBC 2, even though, in order to tempt the wider audience into some of these special interests, the channel followed its older rival in assigning a third of its airtime to material with a popular appeal. The minorities it aimed to serve fell into three broad categories: *cultural* – lovers of opera, ballet, classical music and drama, 'art films', jazz and other kinds of music, serious talks and discussions; *special interest* – enthusiasts of certain sports and hobbies like canoeing or fly-fishing; and *ethnic* – those mostly of Afro-Caribbean and Asian origin, who since the 1950s had become a significant cultural and political presence in Britain.

In some ways the BBC's version of public service broadcasting has been eclipsed by the version which was embodied, for the first ten years or so of its existence, by Channel 4. Though much broader – it seeks to provide something for *everyone* – the former is distinguishable from other kinds of broadcasting only when, like Channel 4's, it serves otherwise neglected minorities. But in a sense public service broadcasting is, and always has been, *only* about programmes for minorities because majority programming is in any system of broadcasting self-funding. Majorities can take care of themselves.

As we have seen, under the BBC's licence system minorities get their own programmes, made as expensively as they need to be made, thanks to part-funding by the majority. These programmes would otherwise be made only in proportion to the size or spending power of those minorities, and therefore be likely to be cheaply and poorly made (much special-interest programming, such as opera, costume drama and documentary, is expensive) – or else they would not get made at all. But Channel 4's public service system went one better by providing expensive, high-quality programmes for minorities which would neither require the majority to part-fund them nor place an impossible financial burden on the minorities themselves. And it could do this because it would be financed not by the viewing public but by the regional companies on the main ITV channel. Its programmes would be paid for by advertisers, but *indirectly* – through a series of institutional and editorial filters. The system was not perfect – some minorities were still unlikely to be served – but it did in its way break that iron link between the quality, or even existence, of programmes and the size or value of their audiences.

Channel 4 was characterized by a second important negative. Not only did the channel not sell its own advertising, it did not even make its own programmes. We have noted that the government entrusted it to the IBA rather than Annan's 'Open Broadcasting Authority'. But the latter had itself grown out of the idea of a 'national television foundation' which had been proposed by Anthony Smith, a research fellow at St Antony's College, Oxford, who had once been a member of the *Tonight* team. The role of the foundation, now assumed by the IBA, was not to produce programmes but *commission* them: to act as a publishing house for outside programme-makers. With this institutional development the history of television recalled that of print, where a somewhat similar division of labour had developed several centuries before between the publishers and those physical producers of books and journals, the printers and binders. The aim of turning Channel 4 into a publisher was to widen creative access to the airwaves and thus improve the quality of programmes for the viewer, for equally significant was the fact that the IBA was required not merely to draw on established programme-makers such as Thames TV or Granada but commission 'a substantial proportion' of material from independent producers. It was to take 35 to 50 per cent of its programmes from the existing ITV contractors; 15 to 35 per cent from the independents; 15 per cent from ITN; and 5 to 14 per cent from foreign sources.

Yet where, under the existing duopoly, would the independent programme-makers come from? The independent sector had begun to flourish in the early 1970s thanks to an expanding overseas market, a growth in demand for industrial training films, and an increased need for TV commercials to fill the extra broadcasting hours. In the event Channel 4 commissioned over 50 per cent of its first year's output from the independents, who in carrying fewer overheads than the ITV contractors were able to offer quality programmes much more cheaply. This was to have important consequences for all the networks, for ITV came under financial and the BBC under political pressure (in radio as well as TV) to make fewer programmes 'in-house' and buy a significant proportion of them from independents.

The rise of the independent houses was made possible not only by the growth of creative talent in a competitive industry which was now almost thirty years old, but by the development of lighter, more compact, more sophisticated, and in real terms cheaper, hardware. This in turn transformed television from a labour-intensive to something approaching a cottage industry. Yet there were also countervailing economies of scale. The independent sector certainly flourished after the launch of Channel 4, but as is often the case in a competitive business there were fatalities, mergers and takeovers, leaving fewer and larger survivors.

Channel 4's first chief executive was Jeremy Isaacs, who had gained extensive experience as a producer with both the BBC and ITV. Since the channel was launched nearly half a century after the establishment of the first British television service, it would perhaps have been unreasonable to expect it to offer many kinds of programming which were genuinely original, but it certainly fulfilled its duty to give expression to new themes and otherwise unheard minority views and values. A summary of its early achievements shows that it presented the traditional genres of television in distinctive and interesting ways.

It attempted to push against the limits of the TV medium by broadcasting in the early evenings a specially extended news programme which was resourced by ITN. This was partly a response to some thoughtful criticisms of the superficial and fitful character of television news which had been expressed by John Birt and Peter Jay in a letter to *The Times* in 1975. Under its young and highly able editor Derrik Mercer, who had been recruited from the *Sunday Times*, *Channel Four News* sought to get nearer than any other programme on the networks to TV's Holy Grail: 'news in depth'. As well as events it covered causes and contexts, and did not shrink from exploring issues of broad contemporary significance, even if these had not been marked by events which were individually 'newsworthy'. The channel also ran a half-hour weekly review programme, *Friday Alternative*, which gave various groups a chance to offer their own perspectives on the week's news coverage. A third innovation came from Isaacs himself, who established the first commissioning editor for film animation, seeing this as a neglected form of minority viewing which the channel could encourage. It was in the field of 'cinematic' film that the greatest early achievements of the channel probably lay. It made a number of co-production deals with the cinema industry, commissioning full-length feature films which involved both TV premieres, in a series called *Film on Four*, and cinema screenings. The channel also bought important 'art house' movies by such directors as Kurosawa, Satyajit Ray, Buñuel and Fassbinder.

Another of its innovations was to proclaim the maturity and self-belief of television by re-running programmes from the medium's own canon, among them vintage series like *The Munsters* and *I Love Lucy* which were quite unknown to the younger generation. It thus made the point that TV was not simply a museum for old movies but had a rich and growing heritage of its own. Finally, the channel continued BBC 2's earlier initiative of popularizing minority sports such as American football.

Sources/further reading

For the social, political and institutional background to independent television during the 1970s see Potter (1989). Briggs (1995) provides similar backgrounding, primarily for the BBC and up to the mid-1970s. For the launch of independent local radio see Baron (1975) and Barnard (1989). The latter also offers an excellent analysis of its early problems, which are further explored in Crisell (1994).

Potter (1990), Briggs (1995) and Day-Lewis (1992) all provide useful details of television programmes during the 1970s. Potter (1989) is illuminating on the background to the Annan Committee, and there is a good summary description of its recommendations in Hood and O'Leary (1990). For the full details, however, see the Annan Report (1977). Curran and Seaton (1997) observe that Annan radically altered public service broadcasting from a cohesive to a pluralistic concept – a view which is broadly endorsed by Scannell (1990) in an interesting discussion of the concept's historical evolution. This evolution can be handily traced in the extracts from Annan quoted in McDonnell (1991).

A useful summary of the ITV contract allocations of 1980 may be found in Tunstall (1983), while Potter (1990) gives helpful details on all the ITV contractors during the 1970s and also provides a fascinating account of the background to, and launch of, breakfast television.

For the background to Channel 4 see Potter (1989). Smith (1976) outlines his idea of the broadcaster as publisher, though he partly attributes it to the Labour politician Tony Benn. There are some sapient remarks on Channel 4 in Wenham (1982). However, the classic account of the background to the channel and its genesis and philosophy are in Lambert (1982). Hood and O'Leary (1990) are also useful on how the channel was set up, and Curran and Seaton (1997) offer some acute remarks on the values which informed it.

Part II

The rise of the active audience

From as early as the second half of the 1950s the history of broadcasting must be seen in the context of momentous developments which were taking place in the economics and technology of reception. Audiences were increasingly able to decide not only *where* they would receive broadcast messages and *how* they would treat them, but even *whether* they would receive them at all – or put their radio and TV sets to other uses.

Since about 1960 the real cost of receivers has fallen to such an extent that radio and television have become not simply *domestic* but *personal* media. The individual can afford a set of her own, and technological advances allow her to use it not just in her own home but almost anywhere she chooses. In Part I we noted a progression from the mass or collective to the private or individual consumption of cultural messages – a process which we termed *atomization*. We saw that it is a recurrent feature of the history of communications, just as it seems to have characterized the general development of modern industrial society. However, individuality of consumption does not always imply individuality of ownership. When they are still fairly new, media and their messages are often so expensive that many of their consumers must resort to devices of corporate purchase. In Chapter 1 we noted the establishment of the relay exchanges for those who were unable to afford their own wireless receivers, and there are still people who rent their television sets.

Perhaps the most striking parallel in media history is that between books and video-cassettes. In the eighteenth century books were too expensive for most people to buy, a fact which explains the contemporary success of the non-proprietary or circulating libraries. The novel was the most 'popular' literary form, as it still is today, yet when the first edition of *Tom Jones* was published in 1749 it cost more than a labourer's average weekly wage. In the late 1970s video was in a similar position: the first commercially pre-recorded cassettes cost between eighty and one hundred pounds. Consequently the vast majority of video films which have been viewed over the past two decades have been borrowed from video rental outlets. But during that time, as the price of video-cassettes has tumbled, increasing numbers have been bought outright. Most commercial videos now retail for ten to fifteen pounds, and it is not unknown for them to be given away to promote the sales of other products.

The development of the 'utility' wireless set in 1944 meant that the great majority of British households could afford a radio by the end of the Second World War, and thanks to rising affluence during the 1950s and 1960s, television sets were acquired much more quickly. Robert Rowland (1982: 88) calculates that whereas it took 100 years for the telephone to reach 75 per cent of British homes, it took only 26 years for radio, and 17 years for television. With the arrival of transistor sets in the 1960s and the subsequent growth of 'in-car entertainment', radio ownership and listening became not simply domestic but *individual* – and even, with the launch of the Sony Walkman personal radio/cassette player in 1979, positively solipsistic.

Much the same thing has happened with television. Even when television sets are not miniaturized or portable, they are often individually owned and watched – the latter process helped, in Britain at least, by that other great technological aid to atomization, central heating, which was installed in an increasing number of homes during the 1970s. Where formerly the family huddled round the sitting-room fire to watch the one television set it owned, its members have now become centrifugal, retreating to their own warm rooms to tune in to personal radio and TV sets. By 1990 25 per cent of the population owned four or more radios and three homes out of five had at least two televisions.

This individualism of consumption and ownership has had considerable implications for media content and effects and for audience judgment. For instance, the increase in the sexually explicit content of TV plays and films and of commercial videos must have been facilitated by the fact that it is less embarrassing to view in private or alone than in public or collectively. On the other hand, the solitary viewing of horror or crime movies may well be an even more frightening experience than watching in a cinema. What is perhaps more significant is that cultural and artistic judgment has become an unprecedentedly singular and subjective business. The viewer of a feature film or television programme can no longer seek guidance from the instantaneous reactions of others sitting around her, and it is probably no coincidence that the rise of that arbiter of 'correct' artistic judgment, the professional critic, dates roughly from the development of the first of the 'atomizing' media, print, which transformed poems and plays into private experiences and spawned a 'private' art form of its own, the novel.

The trend towards individualism of ownership and consumption preceded another development which began during the 1970s: the growth of audience *autonomy*. Technology increasingly enabled the audience to put the television (and less importantly, radio) set to uses other than that which was designated by the broadcasters. The first opportunity to do this was provided by the *remote control*, which had appeared in the 1960s as a device attached to the TV set by a cord, but which grew much more popular when cordless versions became available. Though offering the viewer of live television little more than an easy muting and channel-changing facility, it has had consequences for programme scheduling and content which, as we shall see later, are becoming particularly important in an era of multi-channel TV. Yet even in the old days of three or four channels, the viewer could use the remote control to 'refuse' the programmes which were offered to her by the broadcasters and make her own programme out of the elements they provided. As John Fiske (1987: 105) explains:

> Zapping allows the viewer to construct a viewing experience of fragments, a post-modern collage of images whose pleasures lie in their discontinuity, their

juxtapositions and their contradictions . . . The television text, then, is composed of a rapid succession of compressed, vivid segments where the principle of logic and cause and effect is subordinated to that of association and consequence to sequence.

The next important technology was *teletext*, a secondary broadcasting system introduced in 1974 which delivered to the TV screen continuously updated news and information in the form of print and graphics. The ITV version was called ORACLE (Optional Reception of Announcements by Coded Line Electronics), the BBC's more banally known as CEEFAX ('See Facts'). The Annan Committee viewed teletext as a blend of broadcasting and telecommunications since it was delivered to a mass audience yet allowed an interactive role to the viewer. It was thus an early instance of media convergence which is now becoming much more familiar to us, and meant that for the first time the viewer could opt out of live output and use her television set for news, information and on-screen entertainment – at times which suited *her*. By 1990 a quarter of all viewers had access to teletext.

However, it was the arrival of the *video-cassette recorder* (VCR) which provided the television audience with the most exciting opportunity to opt out of live transmission. We have already looked at the role of video technology in broadcast production – a role which dates back to 1958 – but its impact on viewing has been even more important. The first video recorder for the domestic market, one which allowed the off-air recording of TV programmes for time-shift reception, was a half-inch-cassette machine launched by Philips in 1972. The next eight or ten years saw an international struggle for market dominance which involved not only several manufacturers but several systems or 'formats', discs as well as tapes. Since no single manufacturer could win a significant market share at this time, unit costs remained high. In 1976, for instance, VCRs cost between £450 and £1,000, with sixty-minute blank tapes retailing at around £20, and Annan calculated that no more than about 40,000 VCRs were in use throughout the United Kingdom. The market was finally shared by two incompatible Japanese systems: Sony Betamax; and the eventual outright winner, the VHS format, introduced in Britain in 1978 by JVC, the aptly named Japanese Victor Company. By the 1980s VCRs carried a whole range of features: digital timing, fast forward and rewind, freeze-frame and remote control. They also created a vast new market for the hire and sale of pre-recorded cassettes, and a sturdy demand for video cameras so that viewers could use the TV screen to watch their own filmic endeavours. By the end of 1985, 8.5 million VCRs had been sold in Britain, where the market was especially strong, occupying a place in 40 per cent of the nation's households. A year later virtually half of all households boasted a VCR, and by 1989–90 the figure had risen to 60 per cent.

The appearance of the VCR was a significant moment in the history of television because for the first time the viewer could choose what *she* wanted to see instead of what was being presently provided for her by the broadcasting institutions

– perhaps recordings of live output, but perhaps other material too, such as cinema feature films or home movies she might have created for herself. But just as important as the unprecedented diversity of material that video offered was the fact that such material could be watched *in the viewer's own time*, thus further strengthening individualism of consumption. For video tipped the balance from a situation in which the viewer was obliged to adjust her day's routine to the timing of a programme she wanted to watch to one in which watching could be adjusted to her day's routine. In this respect video has enabled television to become much more like print, whose messages can also be absorbed in the receiver's rather than the sender's time.

Video recording has reduced what from the viewer's standpoint is the negative effect of broadcasting competition since she can simultaneously watch one channel while recording a programme on another. If the viewer is not necessarily watching a programme at the time of its transmission, broadcasters can take a slightly more flexible approach to scheduling. Open University and schools programmes, for instance, are usually transmitted at times when most people, including students, are likely to be asleep. BBC 2's *The Learning Zone* is a series of programmes transmitted between twelve-thirty and seven in the morning. But if the VCR has made programme scheduling in some respects less crucial for broadcasters, it has shifted from broadcasters to audience rather more of the responsibility for what children and young people are able to view. Formerly many children would have been unable to view unsuitable programming simply because it was shown after they had been sent to bed. Though most of it continues to be broadcast at late hours, video-cassettes mean that it is now viewable at any time of the day.

Video technology has had another major social consequence. We have noted that the overall effect of radio and television has been to move messages first into the domestic and then into a personal or individual sphere (something which print achieved from the outset). And we have seen that video and audio recording has further increased audience autonomy by allowing its members to watch and listen in their own time. But as well as this, the purchase of commercial videos and the practice of off-air recording have introduced the virtual ownership of media *messages* as well as of the media *receivers*, the radio and TV sets. Just as several centuries ago books began to move the poetry of Homer or Virgil or the plays of Shakespeare from the public domain not simply into private consumption but private ownership, so video recording is doing the same to the Hollywood movie and the live theatre. Moreover, it has not only turned spectator sports such as soccer matches and athletics meetings into private experiences; it has *fixed* them – transformed them into artefacts which may also be possessed.

That a cinema film or TV programme costing millions of pounds to make – a BBC costume drama, for instance – can be cheaply bought as a video-cassette, or recorded off-air and 'owned' for next to nothing, is a fact so remarkable that it is worth dwelling on for a few moments. In the first place we should remind ourselves that from a time well before the arrival of video, broadcasting has both increased the scope and quality of entertainment and cultural provision beyond all previous imagining and simultaneously reduced its cost to the consumer. (In this respect we may be dwelling in a golden age because it is conceivable that we shall move to a rather more expensive regime of 'pay-per-view' TV in the near future.) On top of this, and at only small cost, video has expanded the material which broadcasting has already provided, afforded absolute flexibility as to when we will view it, and given us the opportunity to 'own' it if we so wish. With respect to broadcast output we might almost say that thanks to the VCR, the TV licence, which was originally a licence to receive media artefacts, has now become a licence both to receive and to *own* them. Second, video technology (to say nothing of information technology, which expanded so rapidly during the 1990s) has meant that the enforcement of copyright law and royalty payments has become so problematical as in many cases to be all but abandoned. Audio-cassette recorders and VCRs, many of which now boast twin decks for the easy copying of tapes, could almost be said to have an illegality of purpose built into them.

The magnitude of the change which has taken place in the relationship between the consumer and certain media products can be appreciated only by those who were alive in the years before video arrived; for they can recall the excitement, the sense of occasion, of being able merely to see a major Hollywood movie in a crowded cinema, and reflect that such movies are now reducible to a collection of cassettes on a shelf – as commonplace as a row of books, privately owned and casually viewable, continuously or discontinuously, at any hour of the day or night. Nowadays it is certainly cheaper to hire a video than to go to the cinema, and it may soon become cheaper to buy one. Like books, cars and even central heating, then, video technology embodies that tendency of modern civilization towards a sense of individual privacy and personal empowerment.

During the 1980s computers followed VCRs in making use of domestic television screens, thus affording audiences another kind of opportunity to opt out of live broadcasts. By 1990 10 per cent of viewers could couple their sets to computers, mostly to play games or solve puzzles, but this meant that the reception of television broadcasts was now only one of *four* functions which the TV set could perform. Such versatility was an early and vivid hint of the multimedia systems which may well transcend both TV sets and computers in the near future.

Sources/further reading

For the cost of books, the social composition of audiences, and the rise of the circulating libraries in the eighteenth century see Watt (1963). The statistics on the quickening pace of new media penetration are in Rowland (1982). The effects of 'zapping' or 'channel surfing', an activity facilitated by the remote control, are explored in Fiske (1987). The discussion of teletext is in the Annan Report (1977), as are the statistics on the early cost of VCRs and tapes and on the number of VCRs in use in the United Kingdom during the mid-1970s.

Armes (1988) gives the best historical account of the development of video technology and of its social implications and applications. The social and political importance of video and of other new media technologies is considered in Hughes (1990) and in Curran and Seaton (1997). Among many others, O'Sullivan, Dutton and Rayner (1994) provide statistics on the growth of VCR ownership during the 1980s and early 1990s, and Seymour-Ure (1996) includes data on the ownership and uses of TV sets during the same period.

Chapter 11

Cables, dishes and government: the duopoly under threat

Cables, dishes and government: the duopoly under threat

Broadcasting technology, economics and politics in the 1980s

In the course of the 1980s new technologies created somewhat contrasting tendencies within broadcasting. Before looking at them we need to distinguish two aspects of it: *production*, or the making of programmes, and *distribution*, the transmission or dissemination of them.

Thanks primarily to the microchip and to video technology, programme-making became easier and cheaper than ever before, a fact attested by the rise of the small production companies which was noted in Chapter 10. For the ITV contractors these companies were to prove a useful ally in their struggle against the power of the unions, but the significance of new technology became dramatically clear during events at Thames Television in 1984. When the station was blacked out by union action a hastily trained skeleton staff recruited from the finance, personnel and other non-broadcast departments was able to restart it after only a day and a half. The effect was a mere 2 per cent drop in ITV's London weekday audience share (Bonner with Aston 1998: 159–60). In 1987–8 a similar sequence of events occurred both at Ulster Television and TV-AM, the holder of the ITV breakfast-time franchise. The latter's attempt to introduce new working practices was resisted by the production staff, all members of the Association of Cinematographic and Television Technicians (ACTT). It therefore locked them out, yet managed to stay on air by using non-technical employees such as secretaries to operate cameras and other equipment.

The 'casualization' of jobs in broadcasting inevitably brought with it a weakening of the once invincible broadcasting unions. Indeed by this time, almost anyone could obtain simple sound-recording and video hardware to make media products in their own private sphere. The lucky few might even reach a conventional media audience, for with such programmes as *Video Diaries* (BBC, early 1990s) home-shot camcorder material began to enter the national broadcasters' repertoire. Some of it could be hugely influential. In 1991 a severe beating which the Los Angeles police gave to a young black man named Rodney King was caught on an amateur video, and its airing on television sparked the city's riots (Humm 1998: 231).

In radio, with its simpler technology and more localized audiences, we shall shortly see that the distribution of media products became just as easy as the production of them. But on the distribution of TV programmes, technology, most obviously in the form of satellites, had the effect of a scaling up rather than a scaling down, for it was during the 1980s that television broadcasting ceased to be a merely regional and national activity and started to become a global one. The satellite links between different national broadcasters and the international co-productions which had developed during the 1960s and 1970s had been but straws in the wind. Henceforth technology would enable a single organization to transmit its programmes around the world.

These contrasting tendencies of technology – the localization, even domestication, of production on the one hand and the internationalization, even globalization, of distribution on the other – were quickly noted by media analysts. In the 1980s Alvarado, Gutch and Wollen (1987: 254) observed that 'video technology offers Western societies the possibility of the production, circulation and consumption of low-cost media products designed for highly specific groups but no way of locking in to large-scale audiences'. A year later Roy Armes (1988: 74) made the similar point that the unprecedented individual access to media production coincided with diminishing access to media distribution, since the latter would be increasingly monopolized by a few large organizations operating on a world-wide basis. Why?

The global audience which satellite technology could deliver meant that media organizations could greatly improve their efficiency and profitability. But only large organizations – or consortia thereof – would be able to bear the enormous start-up costs, including that of hurling a satellite into geostationary orbit some 22,000 miles above the earth's surface. We noted that the original ITV contractors were themselves groups of companies. Now even bigger cartels would be needed to play the global game, and two ITV contractors formed part of the consortium which was to make up British Satellite Broadcasting (BSB). Another and larger member of the consortium, and one which would continue its involvement in broadcasting and multimedia after the early demise of BSB, was the Pearson Group, whose interests outside the media embraced banking, property, the Royal Doulton china company, and even the Château Latour vineyard in France.

There were two disquieting consequences of this necessary enlargement of organizations with ambitions to play a major part in the new age of broadcasting. The first was the growth of cross-media ownership, a process which such bodies as the IBA and the Monopolies Commission could delay yet never wholly prevent. In addition to its involvement in television, Pearson owned two book publishing companies, Penguin and Longman, and a newspaper, the *Financial Times*. A much more conspicuous example was the most successful organization of them all, Rupert Murdoch's News International (later News Corporation), whose interests were largely confined to the media but which included newspapers, book publishing, TV broadcasting and film distribution.

However worrying it might have been, cross-media ownership was a problem which could at least be addressed when the parent company had a specific national identity. But the second consequence of corporate expansion was that the companies perforce raised money and supplied markets on an international scale and were to a large extent outside individual state control. Murdoch himself typified the problem: he was a veritable citizen of the world. Though Australian in origin, he acquired the *News of the World*, the *Sun* and *The Times* in Britain and built another newspaper empire in the United States. He also bought control of Metromedia and Twentieth Century Fox in order to obtain fodder for his satellite channels and readily adopted American citizenship in order to retain control of what he had gained there. His media empire thus spanned three continents.

Quite apart from the unavoidably international character of the satellite broadcasters, the very nature of the technology has made individual state control extremely difficult since the 'footprints' of the satellites – their transmission areas on the earth's surface – mostly transcend national boundaries, causing not just cultural homogenization but problems of regulation and accountability (McQuail 2000: 217). In the early 1990s the British government had difficulty in preventing the reception in this country of a pornographic satellite channel broadcasting quite legally from northern Europe, where the obscenity laws are less stringent. Indeed, as Eric Hobsbawm (1994: 15) observed, the increasing powerlessness of individual states against the globalizing tendencies of both technology and economics was perhaps the most striking characteristic of the end of the twentieth century, affecting not just the broadcasting media but general trade and the movement of capital, physical travel, scientific activity, the traffic in information, and even aspects of private life.

In the Britain of the 1980s there was in any case not much political appetite for state regulation. Sensing that the country was tired of dilatory, inefficient public services, strikes, ubiquitous state intervention and the chronic ravages of inflation, the new Conservative administration under Margaret Thatcher determined to roll back state involvement and state provision. The aim was to 'set business free' from bureaucratic, essentially government, controls. Private enterprise was rediscovered as the engine of the economy, and the old-fashioned, labour-intensive industries which the state had directly or indirectly supported – shipbuilding, steel-making, heavy engineering, coal-mining – were allowed to go to the wall and were replaced by jobs in financial and specialist services, light industry, leisure, tourism and catering, and information technology. On the supply side the aim was leanness and competitiveness, on the demand side consumer sovereignty – and together these qualities created 'the disciplines of the market', the economic panacea for which poverty, deprivation and unemployment seemed to everyone except the growing number of their victims to be a price worth paying.

Like every other publicly funded organization the BBC would soon find itself under scrutiny with the object of determining whether it could be run more efficiently. It received licence income whether or not the public approved of its programmes. Could it be slimmer, more cost-effective and more responsive to those who funded it? Nor would ITV be spared from scrutiny, for how efficient was a commercial system which enjoyed a monopoly of television advertising? It was noted earlier that because the BBC and ITV had separate and assured sources of income the competition between them was not cut-throat. This meant that since audience maximization was not an absolute necessity, both broadcasters could afford to do some programmes of minority interest. The government would now wish to see whether unfettered competition could cater for a similar range of interests. During its first term of office, from 1979 to 1983, it proceeded cautiously: broadcasting policy came under the restraining influence of the Home Secretary, William Whitelaw. He was an admirer of the BBC and was happy to assign the new Channel 4 to the IBA, where it would operate as a public service network which was cushioned against competition. But the government's longer-term aim was to break the 'cosy duopoly' of the BBC and ITV by giving access to other broadcasters and full scope to the new technologies of satellite and cable.

Developments in radio

Though sound broadcasting was no longer a preoccupation of the majority, there was by the early 1980s some dissatisfaction in various quarters with what was being offered by local radio. Despite its vestigial public service obligations, ILR, which consisted of forty-eight stations by 1984, was largely characterized by a diet of pop music. As Radio 1 demonstrated, this was just as easily provided by the networks: there was little that was 'local' about it. And even within that vast section of the public who preferred pop music to any other kind of output, there were many who felt excluded. Why? Most ILR stations based their playlist on the Top 40 because these songs appealed to the greatest number of listeners. But pop and rock had by now fragmented into various sub-genres – reggae, country and folk, heavy metal, soul and dance music, golden oldies from the 1950s, 1960s and early 1970s. Songs of these kinds featured only rarely in the Top 40 but they were favoured by significant ethnic and social minorities, who thus felt that the ILR stations had little to offer them.

Despite continuing to open new stations during the 1970s and early 1980s BBC local radio was even less healthy than its rival. If, in terms of the interest and resources it attracted, network radio was the poor cousin of BBC TV, then BBC local radio was the poor cousin of the networks. Chronically underfunded, it offered a thin diet of news, information and light music and opted into one of the national services, usually Radio 2, for those parts of the day when it could no longer afford to provide a service of its own. Despite the many disclaimers at official level, local radio was regarded within the corporation as existing primarily to feed the networks with new talent and new programme ideas.

Furthermore, public dissatisfaction with local radio was not restricted to *content*: in neither the BBC nor the independent stations had the dream of wider *access* been realized. Both were largely a professionals' closed shop: even the much-vaunted phone-ins were mediated by professional presenters, albeit for unavoidable legal reasons. Whether as members of an ethnic group, devotees of a particular interest, or even as part of one of the more close-knit geographical communities, many people felt that their needs as listeners and potential broadcasters were not being met by local radio as it was presently constituted. Their feelings were sharpened by an awareness that modern technology made sound broadcasting an unprecedentedly cheap and simple matter and afforded room for many more stations on the spectrum. If broadcasting was no longer a scarce commodity, why the need for such tight regulation? Why could the airwaves not be opened up to all tastes and all shades of opinion?

An unprecedented growth of interest in 'do-it-yourself' radio found expression in the launch of the Community Radio Association in 1983, and closed-circuit or in-house stations began to broadcast on college and hospital campuses and even in small communities, such as Radio Thamesmead in south-east London. The government, in the form of the Home Office, was happy to license these because they were piped to closed communities, but in the wider world of the airwaves pirate stations could once more be heard. Most of these were based in London and were of ethnic origin. By the mid-1980s as many as fifty were broadcasting, often relocating and reopening as fast as the Home Office investigators could trace them, raid them and impound their equipment. But neither of the main political parties was unsympathetic to the idea of community radio. The Labour opposition saw it as a forum for local democracy while the Conservative government regarded it as a way of enriching listener choice and fostering business enterprise. A new framework for sound broadcasting was clearly needed which would allow many more stations on to the air. In 1985 the government decided to license a national spread of twenty-one community radio stations on an experimental basis, but then abandoned the plan in order to consider the broader future of radio (and television) – a measure which would culminate in the Broadcasting Act of 1990.

However, in 1989 the IBA seized the initiative by licensing twenty-one 'incremental' stations, so called because under existing legislation they had to be located in areas which were already served by ILR. About a quarter of them were former pirates and most subscribed to the 'community' ideal by appealing, like Spectrum Radio in London, to ethnic groups; by offering specialist music such as Jazz FM and Melody FM, also in London; or by broadcasting to people in small geographical areas, like Wear FM in Sunderland. Unfortunately, the launch of the incrementals coincided with yet another slump in advertising, and those that pinned their faith on 'access' and community-originated programming soon learnt the hard lesson that what the public wants to broadcast is not necessarily what it wants to hear. Within a year over half the stations had been refinanced, lost their original management, or become part of bigger ILR groups transmitting the predictable diet of chart-based pop. What had begun as an exciting attempt to free up the airwaves, to enable them to carry the full range of values, tastes and opinions that shape our society, ended in an increase of stations sounding virtually indistinguishable from one another.

Meanwhile, even the conventional ILR stations had not been thriving, as we saw in the last chapter. They were over-regulated by the IBA, and from the mid-1980s further hit by the pirates who, free from public service obligations, could attract advertisers by targeting their audiences as closely as they wished. The IBA finally moved to ease the sufferings of its licensees. Their public service obligations were lightened: they were allowed to adopt a simple Top 40 and capsule news format. Sponsorship was permitted, transmitter rentals were reduced, and companies with holdings in other media were allowed to run radio stations. Clusters of ownership soon developed, such as Crown Communications, the Capital Radio Group and the East Midlands Allied Press (EMAP). Later the stations were also allowed to split their frequencies – that is, to offer different kinds of music on different wavebands so that they could target audiences more narrowly – and the great majority which did so (eighteen of them in 1988–9 alone) broadcast Top 40 music on FM and golden oldies on the medium wave.

National radio enjoyed a more tranquil existence. For most of the 1980s it was still the preserve of the BBC, though there were occasional hints of a more competitive future. Since Radio 4 was the only network which continued to offer anything like the traditional Reithian diet of separately constructed and varied programmes, it was mostly here that the old favourites continued and new creations appeared. Among the latter were *In the Psychiatrist's Chair* (1981 onwards), in which Professor Anthony Clare cleverly exploited the confessional blindness and intimacy of the medium to probe the psyches of his famous 'patients'; and from 1985 *Loose Ends*, a somewhat anarchic chat show presided over by Ned Sherrin. Two years later Radio 4 unveiled its first soap opera since *The Archers*, but despite being provided with a long runway *Citizens* never quite took off and slithered to a halt in 1991. Another and more successful innovation was that from 1989 Radio 1 suspended pop music once a week and late at night to present a much-acclaimed comedy show, *The Mary Whitehouse Experience*, named in ironic honour of the famous 'clean up TV' campaigner. And to crown a fairly satisfactory decade, all four of the networks acquired FM frequencies between 1988 and 1991, thus affording a quality of reception which matched their high production standards. Nevertheless it was clear that the BBC's near monopoly of national radio could not last much longer. For a brief period in the mid-1980s an offshore pop pirate, Laser 558, had dented Radio 1's audience by minimizing disc jockey chat, promising that 'music is never more than a minute away', and in its Green Paper of 1987 the government signalled its intention to expose the BBC to competition at network as well as local level. This happened sooner than either the government or the corporation anticipated with the launch in September 1989 of Atlantic 252, a long-wave pop and rock station offering big prizes and little chat. Although it provoked protests from ILR, it was the first legal national daytime commercial station to be heard in this country – legal because it was beamed in from the Irish Republic and thus escaped British jurisdiction.

The 1990 Broadcasting Act contained important provisions for radio which embodied the government's guiding principle that deregulation would stimulate competition, increase efficiency and widen consumer choice. In essence this meant leaving BBC radio pretty much as it was while greatly increasing the number of its commercial rivals. These would be licensed at national and regional as well as at local level by a new Radio Authority whose control, however, would be lighter than the IBA's had been. None of the independent stations would henceforth incur the public service obligation to provide 'range' and 'balance', and they would be allowed to own their transmitting facilities instead of having to rent them from the authority.

Three independent stations would present the BBC with competition at national level: one on FM, the others on medium-wave frequencies which the BBC networks would be obliged to vacate now that they had acquired homes on the FM band. The Radio Authority was empowered to prescribe the kind of programming that the new frequencies would carry before it invited bids for them. In the event it decided that at least one of the stations would offer speech-based output and at least one other carry music which was not pop.

The early 1990s were marked by two other events in the world of radio. In their different ways these contrasted with the Broadcasting Act by recalling the past rather than looking to the future. The first was the BBC's launch in August 1990 of Radio 5, an old-fashioned mixed-programme network which was borne of expediency rather than any vision of the modern role of radio. The move to FM by the four existing BBC networks had left two spare medium-wave frequencies which the corporation realized might be assigned to yet other competitors if it failed to improvise a way of filling them. The result, if you were a critic of Radio 5, was a 'ragbag', 'mish-mash' or 'dumping ground' of programmes that did not fit into any of the other networks. But if you were a fan, it was a 'treasure chest' of adult education and schools broadcasts, sports commentaries, stories and magazine programmes.

The second event was the death of the once hugely popular Radio Luxembourg, weakened by waves of competition at, or nearer, home (first the pirates, then Radio 1, then ILR), and now expiring at the prospect of independent national stations. It disappeared from the medium wave in December 1991, but persisted for a few months more as a satellite channel.

Brief mention must be made of a technological development which has enhanced the autonomy of the listener: the Radio Data System (RDS). First incorporated into car radios by Volvo in 1988, RDS transmitted inaudible data alongside the audible radio signal. This data would automatically re-tune the radio to the strongest signal of the station that the listener wished to hear, irrespective of its frequency. People in cars have for many years been an important sector of the listening public and a device which would spare them the need to re-tune constantly to low-power FM transmitters was a real boon. It would also, if they wished, interrupt the signal with information about traffic and travel conditions. While RDS could strengthen station loyalty (always strong on radio since listeners re-tune much less than viewers) another facility could weaken it by replacing it with loyalty to a particular kind of output. The listener could preselect a certain type of programming, such as jazz, news or drama, and the system would search for it among all the stations on the spectrum. RDS was clearly attractive to those who did most of their listening in cars. What was less clear was whether it would appeal to others, since it could more than double the cost of a cheap radio set.

Cable TV

The development of cable TV in Britain has been so interwoven with that of satellite TV that it can sometimes be difficult to distinguish between them. Satellite television has so far had a more spectacular history and gained a larger share of the audience, but cable television, though it largely depends on satellite feeds, may have a bigger future than direct reception from satellite.

We need to begin by reviewing the differences between cable technology on the one hand and the more conventional kinds of broadcasting (including satellite) on the other. Earlier in this book it was observed that conventional broadcasting, whether in the form of radio or television, was a 'wire-less' process: messages were transmitted from sender to receivers 'over the air' or through the atmosphere. Satellite technology is simply an extension of this process: messages or signals are transmitted from the sender up to the satellite and thence beamed down to the receivers, who are usually located on some other part of the globe. The meaning and origins of 'broadcast' are important in this context. An ancient word which had been used to describe the sowing or scattering of seed, it usefully evoked the aerial nature of this new form of communication together with the indefinite plurality of its reception. Its messages would certainly be seen and/or heard by more than one person, but the precise number would be unknown: with the right equipment anyone within a given area could receive them.

'Cable', on the other hand, is a fixed, physical link and implies a rather more specific, less random relationship between sender and receivers. To describe the cable transmission of TV and radio programmes as 'broadcasting' is thus a significant modification of that word, though perhaps acceptable given the widespread nature of their reception. Still, it is clear that cable transmission is at a certain disadvantage when compared to conventional broadcasting, and especially to satellite, its main competitor. Satellite transmissions can be received almost anywhere by means of a 'dish', whereas cable is available only in those areas which are sufficiently populous to justify the huge cost of laying it.

Nevertheless, its reception of the satellite channels is invariably excellent and it has two crucial advantages which, as we shall see, emerged with the development of fibre optic or 'broad band' cable at the end of the 1970s. First, its channel-carrying capacity is vast; second, it can serve as a medium of two-way or *interactive* communication. As well as relaying the conventional radio and television stations, it can give the audience a 'return path' to those stations in order to modify their broadcasts or order supplementary material, and it can provide access to retail services like home shopping, home banking and ticket purchasing. Moreover, it has enormous potential in the field of information technology, and it can offer various forms of telecommunication such as phone and video conferencing.

This ability of cable to carry not only all the broadcasting channels but services for telephones and computers means that the cable companies cannot simply be equated with conventional broadcasters like the BBC or Channel 4. They are also in direct competition with the likes of British Telecom (BT): indeed, telecoms are likely to form the most profitable part of their business. The BBC, ITV and Channels 4 and 5 may make and/or commission programmes and use their own means to disseminate or distribute them, but the cable companies are the providers merely of channels. They are the carriers or distributors of material originated or commissioned by others. If, to take an analogy from the literary world, the conventional broadcasters could be compared to the creators of books in both the artistic and material senses, and also to the publishers, the cable companies could be compared to bookshops, selling a range of wares, including those of the BBC, ITV and Channels 4 and 5. (Moreover, if one recalls their ability to offer other services than broadcasting, they could be compared to those bookshops which sell a range of products in addition to books, such as newspapers and confectionery.) Like the bookshops, they have a broad legal responsibility for what they carry, but they take no direct editorial role in the shaping of programme content; that is the province of the individual broadcasting organizations.

Cable television has existed in Britain since the early 1950s, but the first systems were to be found in places where the reception of conventional broadcasts was likely to be difficult, such as large blocks of flats. The first city-wide cable system opened in Gloucester in 1951, yet until recently cable development in Britain has lagged behind that of certain other countries such as the United States, and for a good reason. In the latter the size and terrain of the transmission areas mean that the conventional broadcasting signal is often so inferior that cable offers a better alternative, whereas with its relative compactness Britain has always enjoyed excellent TV reception. Nevertheless, in the 1970s British cable systems were developed which were similar to the old radio relay system, although they were allowed to carry only the three national networks. They were also an early form of pay TV, the first experiments in which had taken place in London and Sheffield in 1966 – an experience which was quite foreign to most British viewers until the 1990s.

Cable received a boost at the end of the 1970s, when new fibre optic technology produced cables with vastly increased capacity – 250,000 times that of ordinary telephone wire – and the potential for interactivity. Glimpsing its possibilities for computing, the government appointed an information technology advisory panel and conceived the idea that the establishment of a national cable infrastructure would be entertainment-led and privately funded. It also set up the Hunt Committee to consider how this idea could be given institutional shape.

In its 1982 report the committee recommended that cable TV should be seen as supplementary to what it regarded as the public service duopoly of the BBC and ITV, not as an alternative or rival to them. It therefore proposed that the cable companies be required to carry the ordinary BBC and ITV channels as part of the basic programme package they would offer to the viewer in return for a subscription. This proposal, which the government accepted, has become known as the 'must carry' rule. Most of the other programming would be delivered to the companies by the satellite operators; few if any channels would be originated by the companies themselves.

When cable was launched in 1983, eleven regional franchises were offered by the Department of Trade and Industry, whose responsibility for it was taken over in the following year, and in accordance with Hunt's recommendations, by a Cable Authority. By the end of 1985 companies were operating in eight different regions. Only one operator was licensed in each region, but for both the system and the programming, and each offered about twenty channels. Most of the operators, like US West and Videotron, were from the United States or Canada, where cable was already well established.

Thus, as often happens in history, a little-noticed development involving only a tiny section of the public had momentous implications. Cable gave British viewers access for the very first time to live television which was not provided by the BBC/ITV duopoly and thus not part of a system established by the government to serve broad public service objectives. They would now have the option of watching channels which might be 'themed and streamed' instead of carrying a variety of separate programmes. However, the cable operators were not, at first, allowed to offer telephony. This was to enable the newly privatized British Telecom and its fledgling rival Mercury to grow a market which was still in its infancy. Yet by forging partnerships with either BT or Mercury some of the cable operators did manage to provide telephone services. On the other hand, neither of the telecoms companies was permitted to carry or provide broadcast content.

The expansion of the cable infrastructure was bound to be slow, but was made slower by the operators' failure to attract many subscribers in the areas already cabled – a failure which deterred some potential investors. On average, the new service was taken up by fewer than 20 per cent of the homes the cable passed. For this there were three obvious reasons. First, most viewers were quite happy with the four, ostensibly free, channels offered by the BBC and ITV, which between them continued to give fairly good programming range and quality and excellent reception. Second, those viewers who were not happy with them could shortly subscribe to what seemed to be the more flexible technology of a satellite dish. Third, what was by now the wide ownership of VCRs already gave access to alternative sources of viewing.

However, thanks to the 1990 Broadcasting Act the economics of cable somewhat improved when from 1991 the operators were allowed to offer telephony to their customers as well as a wide range of TV and radio channels. This gave them the possibility of doubling their revenue for about a 21 per cent increase in the installation cost.

Satellite TV

The history of satellite TV in Britain has been marked by three overlapping developments. During its first phase, which was outlined in Chapter 6, the BBC and ITV used satellite links as an element within their own earth-based or 'terrestrial' broadcasting. In 1968, for instance, they took pictures from the Mexico Olympics via satellite and then relayed them to the domestic viewers in the conventional way. This use of satellite pictures within terrestrial broadcasts has become increasingly common since its inception in 1962. In the second development, which dates from 1984, whole programmes were originated by satellite broadcasters which bypassed the BBC/ITV duopoly and were relayed to the viewing public via the cable operators. Satellite continues to provide a substantial part of cable TV programming. In the third development, which began in 1989, programmes were originated by satellite broadcasters which bypassed *both* the BBC/ITV duopoly *and* the cable operators, and (in return for a subscription) were beamed direct to viewers via a circular aerial, or 'dish', and a decoder. This was known as direct broadcasting by satellite (DBS).

As a cable supplier satellite TV began a trial service in mainland Europe in October 1981. In the following year it was officially launched as the Sky Channel, transmitting general entertainment programmes for a mere two hours a day to the cable systems there. In 1983 Rupert Murdoch's News International gained control of it and a year later began a service to cable operators in Britain, where the two media fledglings were covered by the Cable and Broadcasting Act of 1984.

However, plans for the third development in satellite technology were already under way, for in 1982 the government had granted the BBC a licence to provide DBS in the United Kingdom. It was intended that the corporation would use a British satellite built by Marconi, GEC and British Aerospace. But the costs proved even more astronomical than the project, and although the IBA was later brought in so that they could be more widely shared it had to be abandoned in 1985. The following year the government asked the IBA to advertise for a contractor to provide a DBS service of three (later five) channels. This would carry certain public service responsibilities and would be expected to go to air before 1990. In due course the franchise was awarded to British Satellite Broadcasting (BSB), a consortium of companies including Virgin (which later dropped out), Pearson, Reed International, and two terrestrial contractors, Granada and Anglia TV. However, the technology required by the IBA was unproven and the start of the new service was repeatedly delayed until suddenly 'scooped' in February 1989 by Rupert Murdoch's Sky Channel, which re-launched as a DBS service.

Murdoch was able to offer DBS to the United Kingdom by leasing four transponders on the Astra satellite, the brainchild of the Luxembourg-based SES company. Unlike BSB he thus avoided the huge expense of having to launch his own satellites – and in offering a non-domestic service he was partly outside the jurisdiction of the IBA (Horsman 1997: 42). The service was mainly funded from subscriptions but with some advertising and at first consisted of just four channels: Sky One, Sky News, Sky Movies and Eurosport. In the meantime BSB was spending £30 million on a pre-launch promotional campaign, marketing its own square receiving dish, which was called a 'squarial', with the tag-line 'It's smart to be square'. It finally went to air in April 1990 but had lost the game almost before it began. Whereas BSB's headquarters and its launch parties smacked of extravagance, Sky TV was a lean outfit with an aggressive sales team who were eager to get dishes on to walls and roofs.

Neither company would easily recoup its huge start-up costs in what was now another economic recession, but Sky had pre-empted BSB by securing rights to all the available major Hollywood movies. Whereas the programmes on Sky One were almost entirely American in origin, BSB was obliged to originate its own programming on all channels. In November 1990 it collapsed. By this time the companies had spent between them some £1.25 billion to persuade a mere one in fifteen households to buy their dishes. As in the case of cable TV, most viewers felt too happy with the abundance afforded by four terrestrial channels and the video suppliers to be tempted to subscribe to an infant DBS service.

Sky immediately absorbed BSB in what was wittily described as a merge-over, and the result was British Sky Broadcasting (BSkyB), a five-channel service which began in April 1991 and consisted of the original Sky package plus a second movie channel. A sixth channel, the Comedy Channel, was added in October. The IBA was, of course, quite unable to prevent or influence the union of Sky and BSB. Because its permission had not been sought, it revoked BSB's licence and ordered it to stop broadcasting by the end of 1992. Had the new company been naive enough to obey, Britain would have been left without a satellite TV service. As things stand, the service is run by a company which is largely outside the regulator's control.

We might conclude this account of the early years of satellite TV with one or two broader observations. The first is that whether it wished to or not, the government was prevented from subjecting satellite to tight control by the knowledge that this would discourage potential operators from incurring the enormous start-up costs that were involved. One consequence of their relative freedom was that, like the cable operators, the satellite companies sought to follow the lead of radio and maximize their audiences not simply by *narrowcasting* – that is, by offering a range of programmes to a specialized audience as BBC 2 and Channel 4 do – but by 'theming and streaming' or *formatting*, providing the specialized audience with only one kind of programme on each of its channels: comedy or sport or movies.

The second point is that satellite TV is essentially a transnational business and therefore hard for governments to bring under control. Its 'footprints' transcend national borders and its operators can ignore the restrictions imposed by some of those countries to which they broadcast. In Britain this has had consequences for terrestrial broadcasting, for the ITV companies have cited the freedom of the satellite operators, with whom they compete for the same audience, to support their own demands for fewer restrictions on ownership and programming. One portent of a more liberal future occurred in 1988, when the IBA allowed the sponsorship of all TV programmes except those relating to news, religion or current affairs.

Government *versus* broadcasters

Curran and Seaton (1997: 306) point out that before the 1970s it was possible to distinguish between the fact that broadcasting was politically accountable and the idea that it could remain independent of political influence. But by the 1980s changes in the political landscape had created something of a cold war between politicians and broadcasters. In Chapter 9 it was noted that politics is no longer a matter of controlled conflict between two or three major political parties: thanks partly to broadcasting itself the wider social sphere has become more highly politicized. Issues and problems such as drugs, housing, the environment, disarmament, law and order and Northern Ireland have somewhat transcended individual party positions, weakening the old notion of consensus and making 'balance' and neutrality ever harder for the broadcasters to achieve. The latter naturally feel obliged to cover these issues yet cannot do so without courting controversy. And since politicians have always regarded broadcasting – rightly or wrongly – as being more influential than the press, those in power began to threaten it when they perceived that its interests were diverging from their own.

Thanks to the government's control over the licence fee, the BBC has always, of course, been especially vulnerable to political pressure. But as Curran and Seaton (1997: 307–8) observe, another historical factor made it even more vulnerable. Its original board of governors had been appointed neither as representatives of the government nor as employees of the BBC but as 'trustees of the national interest'. This was reflected in two promptly established traditions: members of the board would be politically neutral, and as a further way of preventing it from becoming identified with the interest of any one party, the chair and vice-chair would be of contrasting political persuasions. However, the dominant personality of Reith was such that during the 1930s he largely succeeded in bringing the board under his control, making its members in effect the creatures of the BBC. This meant that when, some half a century later, the Conservative government sought to move against the BBC, the idea that its governors were independent guardians of the national interest had long since been lost. The government reasoned that if the board was to be a creature of anybody, it should be a creature of the government rather than of the BBC.

In the course of the 1980s it therefore packed the board with its own supporters. Two successive chairs, Stuart Young (appointed 1981) and Marmaduke Hussey (appointed 1986) were enthusiastic Tories, but so indeed was the vice-chair who served under both, William Rees-Mogg. In Alasdair Milne the BBC at least had a director general with a distinguished and non-political backgound in programme-making. But in 1987 he was sacked by Hussey and replaced first with an accountant, Michael Checkland, and then with the managerial enthusiast John Birt, who had been recruited from London Weekend Television and was eager to subject his new public service charge to the commercial disciplines of the 'internal market'.

Moves against the duopoly (1): the Peacock Committee

The Conservatives thus had two main reasons for wishing to move against the broadcasters. The first could be seen as *ideological*: to make them leaner and more efficient – more responsive to consumer choice and the disciplines of the market. The second could be described as *editorial* – a dissatisfaction with some of the issues the broadcasters felt the need to cover and/or the way in which they covered them. During their first term of office the Tories were largely preoccupied with the launches of Channel 4 and cable television. It was during their second term, from

1983 to 1987, that they turned their attention to the duopoly, seeking to reform it by moving against the BBC (Goodwin 1998: 69).

Mrs Thatcher was angered by what she saw as the BBC's subversively impartial coverage of the Falklands War in 1982 and the miners' strike in 1984; by the publicity it gave to terrorists in its *Real Lives* documentary on the IRA in 1985; and by its critical treatment of the United States' bombing of Libya in 1986. But the trigger appears to have occurred in 1984 when it requested a 41 per cent increase in its licence fee, from £46 to £65. The BBC's case was not only that television programme costs tend to rise faster than the rate of inflation, which was considerable at the time, but that these costs could no longer be partly offset, as they had been during the 1970s, by the huge number of viewers who had switched from black and white to the much more expensive colour licence. Moreover, the BBC had to acquire extra capital to pay for its future operations, which might extend to satellite broadcasting.

The new licence demand sparked an outcry in the press, especially among those newspapers owned by the controller of Sky TV, Rupert Murdoch. The government approved a 26 per cent increase – to £58 – but then appointed a committee under Professor Alan Peacock, an apostle of the new economics, to determine first whether the BBC should take advertising or sponsorship as an alternative or supplement to licence income; and second, what impact such a measure might have on the broadcasting system as a whole. Hence, though primarily a move against the BBC, the appointment of Peacock was also a move against ITV and the duopoly: for if the BBC were forced to take advertising this would not only fatally weaken its public service role but oblige ITV to compete for its source of revenue.

As Paddy Scannell (1990: 22) observes, Peacock was the first parliamentary committee which was not required to treat public service in broadcasting as its primary consideration: it was to think of the audiences simply as 'consumers'. Indeed, its report, which was published in 1986, professed some uncertainty as to what public service meant and made the dismaying claim that even broadcasters were hard put to supply a definition. But in having to consider how those consumers would be served whose tastes were not widely shared, and were thus 'uneconomic', the committee inevitably found itself pondering the meaning of the term. Public service was defined in its report as 'any major modification of purely commercial provision resulting from public policy' (Peacock 1986: 130) – that is, a service that viewers were willing to support as taxpayers and voters but not as consumers. It was a way of providing for what the market itself would not provide for – which is, of course, the whole point of the licence fee. Hence what Peacock did was not so much devise a new concept of public service as find a new way of describing the old concept.

Since public service could not be supported by the conventional laws of the market the committee rejected advertising for the BBC but in most other respects echoed the philosophy of the government. Consumers, it insisted, were the best judges of their own cultural needs and they, not the producers, should determine the character of broadcasting. It accepted that in the short term the licence fee would have to be retained but recommended that in order to subject the BBC to a greater financial discipline the fee should be pegged to the retail price index, which at that time was rising more slowly than programme costs. In the longer term, when multi-channel TV and radio had arrived and the BBC's audience share had significantly fallen, the fee should be abolished and replaced by subscription funding. The committee also proposed that Radios 1 and 2 should be privatized since their output did not, it felt, differ materially from that of the commercial stations.

Impressed by the example of Channel 4, Peacock made one other important recommendation: both the BBC and ITV should commission a quota of their material from independent sources. This would have the twin benefit of undermining their own dominance by giving greater access to outside programme-makers and greater diversity to the viewers; and of reducing their costs by both scaling down their own production facilities and forcing the independents to tender competitively.

Moves against the duopoly (2): *Broadcasting in the 90s*

It may be a pardonable exaggeration to say that Peacock was a gun which the government fired at the BBC but which wounded ITV. In the short term it left the BBC with its licence funding intact, but possibly in the longer term, too, since subscription funding raised economic and technical problems. Even the proposal to privatize Radios 1 and 2 came to nothing because in sharing premises, equipment and personnel with the other networks they were not physically detachable from the rest of the corporation. However, the government was attracted by Peacock's proposals for ITV, notably the idea of auctioning its franchises and requiring Channel 4 to sell its own advertising. On the one hand a franchise auction would cream off some of the gains which the ITV contractors made by restricted entry into a monopoly; on the other hand that monopoly would be weakened, however slightly, by a self-funding Channel 4.

Thwarted in its attempt to reform the BBC, the government therefore turned its attention to ITV, and, as we have seen, there were two more reasons why it was by no means reluctant to do so. Though champions of private enterprise, the Conservatives deplored ITV's monopoly of advertising, believing that among other things the lack of financial competition encouraged it to cave in to the excessive demands of the trade unions. In 1987 Mrs Thatcher denounced ITV as 'the last bastion of restrictive practices', and even though most of these had by now been removed by the contractors' use of the government's new Employment Acts, the remark betrayed her lingering disapproval (Bonner with Aston 1998: 149). Then in 1988 she was incensed by *Death on the Rock*, a Thames Television documentary which suggested that a British army unit in Gibraltar had gunned down several IRA terrorists in cold blood.

After Peacock the BBC, meanwhile, was busily ingratiating itself with the government. The latter was swiftly appeased by the Tory sympathies of the board of governors and senior management, and by the attempts of the Director General, Michael Checkland, and his deputy, John Birt, to make the corporation leaner and more efficient and seek commercial ways of supplementing the licence fee. It should again be emphasized that any government move against ITV would also be a move against the BBC: to expose ITV to more competition meant more competition for the corporation. But ITV was clearly the main target of the government's 1988 White Paper, *Broadcasting in the 90s: Competition, Choice and Quality*. This proposed that Channel 4 should be obliged to sell its own advertising (albeit with a 'safety net' arrangement between it and the main ITV network) and that both should compete with a third commercial channel. The latter would also be funded by advertising and not by subscription, probably in order to appease those business interests who had lost the battle for the BBC (Goodwin 1998: 97). This White Paper was intended to form the basis of a new Act of Parliament which would seek to transform the duopoly in particular and British broadcasting in general.

Those TV times: new programmes, new trends

The 1980s produced many television programmes of merit. Granada's adaptation of Evelyn Waugh's melancholy masterpiece *Brideshead Revisited* (1981), starring Jeremy Irons, John Gielgud and Laurence Olivier, was so lovingly done that to the mingled pride and exasperation of ITV executives it was mistaken in the United States for the handiwork of the BBC. In 1984 Granada began another adaptation which was highly lauded: *The Jewel in the Crown*, based on Paul Scott's *The Raj Quartet*. Among those dramas which were well received across the Atlantic was an elegant detective series featuring the donnish *Inspector Morse* (Central, 1987–93), and on BBC Dennis Potter was able to exploit the unusual idiom he had devised for *Pennies from Heaven* with another success, *The Singing Detective*. But it was hardly surprising that much of the new drama which was needed to fill the continuing expansion of broadcasting hours should take the more workaday form of soap opera. As well as carrying the American imports *Dallas* and *Dynasty*, the networks were growing more soaps of their own. Reacting to the gritty new world of *Brookside* on Channel 4, the BBC launched *EastEnders* in 1985, only to incur the wrath of Mrs Mary Whitehouse, who declared that the series put the nation 'in moral peril'.

Comedy remained a prolific genre, and moreover one which was keen to reflect the contemporary world. The BBC launched *Only Fools and Horses*, another series about shady entrepreneurs, starring David Jason, while Central offered *Auf Wiedersehen, Pet*, tales of British labourers seeking high wages in Germany. From 1984 Central also staged a welcome revival of television satire, though in an original form, for *Spitting Image* attacked its victims not by using comedians to ridicule or mimic them but by caricaturing them in the guise of gruesome latex puppets. Imbued with that rancorous vitality we expect from all good satire, the series made a particular target of an institution whose stature television had already done much to reduce: the royal family.

The middle of the decade saw an interesting development in the broad genre of 'talk' television. Before the 1960s most studio discussion programmes had been the rather stilted preserve of authorities and experts, but *Late Night Line-Up* (BBC 2) gave us the less formal 'talk show', where conversation ranged more widely and was leavened with wit and vivacity. The 1970s were marked by the celebrity 'chat show', in which the likes of David Frost and Michael Parkinson allowed their guests to dilate on cherished subjects: themselves and their careers. Conversely, the discussion programme of the 1980s, though still located in a studio, took the *audience* as its focus, placing them on a discursive par with its guests, who were typically experts rather than celebrities. The audience sat on a sort of studio grandstand, with the experts identified in the front row or else seated on a stage and confronting them. Each programme would focus on one issue, and its host would roam through the assembly, selecting or responding to speakers with a hand-held or boom microphone. It was, of course, cheap to produce and invariably screened outside prime time. Hence its preoccupation with economic, political or sexual matters could assume a serious and 'relevant' air for that growing sector of viewers who had the leisure to watch off-peak television but scrupled to devote it entirely to 'pure' entertainment programmes.

The genre originated in the United States in the late 1960s, and one of its best-known exports was *The Oprah Winfrey Show* (Channel 4, later BBC 2 and Channel 5), which in Britain alone commanded off-peak audiences of over 1.5 million. Of home-grown versions the most popular were *Kilroy* (BBC 1), hosted by the former MP Robert Kilroy Silk; *The Time, the Place* (ITV) with John Stapleton; and *Question Time* (BBC 1), then chaired by Robin Day and sometimes watched by a late night audience of more than 4 million.

The audience-based talk show was a logical development of 'access' programming, which became fashionable during the 1970s, notably with the phone-in, a genre that gave audiences a 'voice' on both radio and TV, though not yet a 'presence'. The talk show now gave the wider public a chance to question and argue with authority on equal terms, to pit first-hand experience against specialist knowledge, common sense against expertise. It was thus an apt expression of that characteristic of television which has frequently been alluded to in this book: its tendency to impugn rank and professional status. In the words of Livingstone and Lunt (1994: 36), it was original because it challenged 'traditional oppositions of programme and audience, producer and subject, expert and laity'. Nevertheless, it is a matter of some dispute whether, even at its best, the audience-based talk show has been a genuine occasion for democratic debate or merely a cheap and trivial way of filling airtime. During the 1990s some versions aimed at nothing more than confrontation and sensationalism. The American-originated *Jerry Springer Show* (Channel 4) was a new concept in bad taste, regularly including such spectacles as child betrothals, admissions of adultery in the presence of the injured parties, and studio brawls, staged or otherwise.

To be comprehensive about the programmes of the 1980s or of any other era is, of course, impossible. It is hoped that this history has already suggested the broad scope and character of the main genres of radio and television, and though new ones are always arising the lineaments of the old ones they combine are usually discernible. As we approach the 1990s and the turn of the millennium, we must focus instead on the new technologies which were emerging and on the various social, political and institutional attempts to come to terms with them. But we will conclude our programme review by noting one other form of content which was becoming more conspicuous on television, and which was sometimes able to exert an influence beyond its own merely recreational nature: pop music.

Television's problem with pop was always how to render in visual terms something which was essentially acoustic. Shots of musicians singing or playing, or of people listening (as in *Juke Box Jury*), were of limited interest. The best images came from dancing, though these seemed to detract somewhat from what was felt to be the centrality of the music. They certainly played an important part in the BBC's *Top of the Pops*, whose popularity had never faltered since its début in 1963. Later cultish shows such as *The Old Grey Whistle Test* (BBC 2, 1971–83) included in-depth interviews with rock musicians, for by the 1970s rock was old enough to take itself seriously – to develop that critical introspection which had long been a characteristic of jazz. Meanwhile, the visual interest of mainstream pop shows was gradually enhanced by the growing sophistication of production techniques and the resources of the medium itself – flashing lights, fancy zooms and camera angles, video film and graphics – not to mention a greater showmanship among such performers as Elton John, Queen and Pink Floyd.

It was not altogether surprising that the biggest media event of the decade should involve pop music, though perhaps remarkable that pop music and television should combine to raise awareness of a distant political problem and attempt to provide a remedy for it. In November 1984 the BBC journalist Michael Buerk presented a TV report on a famine in Ethiopia. Its pictures of the dead and dying horrified the millions who saw it, among them the Irish rock musician Bob Geldof. After making a fundraising record at Christmas, Geldof went on to organize two televised rock concerts which were held in sequence on 7 July 1985 – one at Wembley Stadium, London, the other at JFK Stadium in Philadelphia. Known collectively as Live Aid, their aim was to raise enough money from around the world to feed Africa's starving and to prevent a recurrence of famine. Featuring rock music's élite – Mick Jagger, David Bowie, Queen, Dire Straits, and many more – Live Aid was the biggest media event since the first moon landings. It was watched by 59 per cent of the population of the United Kingdom and by 1.5 billion people in over 160 countries round the globe. The sum raised was £40 million.

In a number of ways the episode of Ethiopia and Live Aid seemed to express the essence of modern television. First there was that shrinkage of the world that the medium both causes and reflects. In covering events in an obscure part of eastern Africa it galvanized first Britain and soon the world. Then, during Live Aid itself, TV made use of satellite technology to link two concerts many thousands of miles apart and both concerts with a global audience. It also demonstrated another kind of technological shrinkage, for viewers saw Phil Collins perform at both. After singing at Wembley he flew to the States on Concorde, and just a few hours later sang again in Philadelphia.

Second, there were the bizarre juxtapositions that television almost inevitably provides. In Chapter 8 we noted the desultory way in which a visual and live medium tends to cover news and current events, one consequence of which is that its momentary and disjointed images, within adjacent items or even a single item, will often 'comment on' one another in unintended ways. This explains the medium's incipient tendency towards irony – in this instance generated by the contrasting yet related pictures of a desperate, naked, starving people and the glitzy world of pop stars, lavish concerts and supersonic gallivantings.

Live Aid also embodied a fusion of show-business and politics that seems achievable only through a medium in which, as we have seen, even serious and informative matter tends to succumb to spectacle and entertainment. Here rock music – the stuff of dreams, wishes and make-believe – became an instrument of collective social action, part of the fight to provide millions with the physical necessities of life. The antithesis was nicely expressed in the Live Aid concert logo – a silhouette of Africa which was treated as the body of a guitar, with a fretboard emerging from the top. Hence in the flippant style of pop culture, a vast geographical and political entity was pressed into the service of rock music; yet at the same time rock music was proposed as a cure for what in essence were the political ills of a continent – a kind of visual pun which was, of course, perfectly suited to television.

Finally, the episode of Ethiopia and Live Aid typified the often huge yet ephemeral effects of the medium. Its images of suffering caused instant and global revulsion: there followed a deluge of generosity; then the TV crews looked for a new story and Ethiopia sank back into oblivion.

In terms of pop music itself, Live Aid coincided with that third phase of its development which had begun several years before. As was noted in Chapter 2, in its initial phase popular music acted mainly as the accompaniment to dance. Thanks to the 'domesticating' effect of records and radio, it then became something which was listened to much more than danced to. Finally, from about the 1970s television managed to transform it into something *visual*. Just two years after Live Aid, in

August 1987, the MTV (Music Television) satellite channel was launched in Britain, at first via cable, later on DBS, and ensured that music could be 'watched' round the clock. MTV was the television counterpart of pop music radio, for whereas the latter broadcast a sequence of pop singles the former broadcast a sequence of video versions of them. Henceforth no singer or band with serious ambitions to be successful could afford to make a record without also providing a video to accompany it. Some of the videos merely show the artists performing their songs in studios or at concerts. But many use the medium to try to express the music more directly and less literally – perhaps by placing the artists in evocative settings where they could not actually be performing even though they might seem to be; or by filming other, sometimes more abstract, subjects; or by intercutting the two. In different ways MTV seems to offer as near a synthesis of pop music and the visual media as is presently conceivable.

Sources/further reading

For a general discussion of the political and policy issues surrounding broadcasting in the 1980s, see Curran and Seaton (1997). The contrasting tendencies in the production and distribution of media products – towards localization or democratization in the former and globalization in the latter – are outlined in Alvarado, Gutch and Wollen (1987) and Armes (1988). Thompson (1995) gives an excellent historical account of the process of media globalization at both the technological and organizational levels. The decline in the power of the broadcasting unions during the 1980s is charted by Sparks (1994) and vividly illustrated by Bonner with Aston (1998). For the impact of amateur video on television broadcasting see Humm (1998). The trend towards conglomeration and globalization in media ownership is described in Seymour-Ure (1996). McQuail (2000) outlines the problems of regulation and accountability raised by satellite broadcasting, while Hobsbawm (1994) stresses the powerlessness of individual states against the broader globalizing pressures of technology and economics.

For a general account of developments in radio during the 1980s see Crisell (1994). Barnard (1989) is excellent on the difficulties and dilemmas of ILR, and Lewis and Booth (1989) helpfully distinguish community radio from the public service and commercial models, looking at developments in all three. For the network radio programmes of the time Donovan (1992) is a useful source of reference.

The authoritative account of the background and establishment of cable TV in Britain is Negrine (1985). The huge capacity of broad band cable is described by Bowen (1994). For the deliberations of the Hunt Committee see McDonnell (1991). The economic consequences of allowing the cable companies to offer telecoms are outlined in Bulkley (1992). Negrine (1994) gives a useful general account of the development of cable and satellite broadcasting, but for more detailed accounts of the latter see Goodfriend (1988) and Negrine (1988). The story of the rise of Sky TV is recounted by Horsman (1997).

Curran and Seaton (1997) explain why the relationship between governments and broadcasters became strained from the 1970s and why this created a particular problem for the BBC. However, my own account draws heavily on Goodwin (1998), which is lucid, well structured and thoroughly researched – the standard work on television under the Conservative governments between 1979 and 1997. Though Hood and O'Leary (1990) provide a good summary of it, the Peacock Report (1986) can easily be read in its entirety, and it is also quoted and glossed by McDonnell (1991). Scannell (1990) includes a discussion of Peacock's particular approach to public service broadcasting.

Day-Lewis (1992) offers lively descriptions of the terrestrial TV programmes of the 1980s. Livingstone and Lunt (1994) provide an exhaustive analysis of the audience-based talk show, while its more recent decline into sensationalism is charted by Matelski (2000). The best-known study of MTV is Kaplan (1987).

The last age of analogue

Chapter 12

The last age of analogue

Background to the 1990 Broadcasting Act

It may already be apparent that there was a certain ambivalence about the Conservatives' broadcasting policy. The effect of this ambivalence, combined with strong criticisms of their 1988 White Paper *Broadcasting in the 90s*, was to produce a new dispensation for broadcasting which although intended to be liberal was in some respects more rigorous than the old one.

How did this come about? We have seen that despite its ideological commitment to less state interference in industry and to privatization, deregulation and competition, the government was loath to leave broadcasters to their own devices. This was partly because it believed that broadcasting exerted a stronger political influence on the public than the press did, and it was more than once vexed by television documentaries which criticized aspects of its performance. Hence, and as we have also seen, the Thatcher regime interfered considerably in the organization and conduct of the BBC. Moreover, it also introduced tighter controls over the moral aspects of broadcasting content. Why? Pragmatically, morals were an easier target than politics. If the government were to complain too loudly about the political content of broadcasting, it would look as if it were unable to take criticism and was seeking to stifle the means by which the electorate could judge it. But the moral stick was a way of threatening the broadcasters which was usefully indirect. Moreover, the government was keen to reassure the electorate that being economically liberal was not the same as being morally *laissez-faire*. Hence in 1981 it set up the Broadcasting Complaints Commission (BCC) and then in 1988 the Broadcasting Standards Council (BSC), which was to deal with public concerns about sex, violence and standards of taste and decency.

Yet (wearing its liberal hat) the government seemed much less interested in programming quality than in subject matter. While proposing in the White Paper that the ITV franchises should in future be put up for auction, it included no quality safeguards whatsoever, an omission which caused much consternation. When George Russell, the incoming chair of the new franchise-awarding body, was asked how he would react if the franchises were merely to be awarded to the bidder with the most cash, he replied that he would be unlikely to take up the job (Bonner with Aston 1998: 377). This forced the government to think again, and the Independent Television Commission, as the new body was called, would be empowered to accept a lower bid in the auction if the quality of programmes it promised was both 'exceptionally high' and 'substantially higher' than that of the highest bidder (Goodwin 1998: 105–6).

These factors help to explain why, despite the claim that the new Broadcasting Act would be a liberalizing and deregulating piece of legislation:

1 The watchdogs, the BSC and the BCC, would remain in place (they were to be merged in 1997 to form the Broadcasting Standards Commission).
2 Neither the BBC nor Channel 4 was to be privatized but would remain in public ownership, and the competitive role of the latter would be mitigated in the short term by a 'safety net' arrangement with the main ITV network.
3 The new ITV franchise holders would not be relieved of the old public service obligation to provide programmes of range and balance.

These factors also help to explain why the new Independent Television Commission, the so-called 'light touch' regulator, would

1 publish detailed programme guidelines that the bidders were obliged to follow;
2 accept only five of the highest bidders for the thirteen ITV regional franchises which were contested in 1992 (Goodwin 1998: 116);
3 subsequently issue public warnings to under-performing franchise holders; and
4 reject the highest bidder in the second auction for the new fifth channel in 1995.

The 1990 Broadcasting Act: details and aftermath

With effect from January 1991 the IBA was split into two separate organizations, the Radio Authority and the Independent Television Commission (ITC). As was noted in the last chapter, the Radio Authority would ensure more commercial stations at local and regional level, and for the first time up to three national stations. The ITC absorbed the old Cable Authority and was also given responsibility for satellite TV, but its control over independent television was in some degree lighter than its predecessor's. Whereas the IBA had been for legal purposes both the broadcaster and regulator in that it transmitted the programmes which the companies provided as well as prescribing their nature and standards, the ITC was merely a regulator. It was not the commission but the companies (henceforth to be known as 'licensees' instead of 'contractors') who had to meet the requirements of the new Act. This also meant that the ITC could not vet the companies' programmes in advance but only exercise a retrospective judgment over programmes that had caused complaint.

As we have seen, the procedure of tendering for the franchises was also radically altered. Henceforth these would be auctioned to the highest cash bids and last for ten years. To prevent the bidders from over-bidding and then either going bankrupt or failing to meet their promises of performance, the bids were payable on a yearly basis, index-linked, and partly took the form of a percentage of advertising revenue (Goodwin 1998: 108). But as a kind of addendum to the auction principle the government included a 'quality threshold'. This was to embrace a range and diversity of output including news, a substantial amount of regional material, and religious and children's programming. Furthermore, the ITC could 'exceptionally' award a franchise to a lower bidder if its quality promise seemed to exceed that of the highest bidder.

However, after 1993 the licensees who collectively made up the main ITV network would no longer enjoy their near monopoly of advertising. In the short term they would have to compete not only with the fledgling cable and satellite channels, as they already did, but with Channel 4, which from that year would be established as a separate corporation and required to sell its own advertising. This plan, which had been mooted in the 1988 White Paper, had also attracted fierce criticism, since by ending their complementary relationship it would also destroy the financial basis on which Channel 4 was able to provide its own form of public service. So the government now retreated somewhat by introducing a 'safety net' arrangement between Channel 4 and the main ITV network. This provided that if Channel 4's revenue fell below 14 per cent of the total advertising income of terrestrial television, the ITV companies would be obliged to intervene and contribute up to 2 per cent of that amount. If, however, Channel 4 acquired more than 14 per cent of total revenue any surplus was to be shared between itself and the ITV companies.

In the longer term the ITV licensees would also have to compete with a network franchise which the ITC was empowered to auction for a new fifth channel. The fact that this would be national and not regional reflected the larger scale on which television broadcasting was now obliged to operate. Indeed, it was unclear whether even a national franchise would be attractive to bidders at a time when broadcasting was an increasingly transnational, global activity.

ITN was another bastion of the ITV system which would be exposed to greater competition, for it was obliged under the Act to change from a supported service to a profit-making business. It would remain the sole supplier of news to the ITV network for a further ten years, though its position was to be reviewed after five.

But its contract with Channel 4 would be at risk after 1993, when the latter became self-financing and free to shop around for its news provider. A predictable consequence of ITN's need to become more competitive was that during the 1990s its approach to the news became rather more populist, more concerned with 'human interest' stories.

The BBC was left relatively untouched by the Act but its charter was renewed until 1996. However, to free up the system yet further (and achieve something of a 'scaling down'), the BBC, the ITV contractors and the future operator of Channel 5 were all required to move slightly in the direction of Channel 4 and S4C by ensuring that not less than 25 per cent of their total programme output was obtained from independent producers.

The Act set out restrictions on the number and nature of the radio and TV franchises that could be held by any one company, and also contained a rather belated and nebulous attempt to make 'programme quality' something more than merely synonymous with 'that which captures the largest audience'. But its main concern was to usher in a new era of multi-channel broadcasting. Nevertheless, new technologies were exerting such powerful economic and institutional pressures that within a year or two of its passage the Act would be in need of revision.

The renewal of the ITV regional franchises on the third channel, which had been delayed until the Broadcasting Act became law, now took place in 1992. The government had originally favoured the idea of an auction partly because 'cash' is a more transparent and measurable criterion than 'quality'. But the belated rein-troduction of 'quality' bedevilled the whole process, reducing the auction to something of a lottery and a farce. The highest successful bid – £43 million for the London weekday franchise – came from Carlton TV, exceeding by £10 million the bid made by the incumbent, Thames Television. At the other extreme was Central Television in the Midlands, which in the absence of a rival was able to renew its franchise with a contemptuous £2,000. Yorkshire TV extended its tenure with a £37 million bid, while Meridian and Westcountry (£7.75 million) replaced TV South and Television South West respectively, neither of whose business plans impressed the ITC, even though TV South outbid Meridian's £36.5 million. Finally, GMTV gained the breakfast television franchise with an offer of £34.5 million – over £20 million more than the then holders TV-AM. It was TV-AM whose lock-out had largely destroyed the power of the broadcasting unions some four years previously, and its defeat now prompted a letter of sympathy from Mrs Thatcher deploring the result of the franchising system her own government had introduced.

Radio: contrasting signals

Following the 1990 Broadcasting Act, scores of new radio stations, nearly all of them commercial, went to air at national, regional and local level. Yet the growth of the medium masked its uncertain health. The choice of listening was huge and there was a boom in radio advertising, but the audience was spreading ever more thinly: the popularity of the medium was static or even slightly in decline. Moreover, only Radio 4 survived as a reminder of the range and plenitude that individual networks once offered, a fine relic of the old Reithian values yet one which, because it was not television, seldom figured in the debate about the BBC and public service broadcasting.

In accordance with the 1990 Act the Radio Authority invited cash bids from aspiring commercial operators for three national wavelengths, and these were duly awarded, though only after one or two initially successful bidders were later deemed unsuitable or failed to meet their undertakings. Classic FM, Britain's first legal, home-based, national commercial radio station finally went to air in September 1992, no less than seventy years after organized radio broadcasting began in this country. It proved a very successful attempt to shape classical music to the format of a pop station and meant keen competition for BBC Radios 2 and 3. It was followed in April 1993 by Virgin 1215, broadcasting music for the older rock fan, and in February 1995 by the self-explanatory Talk Radio UK, both stations occupying medium wavelengths which the BBC had been forced to give up. Each of the national commercial licences was awarded for eight years.

After trying to raise ratings by using 'shock jocks' – presenters who declaim outrageously reactionary views on all the usual chestnuts – crime and capital punishment, race, the role of women – Talk Radio sought to usher in a new post-literary age of stimulating conversation and debate. Neither approach was greatly successful, and after several changes of ownership and attempts to reposition itself, it is now known as TalkSPORT. Virgin 1215 scooped up those older rock fans whom Radio 1 abandoned in its attempt to target a younger listenership, but it was strongly challenged by Atlantic 252 and the ILR stations. The Radio Authority also licensed yet more of the latter, along with several regional stations mostly offering light or popular music.

The consolidation of ownership that had begun during the 1980s continued during the following decade, with most of the stations belonging to one of three big groups: EMAP, Capital and Great Western Radio. This raised the question of how local ILR really was. Some chains were branded with names like Magic and Gold, with no more suggestion of localness than 'Marks and Spencer'. The Radio Authority also awarded a number of restricted service licences (RSLs) which enabled radio enthusiasts to operate low-powered stations, usually for a limited period. The principal beneficiaries of RSLs were hospitals and educational establishments. They gave valuable experience to aspiring broadcasters and 'alternative' output to the tiny section of the public who wanted it.

BBC radio was hit hard by the burgeoning competition from the commercial sector. While Classic FM and Virgin made steady progress through 1994, Radio 1 suffered a spectacular fall in listening figures, its popularity plunging below Radio 2's for the first time. It subsequently rallied somewhat, largely by concentrating on the youth market and ceding older pop music lovers to Radio 2 and the commercial stations. Offering an adroit blend of pop, jazz, country and light classical music along with a few features programmes, Radio 2 was thenceforth able to claim the largest audience of any of the BBC networks. And it had more success than Radios 3 and 4 in the frequent attempts made by all three to widen their appeal beyond loyal but ageing listeners. Yet though Radio 3 held on to its ardent if minuscule audience of classical music lovers, Radio 4 seemed to assume a kind of pre-eminence among the BBC networks by continuing to provide the nation's intelligentsia with a varied diet of substantial and well-crafted programmes. During its first four years BBC Radio 5 was a failure, for the diverse and unpredictable nature of its content, however good in itself, flew in the face of modern listener requirements. In March 1994 it relaunched as Five Live, a populist news and sport network whose evident appeal to a hearty and mainly male section of the public earned it the soubriquet 'Radio Bloke'. This was appreciably more successful than its predecessor: by 1996 Five Live was capturing more than 5 million listeners.

In early 1995 independent radio's audience share overtook the BBC's for the first time. Advertising revenue rose from £141 million in 1992 to £270 million in 1995, and in the three years up to 1996 was showing an annual increase of 23 per cent. The boom was created by aggressive marketing and distinguished by a slight improvement in the quality of the commercials. Previously, most advertising agencies had employed creatives with a background in graphic design, and since they had honed their skills on billboards and TV screens their early efforts in the medium of sound were often amateurish. But after the launch of the national stations radio copywriting became rather more imaginative and persuasive and when the 1996 Broadcasting Act relaxed the rules on cross-media ownership, revenues received a further boost.

In spite of the exciting developments in radio there remained some worrying portents. Total listening remained flat, for the new stations did not so much create a new audience as filch the BBC's old one. It emerged during the 1990s that perhaps 30 per cent of young people *never* listened to what had, in the forty or so years since the upsurge of pop music, been regarded as a mainly young people's medium. The youthful obsession with pop continued unabated, but whereas it had once been satisfied by trannies, then by car radios, and later by ghetto blasters and Walkmans, many youngsters now got their fix from bedroom television sets offering frequent rock shows on the terrestrial channels and an endless stream of MTV on satellite and cable.

The BBC hedges its bets

By the 1990s the government's attitude to the BBC had mellowed. Mrs Thatcher, its arch enemy, had been deposed. Moreover, the fiasco of the ITV franchise auction blunted the Tories' appetite for further reforms to the broadcasting system: issues such as Europe and the party leadership became rather more pressing. Finally, the corporation was already remodelling itself along lines the government liked. Having shed 7,000 staff between 1986 and 1990 it continued to make tough economies. It reduced its overheads by selling off many of its production and transmission facilities, and in accordance with the Broadcasting Act became more of a commissioner or publisher of programmes in the style of Channel 4. John Birt, who was elevated to Director General in 1993, introduced the policies of 'producer choice' and the 'internal market'. These meant that every programme production became an autonomous entity which was obliged to bid for funding against other productions and buy its resources according to the best deal available, whether inside the corporation or from outside suppliers. Moreover, the BBC sought to supplement its licence income with a whole range of commercial activities which it would develop both in its own right and in partnership with the private sector. In 1994 the government rewarded these policies by extending the corporation's charter and licence funding to the year 2002.

Why was it necessary for a public service broadcaster to involve itself in the private sector in this unprecedented way? It will be recalled that by the early 1980s the common understanding of 'public service' was the provision of something for everyone over a range of networks. But the arrival of Channel 4 emphasized that the crucial element in the concept is the provision for *minorities* – that is, and as Peacock acknowledged, the provision of programmes which cannot be delivered by the usual market mechanism. The shift of emphasis is explained in the BBC's policy document, *Extending Choice* (1992):

> In the past, as a dominant provider, the BBC had an obligation to cover all audiences and broadcasting needs: in the future it will have an obligation to focus on performing a set of clearly defined roles that best complement the enlarged commercial sector.
>
> (quoted in Goodwin 1998: 130)

It has often been remarked that the majority of licence payers get from the BBC programmes which could just as easily be paid for from advertising: but they get them as a 'reward' for subsidising programmes for minorities. The BBC's only real public service justification lies in serving minorities which the market would serve either poorly or not at all. It is true that Channel 4, which carries advertising, also served unprofitable minorities, but only because it behaved as if it were a *non-*

commercial broadcaster: it was funded not from the advertising it carried, but from a grant paid for by the regional contractors on the main ITV channel. And in any case, after 1993 it was required by the government to sell its own advertising in order to make the commercial sector more competitive – a change which resulted in the predictable loss of much of its minority programming.

The BBC's problem was that as channels multiplied and it commanded a smaller and smaller share of total viewing, the levy of a universal licence fee would become harder and harder to justify. A point might arrive when the only politically feasible way of retaining it would be to peg or even reduce it. And this is why, at the government's prompting, the BBC began to look for commercial ways of supplementing its licence income. The plan was that it would charge for a variety of what were, in a sense, peripheral services and use the profits thus raised to subsidize its core activity: the provision of a licence-funded and free-to-air service offering programmes for everyone, including unprofitable minorities.

During the 1990s the BBC 'went commercial' in two ways. One was to form partnerships with the private sector in order to secure overseas distribution for its programmes and services. Its commercial partners provided the financial investment and the access to new audiences while the BBC provided the programming, the ideal role for an institution which not only had a longstanding and international reputation for high programme standards but – a trump card this – possessed a huge library of old material with which to feed the burgeoning number of channels at home and abroad. In 1995 it joined forces with Pearson and the American-owned cable and satellite company Flextech to create the nostalgia pay-TV channel UK Gold, which was carried by BSkyB. In 1996 the BBC also made a deal with Flextech's associate, Discovery, to launch channels in the United States. Then in 1997, in a further deal with Flextech, the corporation launched 'UK TV', a package of four pay channels which were offered on both cable and BSkyB. UK Gold carried old favourites from light entertainment; UK Horizons showed documentaries; UK Style offered cookery, gardening and life-style programmes; and UK Arena broadcast film, drama and arts content. Hence, in entering the domestic subscription market the BBC broke with its original public service principle of providing universal access based on the licence fee (Murdock 2000: 130–1).

But, during the 1990s the BBC 'went commercial' even without the help of the private sector. In order to maintain its position as a renowned and trusted broadcaster in other parts of the globe, the corporation had felt a need at the end of the 1980s to offer a world television service to complement its world service in radio. Since the war the latter had been funded not from the licence fee but by a parliamentary grant paid through the Foreign Office. However, the government declined to extend this funding to a television service, so when the latter, soon to be known as BBC World, was launched in 1991 it was paid for entirely from advertising and carried commercials in the conventional way. Then in 1997 the corporation launched its round-the-clock channel, BBC News 24, which was aimed at cable subscribers (yet which viewers of the traditional networks could watch each night and free of charge after BBC 1's service had closed down).

It is clear that this strategy of defending the licence fee through supplementary commercial activities has its hazards. The more closely identified with the private sector the corporation becomes, either by sharing platforms with purely commercial broadcasters or by operating commercial channels in its own right, the greater the risk that it will lose its distinctive 'brand'. And there is the further risk that if the strategy succeeds too well, the commercial tail will soon start to wag the public service dog. Inside the BBC, the talent and big money could be diverted towards creating premium content for its commercial clientele and thus leave an impoverished public service core, in the way that the consequence of private medical care seems to be an impoverished National Health Service. And those outside the BBC might well be prompted by the sight of an organization which was thriving on commercial revenue to ask the naive question, Why does it need any licence funding at all?

Nevertheless, in 1992 the BBC sought to defend the licence fee by unveiling a wholly new concept of 'public service' – and, moreover, one which soon gained considerable currency. It was described in *Extending Choice* as 'Providing the comprehensive, in-depth and impartial news and information coverage across a range of broadcasting outlets that is needed to support a fair and informed national debate' (quoted in Goodwin 1998: 130). There is no historical basis for this definition: indeed, we will recall from Chapter 1 that of all the elements in Reith's mixed progamme diet, news was the weakest. Nor could it be argued that the BBC's modern news provision serves otherwise neglected minorities, since several of its commercial rivals offer extensive news coverage.

Yet there is no doubt that this new formulation of 'public service' was a shrewd move on the BBC's part. Most news and much information are in some sense to do with politics, and in a democracy most of us would agree that if it is not part of public service broadcasting to inform and educate the audience about politics, then it certainly should be. But the aim was primarily to court the politicians, who are interested only in the political content of broadcasting, and who are also aware that in a fully competitive system they would gain nothing like the amount of exposure that they get from the BBC. In such a system some commercial networks would cut their coverage of news and politics to the bone, and even the best would merely play to television's strengths by offering rolling news with a good deal of actuality, location reports and a focus on *events*. What the BBC has always tried to do is to cover *ideas* as well as events, offering endless backgrounding on both its television and radio networks in the form of interviews, debates, discussions and analysis – all of which gives politicians a considerable public platform. The knowledge that this platform could all but disappear might prompt them to work harder to defend a licence fee that they insist is unpopular with the electorate. In 1996 it might even have influenced the government's decision to renew the corporation's charter and licence funding until 2006, when the latter is once more to be reviewed.

A look at some of the BBC's best programmes during this decade could justifiably focus on its sitcoms such as *One Foot in the Grave* (1990 onwards), *Absolutely Fabulous* (1992–6) and *The Royle Family* (1998 onwards), or on its numerous cookery programmes, which seemed to grow from a sudden if belated recognition that food is highly telegenic. But probably the major development was the concept of 'real time' news, which transformed certain kinds of current affairs output from a series of past-tense narratives into something approaching running commentary. The very notion of 'continuous', 'breaking' and 'rolling' news is peculiar to broadcasting and could not have pre-dated it, but the catalyst was the arrival of lightweight recording equipment and easy satellite links which are, of course, used to best advantage by television. CNN pioneered the concept in the United States with a twenty-four-hour cable news channel which aimed to keep abreast of events in the Gulf War of 1990–1. BSkyB followed suit shortly afterwards and the BBC launched its News 24 channel in 1997. The last of these might well have been intended to bolster the corporation's recent and somewhat ahistorical claim that range and quality of news coverage were part of what entitled it to be regarded as a public service broadcaster. In November 1997 the BBC added to its already extensive news provision by launching BBC News Online, a free-to-access internet news service funded from the licence fee.

ITV: a changing landscape

For the ITV licensees life got tougher after 1992. Their advertising revenue was immediately hit by the cable and satellite channels, and then by the change in Channel 4's status. In 1993 the licensees took 78 per cent of all TV advertising, with Channel 4 taking 17 per cent and cable and satellite taking 5 per cent. A year later ITV had lost 3 per cent of the market, 2 per cent of it to Channel 4 and 1 per cent to cable and satellite.

As well as having to compete with all these broadcasters, not to mention BBCs 1 and 2, ITV would soon face a third commercial network, Channel 5, which was to be launched as soon as practicable. These challenges illustrated that if, given the technology and economics of TV broadcasting, it had ever made sense to operate a regional system in a country as small as Britain, it was making much less sense in the 1990s. All the licensees' competitors on the other channels operated on a scale which was at least national, and the government accepted their need to get bigger by relaxing some of the ownership rules that had been enshrined in the 1990 Act.

Consolidation soon followed. In 1992 Yorkshire TV and Tyne Tees Television were allowed to unite. Then in May 1993 LWT paid £14 million for a 14 per cent stake in Yorkshire–Tyne Tees. A month later Granada paid £68 million for a 15 per cent stake in LWT, and at about the same time Carlton took over Central (which already owned 20 per cent of Meridian) as well as having a 20 per cent interest in GMTV. Before the end of the decade a substantial share of the third channel had been carved up by three big operators: Carlton, Granada and United News and Media. In 2000 the last of these was bought out by Granada, which co-owns with Carlton both ITN and the ITV digital operation. Though new legislation would first be needed, it is expected that the whole of the third channel will soon be in the hands of a single licensee.

The history of the bidding for the new Channel 5 suggested that in an era of global and multi-channel broadcasting even a national franchise was too small to be a particularly tempting prospect. Offers were invited in April 1992. At the closing date for the applications three months later, only one bid had been received – from Channel Five Holdings – which the ITC rejected because dissatisfied with its business plan. The franchise was re-advertised and in 1995 awarded for the modest sum of £22 million to Channel 5 Broadcasting, a consortium of Pearson, United News and Media, and CLT, the Luxembourg-based broadcaster. But there were subsequent difficulties and delays. Its transmission area was patchy, covering only 85 per cent of British homes, and even within that area 90 per cent of domestic video recorders would be affected by its signal, committing the company to a costly re-tuning operation. Nor was it allowed to transmit until 90 per cent of the re-tuning was completed. Channel 5 was eventually launched on Easter Sunday, 30 March 1997. It was a commissioner, not a producer of programmes, offering a brash round-the-clock diet of old movies, pseudo-documentary titillation and occasional soccer matches.

A second Broadcasting Act was passed in 1996, one important aim of which was to assist the emergence of British commercial broadcasters big enough to hold their own in the international media market. To this end, companies were no longer restricted to major shareholdings in just two ITV licences but subject to the more flexible limit of a 15 per cent share of the total audience. Moreover, as well as being allowed to hold stakes in several TV broadcasters (Granada and Pearson both had major shareholdings in Rupert Murdoch's BSkyB), companies were subject to much less control on cross-media ownership. At a time of growing media convergence the government's aim was to lump newspapers, TV and radio into a single media market, in which the main restraint was a 'public interest' test that could be flexibly interpreted according to three criteria. If mergers or acquisitions occurred, what economic benefits would result? What would be the effect on competition? And would diversity in information sources be reduced?

Channel 4 at the crossroads

Channel 4 spent its infancy trying 'to give a voice to the new pluralism of the 1980s' (Harvey 1994: 118) – and on most counts it succeeded. Such programmes as *Out on Tuesday* (1988) and *Sex Talk* (1990) explored sexuality of various kinds; *Union World* (1984–5) served the needs of trade unionists; *Handsworth Songs* (1987) and *Looking for Langston* (1990) were the creations of black British filmmakers. From 1987 *The Media Show* was the first series for those who wished to take an informed and critical look at television itself. Perhaps the channel's most extraordinary and famous achievement was the series *Film on Four*, a collaboration with the movie industry to produce feature films for both TV screening and cinema exhibition. It supplied 22 per cent of the budget of *Paris, Texas* (1984) and 100 per cent of the budget of *My Beautiful Launderette* in 1987. In that year alone its screenings of new films included *Letter to Brezhnev*, *Caravaggio* and *The Company of Wolves*.

However, as a result of the 1990 Broadcasting Act the character of the channel changed somewhat. It ceased to be a subsidiary of the IBA and became an independent trust whose board members were nominated by the ITC, and to further the Act's aim of making broadcasting more competitive it was obliged to sell its own advertising from 1993. Since this had been a likely development ever since the publication of the Peacock Report in 1986, the channel's chief executive, Michael Grade, who succeeded Jeremy Isaacs in 1988, gave its schedules a slightly more populist slant. The soap opera *Brookside* swelled the ratings, as did several drama series which were bought in from America: *Cheers*, *The Cosby Show*, *The Golden Girls*, and later *Friends* and *ER*. Audience share rose from 8.8 per cent in 1988 to around 11 per cent in 1993, surpassing BBC 2's. Whereas even in its early years a heartening 50 per cent of the viewing public watched something on Channel 4 in any one week, nearly 80 per cent were doing so in 1991. Its core audience of youngish, affluent professionals was an attractive prospect for many advertisers in 1993, and in any case the channel retained a connection with the main ITV network through the 'safety-net' agreement.

However, its critics insist that after 1993 the slide towards populism accelerated, eroding the channel's distinctive character. In that year it launched a down-market early morning programme, *The Big Breakfast*, which by 1995 generated no less than 10 per cent of the channel's entire advertising revenue of £450 million (Franklin 1997: 206). While the channel was associated with two notable successes in *Four Weddings and a Funeral* and *Trainspotting*, it has also been suggested that after 1993 its funding of cinema films became less adventurous in nature and began to dwindle overall (Hill 1996: 169). In the event, the channel was becoming too successful for its own good. Its advertising income grew so dramatically that in 1995 alone it was obliged under the safety-net agreement to pay £57.3 million to ITV – enough to fund five years of product for *Film on Four* (Grade 1996: 181–2).

With S4C its share of net advertising revenue grew to over 21 per cent by 1997. It was able to keep a larger share of this money after it was released from the safety-net agreement by the 1996 Broadcasting Act.

One could almost argue that Channel 4 suffers from having a 'failure requirement' built into it, in the sense that if it grows its audiences too successfully they will cease to be the minorities it was designed to serve. But in the late 1990s it attracted the more serious criticism that it was using a protected public service status (which it merited less and less) to secure an advantage over its commercial rivals. Though obliged to support itself from advertising from 1993, the channel continued to be subsidized in the sense that, because it had a public service remit, it was alone among the commercial broadcasters in paying nothing to the government for its spectrum. From 1998 it was thus able to launch new broadcasting developments which were extremely well funded: the FilmFour and E4 subscription channels on cable and satellite and the 4Ventures Division in partnership with other enterprises. Its rivals argue that Channel 4 is acceptable either as a commercial broadcaster or as a public service one, but that it should not be allowed to act as both.

Whether or not the channel continues to prosper, it faces much the same danger. If it is hit by the growing competition – in 1996 its share of viewing was overhauled for the first time by satellite and cable, and from 1997 it was threatened by Channel 5's search for a young audience – it could either be forced further into the mainstream or try for a lucrative niche, in either case sacrificing several kinds of minority programming. But if it beats off the competition the outcome could be much the same. By the turn of the millennium the channel was valued at between £2 billion and £3 billion and was still in public ownership. A future government of any hue might be tempted to privatize it – and private ownership could threaten investment in programmes and erode the channel's distinctiveness, especially the provision of programmes for unprofitable minorities. It remains hard to see how as a conventional commercial broadcaster Channel 4 can continue to fulfil the public service remit which was imposed on it in 1982.

Sky without limit: the rise of satellite TV

We noted in the last chapter that satellite TV made slow progress in its early years because viewers were already blessed with an abundance of material from the terrestrial channels, not to mention video rental and retail outlets. Eric Hobsbawm (1994: 12) draws our attention to a stupendous fact that we all too easily overlook: by 1990 people were living in 'a world which could bring more information and entertainment than had been available to emperors in 1914, daily, hourly, into every household'. Not only was the provision lavish beyond the most fervid imaginings of anyone living seventy-five years earlier: after the purchase of a receiver it was – and this is what made it universal – virtually *free*. The achievement of broadcasting, and especially television, was to bring news, sport, drama, comedy, music, and so on, to those otherwise too poor to obtain them through separate cash payments. It was an egalitarian process which appealed to the most radical social reformers on the one hand and to old-fashioned patricians like John Reith on the other. As Hobsbawm (1994: 307) puts it, 'entertainments hitherto only available as personal services to millionaires were now in the most modest of living rooms'. This is the profoundest sense in which television broadcasting in particular is a democratic phenomenon, for it is the precondition of those other democratic effects which we discerned earlier in this book. We noted its tendency to impugn expertise, reduce status and demystify authority, and we observed its power to expose the obscurest political misdeeds of individuals and nations. But it is 'democratic' only because it does these things before millions upon millions of viewers of every social background.

In his mention of households and living-rooms Hobsbawm draws attention to another 'democratic' fact about broadcasting which has been stressed throughout this book: the privacy and individuality of its reception. To avail themselves of this lavish and 'free' facility audiences are not even obliged to go anywhere: it comes to each consumer's own space. She almost invariably owns the receiver and her consumption of broadcasting does not lessen, neither is it lessened by, that of others, no matter how many they number. In the sense that this consumption is atomistic, sometimes solitary, we could say that there is a sense in which the cultural integration, the almost physical sense of national unity, that Reith sought to instil was working against the grain of the medium itself. The private, idiosyncratic nature of listening and viewing has, if anything, been compounded by the increasing choice of channels.

Nevertheless, the rise of satellite television has shown that broadcasting may not be virtually free for much longer since its conditional access technology – the means of allowing or preventing the transmission or reception of its signals – can establish a firm connection between what one watches and what one pays for. As a result we may come to regard the primitive age of terrestrial television as 'the good old days' – an age when despite the limited number of channels the viewer had access to a fair diversity and quality of content that cost her almost nothing. It is in any case worth noting that old viewing habits die hard. In 1997 more than three-quarters of all British viewing was still of the same three channels, BBCs 1 and 2 and ITV, which had been available at the beginning of the 1980s. Even the 30 per cent of all viewers who had home access to multi-channel television still devoted the majority of their viewing to the domestic channels (Goodwin 1998: 156–7).

The only way in which BSkyB could prosper, then, was to offer an even better diet than terrestrial television – or, which came to the same thing, to appropriate the most popular bits of it – for audiences were canny enough to realize that more channels did not necessarily mean more choice. Like ITV's in the mid-1950s, BSkyB's first years were modest and faltering and prompted rash predictions of failure. But by acquiring exclusive rights to big movies and sporting events and by assiduous marketing, mostly through Murdoch's own newspapers, it made steady progress as the decade wore on. During 1992 no fewer than twenty-nine satellite and cable services were launched, and 1993 marked the turn of BSkyB's fortunes, when the previous year's loss of £20.4 million was transformed into a profit of £62.2 million.

Two years later saw one of the most adroit deals in the satellite sector. Though Murdoch himself owned 50 per cent of BSkyB, other major shareholders included Granada, the oldest of the ITV regional operators, with 13.5 per cent, and the Pearson Group, both of which had held shares in BSB, the ill-fated venture that Sky took over. BSkyB now acquired from Granada the rights to 3,000 vintage episodes of *Coronation Street* as part of a plan to launch several new satellite channels in 1996. The channel which recycled old programmes from both Granada and LWT, a company which Granada now owned, would be called Granada Gold Plus. The deal enabled BSkyB to win many more viewers to pay TV, and for Granada it meant swift and cheap elevation to broadcasting on a higher plane. By 1996 about 5 million homes boasted satellite dishes and one in five British households was able to receive BSkyB either directly or via cable. The year was also full of dark omens for the traditional broadcasters. Sky won the exclusive right to televise the world title boxing match between Frank Bruno and Mike Tyson, but to general indignation would beam it only to those of its subscribers who were prepared to pay a ten-pound surcharge. Given Bruno's propensity to become rapidly intimate with the canvas, it was not surprising that the transmission turned out to be poor value.

The company was well aware that it particularly needed to buy up sporting events because unlike movies, its other staple fare, these did not suffer from the disadvantage of being pre-recorded. Thanks to the cinemas and video outlets there was a likelihood that viewers would have seen many of the movies before, although this might change in the future. But a live sporting event was a genuine TV premiere. As BSkyB clinched an increasing number of exclusive deals on sport – and on movies, despite the fact that some of its subscribers had already seen them – the old-fashioned, terrestrial broadcasters began to resemble its poor relations. Even the government grew anxious. It used the 1996 Broadcasting Act to prevent BSkyB and other subscription companies from obtaining the exclusive right to broadcast any of eight major British sporting events, including the FA Cup and the Grand National. Yet it was trying to stop the unstoppable. A few months later both the BBC and BSkyB won rights to screen Premiership soccer until the year 2001. But whereas the BBC could afford to bid only for recorded highlights, Sky bought live transmissions of whole matches.

In global terms Murdoch's was only one of several big organizations operating partly as rivals and partly as cartels with shared strands of ownership (McQuail 2000: 219). As well as the three leading American firms, Time-Warner, Disney and

Viacom, four foreign operators had a big stake in the US media market: Seagram of Canada, Bertelsmann of Germany, Sony of Japan, and of course Murdoch's (originally Australian) News Corporation. Aside from his press interests Murdoch owned Fox, a US television network, and a Hollywood movie studio, held stakes in Australian broadcasting, and kept a majority share in Star TV, the Asian satellite network whose potential for growth was massive. These international holdings had implications for British television as well as that of many other relatively small countries. Material originating from any one part of Murdoch's empire (most of it, in practice, from America) could be transmitted to audiences in all the other parts of it, leading to an ever greater homogenization of media content. And the rules which individual countries might frame so as to restrict foreign programme quotas or in some other way to regulate the nature of what was broadcast would be all but unworkable.

Wiring up: cable TV

We have seen that the special advantages of cable were large capacity and, above all, *interactivity*. The aim was to use it not only for broadcasting but as a simultaneous conduit for telecommunications and information technology. Telephones and linked computers are by their very nature interactive, but the plan was also to make *broadcasting* a two-way process. The audience would be able not only to *respond* to broadcasts within the same medium rather than via a separate telephone network, for instance in voting for a 'man of the match', but to *modify* the broadcasts as they happened by choosing camera angles, frame freezes, re-runs and so on. In the longer term the audience might even be able to *initiate* broadcasts – that is, to choose what programmes to receive, not from published schedules as at present but from a vast library of material of every imaginable kind. Since the 1980s it had been possible to run videos and computer programmes on domestic TV screens, but that was a dedication of the television set to uses other than broadcasting. What was expected to emerge in the next decade was *interactive broadcasting*, something we shall look at more closely in the final section of this book.

After an indifferent start cable was given a boost by the 1990 Broadcasting Act because it allowed the operators to offer telephony to their customers. In 1992 the number of cable franchises providing telecoms jumped from ten to twenty-four, and by 1994 the cable had passed more than a million homes. Two years later 40 per cent of the networks had been built, yet the cable companies had captured only one in five of their potential customers. The problem was that it was hard for them to compete against DBS for the entertainment-led, broadcasting side of their business, while the unique interactive facilities they were promising had still not materialized by 1997 (Goodwin 1998: 68). Most of the TV channels they carried were also available on satellite, and the terms on which they were supplied by BSkyB, an organization that was to a large extent in competition with cable, were stringent. One channel which was exclusive to the latter was SelecTV. Another was L!ve TV, which was supplied by the Mirror Group and whose contribution to broadcasting history was the introduction of topless darts and of someone called News Bunny. Despite these frantic attempts at notoriety the channels soon disappeared, and cable television would continue to be handicapped by a failure to secure its own separate sources of programming.

In 1996 the industry at last sought to become more competitive through a process of consolidation. Cable and Wireless merged its telecoms subsidiary, Mercury, with three of the main cable operators, Bell Cablemedia, Nynex and Videotron, to form Cable and Wireless Communications. Then in May 2000 the latter was bought out by National Transcommunications Limited (NTL), the old ITV transmitter operation which had been privatized in 1990. Now NTL and Telewest are the only major operators left in the field.

The future of cable may well lie in telecoms and other interactive media rather than in conventional broadcasting. But since the latter can be conducted via wire and turned into a two-way medium the difference between them is narrowing, and the cable operators will soon face competition in both from British Telecom, which since the beginning of 2001 has been allowed to offer broadcast content.

Everybody's listing

At the beginning of the decade the deregulation of broadcasting was mirrored by developments in the press: the *Radio Times*'s monopoly of the BBC's programme listings and the *TV Times*'s monopoly of ITV's were ended in 1991.

The first challenge to these giants had been mounted in 1983 by a pygmy, the London magazine *Time Out*; but after a legal battle which cost it some £300,000 their copyrights were upheld. However, in 1989 the government, acknowledging the need for increased consumer choice in all aspects of broadcasting, announced an end to the duopoly. Even so, the battle for deregulation was not quite won, for both the BBC and ITP, the publishers of the *TV Times*, attempted to force rival publications to pay huge fees for the right to reproduce the listings, something it took another copyright tribunal to overturn in 1992. Since then both the *Radio Times* and the *TV Times* have listed the programmes of all the television channels, not merely those of their parent broadcasters, but so have innumerable other publications and the circulation of these quondam giants has dropped.

Sources/further reading

On the background to the 1990 Broadcasting Act see Hood and O'Leary (1990), Negrine (1994) and Bonner with Aston (1998). The main provisions of the Act and its consequences for the ITV franchises are outlined in O'Sullivan, Dutton and Rayner (1994) and subjected to a shrewd analysis by Goodwin (1998). For the changes to ITN see McNair (1994).

The boom in commercial radio is described in Horsman (1996a) and there is a discussion of Classic FM's pop format in Crisell (1994). Garfield (1998) describes the decline in popularity of BBC Radio 1 during the mid-1990s and its attempts to reposition itself in the radio landscape. The decline in radio's popularity among the young is discussed in Brown (1995). There is a good survey of modern sound broadcasting in Barnard (2000).

For discussions about the BBC and public service broadcasting in the context of the 1990s see Smith (1990), Tusa (1994), Garnham (1994), Negrine (1994) and Tracey (1998). The BBC's partnership with Flextech is outlined in Horsman (1996b), and McNair (1998) gives a brief account of the origins of 'rolling news' in television. Harvey (1994) provides a useful potted history of the first ten years of Channel 4; speculations about its future are in Bell (1997). A personal perspective on its first five years is offered by Isaacs (1989). Both Hill (1996) and Franklin (1997) see signs in Channel 4 of a shift towards populism after 1993.

For his remarks on the miraculous abundance and cheapness of broadcasting in 1990 see Hobsbawm (1994). The standard history of BSkyB is Horsman (1997). Turow (1999) and McQuail (2000) contain some useful analysis of the international media conglomerates, and Negrine (1994) and Goodwin (1998) include details of the development of cable during the 1990s.

The dawn of the digital era

The dawn of the digital era

Prestidigitation!

The main reason for the government's desire to bring in the Broadcasting Act of 1996, a mere six years after its predecessor, was to provide the framework for an expansion of broadcasting which would make all previous expansions seem paltry. For most of its history television had been based on *analogue* technology: frequencies were allocated to individual broadcasters, with one frequency needed for each channel. What was now about to replace it was *digital* technology, which could be used by satellite, cable and traditional broadcasters alike, reduced transmissions to a stream of data expressed as a series of ones and zeros, and resulted in a much more efficient use of scarce spectrum space. A single frequency could accommodate several channels, each offering high-quality sound and vision. This meant that there could soon be scores if not hundreds of television channels, with a similar expansion occurring in radio. And since digitization also afforded easy interactivity it was likely that many of these new channels would be provided on a subscription or pay-per-view basis. To receive digital transmissions the viewer would have to acquire either a set-top converter or a new television set, and listeners would need to buy special digital radios. The new technology also provided a successor to video cassettes in the form of digital video discs (DVDs), although these were not to achieve popularity until after the turn of the millennium.

Under the terms of the 1996 Broadcasting Act, bundles of frequencies called *multiplexes* – six of them in television, more in radio – would be allocated to different operators or groups of operators. The most powerful of the TV multiplexes was assigned to the BBC, which uses it to transmit BBCs 1 and 2 along with BBC Choice, BBC Text, BBC News 24, BBC Knowledge and BBC Parliament. The remainder of the multiplexes would be allocated by the ITC.

Since digital technology affords not only an excellent signal but room for many more channels on the spectrum, the plan is that it should not simply coexist with analogue but replace it. However, the year in which the government will switch off the analogue signals depends on how rapidly the public embraces the new technology. The most popular guess is 2010.

The BBC's digital proposals

Since they are able to invest in long-term research and do not need to provide an early return of audiences to advertisers, the national public service broadcasters have been central to the early development of digitization, especially in northern and western Europe (Hendy 2000a: 215). At the same time the BBC, under Director General Greg Dyke, who succeeded John Birt in 2000, has sought to re-affirm the case for a universal licence fee. In television the corporation plans to adjust to the digital future by complementing its two old-fashioned mixed programme networks with several others of a themed nature. There will be eight 'public television' services, all of which would be supported from licence income:

1 BBC 1 – the traditional, mainly populist mixed programme network.
2 BBC 2 – the traditional mixed programme network carrying some content for minorities.
3 BBC 3 – a network offering a mixture of entertainment, comedy and drama which would be targeted at young people. (This part of the plan incurred the government's initial disapproval on the grounds that the network carried insufficiently serious content and duplicated services widely available in the commercial sector.) However, during the day the channel would carry:
4 A service for pre-school children.
5 BBC 4 – a network dedicated to the arts and culture. However, during the day the channel would carry:
6 A service for schoolchildren.
7 BBC News 24 – the continuous news service which is already operating as a subscription channel.
8 BBC Parliament – continuous live coverage of parliamentary debates.

The two latter services could be seen as part of the BBC's recent and unhistorical claim that news and political coverage are a central part of public service provision. BBC Parliament, in particular, which will usually draw only tiny audiences, seems a shrewd attempt to appease those who determine the level, indeed the very existence, of the licence fee.

In radio the proposal is for eleven national and licence-funded channels:

- BBC Radios 1, 2, 3, 4 and 5 Live – together with full UK availability for the World Service.
- A black music and news-based station aimed at young people.
- A station drawing on the BBC's unique archive of musical performances and interviews which have helped to shape popular culture over the past thirty years.
- A speech service of drama, comedy and readings for all generations including children. It would combine original material with archive classics.
- Live Sports Extra – a service bringing more live sport to radio by extending the coverage hitherto offered on 5 Live. (This service was launched in February 2002.)
- A BBC Asian network, serving Asian communities throughout Britain with speech and music.

What are the principles behind this new structure for public service television and radio? It is first of all apparent that the BBC is seeking to hedge its bets by retaining the old radio and TV networks for its more conservative audience, yet providing new services for a public who will be at ease with the new technology and likely to disperse as never before over numerous themed channels. The corporation clearly hopes that these eight TV and eleven radio services will give it a big enough presence on the digital landscape to justify the continuing levy of the licence fee on every owner of a television set. Its aim will be to ensure that there is nothing its rivals can provide which licence funding would not provide to at least as high a standard, and also to carry content for minorities whom its rivals would regard as unprofitable.

Digital terrestrial television: the commercial sector

The five other television multiplexes which the government made available were assigned to the commercial sector, and a distinction was established between the *multiplex operators* and the *programme service providers*. Many of the providers, such as Granada and Channel 4, had already, of course, been licensed by the ITC. But now the latter was also empowered to license the multiplex operators who would buy the services of the providers. The ITC awarded the first multiplex to Digital 3 & 4 Ltd, which carries the conventional terrestrial services of ITV, Channel 4 and teletext. It also offers subscription channels, including ITV 2 and the 'art house' film channel, FilmFour, which launched in 1998.

In 1997 the ITC awarded three multiplexes to British Digital Broadcasting (BDB), a consortium equally owned by Granada, Carlton and BSkyB, but only on condition that the last should withdraw. BDB, later known as ONdigital, launched on 15 November 1998, essentially as a pay-TV operation. Carrying BBCs 1 and 2 and ITV free of charge, it also offered BBC News 24, BBC Choice, ITV 2, Channel 4, Channel 5, S4C, and various other subscription channels – many of them provided by BSkyB. The service failed to thrive. It was afflicted by low audiences and high 'churn' (the cancelling of subscriptions by dissatisfied customers), and was forced to match BSkyB's giveaway of the 'digiboxes' which convert analogue TV sets to digital reception and cost around £130 each. Losses were so enormous that in June 2001 Granada came under pressure from its shareholders to pull out. ONdigital had attracted only a million subscribers in contrast to the 4.5 million who had signed up to BSkyB. Soon after, it re-branded itself as ITV Digital but went into liquidation in April 2002.

The ITC awarded its last multiplex to S4C Digital Networks, which guarantees capacity to the Welsh version of Channel 4 and to Channel 5. It also offers Gaelic programming in Scotland during peak broadcasting hours and carries a number of other new digital services.

Digital satellite television

In the mid-1990s BSkyB formed a consortium called British Interactive Broadcasting with the aim of providing an extended satellite service partly of TV channels and partly of interactive channels which audiences could use via a phone line. The other members of the consortium were British Telecom, Midland Bank and Matsushita, the owners of Panasonic. 'Sky Digital', as it was branded, launched on 1 October 1998. To boost take-up of the new technology the company took the expensive decision to give the digiboxes to its subscribers free of charge. The service comprised the free-to-air terrestrials (though not ITV and ITV 2 until 2001) together with subscription channels and interactive facilities for home shopping.

Because of the costs of converting to digital transmission and acquiring the premium programming which would lure new customers, BSkyB lost £263 million in 1999. The gift of the digiboxes cost it a further £381 million. Moreover, the interactive channels, known collectively as 'Open', were highly unprofitable, leading to speculation that TV sets might not, after all, replace personal computers as the primary home-shopping medium. But having converted its subscribers to the new technology – it switched off its analogue signal in 2001 – BSkyB had several reasons for optimism. First, it had again won the auction for the combined television rights to Premiership soccer. Second, thanks to this and its acquisition of blockbuster movies, it had attracted almost 5 million subscribers by the end of 2001 – a realistic step towards its goal of 7 million by 2003. Third, it had a clear lead in conditional access technology, the subscriber management system by which pay TV is operated. Fourth, it was still the main satellite broadcaster to Britain. And finally, although it was compelled by the ITC to relinquish its shareholding in BDB, later ITV Digital, the latter's licence depended on being able to offer premier sports events and movies – and BSkyB was the sole supplier of these. Hence, although it put no money into ITV Digital it gained a big share of its revenue.

Digital cable television

The cable companies do not operate a digital television service of their own but merely relay the packages of channels made up by the BBC, ITV Digital and Sky. For some time there has been a promise that they would launch their own distinctive digital service, but in an industry not renowned for big profits it is hard to see where the necessary investment will come from. The service would probably be a collaboration between the two main operators, NTL and Telewest, and handicapped by the heavy reliance on satellite feeds that characterizes the present one.

The biggest failure of the cable industry to date has been its inability to exploit those interactive services which are its 'unique selling proposition' – the feature which would give it an advantage over all its competitors. Sky Digital offers interactivity but only by means of a separate telephone line. Cable can in theory offer interactivity through a single conduit which will deliver not only broadcast services but the facility to modify or respond to them and to order supplementary services such as video on demand; and it can also provide telecoms and internet access. But a low take-up rate among potential customers and considerable 'churn' among existing ones are facts which speak for themselves.

Digital radio

Digital radio offers better sound quality than its analogue predecessor, up to six stereo or twelve mono services per frequency, and the potential for supplementary text or simple graphics which the listener can view on a small screen built into the receiver. In September 1995 the BBC set up its own radio multiplex by launching a digital service of all five of its networks. Geographical coverage was limited and, as with television, listeners needed special receivers, so the take-up was minimal – restricted largely to technical enthusiasts and broadcasting personnel. For several years afterwards sales of digital radio sets remained sluggish. Why?

Although digital sound is excellent, FM quality is good enough for most people's purposes. Moreover, analogue receivers can be bought very cheaply and each household typically owns several. Digital receivers are expensive and, in the usual vicious circle, their prices will not fall until they are bought in large numbers, nor will they be bought in large numbers until their prices fall. To replace with digital sets all the analogue sets in a household could prove very costly. But what might lend impetus to domestic sales is the fact that digital radios are now appearing as a standard feature in all new cars.

The slow sales of digital radio sets mean that the analogue broadcasting signals could well be turned off at a later date than would have occurred if television were the only medium. But the commercial operators have also taken the expensive plunge into digital radio. The Radio Authority allocated the first national independent radio multiplex to Digital One, a consortium of Great Western Radio, NTL and

Talk Radio, which began transmission in November 1999. Thirteen local and regional multiplexes were also licensed in 2000 and a further twenty in 2001. Digital One carries the three national analogue commercial stations, Classic FM, Virgin and talkSPORT, together with seven digital-only channels: three offering pop music (Planet Rock, Core and Life); one easy listening (PrimeTime Radio); one drama and readings (Oneword); one news (ITN); and one offering business and financial information (Bloomberg Radio).

The internet would appear to offer enormous possibilities to radio, especially as pure sound needs much less digital capacity than sound combined with vision. From the perspective of the broadcasters

> the great potential of Internet radio is that it has a democratizing effect on the business of broadcasting. Just as anyone, anywhere, can launch a web site, so anyone, anywhere, can start their own radio 'station' and broadcast to the world – without prohibitively high start-up costs or investment in state-of-the-art equipment. For some, this is a return to the pioneer spirit of unregulated, experimental 1920s radio.
>
> (Barnard 2000: 253)

It is now a commonplace irony that stations which have been issued with restricted service licences by the Radio Authority can quite legally use the internet both to reach listeners on the far side of the globe and to continue broadcasting long after their RSLs have expired.

From the listeners' perspective the advantages of internet radio are more ambiguous (Barnard 2000: 253–4). To find stations on the web takes diligence and persistence and congestion can cause poor sound quality. With a conventional analogue receiver it is usually easy to move from place to place while continuing to listen to the radio. But internet radio is almost entirely accessed through a personal computer and thus demands a static listener. It may suit the desk-bound office worker who does not have to pay for her own internet connection, but for many it is not a congenial way of listening. Moreover, because the receiver is a computer it also offers pictures, but 'radio with pictures' runs the risk of losing the virtues of self-sufficient sound broadcasting and instead becomes a visual display which the sound element merely subserves. Nevertheless, technical improvements could soon overcome the problems of portability and sound quality, and while the audiences for internet stations are not necessarily large they may be very widely distributed. Furthermore, unlike conventional radio listeners they have the option of being interactive: they can download music and other material from the web stations, join on-line chat groups and order merchandise.

The history of broadcasting before the 1990s offers us no portent or precedent for internet broadcasting, no way of helping us to understand it or determine how it might best be conducted. Aside from the interactivity it allows it is unquestionably 'broadcasting' in our original sense of enabling a mass audience to receive from a sender live sound (and, increasingly, moving pictures) at the time they are being sent. For this reason separate consideration must be given to the internet, even if its relationship to broadcasting is as indeterminate as it is undeniable.

The internet

The internet may be regarded as a medium in its own right: it is simply an international network of computers operating according to agreed protocols. In Britain dial-up internet access was first provided by Demon – in 1989 according to one source (Crook 1999: 39), 1992 according to another (Cornford and Robins 1999: 118). By January 2000 more than 20 per cent of the UK population had access to the internet (Briggs and Burke 2002: 307) and by the end of that year the *Guardian* newspaper was claiming that the figure was one-third. But perceptions of the internet as a single, integrated medium are inhibited by the fact that it does not conform to previous media models (McQuail 2000: 125). Not only does it combine a multiplicity of codes and functions in a way which makes it look as if it has swallowed every previous medium (it carries music, sound, still and moving pictures, graphics and print and can be used both 'passively' and interactively); it is not owned, organized or controlled by any single body (McQuail 2000: 29). Its penetration is highly variable and there is no simple, composite definition of its function.

Nevertheless, we can identify some of the significant features of the internet. First, its technologies are digitally based: its point of access is commonly the computer, though TV sets and mobile phones are others. Second, because computers, TV sets and phones are affordable to growing numbers of people and because the internet is subject to little or no regulation, the latter is easily and widely accessible. Third, the internet is distinguishable by a lack of *physical* location. In one sense global, national, regional or local, in another sense it is none of these things, creating new communities of interest and a wholly new basis for personal identification. Finally, the internet is characterized by a variety of uses and a heterogeneity of content: it is both an interpersonal, private medium and a public, mass medium and can switch easily between both.

This instantaneous versatility is what makes the internet so difficult to define, and its versatility largely derives, of course, from the degree of interactivity it confers on its users. Given the traditional perception of broadcasting as a one-way process directed at a large and essentially passive audience, it is probably the interactivity which is at the root of our feeling that the internet lacks 'the precision provided by the simultaneous reception of a defined body of information characteristic of [the press and broadcasting]' (Seymour-Ure 1996: 10).

In passing, we might note that the ease of access and personal autonomy which characterize the internet are not without their limitations. By using desk-top software it is easy, for instance, to become an author and publish on the internet because there is no 'gatekeeper' analogous to a book or newspaper editor, whose role is to mediate between writers and readers. But by the same token there is no means for an author to acquire validation, gain distinction or build a reputation. As McQuail (2000: 119) crisply remarks, 'It is not easy to become famous on the Internet.' In this sense there is a kind of impotent, futile democracy about the medium. And with respect to broadcasting, whether over the internet or by any other means, the mass audience is likely to survive, still requiring gatekeeping in both intellectual and recreational matters in order to avoid wasting its time.

Since broadcasting, however informally it may be conducted and however much it may be modified by interactivity, is clearly one function of the internet we must give it some further consideration. So far, internet broadcasting has mostly consisted of radio, since sound occupies much less bandwidth than sound combined with moving pictures. But with the development of broad band technologies – an asymmetrical digital subscription line (ASDL) can give net users much faster access – rudimentary television broadcasting has also developed. Somewhat ironically, web-cams are now installed in the studios of BBC Radios 1 and 2, not to mention in the rooms of countless private dwellings, so that viewers may stare at the occupants in various stages of intimacy.

A significant moment in internet television occurred in July 2001 when singer Elton John teamed up with Microsoft Network (MSN) to web-cast a concert from Turkey. What MSN offered on a pay-per-view basis were video-quality pictures and CD-quality sound, and to ensure uninterrupted reception it limited the internet audience to 130,000. Access was provided on a first-come, first-served basis, just as it normally is to fans who attend such events. The advantages of showing them on the internet are that they can reach a world-wide audience much more cheaply than via satellite, and they can be presented as unique, live occasions which do not have to be squeezed into a conventional TV schedule. On the other hand, internet television presently lacks interesting content and the absence of scheduling and publicity could make it hard to find a regular audience. Of the three big broad band providers, British Telecom, NTL and Telewest, the last has shown the most interest in becoming a supplier of content.

Sources/further reading

Much material in this chapter is contemporary rather than historical and thus likely to become outdated very quickly. The reader should therefore access the BBC, ITC and Radio Authority web-sites, where most of it came from and where the very latest developments are published.

Barnard (2000) offers a useful account of the possibilities and limitations of radio on the internet, while Hendy (2000a) outlines the political economy of digital radio. Many of his observations are equally applicable to digital television. For an excellent analysis of that complex and protean entity the internet, see McQuail (2000).

Part III

From broadcasting to multimedia

This historical study began by noting that from its inception broadcasting was a live medium which was *private* in the sense that it was *domestically* received. From about the 1960s it was becoming even more private because increasing numbers of people could afford their own *individual* radio and television sets – sets whose use was no longer confined to the home. This development was broadly contemporary with another: a growth in audience *activity* which was made possible in the case of radio by the audio-cassette recorder and in the case of television by such new devices as the remote control, teletext and, above all, the VCR. What the more important of these technologies allowed the viewer and listener to do was to opt out of live broadcasting, to use their receivers for messages other than those devised for them by the broadcasters.

At present, another kind of audience activity is developing which was presaged by the arrival of cable television and which we might more helpfully term *inter*activity. The viewer will be able not only to opt out of broadcast content but to modify, respond to, and even initiate it – either within the same medium (cable) or via a separate phone line (terrestrial and satellite). But thanks to the digital technology that we noted in our discussion of the internet, that broadcast content can also be delivered by computers, which are themselves an interactive medium. These developments will have two consequences. First, interactivity will increasingly modify the traditional 'one-way' process of broadcasting. Second, various media are rapidly *merging*: it is conceivable that a single appliance may shortly encompass the range of functions once separately performed by the television, the radio, the computer and the telephone. These two consequences are, of course, closely connected. It is precisely because a TV set can now be digital, cabled up to the broadcaster, and thus enable the viewer to be directly interactive that it is partly indistinguishable from a conventional computer.

In this final section we shall consider how the new technologies of satellite, cable and, most important, digitization will impact on broadcasting: how they will influence audience behaviour, media content and organizations, and raise issues of 'access' for both broadcasters and audiences, and 'control' for both broadcasters and regulators. Inevitably, different questions will be encountered at different levels. Several tendencies will be discussed, all of which seem certain to develop even though some could do so only at the expense of some of the others. Hence, in judicious or perhaps merely cowardly fashion, possibilities will be suggested but firm predictions generally avoided.

Chapter 14

Future history: some speculations

Future history: some speculations

The viewing and listening experience

The whole process of broadcasting is directed at the viewers and listeners so it is from their perspective that this discussion will begin. It will also address the kind of content they will be consuming, on what media, and who will be providing it.

Despite recent technological developments, most viewers own, in addition to their television sets, nothing more than a remote control and a VCR. Thus equipped, and faced with a multitude of digital channels, what and how will they watch?

Digitization, whether via satellite or in the form of the internet, could well increase the global tendency of broadcasting, both that which is aimed at an international audience and that which may be aimed only at a national audience but will be receivable elsewhere. Apart from programming whose appeal transcends linguistic differences, such as sport and rock music, the world domination of the English language means that other nations would be more likely to watch our broadcasts than we theirs. However, there could be considerable cross-national viewing between Britain, Canada and the United States, with the bulk of the output originating, as at present, from the USA. Yet the position of English as the world language of broadcasting will last only as long as the economic and political pre-eminence of the United States, and in the distant future Chinese may replace it.

Digitization may also lead to an increased use of the remote control, for in order to avoid missing out on something good many viewers will 'surf' – sample the output of a range of channels. This potential restlessness may even mean that fewer viewers will be willing to watch whole programmes and could lead to their partial replacement by 'sequences', a tendency that we will explore later. If there are scores of channels through which the viewer may browse with ease, a number of them offering content that is duplicated or triplicated elsewhere, their individual significance is bound to be diminished. Many viewers who are not immediately transfixed by what one channel has to offer will hop to another. Digitization may also mean an increase in the use of television as a secondary medium, for it is conceivable that certain channels will offer nothing but 'moving wallpaper' – landscapes or underwater scenes rather like the interludes which punctuated programmes in the early days of BBC television, and whose aim will be to occupy the idle eyes of customers in bars, shopping centres and airport lounges. (In passing, we might note how even in today's world the visual media are bursting their traditional bounds. In post offices and doctors' waiting rooms our attention is solicited by video monitors and TV sets, presumably in the belief that wherever we go we must have something to gaze at.)

Hence digitization, following upon our ability to put receivers to uses other than live television or radio, means that broadcasting may have to take itself less seriously in the future and will become in certain respects less influential. There would be less reason to require broadcasters who are not funded from the licence fee to observe political balance and editorial impartiality. We will no doubt continue to watch a great deal of TV and listen to a fair amount of radio, but their effects will be diffuse and attenuated. Indeed, and disregarding the cynics who feel this point was reached in 1955, the digital era will probably mark the first time in broadcasting that there will be more channels available than content to fill them. It will certainly create a huge demand for the latter, one which has already been growing over the last twenty-five years.

We have see that the cable operators seem presently more interested in carriage than content, despite needing to find programme sources other than BSkyB. British Telecom, though keen to provide wired television and video-on-demand, seems equally keen to remain a mere carrier and find others to provide its programming. But the likeliest consequence of digitization will be a scramble among broadcasting *carriers* – whether satellite, cable or the traditional operators – to secure distribution rights to the best sources of *content*: indeed they will probably seek to own them outright. The reason Rupert Murdoch acquired Twentieth Century Fox was to feed the growing needs of his satellite channels, and in the near future film and TV production companies could well become targets for one or other of the big carriers. But because broadcasting will be delivered by cable and phone lines as well as in the traditional atmospheric way, and because the first two systems permit an interactive element, *new* carriers may emerge: telecoms operators, TV rental companies, computer manufacturers, internet service providers. It is also conceivable that there may be new producers of broadcastable *content*, such as book publishers.

We can be fairly sure that the increased demand for content will cause an increase in the vast amount of *recycling* which already takes place. For many viewers certain broadcasts have a value which transcends the ephemeral way in which they are experienced. Historically it was easy to prize sculptures, paintings, musical scores and works of literature because they existed in space. It was less easy to prize theatrical, musical or balletic *performances* in the same way because these, the lifeblood of broadcasting, existed only in time. The problem was solved by the arrival of recording technology. (Indeed, it is most probably recording technology which has underpinned the recent growth of academic interest in 'cultural studies', for broadcasting provides much of the material for such studies, and it is surely no coincidence that academic research into British television began just one year after the arrival of Ampex videotape.) Not all recorded output is deemed valuable, of course, and as channels have increased both in number and in transmission hours much recycling has been the result of sheer pragmatism. But with the arrival of digitization the appetite for material will be unprecedented, and given the limits to human originality we can expect a huge growth in recycling.

It is worth reviewing the forms that recycling can take. First, broadcasting makes extensive use of *borrowings* and *adaptations*, which could be seen as recyclings from other media with which many of its audiences will be familiar. The most obvious examples of borrowing are television's screenings of cinema films and (more rarely nowadays) of theatrical plays. Adaptations involve some alteration of the original, as, for example, in BBC television's celebrated dramatizations of Jane Austen's novels. Rather more obvious examples of recycling are those innumerable *programme repeats* – second, third, uncountable showings of what has originated within broadcasting itself. Granada Plus and UK Gold are reminders that whole channels are now being dedicated to repeats, a trend which is bound to intensify. They vividly illustrate the effrontery which distinguishes so much clever marketing for they are invariably subscription channels, thus requiring their viewers to pay for material which is not merely old but which, for the most part, was originally shown free of charge. *Remakes*, updated versions of old broadcasting artefacts, constitute a third form of recycling. A few years ago viewers were able to watch the comedian Paul Merton's not very successful attempt to revive some Galton and Simpson scripts which had first been performed by Tony Hancock. In the early 1990s viewers were also offered remakes of the 1960s classic series *Maigret* and *Dr Finlay's Casebook*, themselves adaptations of the literary endeavours of Georges Simenon and A. J. Cronin respectively.

It is likely that the abundance of digital channels will not only increase demand for content but sharpen competition for *audiences*. With more and more broadcasters chasing a fairly static body of viewers and listeners it will make sense for many to seek a niche through theming or specialization. We can therefore expect a growth in the number of *format* channels – a phenomenon which began with satellite and cable TV in the 1980s. The traditional generalist, mixed programme networks were well suited to an era of broadcasting shortage (hence the old public service rationale of ensuring that a scarce resource offered something to everyone). But when there is a vast choice of channels the audience for such a network can no longer be reliably predicted: mixed programming can create wild fluctuations in its size. In contrast, specialization in a single, recognizable form of output assures constant viewing (and listening) figures and a steady revenue stream, while those who enjoy that form of output are spared the need to hunt for it over scores of channels or wait for a mixed programme network to feature it.

Since it gives you what you want at any time you want it, the format channel can also provide effective competition against the VCR. Its overall appeal to the viewer is, in effect: no need to comb the channels in search of your favourite kind of programme; no need to pre-record it or get a cassette of your favourite movie: it, or its type, is always on air – twenty-four hours a day. Of course the video that the viewer might otherwise have watched could have been taken from the channel's own output, but the benefit to the channel is that it might also have come from somewhere else – and in any case video viewing is not normally reflected in the audience statistics.

Formats have a certain flexibility. While some, such as MTV, are dedicated to a single kind of output others may offer a variety of programmes but one which is unified within a single theme. 'Gold' channels, for example, may provide comedies, dramas, quiz games and so on, but within some such implicit theme as 'nostalgia' or 'classic TV'. The names of satellite and cable channels like Sky Movies, Screensport, MTV, the Comedy Channel, the Arts Channel, the Learning Channel and the Parliamentary Channel evoke the range of interests that format television has already catered for. But digitization will hugely extend it, with numerous channels offering everything from sailing to soft porn and thus rendering broadcasting very similar to a large store like W. H. Smith, where the consumer can find a galaxy of publications ranging from daily newspapers and popular journals to special interest magazines.

Much depends on the content carried by the various TV formats, but since it will be substantially unvarying within a particular channel we can expect to see some replacement of self-contained programmes with the more indeterminate 'sequences' that already typify format radio. In any case, the *segment* or 'bite' of which so much broadcasting content is composed – the interview, rock video, commercial break, comic sketch, brief report, feature, or whatever – may well become the salient or significant feature.

Nevertheless, segmentation on television has a slightly different rationale from that of radio. Radio is a secondary or background medium, and segments allow the listener to 'enter' or 'leave' its content without feeling that she has missed or will miss anything of importance. Segmentation has a similar function on those television channels which can also be treated in a secondary or intermittent way, such as MTV. But whereas *intermittence* is the key to segmentation on the radio, its main aim on television is not only to attract viewers at all times but – because TV is mostly a primary medium – to *hold* them, whether they have just switched on for the first time, have changed channels, or are merely browsing. In effect, however, there is little difference, for on television as on radio segmentation affords continuous accessibility while also seeking to retain its existing audience by providing a constant change of stimulus. We might sum up its function by saying that it seeks to preclude the 'horizontal' desultoriness of the viewer – her inclination to keep browsing among all the channels available to her – by offering 'vertical' desultoriness: a constant change of stimulus within a single channel. But in so doing it strengthens that tendency to treat complex matters in the fitful, superficial way which already seems characteristic of so much television.

This aspect of viewing behaviour and the measures which TV channels take to counter it should not be exaggerated. Not all viewers are compulsive channel switchers, nor is all format television obviously segmented: movies, for instance, and some sport require sustained attention. But since the television set, with its myriad broadcasting channels and accompanying video facility, is the main if not the only cultural and intellectual source for so many, the often fragmentary nature of the experiences it offers is a matter for some concern. In a single well-loaded sentence one eminent historian reviews some of the remarkable advantages that the modern media have brought, yet sounds a cautionary note:

> It is barely possible for someone who has been brought up in the age when electronic and mechanically generated music is the standard sound heard on live and recorded pop music, when any child can freeze frames, and repeat a sound or visual passage as once only textual passages could be re-read, when theatrical illusion is as nothing to what technology can do in television commercials, including telling a dramatic narrative in thirty seconds, to recapture simple linearity or sequentiality of perception in the days before modern high-tech made it possible to move within seconds through the full range of available television channels.
>
> (Hobsbawm 1994: 502)

What does television do for patience, concentration, the ability to construct meaning through sustained narrative or argument? With the help of the remote control, interactivity can simply mean hyperactivity and suggests that old-fashioned 'passive' viewing may have its virtues after all.

Because multi-channel, largely formatted broadcasting may soon join video in providing us with what we want whenever we want it, it is possible to see a further weakening of the link between entertainment and cultural consumption on the one hand and what we might term 'the sense of occasion' on the other: a weakening which has been taking place over several centuries. Historically, the business of being entertained or culturally edified has been more or less separate from the banalities of existence.

From the brief glance at the evolution of the media which we allowed ourselves in Part I it can be seen how the loss of occasion began with print, because print enabled the consumer to replace attendance at a poetic recitation or dramatic performance in a public space and at a certain time with the activity of reading in her own space and time. But, especially important in the case of drama, the temporal elements – sound and moving vision – were lost in the substitution. With broadcasting the sense of occasion was further eroded because many more of the original elements of the event could be transposed to the consumer's own space. First, sound could be conveyed on the radio, then both sound and moving vision on television. Finally, since the 1980s television has, thanks to formatting, emulated video in enabling the consumer to view what she wants *in her own time* – an important effect of which is to 'banalize' entertainment, to assimilate it more closely than ever before to the daily routines of the individual.

In a previous chapter we hinted that from the early 1970s, when the restriction on broadcasting hours was lifted, television moved nearer to the rhythms of ordinary life: cookery, hobbies and education were covered during the day, children's programmes were broadcast at teatime, general entertainment was provided in the evening. What TV was doing, of course, was reflecting the fact that the consumption of certain cultural artefacts, or the attendance at certain cultural events, has traditionally been associated with particular times of the day: we speak of a film or theatre 'matinée', for instance. However, format TV takes this assimilation even further by affording much greater autonomy to the individual viewer; for she might now, if she prefers, watch a Humphrey Bogart film on Sky Movies or a cycle race on Eurosport not in the afternoon or evening but over breakfast. Nor need this preference be merely eccentric: the life-style of the modern individual may diverge from the traditional pattern either because she has more free time through being unemployed or because the recent revolution in the nature of employment (now often home-based and occurring at flexible and irregular hours) has resulted in unusual and irregular periods of leisure.

What has made the continuous and specialized nature of modern television so much easier to provide is, of course, the increasingly global conduct of broadcasting: we can watch live cycle racing over breakfast because it is being transmitted in the early evening from Australia. Yet the experience can be disorientating. Before broadcasting became global we were used to pre-recorded elements within it which were of such high quality that we could not tell them from live transmissions. Now, because we might be sitting in broad daylight watching an event which is evidently taking place in darkness, or vice versa, live transmissions often look as if they are recordings. Hence, as O'Sullivan, Dutton and Rayner (1994: 283) acutely point out:

In the 'global village' differences of time and space are eroded as the result of the 'instantaneous' nature of modern communications. We are all synchronised into a randomised 'world time' and to a 'cocktail' of programme content – places, events, personalities, narratives, aesthetic values. We have been dislocated and resynchronised into a new kind of simulated and 'hyperspace' world.

In one respect, then, we can make television subserve our individual needs and whims. In another it lures us into a free-floating world of its own, untrammelled by the normal laws of time and space.

The increasing subjugation of broadcasting to the individual life-styles of its audience in one sense devalues the culture and entertainment that it offers. We often speak of television not so much as a source of entertainment in itself but as a poor alternative to 'real' entertainment ('I think I'll just stay in and watch the telly tonight'). And this despite the fact that what it offers us – its scripted and unscripted discourse, its aesthetic experiences, its visual wonders, its technical and production standards, the calibre of its performers, its ability to reproduce artefacts which originated in other media, including the entire oeuvre of the cinema – is of a magnitude, range and quality unimaginable to previous generations. Perversely, what we consider as 'real' entertainment is often bound up with a sense of occasion, something we have to make an effort to *get to* rather than that which we can consume in our own space at any time.

But if digitization means that the cultural content of television will be treated even more 'functionally' than before – as a casual and basic resource rather like the gas or water supply – this may encourage the medium's more *obviously* functional possibilities. Traffic, travel, weather and home-shopping formats already exist on satellite and cable but as the last of these implies, much functionality requires an ability to use the TV set in an interactive way, either by responding directly to the broadcasts or by using it instead for booking, banking or access to the internet. This brings us back to an issue that we addressed at the beginning of this section: if TV sets can be used as a two-way medium and dedicated to purposes other than the reception of broadcasts, what distinguishes them from computers?

Interactivity and media convergence

We noted earlier that many viewers still possess no more than a television set, a remote control and a VCR. The latter two devices enable us to opt out of live broadcasting and use the television to watch teletext or videotapes. Now technology enables us not only to *opt out* of live broadcasting but to *control* it in the sense of being able to modify or adapt it to suit our particular purposes. Of course, in a basic, absolute sense we have always been able to control live output merely by pressing the on/off button or playing with the controls on the TV set to darken the picture, mute the sound, switch channels and so on. Later, the remote control enabled us to do these things without leaving the armchair. But thanks largely to digitization we are – or soon will be – able to do very much more. We will be able to preselect programmes from an evening's schedule and rearrange their sequence to suit our own tastes. Certain kinds of content, such as sport, will allow us to choose our own camera angles and action replays, and we will be able to play alongside the contestants in quiz shows like *Mastermind* or *Who Wants to be a Millionaire?* in a far more intimate way than previously, so that the sensation of sitting in the 'hot-seat' will be heightened to an unprecedented level.

Two new developments are of particular interest in allowing the broadcasters themselves (and not just video retailers and home camcorder owners) to offer alternative content to live broadcasts which is nevertheless contemporaneous with them – that is, which is not content that the viewer has previously taken off air. First, the viewer will be able to access material which is supplementary to the programme being broadcast but which is not included in the transmission itself. Second, video- or near-video-on-demand (NVOD) gives pay-per-view access to various films which are continuously screened at staggered starting times to allow the viewer a choice of when to watch them. In the longer term this facility may enable the viewers to access a whole portfolio of programmes at times entirely of their own choosing.

These developments serve to call into question what broadcasting is. In its brief history it seems to have gone through at least four phases:

1 The broadcaster transmits *live* material which is instantaneously received and consumed by a mass audience.
2 The broadcaster transmits *pre-recorded* material (old cinema movies, programme repeats) as well as, or instead of, live material, which is instantaneously received and consumed by a mass audience.
3 The broadcaster transmits live and/or pre-recorded material which is instantaneously received and consumed by a mass audience, but which can also be *stored* (using VCRs and TiVo) by individual members of that audience for consumption at times which suit them. TiVo is a new video-recording technology which builds up a profile of its user's tastes and automatically pre-records what it thinks she will like.
4 As well as transmitting live and/or pre-recorded material which is instantaneously received and consumed by a mass audience, or which its members can store for later consumption, the broadcaster holds material which can be *accessed at different times* (using NVOD and other new digital technologies) by *individuals* or *small sections of the audience* for consumption either at the time of reception or at times which suit them.

Hence, unlike the material viewed in phase one, the material which is viewed in phase four is

- not always transmitted in live form;
- not always consumed at the moment it is received;
- not always 'offered' by the broadcaster so much as sought by individual viewers (who may not even amount to a 'mass' audience in any meaningful sense).

Can the activity described in phase four still be regarded as broadcasting? Furthermore, it is not simply that broadcasting has changed so much since its inception that perhaps it needs a different name: it now involves media which previously served only *non-broadcast* purposes. Indeed, since we have already noted that by providing us with certain interactive features TV sets are looking more and more like computers we can see that the different communications media are undergoing a *convergence* of functions.

Developing in parallel with broadcasting technology, the computer is the major product of the digital revolution: interactivity is at its heart. Yet since each computer can be linked with countless others to form the internet, and since it uses not only printed text but sound and, increasingly, moving images, it too can serve as a medium of broadcasting. When bandwidth increases, the internet may well revolutionize broadcasting at all levels – the political, the economic and the institutional, as well as those of content and audiences – but it is presently too early to say in which directions. The Elton John web concert which was referred to earlier may well be a portent: it was among the first TV shows that could be watched only on a computer.

Nevertheless, we need to be clear about what kind of media convergence is significant. The radiogram, which first appeared in 1927, is a reminder that it has long been possible to create convergence of a kind simply by putting two different media in the same box. Moreover, there has always been some overlap of features between different media: to give only one obvious example, sound is a property of both radio and television. But thanks to the common binary code of digital technology, what is now occurring is an *interchangeability* of media, an unprecedented versatility within each medium which allows it to assume the character and many of the essential functions of the others. Here are some examples:

- Through NVOD and TiVo the *television set* incorporates the functions of the *VCR*.
- The *television set* can resemble the *computer* in offering e-mail, internet access and home shopping, while through 'web-casting' the *computer* can also offer a form of *television*.
- Internet radio is heard mostly on *computers* not *radio sets*. (Listeners can not only hear live radio but choose a playlist by voting records on or off the air; join

on-line discussion groups; access supplementary material from station web-sites, such as interviews with musicians or music from a CD database; and order merchandise.)

- Through a technology known as 'wireless application protocol' (WAP), which allows callers to access the internet, *mobile phones* are acquiring some of the functions of both *computers* and *radios*.
- *Computers* are also *audio recorders* when used to download music files from the internet.

Of all these merging media, computers are perhaps the most glamorous because they are the newest and most versatile: they combine the functions of virtually all the others. It is thus not surprising that television and radio seem to be acquiring 'computer manners'. The Sky channels, in particular, imitate the 'busy screens' of computers, making much use of split images, rolling text and various kinds of graphics. Moreover, on Sky News viewers might be invited to 'press the red button' if they want the full text of a political speech from which the on-air bulletin is taking only sound bites. This provision of a more extended coverage seeks to emulate not only the computer's ability to store vast amounts of information but the strengths of the traditional print media, enabling television to offset some of the quantitative advantages of newspapers that were outlined in Chapter 8.

Even those television and radio stations which are unable to provide the quasi-interactive, computer-like facilities of Sky News show an increasing multi-media consciousness in their programming by referring the audience to their own web-sites. Hence by turning to their computers and accessing the site viewers and listeners may be able to learn more about a station and its output; to e-mail instant feedback to on-air programmes (as in the *Jimmy Young Show* on BBC Radio 2); to take part in on-line, though off-air, discussions with other members of the audience; to order the station's merchandise; and to access the web-sites of any other organizations which the station has publicized in its programming.

We have already suggested that the convergence of the various media may mean that in the fairly near future one single item of domestic equipment could combine the different functions of the computer, the TV set, the radio, the telephone, the VCR, the fax machine and so on, serving the needs of both work and leisure in a way that computers already do rather more successfully than televisions. And even if they are more likely to complement rather than merge with one another, it still makes some sense to have a single regulating body for all the electronic media. This is why it is widely believed that in addition to its responsibility for telephony the Office of Telecommunications (OFTEL) may shortly be placed in charge of radio and television broadcasting, both public service and commercial, and whether satellite, cable or terrestrial, as well as of internet service provision. But prediction is a dangerous game. In terms of broadcasting, a rosily democratic picture has been painted here of an alert and busy audience with an almost baffling choice of content and of means by which to mediate it. But a closer look reveals conservative factors both in the economic laws which will shape the development of the new technologies and in the attitudes and behaviour of the audience.

Control, access and broadcasting content

Who will own and operate the scores of digital channels? Who will regulate them? Who will be able to watch and listen to them, and on what terms? And what sort of content will they be able to watch and listen to?

In Chapter 11 we noted that because media markets are becoming increasingly transnational – and, indeed, global – the only way that British broadcasting organizations can raise the capital to stay competitive with the likes of BSkyB is to get bigger in themselves and/or to form large consortia. This is why the government has relaxed many of the restrictions on multiple franchise holdings and cross-media ownership. Broadcasters are now fewer and bigger than before, and over the last twenty years foreign companies have taken a considerable stake in British commercial radio and television. Nevertheless, the fiasco of the Sky/BSB merger in 1990 vividly illustrates how hard it has become for governments to regulate broadcasting which originates outside the UK if at least one of the parties responsible for it is also based abroad. How will such broadcasters be regulated in the future, when much that is viewed and heard in Britain might be transmitted from America or any other part of the world?

The regulation of foreign broadcasts is felt to be necessary mainly because of fears that 'the law of the jungle' could prevail. A few media giants such as AOL/Time-Warner, Disney and News Corporation may conceivably devour the smaller operators and pose that threat known as 'cultural imperialism', by which, with the help of satellite television, the culture of politically dominant nations (America is invariably meant) is alleged to 'swamp' that of less powerful peoples. To resist it, several European countries have for many years imposed quotas on the number of foreign programmes they allow their home-based broadcasters to transmit. Yet aside from the fact that the cultural imperialism thesis is open to a number of objections (Thompson 1995: 166–73; McQuail 2000: 232–5), the channels afforded by digital technology could be so numerous that, as in press and magazine publishing, where a few companies monopolize the most popular titles, there could still be room for a shoal of independent operators at the margins. And many of these operators would no doubt affirm their independence by promoting counter-cultures or at any rate distinctive cultures. Indeed, the digital expansion, especially as embodied in the internet, gives cause for considerable optimism. For twenty years or more, video camcorders have enabled 'ordinary people' to make their own TV programmes yet with virtually no prospect of showing them to a wider public. Henceforth, a vast increase in outlets could offset the otherwise global tendency of broadcasting by allowing some of these programme-makers to gain access to a mass, if modestly sized, audience – yet another instance of the democratizing effects of broadcasting. In other words, thanks to digitization, a technology of cheap distribution could at last catch up with the technology of cheap production.

Because they could be numerous, transient, and of uncertain provenance yet global reach, the independent operators could prove every bit as hard to regulate as the transnational giants. Yet regulation may be just as necessary in order to resist not cultural imperialism but propaganda, obscenity and violence. On the other hand, we may well find that in the new digital era there will be relatively little room for independent operators, that the growth of content may not keep pace with the growth of channels, and that after an initial expansion even the latter may turn out to be less numerous than is anticipated. The digital era may prove to be just as subject as its analogue predecessor to strong conservative pressures at the levels of institutions, programming and audiences. Why?

Let us first consider conventional broadcasting. Since the dominant broadcasters are the only ones who can afford the high cost of investment in digital technology, their dominance is likely to be maintained. Economies of scale will intensify (Graham 1998: 32). The fixed costs of programme-making will remain high while distribution costs will fall considerably. Hence, and as we noted earlier, content will be at a premium. For the broadcasting institutions the logical way to recoup their costs will be to take over the smaller operators and thus acquire more channels through which to diffuse what is essentially the same body of material. But these are likely to be channels not just of one particular medium, whether radio or television, but a *range* of media: radio, television, print and so on. Why?

Thanks to the binary code which all digital technologies use there is a high degree of interchangeability between media: TV programmes can be delivered by computer, internet messages via mobile phones, and so on. But of course the interchangeability is not absolute: it is impossible, for instance, to deliver TV programmes via a radio set. Moreover, not everyone who has a radio set has a computer – or wishes to receive radio programmes via her computer even if she can. Nevertheless, the binary code allows not only an artefact designed for one medium to be delivered by another but, as David Hendy (2000a: 224) points out, a single body of material to be simultaneously packaged for different artefacts in different media. Hendy observes that the stories, interviews, features and music sessions which are suitable for a radio programme could just as easily be turned into a newspaper article, a web-site, a CD, a television documentary, a video, and so on. In future, then, whether an artefact made for one medium is transmitted through several media, or whether a single body of material is simultaneously fashioned into different artefacts in different media, content will not only be at a premium but regarded as 'content' pure and simple. In other words, it will be conceived not primarily in terms of 'radio' or 'television' but simply as material whose mode of delivery – be it radio, TV, or whatever – will be a secondary consideration. This versatility, along with media convergence, prompts the thought that if the various media do remain distinct, their distinctions may rest upon the different situations in which they are used rather than on any inherent differences of function.

Digitization has, of course, been the reason why the BBC has in recent years been so keen to provide its staff with 'bi-media' production skills. But, more to the point, it strengthens the rationale for the formation of the multi-media conglomerates – companies with interests not only in radio and television but in newspapers, magazines, records, film production and internet services. For audiences, however, it could mean rather less genuine variety of content and rather more in the way of superficial variations on the same body of content which they will encounter across a range of media. The sheer limits on human creativity combined with a technology driven by economic considerations will ensure that rather than attempt to offer something different on each channel, broadcasters will spread a limited amount of content over a greater number of channels. And aside from being able to switch material from one medium to another, they will duplicate content that exists elsewhere if this will yield higher profits than going for a new niche. The recent proliferation of commercial radio stations has not brought with it a commensurate increase in choice. The great majority offer the same few safe and predictable music formats: adult contemporary, 'gold' and Top 40 (Hendy 2000b: 35). It has also been noted that the new drama and spoken-word channel on Digital One carries almost no original material but relies instead on adaptations of existing and well-known works, many of them purchasable as audio books in the shops (Hendy 2000a: 228).

So while it could be said on the one hand that digitization will bring in a multitude of channels, an abundance of broadcasters and a variety of content, it could be argued on the other that because of the high investment costs there will be fewer and bigger broadcasters than ever, and that the convertibility of the digital code means that the choice of content will not be nearly as great as the range of channels. Moreover, even if this convertibility allows content to go further than it otherwise would, economic forces are likely to exert a reductive pressure on the number of channels that technology has made possible. Why?

First, there is little scope for an increase in the overall size of the broadcasting audience – and there are severe limits to the extra time that it could give to viewing and listening. This means that as the number of broadcasting channels increases the audience will fragment. Each channel will capture a smaller following than the few channels did in the old era of scarce broadcasting, thus attracting less advertising or subscription revenue; and for many channels these factors will lead to cheaper and poorer content, and, in a spiralling decline of audiences and revenue, to a likelihood of closure. The big commercial networks will probably do reasonably well, but least vulnerable would be a system of broadcasting in which revenue is not closely tied to audience size: the public service system. Hence, while seeming to promise golden opportunities for commercial broadcasters and to threaten the future of the universal licence fee, the digital expansion of broadcasting may actually give a new lease of life to the BBC.

These economic laws may apply less severely to the internet, where the cheapest and most banal forms of broadcasting are likely to be found. But although many viewers seem quite happy to gaze at street scenes or at people getting dressed and brushing their teeth, it would appear that the great majority prefer the more carefully constructed forms of entertainment that network television has traditionally provided – and this could prove to be another conservative factor in the future of broadcasting. As Denis McQuail (2000: 410) points out, the economics of scale push towards one-way mass communications rather than two-way narrowcast channels. Audiences can press buttons if they wish, but most of the time they like to sit back and be entertained. They like the big 'production values' inherent in pop music and dance extravaganzas, comedy shows, costume dramas, blockbuster movies, top sporting events and wildlife documentaries. They dislike television that looks cheap. This suggests that, notwithstanding their potential for convergence, TV sets and computers may well remain separate entities in the future, with the former being used primarily for entertainment and recreation and the latter for functional purposes – for doing 'the world's work' – in addition to providing the more interactive forms of entertainment.

Furthermore, in spite of its promise of democratic access and an unprecedented diversity of content, even broadcasting on the internet could fall victim to constriction and consolidation. Power will lie with those who control the 'gateways' or *portal sites* – the means by which the audience can locate the countless web-casters who could not otherwise alert it to what they have to offer. For providing this facility, along with services such as format guides and programming details, the portal controllers could well charge a fee to both web-casters and audiences – and it is conceivable that they may use their position to impose editorial constraints on the former. Since owning or controlling a portal site will be as powerful as operating a multiplex (Hendy 2000a: 226) it seems likely that those who do so will be the multi-media conglomerates. Moreover, because the interactivity which digitization affords makes conditional access very easy to impose, while both the technology itself and the content it will need are expensive, it also seems likely that a significant, perhaps the greater, part of broadcasting will no longer be free at the point of use.

Public service: enduring ideal or heroic red herring?

Let us try to summarize what digital broadcasting may shortly be like. We will refer mostly to television but what we allege of it will also apply to radio. Even if there is some economic pressure towards consolidation there will be an abundance of channels, certainly in comparison with the analogue era. The content of many of these is likely to be subject to conditional access, either because they are subscription channels or they carry pay-per-view programmes which the subscriber can cull from numerous different channels and arrange into her own private schedule. Among the free-to-air services will be the BBC's eight television and eleven radio networks, seeking despite their relative fewness to carry everything that it is both possible and worthwhile for broadcasting to offer, including content that is not economic for other broadcasters to provide.

If the competitive, specifically commercial ethos prevails, the abundance of channels, combined with a close link between what the viewer sees and what she pays for, could increase the tendency towards populist entertainment, leaving only a minimal provision of news and current affairs. And if enough viewers resent paying the licence fee for channels they seldom watch because they are already having to pay for channels that they do watch, it could mean the end of the BBC as a genuine public service broadcaster. Perceptions that this full-bloodedly competitive ethos is already developing have led to pronouncements that British broadcasting *was* excellent, *is* crumbling, and *will be* awful. But it is also arguable that Reith's public service vision was never much more than a heroic red herring, that he set too much store by broadcasting as a force for cultural and intellectual enlargement. However edifying it can be, its content is largely ephemeral, its consumption passive, its effects uncertain. And if in the old days of limited educational opportunity and spectrum scarcity broadcasting was such a force, perhaps we should no longer expect it to be but should simply treat it as a medium of light entertainment, and for our more serious needs turn to outlets such as broadsheet newspapers or books, of which there is no shortage. This is pretty much what already happens in the United States. On the other hand, if the public service ideal can survive in an era of relentless and often trivial entertainment, providing a forum for the nation among all those narrowcast pay channels, its insistence that broadcasting can serve higher needs and that value is not merely to be judged by popularity could prove to be more eloquent than ever.

Sources/further reading

A useful discussion of media convergence can be found in Briggs and Burke (2002). My discussion of sequences and segmentation owes a large debt to Williams (1974) and Ellis (1982), even though the three of us discuss these phenomena in slightly differing ways. The remark about the effect of modern television on human perceptions is in Hobsbawm (1994), while the hyperspace world created by modern global broadcasting is neatly evoked in O'Sullivan, Dutton and Rayner (1994).

For a helpful description of media globalization see Abercrombie (1996), and for 'cultural imperialism' see Thompson (1995) and McQuail (2000), both of whom point to the factors which resist as well as promote it. Graham (1998) argues cogently that digitization will increase rather than reduce the concentration of ownership in the media. My discussion of the generic versatility of the binary code and the other reasons why choice of content may not keep pace with the numbers of digital channels is largely indebted to Hendy (2000a, 2000b). Though his subject is radio, his arguments are applicable to broadcasting in general.

Timeline of British broadcasting

1843	Transmission of Morse's first telegraph message, using Morse code.
1864	Maxwell expounds his theory of electromagnetic waves.
1876	Bell's telephone transmits over a distance of two miles in the USA.
1877	Edison develops his phonograph.
1880	Hertz describes radio waves.
1884	Nipkow devises a revolving disc as the basis of a system of television.
1897	Marconi founds Wireless Telegraph and Signal Company. Karl Braun invents cathode ray tube.
1900	Fessenden broadcasts voice messages.
1901	Marconi transmits messages from Cornwall to Newfoundland.
1904	Wireless Telegraphy Act.
1905	Elster and Geitel devise the photo-electric cell.
1906	Fessenden broadcasts words and music.
1914–18	First World War.
1915	The American Telephone and Telegraph Company sends a speech signal 3,500 miles, from the USA to France.
1920	Dame Nellie Melba broadcasts from Writtle, near Chelmsford.
1922	Marconi Company begins regular radio broadcasts from Writtle. Formation of the British Broadcasting Company. John Reith is appointed General Manager.
1923	Publication of the Sykes Report on the British Broadcasting Company's finances.
1925	Baird demonstrates his television system in Selfridge's department store, London.
1926	Publication of the Crawford Report on the future of public service radio. The General Strike, 3–12 May.

1927	The British Broadcasting Company becomes the British Broadcasting Corporation. Reith is appointed Director General.
1928	Baird sends the first intelligible TV signal across the Atlantic.
1929	The BBC begins the first experimental television transmissions.
1931	Radio Normandie begins broadcasting from the European mainland.
1932	The BBC moves into the purpose-built Broadcasting House. Launch of the BBC's Empire Service.
1933	Radio Luxembourg begins broadcasting.
1935	The Selsdon Report recommends that BBC television should be funded from the existing licence fee.
1936	The Ullswater Report on the BBC's finances. Launch of the BBC television service, using both the Baird and EMI systems. Transmissions are in black and white on 405 lines/VHF.
1937	The Baird television system is dropped. The coronation procession of King George VI is televised.
1938	Resignation of Sir John Reith as Director General of the BBC.
1939–45	The Second World War.
1939	Suspension of television service. Radio networks combined into a single Home Service.
1940	Launch of the Forces Programme.
1942	Launch of the General Forces Service for British troops stationed overseas.
1943	Launch of the American Forces Network for US troops stationed in Britain.
1944	The two British forces networks are combined to form the General Forces Programme. The government and the BBC agree the 'fourteen-day rule'.
1945	Launch of the BBC Light Programme.
1946	Launch of the BBC Third Programme. Resumption of the BBC television service. Resumption of Radio Luxembourg after wartime closure.
1947	Transistor devised in the Bell Laboratories, USA.
1951	The Beveridge Report on the status and financing of the BBC.
1952	The first full Eurovision link between Britain and the continent.
1953	The coronation of Queen Elizabeth II, the first real 'media event'. Television supersedes radio as the major medium of broadcasting.
1955	The launch of commercial ('independent') television (ITV) under the control of the Independent Television Authority (ITA). The beginning of VHF/FM radio broadcasts. UHF waves first generated at Massachusetts Institute of Technology.

1956	The Suez crisis: end of the fourteen-day rule. The Soviet invasion of Hungary. The arrival in Britain of the transistor radio and rock music.
1957	Russia launches Sputnik, the first man-made satellite.
1958	First extended television coverage of a by-election (at Rochdale). First live TV coverage of the state opening of Parliament. Income from TV advertising surpasses that of the press.
1959	Sales of transistors exceed the sales of valves.
1962	Publication of the Pilkington Report on the future of British broadcasting. The first transatlantic TV transmissions, using the Telstar satellite.
1964	Launch of BBC 2 with a higher-definition picture on 625 lines/UHF. The launch of several offshore pirate radio stations, notably Radio Caroline and Radio London.
1967	BBC 2 begins regular colour TV transmissions. The pirate radio stations are forced off the air by the Marine Broadcasting (Offences) Act. Launch of Radio 1. The Light Programme becomes Radio 2, the Third Programme Radio 3, and the Home Service Radio 4. Launch of BBC local radio.
1969	Colour TV is extended to BBC 1 and ITV. Sony introduces videotape cassettes. Publication of *Broadcasting in the Seventies* on the future of BBC radio. First man lands on the moon.
1971	The government abolishes the radio-only receiving licence.
1972	The government lifts the restriction on TV broadcasting hours. The Sound Broadcasting Act: the ITA becomes the Independent Broadcasting Authority (IBA) with responsibility for both commercial radio and commercial television. Domestic video-cassette recorders (VCRs) on sale.
1973	The first independent local radio stations go to air.
1974	Launch of teletext: Ceefax on BBC, Oracle on ITV.
1975	Fibre optics developed.
1976	Radio is allowed to relay the proceedings of both the House of Commons and the House of Lords.
1977	Publication of the Annan Report on the future of British broadcasting.
1979	VCRs begin to be bought in large numbers: the two main formats are Sony Betamax and VHS.
1981	The first trials of satellite television as a cable supplier – on the European mainland only.
1982	Rupert Murdoch gains control of Sky TV, the main European satellite operator. Publication of the Hunt Report on the future of cable television. Launch of Channel 4.
1983	Breakfast TV begins on both BBC and ITV.

1984	The Cable and Broadcasting Act places broad band cable TV under the control of the Cable Authority: Sky TV provides a large amount of its programming. The first camcorder is marketed.
1985	Television cameras are allowed into the House of Lords.
1986	Publication of the Peacock Report on the future financing of the BBC. Nearly half of all TV homes now have VCRs.
1988	Programme sponsorship is allowed on ITV.
1989	Sky TV launches its British direct-to-home (DBS) satellite service. Television cameras are allowed into the House of Commons.
1990	British Satellite Broadcasting (BSB) launches its British DBS service. It collapses after seven months and is absorbed by Sky. Launch of BBC Radio 5. The Broadcasting Act of 1990: the IBA is divided into the Independent Television Commission (ITC) and the Radio Authority.
1991	Sky re-launches as British Sky Broadcasting (BSkyB). BSkyB follows CNN in launching a continuous news channel. BBC World launched – funded entirely from advertising. Radio Luxembourg closes down.
1992	Launch of Classic FM – Britain's first legal, national, domestically based commercial radio station. For the first time the ITV franchises are awarded by auction.
1993	Launch of Virgin 1215, a second national commercial radio station.
1994	BBC Radio 5 re-launches as a news and sport format called Five Live.
1995	Launch of Talk Radio UK, a third national commercial radio station. The BBC launches a digital radio service of its five networks. The BBC launches pay-TV cable and satellite channels with commercial partners.
1996	The Broadcasting Act of 1996 relaxes the rules on cross-media ownership and provides a blueprint for digital broadcasting.
1997	Launch of Channel 5. The BBC launches its News 24 channel. BBC News Online launched, a free-to-access internet news service. The ITC allocates multiplexes for digital television.
1998	Launch of ONdigital, ITV's digital terrestrial television service. BSkyB launches Sky Digital, a digital satellite TV service.
1999	The first multiplex for national commercial radio begins transmission.
2001	ONdigital re-launches as ITV Digital. BSkyB switches off its analogue signal. The first major TV web-casts.
2002	ITV Digital goes into liquidation.

Bibliography

Abercrombie, N. (1996) *Television and Society*, Cambridge: Polity Press.

Alvarado, M., Gutch, R. and Wollen, T. (1987) *Learning the Media*, London: Macmillan Education.

Ang, I. (1985) *Watching Dallas: Soap Opera and the Melodramatic Imagination*, London: Methuen.

Annan Committee, The (1977) *Report of the Committee on the Future of Broadcasting, 1977*, Cmd 6753.

Armes, R. (1988) *On Video*, London: Routledge.

Bakewell, J. and Garnham, N. (1970) *The New Priesthood: British Television Today*, Harmondsworth: Allen Lane/The Penguin Press.

Barendt, E. (1998) 'Judging the media: impartiality and broadcasting' in Seaton, J. (ed.) *Politics and the Media: Harlots and Prerogatives at the Turn of the Millennium*, Oxford: Basil Blackwell.

Barnard, S. (1989) *On the Radio: Music Radio in Britain*, Milton Keynes: Open University Press.

—— (2000) *Studying Radio*, London: Edward Arnold.

Barnouw, E. (1966) *A Tower in Babel: A History of Broadcasting in the United States to 1933*, New York: Oxford University Press.

—— (1977) *Tube of Plenty: The Evolution of American Television*, New York: Oxford University Press.

Baron, M. (1975) *Independent Radio*, Lavenham: Dalton.

Bates, A. (1984) *Broadcasting in Education: An Evaluation*, London: Constable.

BBC (1967) *Handbook 1968*, London: British Broadcasting Corporation.

—— (1969a) *Broadcasting in the Seventies*, London: British Broadcasting Corporation.

—— (1969b) *Handbook 1970*, London: British Broadcasting Corporation.

Bell, E. (1997) 'Panic station as Channel 4 faces an ungraded future', *Observer*, 2 February.

Beveridge Committee, The (1951) *Report of the Broadcasting Committee, 1949*, Cmd 8116.

Black, P. (1972a) *The Biggest Aspidistra in the World*, London: British Broadcasting Corporation.

—— (1972b) *The Mirror in the Corner*, London: Hutchinson.

Blain, N. and Boyle, R. (1998) 'Sport as real life: media sport and culture' in Briggs, A. and Cobley, P. (eds) *The Media: An Introduction*, Harlow: Addison Wesley Longman.

Bonner, P. with Aston, L. (1998) *Independent Television in Britain: Volume V – ITV and the IBA, 1981–92*, London: Macmillan.

Booker, C. (1970) *The Neophiliacs*, London: Fontana Books.

Bourdieu, P. (1998) *On Television and Journalism*, trans. Priscilla Parkhurst Ferguson, London: Pluto Press.

Bowen, D. (1994) 'After the media earthquake', *Independent*, 6 March.

Boyle, A. (1972) *Only the Wind Will Listen*, London: Hutchinson.

Bridson, D. (1971) *Prospero and Ariel*, London: Gollancz.

Brierley, S. (1998) 'Advertising and the new media environment' in Briggs, A. and Cobley, P. (eds) *The Media: An Introduction*, Harlow: Addison Wesley Longman.

Briggs, A. (1961) *The History of Broadcasting in the United Kingdom: Volume I – The Birth of Broadcasting*, London: Oxford University Press.

—— (1965) *The History of Broadcasting in the United Kingdom: Volume II – The Golden Age of Wireless*, London: Oxford University Press.

—— (1970) *The History of Broadcasting in the United Kingdom: Volume III – The War of Words*, London: Oxford University Press.

—— (1979) *The History of Broadcasting in the United Kingdom: Volume IV – Sound and Vision*, Oxford: Oxford University Press.

—— (1985) *The BBC: The First Fifty Years*, Oxford: Oxford University Press.

—— (1995) *The History of Broadcasting in the United Kingdom: Volume V – Competition*, Oxford: Oxford University Press.

Briggs, A. and Burke, P. (2002) *A Social History of the Media: From Gutenberg to the Internet*, Cambridge: Polity Press.

Briggs, S. (1981) *Those Radio Times*, London: Weidenfeld and Nicolson.

Brown, M. (1995) 'Warning: your wireless is exploding', *Independent*, 19 January.

Brunsdon, C. and Morley, D. (1978) *Everyday Television: 'Nationwide'*, London: BFI Television Monograph, 10.

Buckingham, D. (1996) '*EastEnders*: creating the audience' in Marris, P. and Thornham, S. (eds) *Media Studies: A Reader*, Edinburgh: Edinburgh University Press.

Bulkley, K. (1992) 'Telephone support for infant cable', *Independent*, 30 June.

Burns, T. (1977) *The BBC: Public Institution and Private World*, London: Macmillan.

Buscombe, E. (1991) 'All bark and no bite: the film industry's response to television' in Corner, J. (ed.) *Popular Television in Britain*, London: BFI Publishing.

Camporesi, V. (1994) 'The BBC and American broadcasting, 1922–55', *Media, Culture and Society*, 16.

Cannon, J. (ed.) (1997) *The Oxford Companion to British History*, Oxford: Oxford University Press.

Cardiff, D. (1980) 'The serious and the popular: aspects of the evolution of style in the radio talk, 1928–39', *Media, Culture and Society*, 2.

—— (1988) 'Mass middlebrow laughter: the origins of BBC comedy', *Media, Culture and Society*, 10.

Cardiff, D. and Scannell, P. (1981) 'Radio in World War II', *Open University*, U203 Popular Culture, Block 3, Unit 8.

Carpenter, H. (1996) *The Envy of the World: Fifty Years of the BBC Third Programme and Radio 3*, London: Weidenfeld and Nicolson.

Caughie, J. (1991) 'Before the golden age: early television drama' in Corner, J. (ed.) *Popular Television in Britain*, London: BFI Publishing.

—— (2000) *Television Drama: Realism, Modernism, and British Culture*, Oxford: Oxford University Press.

Chaney, D. (1993) *Fictions of Collective Life: Public Drama in Late Modern Culture*, London: Routledge.

Chapman, R. (1992) *Selling the Sixties: The Pirates and Pop Music Radio*, London: Routledge.

Collini, S. (2000) 'From sages to celebrities', *Guardian*, 11 November.

Corner, J. (1991) 'General Introduction: television and British society in the 1950s' in Corner, J. (ed.) *Popular Television in Britain*, London: BFI Publishing.

—— (1995) *Television Form and Public Address*, London: Edward Arnold.

—— (1996) *The Art of Record: A Critical Introduction to Documentary*, Manchester: Manchester University Press.

—— (1999) *Critical Ideas in Television Studies*, Oxford: Oxford University Press.

Corner, J., Harvey, S. and Lury, K. (1994) 'Culture, quality and choice: the re-regulation of TV 1989–91' in Hood, S. (ed.) *Behind the Screens: The Structure of British Television in the Nineties*, London: Lawrence and Wishart.

Cornford, J. and Robins, K. (1999) 'New Media' in Stokes, J. and Reading, A. (eds) *The Media in Britain: Current Debates and Developments*, Basingstoke: Macmillan.

Crawford Committee, The (1926) *Report of the Broadcasting Committee, 1925*, Cmd 2599.

Crisell, A. (1986) *Understanding Radio*, London: Methuen.

—— (1991) 'Filth, sedition and blasphemy: the rise and fall of television satire' in Corner, J. (ed.) *Popular Television in Britain*, London: BFI Publishing.

Crisell, A. (1994) *Understanding Radio*, London: Routledge, second edn.

Crook, T. (1999) *Radio Drama: Theory and Practice*, London: Routledge.

Cumberbatch, G. and Howitt, D. (1989) *A Measure of Uncertainty: The Effects of the Mass Media*, London: John Libbey.

Curran, J. and Seaton, J. (1997) *Power without Responsibility*, London: Routledge, fifth edn.

Curran, J., Smith, A. and Wingate, P. (eds) (1987) *Impacts and Influences: Essays on Media Power in the Twentieth Century*, London: Methuen.

Dahlgren, P. (1995) *Television and the Public Sphere: Citizenship, Democracy and the Media*, London: Sage.

Davis, A. (1976) *Television: Here is the News*, London: Independent Television Books.

Day-Lewis, S. (1992) *TV Heaven: A Review of British Television from the 1930s to the 1990s*, London: Channel Four Television.

Doherty, M. (2000) *Nazi Wireless Propaganda: Lord Haw-Haw and British Public Opinion in the Second World War*, Edinburgh: Edinburgh University Press.

Donovan, P. (1992) *The Radio Companion*, London: Grafton.

—— (1997) *All Our Todays: Forty Years of the Today Programme*, London: Jonathan Cape.

Drakakis, J. (ed.) (1981) *British Radio Drama*, Cambridge: Cambridge University Press.

Dyer, R. (1973) *Light Entertainment*, London: BFI Monograph, 2.

Ellis, J. (1982) *Visible Fictions*, London: Routledge and Kegan Paul.

Ezard, J. (2000) 'How the British lag behind in reading, but lead the world at watching TV', *Guardian*, 15 June.

Fink, H. (1981) 'The sponsor's v. the nation's choice: North American radio drama' in Lewis, P. (ed.) *Radio Drama*, London: Longman.

Fiske, J. (1987) *Television Culture*, London: Methuen.

Fornatale, P. and Mills, J. (1980) *Radio in the Television Age*, Woodstock, NY: The Overlook Press.

Foster, A. and Furst, S. (1996) *Radio Comedy 1938–1968: A Guide to 30 Years of Wonderful Wireless*, London: Virgin.

Franklin, B. (1997) *Newszak and News Media*, London: Edward Arnold.

Frith, S. (1983) 'The pleasures of the hearth: the making of BBC light entertainment' in Donald, J. (ed.) *Formations of Pleasure*, London: Routledge and Kegan Paul.

Frye, N. (1971) *Anatomy of Criticism*, Princeton: Princeton University Press.

Gaber, I. (1998) 'Television and political coverage' in Geraghty, C. and Lusted, D. (eds) *The Television Studies Book*, London: Edward Arnold.

Gable, J. (1980) *The Tuppenny Punch and Judy Show*, Harmondsworth: Michael Joseph.

Garfield, S. (1998) *The Nation's Favourite: The True Adventures of Radio 1*, London: Faber and Faber.

Garnham, N. (1994) 'The broadcasting market and the future of the BBC', *Political Quarterly*, 65.

Geraghty, C. (1996) 'The continuous serial: a definition' in Marris, P. and Thornham, S. (eds) *Media Studies: A Reader*, Edinburgh: Edinburgh University Press.

Gielgud, V. (1957) *British Radio Drama, 1922–1956*, London: Harrap.

Gifford, D. (1985) *The Golden Age of Radio*, London: Batsford.

Gillard, F. (1964) *Sound Radio in the Television Age*, BBC Lunch-time Lectures, second series, no. 6.

Goddard, P. (1991) '"Hancock's Half Hour": a watershed in British television comedy' in Corner, J. (ed.) *Popular Television in Britain*, London: BFI Publishing.

Goldhamer, H. (1971) 'The social effects of communication technology' in Schramm, W. and Roberts, D. (eds) *The Process and Effects of Mass Communication*, Urbana, Ill.: University of Illinois Press, revised edn.

Goldie, G. (1977) *Facing the Nation: Television and Politics, 1936–1976*, London: The Bodley Head.

Golding, P. (1974) *The Mass Media*, London: Longman.

Golding, P., Murdock, G. and Schlesinger, P. (1986) *Communicating Politics: Mass Communications and the Political Process*, Leicester: Leicester University Press.

Goodfriend, A. (1988) 'Satellite broadcasting in the UK' in Negrine, R. (ed.) *Satellite Broadcasting: The Politics and Implications of the New Media*, London: Routledge.

Goodwin, P. (1998) *Television under the Tories: Broadcasting Policy 1979–1997*, London: BFI Publishing.

Gorham, M. (1952) *Broadcasting and Television since 1900*, London: Andrew Dakers Ltd.

Grade, M. (1996) 'Getting the right approach: Channel Four and the British film industry' in Hill, J. and McLoone, M. (eds) *Big Picture, Small Screen: The Relations between Film and Television*, Luton: John Libbey Media/University of Luton Press.

Graham, A. (1998) 'Broadcasting policy and the digital revolution' in Seaton, J. (ed.) *Politics and the Media: Harlots and Prerogatives at the Turn of the Millennium*, Oxford: Basil Blackwell.

Harris, P. (1970) *When Pirates Ruled the Waves*, London and Aberdeen: Impulse Books, fourth edn.

Harvey, S. (1994) 'Channel 4 television: from Annan to Grade' in Hood, S. (ed.) *Behind the Screens: The Structure of British Television in the Nineties*, London: Lawrence and Wishart.

Harvey, S. and Robins, K. (1994) 'Voices and places: the BBC and regional policy', *Political Quarterly*, 65.

Hendy, D. (2000a) 'A political economy of radio in the digital age', *Journal of Radio Studies*, 7.

—— (2000b) *Radio in the Global Age*, Cambridge: Polity Press.

Hill, J. (1991) 'Television and pop: the case of the 1950s' in Corner, J. (ed.) *Popular Television in Britain*, London: BFI Publishing.

—— (1996) 'British television and film: the making of a relationship' in Hill, J. and McLoone, M. (eds) *Big Picture, Small Screen: The Relations between Film and Television*, Luton: John Libbey Media/University of Luton Press.

Hilton, J. (1938) *This and That*, London: George Allen and Unwin.

Hobsbawm, E. (1994) *Age of Extremes: The Short Twentieth Century*, Harmondsworth: Michael Joseph.

Hobson, D. (1982) *Crossroads: The Drama of a Soap Opera*, London: Methuen.

Hood, S. (1975) *Radio and Television*, Newton Abbot: David and Charles.

—— (1980) *On Television*, London: Pluto Press, second edn.

Hood, S. and O'Leary, G. (1990) *Questions of Broadcasting*, London: Methuen.

Horsman, M. (1996a) 'On radio advertising's boom', *Independent*, 16 April.

—— (1996b) 'BBC plans eight pay channels', *Independent*, 28 September.

—— (1997) *Sky High: The Inside Story of BSkyB*, London: Orion Business Books.

Hughes, P. (1990) 'Today's television, tomorrow's world' in Goodwin, A. and Whannel, G. (eds) *Understanding Television*, London: Routledge.

Hughes, R. (1995) 'Who wants to watch it anyway?', *Television*, 32.

Humm, P. (1998) 'Real TV: camcorders, access and authenticity' in Geraghty, C. and Lusted, D. (eds) *The Television Studies Book*, London: Edward Arnold.

Isaacs, J. (1989) *Storm over Four: A Personal Account*, London: Weidenfeld and Nicolson.

Jacobs, J. (2000) *The Intimate Screen: Early British Television Drama*, Oxford: Oxford University Press.

Kaplan, E. (1987) *Rocking around the Clock: Music Television, Postmodernism and Consumer Culture*, New York and London: Routledge.

Kermode, F. (1967) *The Sense of an Ending*, New York: Oxford University Press.

Kerr, P. (1990) 'F for Fake? Friction over faction' in Goodwin, A. and Whannel, G. (eds) *Understanding Television*, London: Routledge.

Kilborn, R. and Izod, J. (1997) *An Introduction to Television Documentary: Confronting Reality*, Manchester: Manchester University Press.

Laing, S. (1991) 'Banging in some reality: the original "Z Cars"' in Corner, J. (ed.) *Popular Television in Britain*, London: BFI Publishing.

Lambert, S. (1982) *Channel Four: Television with a Difference?*, London: BFI Publishing.

Levin, B. (1972) *The Pendulum Years: Britain and the Sixties*, London: Pan Books.

Lewis, J. (1990) 'Are you receiving me?' in Goodwin, A. and Whannel, G. (eds) *Understanding Television*, London: Routledge.

Lewis, P. (1981) 'Radio drama and English literature' in Lewis, P. (ed.) *Radio Drama*, London: Longman.

Lewis, P. M. and Booth, J. (1989) *The Invisible Medium: Public, Commercial and Community Radio*, London: Macmillan.

Lezard, N. (2000) 'Is America bad for us?', *Guardian*, 11 November.

Livingstone, S. (1990) *Making Sense of Television: The Psychology of Audience Interpretation*, Oxford: Pergamon Press.

Livingstone, S. and Lunt, P. (1994) *Talk on Television: Audience Participation and Public Debate*, London: Routledge.

MacCabe, C. and Stewart, O. (eds) (1986) *The BBC and Public Service Broadcasting*, Manchester: Manchester University Press.

McDonnell, J. (1991) *Public Service Broadcasting: A Reader*, London: Routledge.

McIntyre, I. (1993) *The Expense of Glory: A Life of John Reith*, London: Harper-Collins.

MacKenzie, J. (1987) 'Propaganda and the BBC Empire Service, 1932–42' in Hawthorn, J. (ed.) *Propaganda, Persuasion and Polemic*, London: Edward Arnold.

McLuhan, M. (1962) *The Gutenberg Galaxy*, London: Routledge and Kegan Paul.

McNair, B. (1994) *News and Journalism in the UK*, London: Routledge.

—— (1998) *The Sociology of Journalism*, London: Edward Arnold.

McQuail, D. (2000) *McQuail's Mass Communication Theory*, London: Sage, fourth edn.

McQueen, D. (1998) *Television: A Media Student's Guide*, London: Edward Arnold.

Mansell, G. (1982) *Let Truth Be Told: 50 Years of BBC External Broadcasting*, London: Weidenfeld and Nicolson.

Matelski, M. (2000) 'Jerry Springer and the wages of fin-syn: the rise of deregulation and the decline of TV talk', *Journal of Popular Culture*, 33.

Mepham, J. (1990) 'The ethics of quality in television' in Mulgan, G. (ed.) *The Question of Quality*, London: BFI Publishing.

Mercer, D. (ed.) (1988) *Chronicle of the Twentieth Century*, London: Longman.

Moores, S. (1988) '"The box on the dresser": memories of early radio and everyday life', *Media, Culture and Society*, 10.

—— (1993) *Interpreting Audiences: The Ethnography of Media Consumption*, London: Sage Publications.

—— (2000) *Media and Everyday Life in Modern Society*, Edinburgh: Edinburgh University Press.

Morley, D. (1992) *Television, Audiences and Cultural Studies*, London: Routledge.

Mulgan, G. (1990) 'Television's holy grail: seven types of quality' in Mulgan, G. (ed.) *The Question of Quality*, London: BFI Publishing.

Murdock, G. (2000) 'Money talks: broadcasting finance and public culture' in Buscombe, E. (ed.) *British Television: A Reader*, Oxford: Oxford University Press.

Nathan, D. (1971) *The Laughtermakers*, London: Peter Owen.

Negrine, R. (1985) 'Cable television in Britain' in Negrine, R. (ed.) *Cable Television and the Future of Broadcasting*, London and Sydney: Croom Helm.

—— (1988) 'Satellite broadcasting: an overview of the main issues' in Negrine, R. (ed.) *Satellite Broadcasting: The Politics and Implications of the New Media*, London: Routledge.

—— (1994) *Politics and the Mass Media in Britain*, London: Routledge, second edn.

Ong, W. (1982) *Orality and Literacy*, London: Methuen.

O'Sullivan, T., Dutton, B. and Rayner, P. (1994) *Studying the Media: An Introduction*, London: Edward Arnold.

Paget, D. (1998) *No Other Way to Tell It: Dramadoc/Docudrama on Television*, Manchester: Manchester University Press.

Parker, D. (1977) *Radio: The Great Years*, Newton Abbot: David and Charles.

Paulu, B. (1956) *British Broadcasting: Radio and Television in the United Kingdom*, Minneapolis: University of Minnesota Press.

—— (1961) *British Broadcasting in Transition*, Minneapolis: University of Minnesota Press.

—— (1981) *Television and Radio in the United Kingdom*, London: Macmillan.

Peacock Committee, The (1986) *Report of the Committee on Financing the BBC, 1986*, Cmd 9824.

Pegg, M. (1983) *Broadcasting and Society, 1918–1939*, London: Croom Helm.

Persaud, R. (2000) 'Car-crash television', *Guardian*, 17 July.

Philo, G. (1990) *Seeing and Believing: The Influence of Television*, London: Routledge.

Pickering, M. (1994) 'Race, gender and broadcast comedy: the case of the BBC's *Kentucky Minstrels*', *European Journal of Communication*, 9.

—— (1996) 'The BBC's Kentucky Minstrels, 1933–1950: blackface entertainment on British radio', *Historical Journal of Film, Radio and Television*, 16.

Pilkington Committee, The (1962) *Report of the Committee on Broadcasting, 1960*, Cmd 1753.

Pimlott, B. (1998) 'Monarchy and the message' in Seaton, J. (ed.) *Politics and the Media: Harlots and Prerogatives at the Turn of the Millennium*, Oxford: Basil Blackwell.

Plomley, R. (1980) *Days Seemed Longer*, London: Eyre Methuen.

Poster, M. (1995) *The Second Media Age*, Cambridge: Polity Press.

Postman, N. (1986) *Amusing Ourselves to Death*, London: Heinemann.

Potter, J. (1989) *Independent Television in Britain: Volume III – Politics and Control, 1968–80*, London: Macmillan.

—— (1990) *Independent Television in Britain: Volume IV – Companies and Programmes, 1968–80*, London: Macmillan.

Reid, C. (1987) *Action Stations: A History of Broadcasting House*, London: Robson Books.

Reith, J. (1924) *Broadcast over Britain*, London: Hodder and Stoughton.

—— (1949) *Into the Wind*, London: Hodder and Stoughton.

Riddell, P. (1998) 'Members and Millbank: the media and Parliament' in Seaton, J. (ed.) *Politics and the Media: Harlots and Prerogatives at the Turn of the Millennium*, Oxford: Basil Blackwell.

Rowland, R. (1982) 'Video education' in Wenham, B. (ed.) *The Third Age of Broadcasting*, London: Faber and Faber.

Russell, J. (1999) 'Di/crash' in Stokes, J. and Reading, A. (eds) *The Media in Britain: Current Debates and Developments*, Basingstoke: Macmillan.

Scannell, P. (1979) 'The social eye of television, 1946–1955', *Media, Culture and Society*, 1.

—— (1980) 'Broadcasting and the politics of unemployment, 1930–1935', *Media, Culture and Society*, 2.

—— (1981) 'Music for the multitude? The dilemmas of the BBC's music policy, 1923–1946', *Media, Culture and Society*, 3.

—— (1986) '"The stuff of radio": developments in radio features and documentaries before the war' in Corner, J. (ed.) *Documentary and the Mass Media*, London: Edward Arnold.

—— (1990) 'Public service broadcasting: the history of a concept' in Goodwin, A. and Whannel, G. (eds) *Understanding Television*, London: Routledge.

—— (1996) *Radio, Television and Modern Life*, Oxford: Basil Blackwell.

Scannell, P. and Cardiff, D. (1982) 'Serving the nation: public service broadcasting before the war' in Waites, B., Bennett, T. and Martin, G. (eds) *Popular Culture: Past and Present*, London: Croom Helm.

—— (1991) *A Social History of British Broadcasting: Volume I 1922–1939: Serving the Nation*, Oxford: Basil Blackwell.

Schlesinger, P. (1978) *Putting 'Reality' Together*, London: Constable.

Scott, R. (1967) *Radio 1 and Radio 2*, BBC Lunch-time Lectures, sixth series, no. 1.

Selby, K. and Cowdery, R. (1995) *How to Study Television*, London: Macmillan.

Selsdon Committee, The (1935) *Report of the Television Committee, 1935*, Cmd 4793.

Sendall, B. (1982) *Independent Television in Britain: Volume I – Origin and Foundation, 1946–1962*, London: Macmillan.

—— (1983) *Independent Television in Britain: Volume II – Expansion and Change, 1958–1968*, London: Macmillan.

Seymour-Ure, C. (1996) *The British Press and Broadcasting since 1945*, Oxford: Basil Blackwell, second edn.

Sherrin, N. (1983) *A Small Thing – Like an Earthquake*, London: Weidenfeld and Nicolson.

Sieveking, L. (1934) *The Stuff of Radio*, London: Cassell.

Silverstone, R. (1994) *Television and Everyday Life*, London: Routledge.

Silvey, R. (1974) *Who's Listening?*, London: George Allen and Unwin.

Smith, A. (ed.) (1974) *British Broadcasting*, Newton Abbot: David and Charles.

—— (1976) *The Shadow in the Cave*, London: Quartet Books, revised edn.

—— (1990) *Broadcasting and Society in 1990s Britain*, London: W. H. Smith Contemporary Papers, no. 4.

Snagge, J. and Barsley, M. (1972) *Those Vintage Years of Radio*, London: Pitman.

Sparks, C. (1994) 'Independent production: unions and casualization' in Hood, S. (ed.) *Behind the Screens: The Structure of British Television in the Nineties*, London: Lawrence and Wishart.

Street, S. (2000) 'BBC Sunday policy and audience response', *Journal of Radio Studies*, 7.

Stuart, C. (ed.) (1975) *The Reith Diaries*, London: Collins.

Sykes Committee, The (1923) *Broadcasting Committee Report, 1923*, Cmd 1951.

Thompson, J. (1995) *The Media and Modernity: A Social Theory of the Media*, Cambridge: Polity Press.

Took, B. (1976) *Laughter in the Air*, London: Robson Books/BBC.

Tracey, M. (1983) *A Variety of Lives: A Biography of Sir Hugh Greene*, London: The Bodley Head.

—— (1998) *The Decline and Fall of Public Service Broadcasting*, Oxford: Oxford University Press.

—— (2000) 'The BBC and the General Strike: May 1926' in Buscombe, E. (ed.) *British Television: A Reader*, Oxford: Oxford University Press.

Trethowan, I. (1970) *Radio in the Seventies*, BBC Lunch-time Lectures, eighth series, no. 4.

Tunstall, J. (1983) *The Media in Britain*, London: Constable.

Turow, J. (1999) *Media Today: An Introduction to Mass Communication*, Boston and New York: Houghton Mifflin.

Tusa, J. (1994) 'Implications of recent changes at the BBC', *Political Quarterly*, 65.

Ullswater Committee, The (1936) *Report of the Broadcasting Committee, 1935*, Cmd 5091.

Walker, A. (1992) *A Skyful of Freedom: 60 Years of the BBC World Service*, London: Broadside Books.

Ward, K. (1989) *Mass Communications and the Modern World*, London: Macmillan.

Watt, I. (1963) *The Rise of the Novel*, Harmondsworth: Penguin Books.

Wenham, B. (1982) 'Into the interior' in Wenham, B. (ed.) *The Third Age of Broadcasting*, London: Faber and Faber.

Wernick, A. (1991) *Promotional Culture: Advertising, Ideology and Symbolic Expression*, London: Sage Publications.

Whale, J. (1969) *The Half-Shut Eye*, London: Macmillan.

Whannel, G. (1990) 'Winner takes all: competition' in Goodwin, A. and Whannel, G. (eds) *Understanding Television*, London: Routledge.

—— (1991) '"Grandstand", the sports fan and the family audience' in Corner, J. (ed.) *Popular Television in Britain*, London: BFI Publishing.

Williams, K. (1998) *Get Me a Murder a Day!: A History of Mass Communication in Britain*, London: Arnold.

Williams, R. (1974) *Television: Technology and Cultural Form*, Glasgow: Fontana.

Wilmut, R. (1980) *From Fringe to Flying Circus*, London: Book Club Associates.

Winston, B. (1998) *Media Technology and Society*, London: Routledge.

Worsley, F. (1948) *ITMA*, London: Vox Mundi.

Index